The Plough Woman

The Plough Woman

Records of the Pioneer Women of Palestine

A Critical Edition

Edited and annotated by
Mark A. Raider and Miriam B. Raider-Roth

Brandeis University Press

Published by University Press of New England

Hanover and London

BRANDEIS UNIVERSITY PRESS

Published by University Press of New England, One Court St., Lebanon, NH 03766

© 2002 by Brandeis University Press

Printed in the United States of America

5   4   3   2   1

Library of Congress Cataloging-in-Publication Data

Katznelson-Shazar, Rachel, 1888–1975.
    [Divre poalot. English]
    The plough woman : records of the pioneer women of Palestine :
a critical edition / edited by Mark A. Raider and Miriam B. Raider-Roth.
      p.   cm. — (Brandeis series on Jewish women) (The Tauber
Institute for the Study of European Jewry series)
    Includes bibliographical references and index.
    ISBN 1–58465–183–0
    1. Women—Palestine—Biography. 2. Labor Zionism. I. Raider,
Mark A. II. Raider-Roth, Miriam B. III. Title. IV. Series. V. Tauber
Institute for the Study of European Jewry series (Unnumbered)
HQ1728.5.Z75 A3 2002
305.48'892'4—dc21   2002003708

This book was published with the support of The Lucius N. Littauer Foundation, Inc.,
the Hadassah International Research Institute on Jewish Women at Brandeis University,
the Jacob and Libby Goodman Institute for the Study of Zionism and Israel, and the
Amy Adina Schulman Memorial Fund.

BRANDEIS SERIES ON JEWISH WOMEN

Shulamit Reinharz, General Editor
Joyce Antler, Associate Editor
Sylvia Barack Fishman, Associate Editor
Susan Kahn, Associate Editor

The Hadassah International Research Institute on Jewish Women, established at Brandeis University in 1997 by Hadassah, the Women's Zionist Organization of America, Inc., supports interdisciplinary basic and applied research as well as cultural projects on Jewish women around the world. Under the auspices of the Institute, the Brandeis Series on Jewish Women publishes a wide range of books by and about Jewish women in diverse contexts and time periods.

MARJORIE AGOSÍN
Uncertain Travelers: Conversations with Jewish Women Immigrants to America, 1999

RAHEL R. WASSERFALL
Women and Water: Menstruation in Jewish Life and Law, 1999

SUSAN STARR SERED
What Makes Women Sick: Militarism, Maternity, and Modesty in Israeli Society, 2000

LUDMILA SHTERN
Leaving Leningrad: The True Adventures of a Soviet Émigré, 2001

PAMELA S. NADELL AND JONATHAN D. SARNA, editors
Women and American Judaism: Historical Perspectives, 2001

JAEL SILLIMAN
Jewish Portraits, Indian Frames: Women's Narratives from a Diaspora of Hope, 2001

CHAERAN Y. FREEZE
Jewish Marriage and Divorce in Imperial Russia, 2002

MARK A. RAIDER AND MIRIAM B. RAIDER-ROTH, editors
The Plough Woman: Records of the Pioneer Women of Palestine, 2002

JUDITH R. BASKIN
Midrashic Women, 2002

THE TAUBER INSTITUTE FOR THE STUDY OF
EUROPEAN JEWRY SERIES

Jehuda Reinharz, General Editor
Sylvia Fuks Fried, Associate Editor

The Tauber Institute for the Study of European Jewry, established by a gift to
Brandeis University from Dr. Laszlo N. Tauber, is dedicated to the memory of
the victims of Nazi persecutions between 1933 and 1945. The Institute seeks to
study the history and culture of European Jewry in the modern period. The
Institute has a special interest in studying the causes, nature, and consequences
of the European Jewish catastrophe within the contexts of modern European
diplomatic, intellectual, political, and social history.

The Jacob and Libby Goodman Institute for the Study of Zionism and Israel was
founded through a gift to Brandeis University by Mrs. Libby Goodman and is
organized under the auspices of the Tauber Institute. The Goodman Institute
seeks to promote an understanding of the historical and ideological development
of the Zionist movement, and the history, society, and culture of the State of Israel.

GERHARD L. WEINBERG, 1981
*World in the Balance: Behind the Scenes
of World War II*

RICHARD COBB, 1983
*French and Germans, Germans and
French: A Personal Interpretation
of France under Two Occupations,
1914–1918/1940–1944*

EBERHARD JÄCKEL, 1984
Hitler in History

FRANCES MALINO AND BERNARD
WASSERSTEIN, editors, 1985
The Jews in Modern France

JEHUDA REINHARZ AND WALTER
SCHATZBERG, editors, 1985
*The Jewish Response to German Culture:
From the Enlightenment to the Second
World War*

JACOB KATZ, 1986
*The Darker Side of Genius:
Richard Wagner's Anti-Semitism*

JEHUDA REINHARZ, editor, 1987
*Living with Antisemitism:
Modern Jewish Responses*

MICHAEL R. MARRUS, 1987
The Holocaust in History

PAUL MENDES-FLOHR, editor, 1987
The Philosophy of Franz Rosenzweig

JOAN G. ROLAND, 1989
*Jews in British India: Identity in
a Colonial Era*

YISRAEL GUTMAN, EZRA
MENDELSOHN, JEHUDA REINHARZ,
AND CHONE SHMERUK, editors, 1989
*The Jews of Poland Between Two
World Wars*

AVRAHAM BARKAI, 1989
*From Boycott to Annihilation: The
Economic Struggle of German Jews,
1933–1943*

ALEXANDER ALTMANN, 1991
*The Meaning of Jewish Existence:
Theological Essays 1930–1939*

MAGDALENA OPALSKI AND
ISRAEL BARTAL, 1992
Poles and Jews: A Failed Brotherhood

RICHARD BREITMAN, 1992
The Architect of Genocide: Himmler and the Final Solution

GEORGE L. MOSSE, 1993
Confronting the Nation: Jewish and Western Nationalism

DANIEL CARPI, 1994
Between Mussolini and Hitler: The Jews and the Italian Authorities in France and Tunisia

WALTER LAQUEUR AND RICHARD BREITMAN, 1994
Breaking the Silence: The German Who Exposed the Final Solution

ISMAR SCHORSCH, 1994
From Text to Context: The Turn to History in Modern Judaism

JACOB KATZ, 1995
With My Own Eyes: The Autobiography of an Historian

GIDEON SHIMONI, 1995
The Zionist Ideology

MOSHE PRYWES AND HAIM CHERTOK, 1996
Prisoner of Hope

JÁNOS NYIRI, 1997
Battlefields and Playgrounds

ALAN MINTZ, editor, 1997
The Boom in Contemporary Israeli Fiction

SAMUEL BAK, painting
LAWRENCE L. LANGER, essay and commentary, 1997
Landscapes of Jewish Experience

JEFFREY SHANDLER AND BETH S. WENGER, editors, 1997
Encounters with the "Holy Land": Place, Past and Future in American Jewish Culture

SIMON RAWIDOWICZ, 1998
State of Israel, Diaspora, and Jewish Continuity: Essays on the "Ever-Dying People"

JACOB KATZ, 1998
A House Divided: Orthodoxy and Schism in Nineteenth-Century Central European Jewry

ELISHEVA CARLEBACH, JOHN M. EFRON, AND DAVID N. MYERS, editors, 1998
Jewish History and Jewish Memory: Essays in Honor of Yosef Hayim Yerushalmi

SHMUEL ALMOG, JEHUDA REINHARZ, AND ANITA SHAPIRA, editors, 1998
Zionism and Religion

BEN HALPERN AND JEHUDA REINHARZ, 2000
Zionism and the Creation of a New Society

WALTER LAQUEUR, 2001
Generation Exodus: The Fate of Young Jewish Refugees from Nazi Germany

YIGAL SCHWARTZ, 2001
Aharon Appelfeld: From Individual Lament to Tribal Eternity

RENÉE POZNANSKI, 2001
Jews in France during World War II

JEHUDA REINHARZ, 2001
Chaim Weizmann: The Making of a Zionist Leader

JEHUDA REINHARZ, 2001
Chaim Weizmann: The Making of a Statesman

CHAERAN Y. FREEZE, 2002
Jewish Marriage and Divorce in Imperial Russia

MARK A. RAIDER AND MIRIAM B. RAIDER-ROTH, editors, 2002
The Plough Woman: Records of the Pioneer Women of Palestine

ALAN MINTZ, editor, 2002
Reading Hebrew Literature: Critical Discussions of Six Modern Texts

TO OUR MOTHERS

ELIZABETH J. RAIDER

AND

CHAYA H. ROTH,

PLOUGH WOMEN IN THEIR OWN RIGHT

Contents

PART III   At Work

PART IV   With Children

PART V   The Departed

Illustrations

Illustrations appear following page 110.

Editors' Note

The present critical edition of *The Plough Woman* seeks to strike a balance between honoring the integrity of Maurice Samuel's masterful translation and restoring significant information that was lost in the volume's evolution from the original Yiddish edition in 1931 to its subsequent English printings in 1932 and 1975. To this end, we have here reinserted substantial material from the first English edition that was jettisoned by the second. For example, we reintroduced the section entitled "The Departed," a necrology of six women Zionist pioneers who died untimely deaths. We also reinserted twenty-two illustrations that comprise a remarkable photographic essay. The former reflects the dramatic tension at the core of the women pioneers' experience and throws light on the complexity of the period. The latter amplifies the narrative in important ways and will be of special interest to students of the semiotics of Zionism.

The new volume reinstates a sizable quotient of material derived from the Yiddish text; such information appears in bracketed form throughout the book. However, we did not elect to translate whole sections that Samuel himself passed over when composing his English translation (e.g., letters, speeches, and prose interspersed throughout the Yiddish volume). Meanwhile, we deliberately reinserted precise terminology such as *kvuzah*, *haver*, and *shtetl* instead of using "colony," "comrade," or "village"—the simplified phraseology characteristic of Samuel's translation. These terms are the ones most often used in the original Yiddish text. In a related vein, wherever possible we inserted, in brackets, the married and/or Hebraized surnames by which many figures who contributed to the volume would later become known (e.g., "Rahel Yanait [Ben-Zvi]," "Golda [Meir]," etc.); likewise, we attempted to substitute complete names for initials. In this way, we sought to be alert to the historical dimensions of the volume as a whole but also sensitive to the intentionality and self-identification of the writers themselves. Moreover, in an effort to both preserve and excavate the Yiddish and English texts, the present volume retains and annotates the prefatory and explanatory materials found in previous editions.

A word is in order concerning stylistic changes. Wherever necessary, we made minor emendations and adjustments in order to unify and enhance the text overall. For example, we modified somewhat the orthography and transliteration of Hebrew and Yiddish, to give English-speaking readers as clear a phonetic equivalent as possible without introducing complex diacritical marks and special linguistic values. Exceptions in this regard are terms and names for which a different usage is highly familiar (e.g., *kibbutz*, *yiddishkeit*, etc.). In other instances, we reinserted Palestinian and/or Zionist locutions employed in the Yiddish text because of their cultural and historic value. Thus, throughout the narrative we replaced "Palestine" with "Erez Israel," "workers' movement" with "Histadrut," "circle dance" with "*hora*," etc. Meanwhile, some common English spellings have been retained for the sake of ease and readability (e.g., "Tiberias," "Nablus," "Jaffa," etc.). It is important to note that there are several women in this volume for whom biographical information could not be found. Their absence from the glossary reflects the complex enterprise of reconstructing the lives of Zionist pioneer women in the Yishuv. It is also worth noting that although the glossaries attempt to be fairly comprehensive, they do not include phraseology and terms that appear infrequently in the book. Rather, to assist the reader, this information has been inserted in the text.

Last, unless specifically stated otherwise, the annotations and glossaries throughout this volume are new to this edition. For the data summarized therein, we have, in part, adapted and drawn from several key sources listed in the Selected Bibliography as well as *The Plough Woman* (Second Edition, 1975). Readers are referred to these texts for additional detailed information.

Acknowledgments

We are grateful to the many individuals, colleagues, and institutions that assisted and supported us in bringing this book project to fruition. We thank Naamat USA and the Herzl Press for recognizing the significance of *The Plough Woman* and granting us permission to reissue it in its present form. From the outset, Shulamit Reinharz, Director of the Hadassah International Research Institute on Jewish Women at Brandeis University, showed keen interest in this undertaking and offered us steadfast encouragement. Pamela Ween Brumberg of the Lucius N. Littauer Foundation was also enthusiastic about this volume. Phyllis Deutsch, our editor at the University Press of New England, played a key role in seeing the book through to publication.

Several individuals have provided valuable research, editorial, and scholarly assistance along the way. Judith A. Sokoloff of Naamat USA was helpful in identifying useful archival materials. Morris Levy and Tracy Metcalf provided diligent research and editorial assistance. Neil A. Tevebaugh-Kenwryck's computer expertise enabled us to scan previous editions of the book and create a new composite manuscript, including the digitized photographs and images reprinted here. Thanks are also due to friends and colleagues who fielded numerous inquiries in our quest to clarify aspects of the manuscript: Robert Alter, Judith R. Baskin, Leon A. Jick, Daniel Ornstein, Piotr Pienkowski, Anna Rosen, Jonathan M. Rosen, Jim Rosenbloom, Zohar Segev, Gregory Stevens, and Aryeh Wineman. We thank Anita Shapira for graciously allowing us to reprint the map of Palestine. We owe a special debt of thanks to Sylvia Barack Fishman, Harriet K. Cuffaro, Sylvia Fuks Fried, Carol Gilligan, Jehuda Reinharz, and Carol R. Rodgers, each of whom was generous with their time and energy, offering crucial expertise and feedback concerning the introductory essays and the manuscript. We would especially like to thank Mishael M. Caspi and Muki Tsur, who devoted considerable energy and attention to this project, sharing with us their vast knowledge of Jewish history, biblical tradition, and the Yishuv.

This undertaking also benefited from significant grants and subventions provided by the Amy Adina Schulman Foundation, the Hadassah

International Research Institute on Jewish Women, the Lucius N. Littauer Foundation, the Jacob and Libby Goodman Institute for the Study of Zionism and Israel, and the University at Albany, State University of New York. We are grateful to the aforementioned foundations and agencies, without whose support the project would not have been feasible.

Finally, we thank our children, Jonah, Emma, and Talia, for their patience, humor, and thoughtful questions that help us to remember the purpose of our work.

MARK A. RAIDER & MIRIAM B. RAIDER-ROTH
Albany, 2002

Foreword to the Second Edition

Marie Syrkin (New York, 1975)

The Plough Woman originally appeared in English in 1932 and has long been out of print. The present edition once more makes available a fascinating chapter in the history of pioneer Palestine. In addition, in view of the current feminist vogue, it is of special, timely interest.

The title is revealing. "Ploughwoman" is found in neither the Oxford nor Webster dictionaries. "Ploughman" and even "ploughboy" appear under the proper letter, as might be expected, but "ploughwoman" has not made the grade. Conceivably, under the pressure of Women's Lib, which has added non-sexist terms such as the less than felicitous "chairperson" to the language, dictionaries will be revised to include "ploughperson." In any case, it is worth noting that the women workers of Palestine introduced a new concept and a new term into our vocabulary more than fifty years ago. Without any of the fanfare that has accompanied present manifestations of a heightened feminist consciousness, these young women in a desolate corner of the Middle East were a revolutionary vanguard of the movement to liberate women not only politically, but from their own enslavement to conventional attitudes as to the role of women in society.

The young pioneers who came to Palestine in the early decades of the twentieth century shared the dream of their male comrades: they would create a new egalitarian society in a Jewish homeland, reclaimed through their labor. To this they added still another dimension—the full emancipation of women. In the great task of rebuilding Palestine, women were not to be shunted aside into the traditional feminine roles. In her account ("Stages") Rahel Yanait [Ben-Zvi] describes the disillusionment that set in when the women discovered that in the tough work of founding a *kibbutz* in marsh or wasteland, the men undertook the backbreaking jobs of digging roads and clearing rocks, while girls were relegated to the kitchen and laundry. Such was the indignation of the more ardent feminists among the pioneers that for a brief period *kibbutzim* consisting solely of women workers sprang up in Galilee, the [Jezreel Valley], and on the sands of Judea. In such *kibbutzim* there was no danger that women would be denied complete equality in all of the forms of physical labor. As Rahel puts it, "Nor did they find it so hard to break in the naked soil of the wilderness, if thereby they could slake their thirst for work on the land."[1] The women's *kibbutzim* were abandoned because they were not practical. A viable agricultural collective required both men and women for psychological as well as economic reasons. This the idealistic young women themselves soon realized, though they did not regret their attempt.

Shortly before the close of World War I, the women suffered another disappointment. When the Jewish Legion was formed, hundreds of young women sought to enlist like the men. Their rejection was a bitter blow: "That rebuff left us flat and wearied; we were not to participate in that great moment."[2] (In this connection we should note that women now serve in the Israeli army, though not in combat.[3])

In time, early feminist extravagances were outgrown. In the course of the subsequent development of Palestine and the *kibbutzim*, women were to play many and varied roles, as *The Plough Woman* makes clear. Most women themselves stopped demanding the privilege of hewing roads, but neither was the kitchen to be their sole domain. Men took their turn at washing dishes, while women worked in the fields and orchards and developed skills in accordance with their capacities.

Not that the respective roles of women and men were ever sorted out to everybody's satisfaction. The voices heard in *The Plough Woman* keep harping both on the difficulty of fulfilling the desire of women for absolute equality in the choice of work, as well as on the hardships and unforeseen complexities of an existence in which this desire was fulfilled.

As marriages were contracted and children born, the whole nexus of problems related to child-rearing compelled women to reassess their roles. Pregnancy and nursing could not be viewed as discriminatory except at the hand of nature. The establishment of collective children's homes offered an obvious solution to the problem of freeing from total confinement to private family concerns. Yet while the children's home enabled women to play their part in the total life of the *kibbutz*, women, not men, were entrusted with the care of young children. This division

1. See pages 109–110.
2. See Rahel Yanait Ben-Zvi's essay, "Stages," in part III, p. 110.
3. A contemporary account of women and the Israel Defense Forces is revealing. It states: "Women have played their role in the defense of the country . . . There is a difference, however, in the Israel army's recognition of women's special characteristics: they do not fight. Most perform clerical, medical, housekeeping, and communications duties. Some pack parachutes, teach, or do cultural work in development areas. Unmarried women from 18 to 26 are conscripted for 20 months. Orthodox girls with scruples about army service are exempt." *Encyclopaedia Judaica* (1971), vol. 16, p. 628.

of labor coincided with the desires of most women and sprang from their intimate experience as mothers.

Some of the problems examined by the writers sound as modern as the latest issue of *Ms.* magazine.[4] Women drawn to political activities and with no recourse to the shelter of the *kibbutz* were tormented by a familiar theme: Were they sacrificing their families to their careers? In the brief chapter, "Borrowed Mothers," the writer describes her maternal anguish at leaving her children for tasks she views as important. With devastating honesty she admits that a "borrowed mother," even if kind and efficient, is not a wholly satisfactory substitute and that her children suffer. She writes: "The modern woman asks herself: Is there something wrong with me if my children don't fill up my life? . . . Can we today measure devotion to husband and children by our indifference to everything else?"[5] The signatory is "G.M.," Golda Meyerson, later to be known as Golda Meir.

The Plough Woman is a vivid, personal record of remarkable women in a heroic time. The present edition has not been revised or updated. It speaks for itself. The only change from the original has been the omission of a section, "The Departed," consisting of memorials to young comrades who died or were killed in the arduous period which the book so movingly records. To make *The Plough Woman* more useful to the contemporary reader, biographical notes and a glossary, prepared by Gertrude Hirschler, assistant editor of the Herzl Press, have been added, as well as an epilogue by Beba Idelson, long the head of Moezet Hapoalot, the Council of Women Workers of Israel.

4. *Ms.*, the first feminist periodical in the United States with a national readership and the first mass-market women's magazine with a radical political agenda, was co-founded in 1971 by Gloria Steinem (b. 1934) and other American feminist leaders.

5. See page 165.

Epilogue to the Second Edition

Beba Idelson (Tel Aviv, 1975)

Those interested in knowing what became of the *haverot* who contributed their stories to the original edition of *The Plough Woman* can find some of them spending their old age in *kibbutzim*, *moshavim*, and cities; a few are now residents in homes for the aged; many are no longer among the living. But in this book, which is a personal and intimate account, they not only left us memories of their personal aims and struggles and a collective image of women rich in spirit and ready to make any sacrifice for their ideals, but they also succeeded in expressing the spirit of an entire era.

The period they describe, starting with the Second Aliyah which began during the first decade of our century, witnessed a one-time miracle: the renascence of young Jews returning to their ancient land to create a new society.

Nearly half a century has passed since *The Plough Woman* was first published. Since then, endless changes have taken place in the world, in Israel, and in the working women's movement, but that unique period left an indelible mark, and it still forms the foundation on which our movement built and has continued to shape its activities to this day. The same spirit of endeavor and dedication still marks every phase of our work today.

During these past decades, our movement has absorbed hundreds of thousands of *haverot*. Some came to Israel as *haluzot* after *hakhsharah* on training farms in the diaspora; others prepared for their new life at the *mishkei poalot* which we set up for them in Israel. Others, later on, came as survivors of the Holocaust, bringing with them the agony of the death camps, or the heroism of participation in partisan and resistance groups. To all these, the working women's movement gave guidance and assistance in their various paths towards absorption in the homeland.

As time went by, the working women's movement established a remarkable network of branches and institutions, covering the entire land of Israel—in cities, villages, *kibbutzim*, *moshavim*, development towns, and workers' settlements. We now have more than 600,000 members and maintain over 1,000 institutions and have thus become an important factor in the life of the country. In our institutions and *kibbutzim* we have helped absorb boys and girls who were torn from the arms of their parents and who finally found a warm and loving home with us in Israel. We have also raised and educated children from underprivileged homes in Israel, helping them to find their way to a wholesome life, thus narrowing the social gap in the country.

Our movement has also done its share in the defense of the homeland. We stood up to Arab riots which afflicted us at various periods and endured four wars of survival. Our *haverot* took an active role in Hashomer [The Watchguard], the group which guarded the early settlements, [the] Haganah [Defense], the defense force of Palestine Jewry, and the Palmah[1] commando units. During World War II, some of our members joined the British Auxiliary Territorial Service (A.T.S.)[2] to help in the Allied war effort. Since the establishment of the [Jewish] state, our *haverot* have served in Hen,[3] Israel's women's army corps, Nahal,[4] which helps till the soil and defend the land, and the civil defense corps, which guards and defends life and property in our towns and cities.

During this entire period, we continued to educate women toward equality and independence, toward acquiring a profession and becoming active in public life, and toward the role of equal partners in the structure of the country in general and the labor movement in particular. We have also aided Arab women in Israel in achieving personal and social progress; some of them have, in fact, become active in our movement.

We have been concerned also with the civic and political position of women. Since the establishment of the State of Israel, our *haverot* in the Knesset, Israel's parliament, have been instrumental in the enactment of many laws to advance the status of women in society, at work and in the family. Our legislative achievements have placed Israel in the front

1. Palmah is an acronym for *plugot mahaz* [shock troops], who performed the clandestine military defense work associated with the Haganah forces in pre-state Israeli society.

2. The British Auxiliary Territorial Service (A.T.S.), a Jewish women's brigade, was stationed in Palestine during World War II.

3. Hen, the acronym for Heil Nashim [Women's Army] was an auxiliary military organization supporting the armed forces in many fields. It supplied women for duties in communications, hospitals, teaching duties, and many headquarters functions. Its purpose was, in part, to relieve men of the country for active combat.

4. Nahal, the acronym for Noar Haluzei Lohem [Fighting Pioneer Youth], is a special corps that conducts military and agricultural training and engages in the establishment and reinforcement of border settlements. The corps serves as a channel for infusing *kibbutzim* with new members, i.e., former Nahal soldiers stationed at the *kibbutz* who choose to remain following their tour of duty. Historically, the Nahal was responsible for setting up new *kibbutzim* under difficult conditions, and building them up until they were ready to be transferred to civilian authority.

ranks of the enlightened nations of the world and have strengthened our appearances on the international scene.

Ours is the only women workers' movement in the world that numbers among its members not only women who are working outside the home for pay but also housewives who are not part of the labor force. The latter have become an important factor in our movement through their own group, Irgun Imahot [Ovdot][5] [Working Mothers' Organization], making their distinct contribution in culture, education, and social service as volunteers.

From its dynamic beginnings, Pioneer Women in the United States and Canada, our sister organization in the diaspora, has grown into a strong movement with branches in twelve countries. Together with [Moezet Hapoalot] in Israel, it is the largest women's organization within the Zionist movement. It supports us in our immense task of creating a better society from the melting pot of immigrants ingathered in the Jewish homeland. The educational and cultural activities of Pioneer Women in the diaspora communities have been an important factor in Jewish life outside Israel.

All these and other achievements make up a glowing canvas which justified our celebrating, with satisfaction and pride, the fiftieth anniversary of Moezet Hapoalot two years ago, and now, in 1975, the jubilee of the Pioneer Women's movement in the diaspora.

The English title of this book, *The Plough Woman*, conveys a twofold meaning: literally, the desire of the early *haluzot* to become tillers of the soil as a primary basis for the healthy existence of a nation, and symbolically, the cultivation of a new society in a rebuilt homeland.

Both these meanings are still valid today. Even though agriculture plays a relatively small role in the modern economy, the agricultural settlements continue to be an influential and inspiring element in Israel, and our movement has continued its work of "ploughing" in the sense of education and guidance with the same fervor as in the early days.

The early pioneering days are long past, but they are still fresh in the memory of our movement, and they continue to inspire its activities. They will continue to serve as guidelines to us and to future genera-

---

5. Established in 1935 as an auxiliary of Moezet Hapoalot, Irgun Imahot [Ovdot] [Working Mothers' Organization] was created to give political representation to housewives in private households throughout the Yishuv. The organization grew to include a varied program of social and educational services and child care facilities, with the general purpose of providing assistance during the hours when mothers were at work. Over the years, the organization became a major social and political force in urban life. It sustained a wide array of educational and recreational activities, pre-school facilities, children's clubs, and summer camps that were operated under the aegis of Moezet Hapoalot and sponsored by the Histadrut.

tions, as women and as members of the Israeli and worldwide Labor Zionist movement, striving for the rebirth of our nation and a creative life in a peaceful world. Therein lies the value of *The Plough Woman*.

Last, but not least, we wish to express our tribute of admiration to our *haverah* Rahel Kaznelson-Shazar, who edited this book and who served as an inspiration to the women whose names appear as contributing authors in *The Plough Woman*.

Introduction to the First Edition

Rahel Kaznelson-Rubashov [Shazar] (Palestine, 1931)

This book is, in form and content, the mirror of a great episode in the history of Jewish womanhood. It is not a literary enterprise. It is a simple collection of human documents, a cooperative effort to record, in direct personal reports, the spirit and achievements of a generation of women.

For the last few years the Jewish women workers of Erez Israel have felt a deep inner need to set down in writing the story of their movement; and in 1928 the Moezet Hapoalot [Council of Women Workers] of Erez Israel decided to issue the collective volume *Divrei poalot* [Women Workers Speak], which here appears in English under the name of *The Plough Woman*. Four leading motives were responsible for this resolution. First, the desire to make an accounting of the achievements of the women workers of Erez Israel and to arrive at an accurate evaluation of their worth; second, to put into permanent form certain important incidents in the history of the new Erez Israel; third, to acquaint the Jewish youth throughout the world with that part of our labor history which is represented by the Second and Third Aliyah (1904–1924); fourth, to achieve a greater degree of self-understanding by means of self-expression.

It would have been impossible to achieve these ends merely through a series of abstract articles by specialists. We needed the personal records of those who had been a living part of the process. And therefore some fifty women comrades, nearly all of them engaged in agricultural work—in *kvuzot*, *kibbutzim*, *moshavei ovdim*, *mishkei poalot*, and *havurot hapoalot*—were invited to participate in what might be called the upbuilding of the book. The eagerness with which the Jewish public in Erez Israel and outside has accepted the Hebrew and Yiddish editions has convinced us that the method which was employed in putting together these records was the right one.

The original work was naturally in Hebrew, and was issued by the Moezet Hapoalot in Erez Israel; the first translation, in Yiddish, was published in America under the auspices of the Pioneer Women's Organization. This body is also responsible for the publication of the work in English. In this way an original source is opened to the English reading public which may acquaint itself at first hand with the Jewish women workers and life in Erez Israel, one of the most important and fascinating chapters in the new history of that country.

In the structure of the book an attempt is made to cover systematically the principal problems and aspects of the women workers' movement.

The first section, "In the Beginning," covers the period of the Second Aliyah (1904–1914). It deals with the struggle of the Jewish woman who was adapting herself to a new form of physical labor, with her acclimatization to a new world, a new nature, and new life-forms.

The section "With the Group" deals with the relationship of the individual woman to the Palestinian labor movement in general, and to the specific group to which she happened to be attached in particular. It is a singular story of the self-sacrifice of the one for the many, of the integration of personal lives with the larger life of the community.

"At Work" describes the struggle of the woman worker to find an acknowledged place in the ranks of labor, the rise of her specific forms of settlement—the *mishkei poalot* and *havurot hapoalot*—and her economic and social achievements. To some extent, this section overlaps with the one that follows—"With Children"—for the problems of the family, of the upbringing of children stand in close and inevitable relationship to those of work and social achievement.

The last section, "In the Literature," does not purport to give anything like a picture of the cultural productivity of the Jewish women workers. It is a reminder, rather than a record. For it was impossible to make the book complete without such a reminder and equally impossible to do anything more within these limits. In the same way, the section "The Departed" is the briefest indication, chosen out of a long list of heroic figures, of the sacrifices which have been laid on the altar of Jewish freedom. The women whose lives were broken in the struggle are legion; the few remembered here are representative and not exceptional.

Translator's Note

Maurice Samuel (New York, 1932)

The translation of this book was at once easy and difficult. It was easy because this is a forthright and simple record, without affectations and attempts to be impressive; it was exceptionally difficult because of the recurrence of terms which can be translated literally but cannot be made to convey their true meaning.

The new Jewish homeland has already produced a life with traditional forms: and formal names for certain institutions have already become charged with a unique and intransferable quality. The word *shomer* can only be translated as "guard," or "watchman"; and yet the bald translation is quite as meaningless for the English reader, quite as void of the significance of the term as, let us say, a literal translation of the word "cowboy" into French or German. For the American cowboy of the past is not just a function; he is a tradition, a part of history, a heritage and a peculiarity. He is a unique type and institution. And the *shomer* of Palestine represents now in Jewish life a similar untranslatable phenomenon, a unique product of time and place and will, concentrating within himself a whole world of memories and experiences. He was a symbol of Jewish self-defense, of Jewish emergence from dependence, of Jewish pride. The thrill of the word must be understood not against the background of romantic adventurousness, but against a more significant background of a national renaissance and a repudiation of an unhappy past. For the word *kvuzah* I have occasionally used the literally exact but spiritually inadequate translation "commune." But the *kvuzah* and the *kibbutz*, two Palestinian forms of commune, have a special power in their own setting, and to reach that power the whole setting must be understood. They are, in social form, communes, but their relation to the Jewish national movement, to the cultural revival, to the Palestinian life, turned them into rich, new human experiments; they have acquired, for the Palestinian Jew, inner, subtle values which simple translation cannot convey.

And for this reason I have found myself compelled to leave the words in the original, adding explanations from time to time,[1] and trusting

1. Samuel's discursive "explanations" have been omitted from the present version of the English text. For a discussion of the rationale in this regard, see the Editors' Note.

that the total effect of this book will ultimately convey the full power of these words. A time may come when these words will acquire a certain international currency, when the world will be sufficiently acquainted with the Jewish homeland in Palestine to have direct access to its values; when the *haluz* will be something more than a pioneer, the *shomer* more than a guard, the *kvuzah* more than a commune, the *meshek hapoalot* more than a women's training farm. Every civilization produced high types and institutions which, in their ideal form, are added to the world's collection of models: among these are to be found, to this day, the products of the Palestinian Jewish life of two thousand years ago; among these, in the future, will also be found the products of the Palestinian Jewish life of today. It is therefore perhaps as well to anticipate that time by accepting their word-symbols now.

The casual reader will occasionally be puzzled by differences the existence of which he did not suspect—the difference, for instance, between a "colonist" and a "worker." Here again the historic background is needed as explanation. The Jewish labor movement of Palestine began only in the twentieth century; Jewish colonization before that time was almost exclusively of the "planter" type. The struggle of the Jewish land-worker to find a place for himself in the agricultural economy ran up against the opposition of the old individualist planters who had built their system on the use of cheap, exploited, and unorganized Arab labor. In the twentieth century, the two types of Jewish colonization went on side by side, with the worker type (representing also a specific social idealism cast in specific forms) on the increase. The struggle between the two types is recorded, among other things, in these pages, and the gradual infiltration of Jewish labor into Jewish colonies is an important chapter in the integration of the Jewish homeland.

At one extreme was the *moshavah*, the settlement of purely individualist farms and planters; at the other extreme the *kvuzah*, or commune; in between was the *moshav ovdim*, the individualist settlement in which each family worked its own plot, did not exploit the labor of others, and developed a high degree of cooperation with the other families in the settlement. Behind these colonies must be understood also the background of the national institutions, the [World] Zionist Organization, the Jewish Labor Federation of Palestine,[2] and the various instruments of these organizations. It would confuse rather than help the reader to load his attention at the outset with lists and glossaries. It happens that the pages which follow are so fascinating in a purely human way that the reader's attention will be held even where he cannot always pick his

2. The reference is to the Histadrut.

way through the allusions. As he reads on, however, the picture will clarify itself in his mind; he will gradually and without effort acquire a general picture of the country behind the individual figures which will claim his first attention. More than that, he will begin to appreciate, perhaps for the first time, the extraordinary folk-depths of the movement, the deep and inexhaustible sources of a renaissance which, in effect, is only at its beginning.

Mission Statement of the Pioneer Women's Organization (1932)

The Pioneer Women's Organization, under whose auspices this book is published, was founded in 1925 in New York. At the present time (beginning of 1932) it has a membership of three thousand, comprising sixty clubs throughout the United States and Canada. Until recently the membership consisted of women between the ages of 30 and 50; at the last biennial convention, held in Detroit in October, 1930, it was decided to extend the activities of the organization to younger groups. Ten clubs are now in existence in which the ages of the members are between 18 and 30.

The program of the Pioneer Women's Organization consists of the following:

1. To work for the re-establishment of the Jewish Homeland in Palestine along cooperative and socialistic lines.
2. To assist the Jewish working woman in finding her place in Palestine and in improving her economic and social position.
3. To aid in the training of such types of women pioneers as shall fit, in the industrial and agricultural fields, into the cooperative life in Palestine.
4. To bring about a closer relationship between the working women of Palestine and the working women of the Diaspora.
5. To conduct a constructive cultural activity among the Jewish working women of America, with special reference to the study of the Jewish people, its history, literature and culture generally: to organize and subsidize Jewish folk-schools in America on the basis of the foregoing program.

The Pioneer Women's Organization is affiliated with the Poalei Zion party, and through it with the Socialist International.[1] The Organization is in close contact with the Council of Women Workers of Palestine [Moezet Hapoalot], and with the Histadrut, the General Federation of Labor in that country.

The Organization is headed by a National Executive and a National Secretary, with headquarters at 1133 Broadway, New York.

1. An international consortium of social democratic parties founded in 1923.

Mission Statement of Pioneer Women (1975)

Pioneer Women, the Women's Labor Zionist Organization of America, was founded in New York in 1925 to promote the national and social ideals of Labor Zionism in Israel and the United States.

Pioneer Women has chapters in most of the major cities in the United States, committed to the same ideals around which the organization was founded: the equality of women, the dignity of labor, the importance of the Jewish homeland and the continuity of Jewish life in the United States. Pioneer Women is the sister organization of Moezet Hapoalot, the Working Women's Council in Israel. Its basic program is:

1. To train and educate Israeli women to lead full productive lives, and to provide the social services and educational tools needed to achieve this goal.
2. To educate American Jewish women for a more active involvement in Jewish communal life and in the establishment of a more egalitarian and progressive society in the United States.

In Israel, Pioneer Women operates a large network of social service installations for the women, children, and young people of the country.

In the United States, Pioneer Women actively supports Jewish educational activities, youth programs, and community agencies.

Pioneer Women also maintains close contacts with sister groups in Canada, Argentina, Australia, Brazil, Chile, France, Belgium, Great Britain, Mexico, Peru, and Uruguay, which are similarly dedicated to Jewish education and culture, the promotion of social legislation, and the protection of Jewish rights in general and women's rights in particular.

National headquarters: 315 Fifth Avenue, New York, NY 10016.

Between Text and Context

The Plough Woman in Historical Perspective

Mark A. Raider (Albany, 2002)

Today, it is unthinkable that a university library would not include substantial holdings in women's history and, likewise, the history of Zionism and Israel. This is significant, for it has not always been the case. Indeed, only recently have these fields emerged as important and legitimate disciplines. And yet, it is still difficult to find more than a handful of useful volumes on the history of Zionist women in the library stacks.[1] Where such a corpus does exist, it almost certainly includes a tattered copy of *The Plough Woman: Records of the Pioneer Women of Palestine* (1932) or perhaps its successor, an abridged reprint published in 1975.

It was the paucity of resources on women and Zionism—impressed upon me time and again by students researching the topic—that prompted my interest in *The Plough Woman*. Moreover, when I used selections from the book in my classes, where it sparked lively discussion and debate, I began to wonder aloud, with my students, about the text's publication history. Who published it and why? Who were the authors and where did the selections come from? What connection does it have, if any, to contemporary perceptions of Jewish women? Put somewhat differently, how might an expanded understanding of these women pioneers, known in Hebrew as *haluzot*, refine and revise what we know about Zionist history and Jewish women's history? Could such knowledge prompt a redefinition of "our very conceptions of what Jews and Judaism were and continue to be about"?[2]

The Plough Woman is a veritable treasure trove of information about the nexus between women and Zionism. An extraordinary and compelling amalgamation of memoirs, prose, reflections, diary entries, testimonials, and letters, it is, at once, uplifting and tragic, dramatic and seemingly banal, public and private. The collection vividly depicts and records the reality, experiences, and perspectives of a cohort of East European Jewish women who matured in the turbulent decades spanning the nineteenth and twentieth centuries, and whose lives were forged in the crucible of *pogroms* [anti-Jewish riots], revolution, and state building.

Rahel Kaznelson-Shazar, an emissary of the Jewish labor movement in Palestine, first introduced the volume to the American Jewish scene in 1931. Since then, like American Jewry itself, the book has been in perpetual motion. Reprinted three times between 1931 and 1975, it was on each occasion deliberately edited and refashioned to suit the dynamic American Jewish milieu. During this period, American Jews experienced swift acculturation and upward mobility, the shock of World War II and the Holocaust, the rise of Israel, the dramatic changes brought on by the cold war and the civil rights era, the euphoria of the Six-Day War (1967) and the near disaster of the Yom Kippur War (1973), and, finally, the community-wide struggle to free the Jews of the now former Soviet Union. Against this backdrop, the book's changing interior landscape can be viewed as a reflection of the dynamic relationship between American Jews and the Land of Israel, American Jewry's shifting attitudes toward Zionism and Jewish political activism, and the struggle by Jewish women for social equality.

That *The Plough Woman* evolved over time is, perhaps, a commonplace observation. To appreciate this evolution, however, one must be mindful of the complexity of the period in which the women pioneers produced their writing *and* the fact that the book has had a "life" of its own. Whether deployed as a propaganda tool, used by Zionist organizations for recruitment purposes, enlisted for adult Jewish education, or probed by college students, the volume has fulfilled a unique role as virtually the only portrayal available in American society of women's experiences in prestate Israel. The volume thus is a rich documentary record of Zionism and a barometer of American Jewish interest in and writing about women, Zionism, and the Land of Israel.

I.

Generally regarded as a classic of Zionist and Jewish women's literature, *The Plough Woman* is an eclectic anthology drawn from a variety of sources written between 1915 and 1928. Originally published in Yiddish as *Vos arbeterns derzeyln: a erez yisroel bukh* [The Woman Worker Speaks: An Erez Israel Book] (1931) and edited by the Labor Zionist leader Rahel Kaznelson-Shazar, the book seeks to document the experience of Zionist women pioneers in the new Jewish society-in-the-making in Palestine. As such, it surveys Jewish life in the colonies, rural communes, and agricultural cooperative farms of the period. It also bears witness to the hardship of Jewish life in Palestine during World War I and records numerous personal impressions of the philosopher Aharon David Gordon, the writer Yosef Hayim Brenner, the poet

Rahel Blaustein, and other notable figures of the Yishuv (the Jewish community in Palestine before 1948). It describes and examines Arab-Jewish relations in the twilight of the Ottoman Empire and, after 1920, under the British Mandate. Finally, it offers a firsthand account of gender relations, parent-child relations, and the status of women in the various settlement frameworks of the Palestine Jewish labor movement.

Key segments of the Yiddish volume first appeared in Hebrew under the title *Divrei poalot* [Women Workers Speak] (1928). Several of the latter previously appeared in *Dvar hapoelet* [The Woman Worker Speaks], the central journal of the women's movement in Palestine. Initially, it was Kaznelson-Shazar herself who lit on the idea of publishing an expanded version of *Divrei poalot* in Yiddish, German, English, and Bulgarian translation. Like her activist contemporaries Manya Shohat and Chaim Arlosoroff, who also spent extended time in Europe and America as emissaries of the Palestine labor movement, Kaznelson-Shazar viewed the Yiddish-speaking immigrant communities of the West as a reservoir of support for the Yishuv. Her plan dovetailed neatly with the agenda of the Pioneer Women's Organization,[3] which in 1931 undertook an educational campaign aimed at both Yiddish- and English-speaking Jewish women in the United States.

In fact, the way for *Vos arbeterns derzeyln* already had been paved by a couple of the Labor Zionist movement's previous Yiddish publications designed for American consumption: *Yizkor* [Remember] (1916), a memorial book to the fallen Jewish watch guards of Palestine; and *Erez yisroel* [Land of Israel] (1918), which described the geography and inhabitants of the country.[4] Like these volumes, *Vos arbeterns derzeyln* attracted considerable attention among East European Jewish immigrant quarters. Owing to its positive reception, Pioneer Women subsequently published the abridged 306-page English translation in 1932.

The English translation was composed by Maurice Samuel, a celebrated Jewish intellectual, publicist, and lecturer, who was deeply sympathetic to Labor Zionism and the pioneering movement in Palestine.[5] Samuel's masterful translation of *The Plough Woman* conveys much of the richness, passion, and lyrical quality of the original Yiddish and Hebrew prose. In the process of translating and editing, however, he also elected to simplify the complexity of the original Yiddish volume. Frequently, such simplification assumed the form of distilling whole paragraphs into a few lines. For example, whereas an essay in the original Yiddish volume might contain a lengthy discussion of rivalry among Jewish political parties, replete with detailed information about various groups and individuals, Samuel's English translation offers a summary, often capturing the gist but not the substance of the writer's remarks. In other instances, Samuel jettisons entire sections from the text.[6]

We may never know the precise rationale for Samuel's editorial decisions. Was he instructed to condense the volume as a cost-saving strategy? Was he seeking to eliminate "unnecessary" duplication? Or was he intent on simplification, as appears to be the case in some instances, for the sake of an Americanized audience that had a remote understanding of Jewish life in Palestine? Whatever the actual reasons, it is clear that Samuel's choices were deliberate. A perspicacious reader and skilled publicist, he clearly recognized the complexity and tensions inherent in the text. In the translator's note, for example, he stressed the volume's significance as an encoded portrait of Jewish life in Palestine. He also asserted that the text was, in part, untranslatable—that it could only be fully understood as an expression of existential questions derived from the life experience of modern Jewry. "The translation of this book was at once easy and difficult," he wrote.

It was easy because this is a forthright and simple record, without affectations and attempts to be impressive; it was exceptionally difficult because of the recurrence of terms which can be translated literally but cannot be made to convey their true meaning. The new Jewish homeland has already produced a life with traditional forms . . . The word *shomer* can only be translated as "guard" or "watchman"; and yet the bald translation is quite as meaningless for the English reader, quite as void of the significance of the term as, let us say, a literal translation of the word "cowboy" into French or German. For the American cowboy of the past is not just a function; he is a tradition, a part of history, a heritage and a peculiarity. He is a unique type and institution. And the *shomer* of Palestine represents now in Jewish life a similar untranslatable phenomenon . . . He was a symbol of Jewish self-defense, of Jewish emergence from dependence, of Jewish pride. The thrill of the word must be understood not against the background of romantic adventurousness, but against a more significant background of national renaissance and a repudiation of an unhappy past.[7]

Samuel went on to explain the alleged profundity of the terms *kvuzah* [commune], *kibbutz* [cooperative], *haluz* [Zionist pioneer], and *meshek hapoalot* [women's training farm]. Such "word-symbols," he asserted, reveal the "extraordinary folk-depths of the [Zionist] movement, the deep and inexhaustible sources of a renaissance which, in effect, is only at its beginning."[8]

Samuel's comments underscore the problematic of reading, decoding (or unpacking), and understanding *The Plough Woman*. In attempting to discern the strategy behind Samuel's translation, it is worth considering whether his reconstruction of the Yiddish text was not also a meditation on the original, an innovative interpretation that reshaped the narrative according to his worldview. To be sure, the English text was meant to be more than simply a literal translation of the Yiddish. Appearing at the height of the Depression, a period that coincided with the Yishuv's rapid growth and economic expansion, *The Plough Woman* presented a poignant alternative to the misery and hardship of American society and the Jewish working class in the United States. It purported to point the way to individual fulfillment and collective national redemption, and it was tailored to appeal to an East European Jewish immigrant community increasingly sympathetic to the aims and ideals of Labor Palestine. It gave concrete expression to the concerns of a wide array of Jewish women confronted by the universal challenges of modernity—in the American, Jewish, immigrant, and Zionist settings.

As editor of the volume, Rahel Kaznelson-Shazar was also cognizant of the seemingly irrepressible desire to hone and reshape the text into a unified entity with a distinct message. Consider, for example, her explanation that the volume was "in form and content, the mirror of a great episode in the history of Jewish womanhood . . . It is not a literary enterprise," she insisted. "It is a simple collection of human documents, a cooperative effort to record, in direct personal reports, the spirit and achievements of a generation of women . . ." She continued:

Four leading motives were responsible for this [book]. First, the desire to make an accounting of the achievements of the women workers of Palestine and to arrive at an accurate evaluation of their worth; second, to put into permanent form certain important incidents in the history of the new Palestine; third, to acquaint the Jewish youth throughout the world with that part of our labor history which is represented by [the Second and Third *Aliyot*]; fourth, to achieve a greater degree of self-understanding by means of self-expression . . .[9]

Of course, despite protests to the contrary, Kaznelson-Shazar's statement hints at the paradox of the enterprise as a whole and the multitude of personal and public strands woven into the fabric of the text. Her dual insistence that the volume was intended as an unadorned account *and* a "mirror of a great episode in the history of Jewish womanhood" is a reminder that, in actuality, the autobiographical vignettes of the Zionist women pioneers are impressionistic prose. They are not merely historical accounts, but rather literary and psychological constructs—imagined realities—in which the writers choose to be self-reflective. In the final analysis, the individual contributors' writings, possessed of the limitations and possibilities of a "specific situational context," are edited and compiled so as to exemplify and thematize the lives of Zion-ist women pioneers in the Yishuv.[10]

The Plough Woman also may be profitably compared to the contem-poraneous writings of other East European Jewish women. In another context, it has been demonstrated that the Polish Yiddish weeklies *Froyen-shtim* [Women's Voice] and *Di froy* [The Woman] "featured pri-marily female authors and proclaimed the importance of what we may call self-emancipation." *Di froy*, in particular, sustained a "specific Jew-ish orientation [that] was Zionist as well as feminist, [as] indicated by its . . . focus on pioneering in Palestine and the building of a new life based on Jewish national culture."[11] Similarly, the Yiddish poet and Zionist activist Aliza Greenblatt, who lived in the United States, constructed her autobiography *Baym fentster fun a lebn* [At the Window of a Life] in order to position herself "at the center" of the Jewish public arena, underscoring the value of authorship as "a key component" of the social hierarchy. Her autobiography, in other words, was intended to be "both personal memoir and collective history."[12] Like *Froyen-shtim*, *Di froy*, and *Baym fentster fun a lebn*, *The Plough Woman* illustrates not a new female identity per se, but rather "the confused outline of merging worlds—a new sense . . . of the bounds of geographic, social, and psy-chological representations."[13] The text invites us to explore the chang-ing self-perceptions of Zionist women and reimagine the world in terms of the protean social and political possibilities they imagined in their everyday lives.

Nowhere is the dissonance between the text's intentional and inad-vertent dimensions more readily transparent than the photographs that punctuate the early Yiddish and English editions of the book. (The series is reproduced here in its entirety in a consolidated format.) The 1931 Yiddish volume included twenty photographs, seven of which were portraits of Zionist women pioneers. The series, an intricate kaleido-scope of individual and collective images, alternates between illustra-tions and messages that are subtle and overt, intimate and public, gen-tle and rugged. Like a play-within-a-play, this text-within-a-text seeks to anchor and focus the written narrative. It amplifies the volume's overarching themes of personal transformation, collective fulfillment, national renaissance, the value of labor, liberation of the self, etc. Para-doxically, however, it also brings the volume's dualism into sharp relief and highlights the disjunction between the lofty idealism and harsh reality of Zionist pioneering in Palestine.

For example, figure 3 documents the founding in 1910 of the first *kibbutz*, Dagania, located on the shore of Lake Kineret. Here, women seemingly share an equal role with men, sitting atop the thatched roof of the colony's sole building, among a group of rugged, youthful pioneers. It is noteworthy, however, that the women (all seated in the background) are relegated to the rear of the scene, and identifiable, in part, by their rather traditional dress (they wear dresses and kerchiefs). Meanwhile, the central activity and story of this moment revolves around men: two men sit on horseback; others stand in the foreground and on a staircase; a few brandish weapons and working implements; one is dressed in Bedouin garb (a romantic imitation of Arab life in the Palestinian wilderness). In order to counterbalance such images, *The Plough Woman* deploys photos like that of a woman worker saddling a horse (fig. 9) and Rahel Zisle-Lefkovich resolutely tilling a field in Ein Harod (fig. 20). Yet these are, in fact, photographs of women engaged in isolated activities. The female figures singled out here occupy center stage as much by default as by design.

In fact, the isolated quality of the photographs pervades the narrative as a whole, as when Rivkah Danit notes in "With a Kvuzah of Shepherds":

It was with the utmost difficulty that I, a woman, could persuade [them] to take me along. There were all sorts of objections. The work was too much for a girl. It wasn't nice for a Jewish girl to be working on the open road. There was even one *haver* [comrade] who believed that it would be a national crime! But another girl and I stuck it out for the first week and, in spite of renewed objections, stayed on. At the end of the first month, there was a whole group of women at work on the road.[14]

In the foregoing account of road building in the lower Galilee, Danit literally and figuratively pushes beyond the "objections" and obstacles of her male comrades. She prevails and, in the end, is joined by "a whole group of women." In the development of her narrative, Danit ultimately reconstructs the male-dominated world of the Palestine Jewish labor movement and asserts her own desired centrality and legitimacy as a laborer (a narrative version of figs. 8 and 10)—a kind of end-goal realized in the context of struggle.

In general, the examples above briefly illustrate the overarching structure and pattern of the volume. In response to the reality of gender differentiation that permeates the book, the editors carefully and deliberately inject the narrative with a countervailing imagined reality. They skillfully and artfully place the photographs so as to accentuate women's physical abilities and, in other instances, to shore up the image of their worth and devotion as mothers. Six photographs explicitly associate women with various traditional and domestic tasks, especially in child-rearing settings—for example, a children's house in Kibbutz

Ein Harod, dated 1929 (fig. 5); child-care in the first cooperative farm at Nahalal (fig. 7); children swimming in Lake Kineret (fig. 11); children at Kibbutz Ein Harod on an outing (fig. 12); cooking in a Moezet Hapoalot-sponsored children's house in Tel Aviv, dated 1928 (fig. 13); children being tucked into bed in a Moezet Hapoalot-sponsored children's house in Hederah, dated 1930 (fig. 14).

Parallel to the photographs, the narrative tells a much richer and more complex tale, throwing light on the women's frequent admissions of ambivalence, uncertainty, self-doubt, and self-recrimination. As if to offset questions raised by the female pioneers about their position in and sense of belonging to the new Jewish society, the volume deliberately strikes a balance between images of traditional and nontraditional female roles. In all, six illustrations depict women performing arduous physical and outdoor tasks—e.g., tending a flock of sheep in the Upper Galilee (fig. 2); planting trees in a women's training farm in Jerusalem (fig. 6); tending emaciated cattle in a women's training farm in Nahlat Yehuda (fig. 8); harnessing a mule (fig. 9); paving a road (fig. 10); tilling a field with a hoe (fig. 20). The illustrations belie the women's struggles, especially the tensions inherent in their multidimensional lives as radicals, workers, and homemakers.

The remaining seven illustrations—a mostly sober and austere set of portraiture—anchors a group of memorials to "departed" (read: deceased) comrades. A few of the photographs were clearly taken before the individuals immigrated to Palestine. Three are composed in a traditional and reserved manner, namely, those of Shoshana Bogen (fig. 15); Dvorah Drakhler (fig. 16); and Pessie Abramson, dated 1914 (fig. 18). Three others reveal a nontraditionalist attitude and strong sense of independence: Sarah Chizhik, dressed as a nurse, dated 1919 (fig. 17); Sarah Lishansky, clothed in a dark Russian outfit with an embroidered collar, dated 1907 (fig. 19); and Rahel Zisle-Lefkovich, wearing short pants and short-sleeves, tilling the fields of Kibbutz Ein Harod (fig. 20). The final portrait, located in a place of honor (and putting closure on the volume), is reserved for Rahel Blaustein, the famous poet of the Second Aliyah (fig. 21). Seated beside her comrades, listening intently to a discussion, Blaustein's measured, calm, and youthful visage suggests an air of quiet confidence and resolute determination.

The Plough Woman, with its veneration of the Zionist women pioneers, was something of a cross between an account of everyday life and a sacred text. True believers revered these women as exemplars of the new irreligious Jewish religion (the text is replete with expressions of their holiness and saintly behavior); Rahel Kaznelson-Shazar, Manya Shohat, and others were its high priests; and "departed" comrades like

Sarah Lishansky, Pessie Abramson, and Rahel Blaustein were anointed as its martyrs.[15] Maurice Samuel accentuated the valorization of the Zionist women pioneers in his English translation. Consider, for example, some of the important ways in which Samuel's reconstruction altered the Yiddish text, thereby emphasizing the mythic qualities of the Zionist women pioneers. First, in the transition from *Vos arbeterns derzeyln* to *The Plough Woman*, the writers' individual names were dropped from the table of contents.[16] Each entry thereby acquired an aura of universal, rather than merely personal, significance. Second, the number of entries in each section was reduced. Parts I ("In the Beginning"), II ("With the Group"), and III ("At Work") were lightly edited —one entry was dropped from parts I and II each; two entries were deleted from part III. Part IV ("The Child in Group Upbringing") was reduced from eight to five entries in all. Such changes had a cumulative effect of streamlining the text.

Most striking, however, is the extent to which the latter parts of the book were substantially edited. Part V ("The Departed"), a necrology comprising memorials about and writings by the deceased women themselves, initially contained entries by many contributors. Whereas the length and style of the entries in the Yiddish text varied considerably, the English translation significantly reduced, modified, and reconfigured the narratives for uniformity. Instead of appearing as composites of contributions by eighteen different writers, each entry was subsumed under the name of the Zionist woman pioneer alone. The distinctive voices of individuals thus were muted and submerged into the larger text. In the process, "The Departed" was transformed from a series of nuanced and diversified writings into a relatively homogeneous and unidimensional whole.

As part of the effort to create a pantheon of giants, the English edition retains all seven photographic portraits (while reducing the series as a whole to fourteen photographs). Meanwhile, little is made of the inglorious deaths of these young women. The editorial silence in this regard and the book's general deemphasis of the hardships of life in the Yishuv—including diseases, fatal accidents, skirmishes with Arabs, and suicides so tragically prevalent in this period—serves to amplify the narrative's epic quality. It also explains, in part, another fundamental change in the English edition: the total omission of a thirty-three–page section of the Yiddish text (part VII) entitled *"Fun briefe un tagbikher"* [Diaries and Letters]. Clearly, the English edition is less concerned than the Yiddish text with the real life experiences of the Zionist women pioneers. Its focus is instead trained on an American readership to be won over by a mythology of Jewish pioneering in Palestine.

Like the plethora of Zionist propaganda and iconography that steadily penetrated the Jewish public arena in this period, *The Plough Woman* was calculated to evoke sympathy and identification with the Zionist pioneers and the Yishuv.[17] As shown here, however, although the Zionist pioneer was a unique Labor Zionist creation, the image of the pioneer was far from monolithic. It was adapted and used to exploit a range of complex attitudes to modern Jewish life, including broad themes that resonated with the experiences of Jewish immigrant women in the United States. In sum, such images gave concrete expression to the mythology of Zionist women—on the one hand, brawny, weather-beaten, rugged pioneers living off the land; on the other, maternal, nurturing, feminine caretakers whose domestic roles were transvalued to suit the needs of the new Jewish society-in-the-making. This dualism helped to elevate the notion of *haluziut* [pioneering] to the position of a hallowed Zionist and Jewish feminist ideal.

II.

The Plough Woman's impact in the 1930s appears to have been limited to Zionist and Jewish immigrant quarters. Indeed, general awareness of the topic did not resurface for several decades. The Pioneer Women's Organization itself did not reprint the volume until 1975. In trying to account for the sharp decline in interest, it is worth considering external social pressure that militated against a widespread appreciation of the radical Jewish sensibility heralded by the volume. A brief list of such items would surely include the following: the speedy acculturation and swift upward mobility of America's Jews, which placed American Jews at arm's length from the socialist orientation of the Palestine labor movement; the trend toward domesticity and *embourgeoisement* among middle-class American Jewish women, which contrasted sharply with the attitudes of Zionist women pioneers; and the text's glorification of revolutionary and communist values, which quickly went out of fashion as a result of the Red Scare and the McCarthy era.

In the 1960s and 1970s, however, against the backdrop of the Six-Day War of June 1967 and the rise of the counterculture movement, American Jews generally and Jewish feminists in particular displayed renewed interest in the lives of heroic Jewish women.[18] The burgeoning publications of the period are evidence of this trend as well as a pervasive desire to reorient perceptions of women in Jewish life. Consider, for example, a few disparate works that illustrate such shifts in the American Jewish outlook. First, *The Jewish Catalog* (1973), an enormously popular do-it-yourself guide to Judaism and Jewish life in American society, contained a chapter on Jewish women emphasizing "consciousness raising" and suggesting new "areas of priorities for interested Jewish women."[19] Second, *Women in the Kibbutz* (1975), a controversial multigenerational study by the sociologists Lionel Tiger and Joseph Shepher, focused attention on the unique experiment of Israeli communal living and, in the words of the publisher, raised "new questions about the goals of the Women's Liberation Movement."[20] Third, Anne Lapidus Lerner's "'Who Hast Not Made Me a Man': The Movement for Equal Rights for Women in American Jewry," a significant contribution to the *American Jewish Year Book* of 1977, accurately pointed to the vitality and durability of feminism in contemporary American Jewish life. The sentiment of the period was summed up in Lerner's bold assertion that "Queen Esther no longer reigns supreme in the hearts of young Jewish women. More and more of them are admiring Vashti's spunk instead." In the final analysis, she optimistically intoned, as "the image of Queen Esther is becoming less persuasive . . . the new Jewish feminism must be confronted and accommodated to ensure the survival of American Jewry."[21]

As participants and observers alike created a new literature and public arena about Jewish women and for feminist discourse—e.g., Trude Weiss-Rosmarin's "The Unfreedom of Jewish Women" (1970); *Lillith* magazine, established in 1976 by Susan Weidman Schneider and Aviva Cantor; Blu Greenberg's *On Women and Judaism* (1979); etc.—some female scholars turned to history in order to discern "models from [the] past." "From them we learn," explained Elizabeth Koltun in *The Jewish Woman: New Perspectives* (1976) "that we are not the first Jewish women discontent with 'women's place' and that, concomitantly, Jewish feminism does not, in fact, represent the total break with our past which our critics would have us believe."[22] A cursory review of such models, though incomplete, adumbrates the emergent Jewish feminist movement and the place occupied by Zionist heroes in the mind of American Jewish women. For example, of the four role models featured in Koltun's anthology, two were distinguished Zionists: Henrietta Szold, the American founder of Hadassah and head of Youth Aliyah; and Rahel Yanait Ben-Zvi, a Labor Zionist leader and founder of the Hashomer self-defense organization in Palestine. Likewise, a bibliographic "Guide to Jewish Women's Activities" in *The Jewish Catalog* begins with five autobiographical works written and edited by Zionist women activists: Rahel Yanait Ben-Zvi, Geula Cohen, Irma L. Lindheim, Rahel Kaznelson-Shazar, and Ada Maimon. It also contains numerous references to women in the Zionist movement, the Yishuv, and contemporary Israel. In another instance, a slim volume entitled *Sisters of Exile* (1974), published by the American Zionist youth movement Habonim, focused on the lives of significant women in Jewish history and elevated Zionist activists to the pantheon of modern Jewish heroes. *Sisters of Exile* is also noteworthy, because it found its way into many Jewish studies classes on American college campuses during an era when such information was still largely ignored and inaccessible. Finally, it is worth noting Golda Meir's best-selling autobiography, *My Life* (1975), that enjoyed a mass distribution in the United States.

Viewed in the wider context of American Jewish life, the developments described above are not surprising. The growing identification of Jewish women with Zionism and Israel in this period—despite the checkered track records of both vis-à-vis the equality and empowerment of women—was a self-defining characteristic of American Jewish feminism in the 1970s. In fact, despite external pressures many Jewish feminists refused to sever their links to Zionism.[23] Adding further weight to this view, the strong similarities between Jewish feminism and Zionism can be explained from a historical perspective:

Like Zionism, Jewish feminism emerged from an encounter of Jews who were deeply concerned with the fate of their group with secular Western culture . . . Jewish feminism, too, did not spring in an unmediated way from Jewish tradition . . . It took secularized Jews, influenced by the rise of feminism in America in the 1960s, to establish a Jewish feminist movement that provided a radically modern form to strivings for gender equality.[24]

In 1975, the Pioneer Women's Organization, in collaboration with Herzl Press of the American Zionist movement, reprinted an abridged edition of *The Plough Woman* using a subtly modified subtitle: "Memoirs of the Pioneer Women in Palestine." The volume's rationale was updated and rearticulated by Marie Syrkin and Beba Idelson who wrote, respectively, the new book's foreword and epilogue. Calling *The Plough Woman* "a vivid, personal record of remarkable women in a heroic time," Syrkin, a noted Zionist polemicist and the daughter of the seminal Labor Zionist ideologue Nahman Syrkin, asserted that "some of the problems examined by the writers sound as modern as the latest issue of *Ms.* magazine."[25]

These young women in a desolate corner of the Middle East were a revolutionary vanguard of the movement to liberate women not only politically, but from their own enslavement to conventional attitudes as to the role of women in society . . . The young women pioneers who came to Palestine in the early decades of the twentieth century shared the dream of their male comrades: they would create a new egalitarian society in a Jewish homeland, reclaimed through their labor. To this they added still another dimension—the full emancipation of women. In the great task of rebuilding Palestine women were not to be shunted aside into the traditional feminine roles . . . Not that the respective roles of women and men were ever sorted out to everybody's satisfaction. The voices heard in *The Plough Woman* keep harping on both the difficulty of fulfilling the desire of women for absolute equality in the choice of work as well as on the hardships of and unforeseen complexities of an existence in which this desire was fulfilled.[26]

In a similarly filiopietistic vein, Idelson waxed poetic about the "*haverot* [comrades] who contributed their stories to the original edition of *The Plough Woman*." The title of the book, she explained, "conveys a two-fold meaning:"[27]

Literally, the desire of the early *haluzot* [women pioneers] to become tillers of the soil as a primary basis for the healthy existence of a nation, and symbolically, the cultivation of a new society in a rebuilt homeland. Both these meanings are still valid today . . . Our movement has continued its work of "ploughing" in the sense of education and guidance . . . The early pioneering days are long past, but they . . . will continue to serve as guidelines to us and to future generations, as women and as members of the Israeli and worldwide Labor Zionist movement, striving for the rebirth of our own nation and a creative life in a peaceful world. Therein lies the value of *The Plough Woman*.[28]

The assessments by Syrkin and Idelson point to *The Plough Woman*'s resonance and appeal for Jewish women nearly half a century after it first appeared. For Zionist stalwarts of Syrkin's generation who were ambivalent about the "current feminist vogue" and "the pressure of Women's Lib," the reprint served as a legitimator of long-cherished values and a touchstone in a rapidly changing world. Meanwhile, for younger women it provided a multifaceted model of "the new Jewish woman they hoped to create through the feminist movement and Jewish feminism."[29]

The volume's inclusion of Beba Idelson established a living link between the halcyon era of Zionist pioneering and the more recent decades of the 1960s and 1970s. A member of the Israeli Parliament and Moezet Hapoalot's secretary general for over four decades, Idelson literally embodied the values and goals of Jewish feminism and the Zionist movement. One can only surmise the reason Idelson was asked to contribute to the volume rather than Golda Meir, who was herself a product of American Labor Zionism. Yet, it is a distinction laden with symbolism, one that underscores the admiration of American Jewish women for so-called "authentic" Israelis. Generational differences notwithstanding, the inclusion of Idelson was a kind of imprimatur and a shrewd choice. Framed by Syrkin and Idelson, the reissued "memoirs of the pioneer women," including basic explanatory notes about the contributors and a glossary of places and terms, were reconfigured to service Labor Zionist veterans and uninitiated readers alike.

Sadly, the new edition included only six poorly reproduced illustrations and one portrait (Rahel Blaustein), sandwiched together at the end of the book. Whereas the photographic series once conveyed a compelling and dynamic story parallel to that of the narrative, by 1975 the illustrations had become mere appendages, shorn of real value. The reprint also jettisoned the section entitled "The Departed," thus omitting some of the most important (albeit complex and ambivalent) moments in the text. In its glorification of "heroic women in a heroic time," the new edition heightened the mythology of the Zionist pioneer women. Despite the dust jacket's professed goal to "make available a fascinating chapter in the history of pioneer Palestine," the simplified version of the text and new cover illustration (fig. 22) actually promoted an ahistorical myth.[30] To be sure, the real rationale for republishing the volume was not historical but organizational. The Pioneer Women group sought to exploit growing interest in Jewish feminism and recruit new members to its ranks. Little thought was given to the value of the text from a documentary perspective. To the extent that such awareness did exist, it was surely minimal, or, to paraphrase one scholar, motivated by antiquarian conceptions of "contribution" and "compensatory history"—early feminist conceptualizations of history primarily concerned with recounting, rather than analyzing, the place of women in society.[31] The updated "plough woman" supplied an image that compelled respect, not necessarily by its truth, but because it was needed by those who believed in the transcendent power of Israel and Zionism. Indeed, as Marie Syrkin makes plain in her disdain for "the fanfare that has accompanied present manifestations of a heightened feminist consciousness," the time was not yet ripe to "test familiar generalizations and rewrite the historical narrative" of women and Zionism.[32]

The irony of this prevailing mythos was not lost on contemporary observers of Zionism and Jewish life. In 1975, for example, Tiger and Shepher argued that the experiment of kibbutz living was "substantially less successful" for women than men. "Though such a conclusion will be painfully unpopular just now," they wrote, "we estimate that our data about women in the kibbutz are in accord with the data of others about human and mammalian sex differences."[33] Meanwhile, Lesley Hazleton derisively pointed to the mythology of the "liberation of Israeli women" as the logical outcome of the hegemony of Zionist patriarchal attitudes and values.

The multifaceted manifestations of the myth include the woman soldier just landed from a parachute jump . . . the tough kibbutz woman working the fields alongside men . . . the sexually uncomplicated urbanite who takes what she wants with no misgivings; and of course, the tough, wizened politician taking her place in the arena of international politics . . . Surrendering their real identity to the "cover identity" ascribed them by ideology, [Israeli women] move in a male world of reality in the false guise of equals.[34]

The veracity of the claims made by Tiger and Shepher or Hazleton is not at issue here. What their positions do throw light on, however, is the bipolar tension that underlies perceptions of Jewish women in the modern period. As argued in this essay, one way of contextualizing this debate is to consider the changing worldviews of *The Plough Woman*'s Yiddish- and English-speaking readers over time. Additionally, a comparative analysis of the volume's several versions reveals multiple layers of meaning embedded in the text. This also brings into focus some of the Jewish, Zionist, and feminist views refracted by the book at different junctures. Last, excavating *The Plough Woman* and mining the women's voices at its core require, in part, analytic tools derived from feminist qualitative methods. Miriam B. Raider-Roth undertakes this challenge in the accompanying introductory essay.

It has been argued that examining the situational context of women's writing, while fraught with difficulty, "yields a sense of the writer's character and personality as she shapes her self-image through her writing."[35] It is my contention that such an approach can be expanded to address not only the question of individual writers but anthologies such as *The Plough Woman* in toto. That is to say, each American edition of *The Plough Woman*, though a composite of personal reflections and structurally different, is in fact part of a complex web whose strands cannot be fully disentangled or viewed in isolation. Each text possesses its own integrity, but none can be fully understood outside the context of the common *mentalité* of female Zionist pioneering that pervades the corpus as a whole.

The Plough Woman presents a unity of interrelated experiences and reveals a *mélange* of secular, modern, radical, and feminist attitudes to women, Judaism, Zionism, and Israel. In its multiple versions, the text impels an important methodological innovation and function: it demands that we broaden our perspective on modern Jewish life and alter our field of historical vision. With its myriad linguistic, stylistic, artistic, historical, and relational dimensions, *The Plough Woman* is ideally suited to this purpose.

III.

Surveying the state of the Zionist historiography, Ben Halpern and Jehuda Reinharz have observed that "the growing body of literature" on the rise of Jewish nationalism and Israel is "voluminous."[36] Curiously, despite the field's swift growth, only scant attention has been paid to the subject of women and Zionism. For example, even after a century of unmatched organizational activity and fundraising, there is still no comprehensive analysis of Hadassah, the largest American Zionist group, and one of the most important women's groups in the United States. Nor have historically significant Zionist leaders like Henrietta Szold, Manya Shohat, and Golda Meir yet emerged as the objects of full-scale scholarly biographies. Lack of interest in women and Zionism is all the more striking when contrasted with the general arena of women's history, where the trajectory of feminist scholarship has been nothing short of meteoric. Here, too, however, for a variety of reasons —including ideological antipathy—interest in Zionist women is practically nonexistent. Whether we think of women and Zionism as a subfield of Zionist history or a branch of women's history, the topic remains, in many ways, a stepchild.

The present critical edition proposes a new treatment of the subject. Although it is, in some ways, yet another retrieval and transmission of women's voices, the focus here is on making *The Plough Woman* available in an unexpurgated format and probing the text from an interdisciplinary scholarly perspective. In short, we contend that *The Plough Woman* merits scrutiny and attention as a singularly valuable historical resource and methodological tool. We trust that this volume will be a modest contribution to the pioneering efforts of others who, in recent years, have boldly thrown a bridge over the chasm that separates the fields of Jewish history and women's studies.

Notes

1. See the bibliographic essay in *Partners to Palestine and Israel: American Jewish Women and the Zionist Enterprise*, ed. by Shulamit Reinharz and Mark A. Raider (Hanover and London: University Press of New England), forthcoming.

2. *Jewish Women in Historical Perspective*, ed. by Judith R. Baskin, 2nd ed. (Detroit: Wayne State University Press, 1998), p. 21.

3. For a brief organizational history, see Mark A. Raider, "Pioneer Women" in *Jewish Women in America: An Historical Encyclopedia*, ed. by Paula E. Hyman and Deborah Dash Moore, vol. 2 (New York and London: Routledge, 1997), pp. 1071–77.

4. Mark A. Raider, *The Emergence of American Zionism* (New York and London: New York University Press, 1998), pp. 85–88.

5. For an analysis of Maurice Samuel's interest in Labor Zionism, see ibid., chap. 4.

6. Samuel deleted, for example, Shoshanah Bogen's meditations on the Jewish Legion (the Jewish military force that served under British auspices in World War I) from the midst of her stream-of-consciousness piece; Yoheved Bat-Rahel's poignant reminiscence "*A farshterter yom-tov*" [A Marred Holiday]; all of part VII of the Yiddish volume, a sampling of anonymous letters and diary entries by *haluzot*; and the concluding essay on "The Pioneer Women's Organization in America" by Rahel Yanait Ben-Zvi. See *Vos arbeterns derzeyln: a erez yisrael bukh*, ed. by Rahel Kaznelson-Rubashov (Tel Aviv: Ahdut, 1931), pp. 107–8, 214–16, 333–65, 366–70.

7. *The Plough Woman*, ed. by Rahel Kaznelson-Shazar (Rubashow), 2nd ed., p. xv.

8. Ibid., pp. xvi–xvii.

9. Ibid., pp. xi–xii.

10. Suzanne L. Bunkers, "Midwestern Diaries and Journals: What Women Were (Not) Saying in the Late 1800s" in *Studies in Autobiography*, ed. by James Olney (New York and Oxford: Oxford University Press, 1988), p. 193.

11. Paula Hyman, "East European Jewish Women in an Age of Transition, 1880–1930" in *Jewish Women in Historical Perspective*, ed. by Judith R. Baskin, pp. 280–281.

12. Susanne A. Shavelson, "Anxieties of Authorship in the Autobiographies of Mary Antin and Aliza Greenblatt," *Prooftexts*, 18 (1998), pp. 162, 184.

13. Germaine Brée, "Autogynography" in *Studies in Autobiography*, ed. by James Olney (New York and Oxford: Oxford University Press, 1988), p. 177.

14. See Rivkah Danit, "With a Kvuzah of Shepherds," in this volume; part I, p. 39.

15. See Anita Shapira, "The Religious Motifs of the Labor Movement" in *Zionism and Religion*, ed. by Shmuel Almog, Jehuda Reinharz, and Anita Shapira (Hanover: University Press of New England, 1998), pp. 251–72.

16. The names of individual writers have been reintroduced in this edition.

17. See Mark A. Raider, *The Emergence of American Zionism*, chap. 3.

18. See Paula E. Hyman, "Jewish Feminism" in *Jewish Women in America: An Historical Encyclopedia*, ed. by Paula E. Hyman and Deborah Dash Moore, vol. 1 (New York and London: Routledge, 1997), pp. 694–98.

19. *The Jewish Catalog*, ed. by Richard Siegel, Michael Strassfeld, and Sharon Strassfeld (Philadelphia: Jewish Publication Society of America, 1973), pp. 252, 258–60.

20. Lionel Tiger and Joseph Shepher, *Women in the Kibbutz*, paperback ed. (New York and London: Harcourt Brace Jovanovich, 1975), back cover.

21. Anne Lapidus Lerner, "'Who Hast Not Made Me a Man': The Movement for Equal Rights for Women in American Jewry," *American Jewish Year Book* (1977), pp. 3, 38.

22. *The Jewish Woman: New Perspectives*, ed. by Elizabeth Koltun (New York: Schocken Books, 1976), p. 137.

23. Sylvia Barack Fishman, *A Breath of Life: Feminism in the American Jewish Community* (New York and Toronto: The Free Press, 1993), pp. 9–10, 242–43.

24. Paula E. Hyman, *Jewish Feminism Faces the American Women's Movement: Convergence and Divergence* (Ann Arbor: Jean and Samuel Frankel Center for Judaic Studies, University of Michigan, 1997), p. 2.

25. *The Plough Woman*, ed. by Rachel Kaznelson Shazar (Rubashow), 2nd ed., p. ix.

26. Ibid., pp. vii–viii.

27. Ibid., p. 265.

28. Ibid., pp. 267–68.

29. Deborah Dash Moore, "Hadassah" in *Jewish Women in America: An Historical Encyclopedia*, ed. by Paula E. Hyman and Deborah Dash Moore, vol. 1 (New York and London: Routledge, 1997), p. 581.

30. *The Plough Woman*, ed. by Rachel Katznelson Shazar (Rubashow), 2nd ed., dust jacket.

31. *Women's America: Refocusing the Past*, ed. by Linda K. Kerber and Jane Sherron DeHart, 4th ed. (New York and Oxford: Oxford University Press, 1995), pp. 4–5.

32. *The Plough Woman*, ed. by Rachel Katznelson Shazar (Rubashow), p. vii; *Women's America*, ed. by Linda K. Kerber and Jane Sherron DeHart, p. 5.

33. Lionel Tiger and Joseph Shepher, *Women in the Kibbutz*, p. 280.

34. Lesley Hazleton, *Israeli Women: The Reality Behind the Myths* (New York: Simon and Schuster, 1975), pp. 20–22. Hazleton further noted: "For nearly three decades Israeli women have been the paradigm of women's liberation, the only example of feminism achieved in a world that has yet to awaken fully to the meaning of the word. They have made an essential contribution to Israel's self-image as good and progressive . . . It is an inspirational myth, and such myths die hard. They make good journalistic copy. They are exciting. They appeal to the idealist in all of us. Thus, Western feminists have been no more immune to the power of the myth than others. The pride in Golda Meir, Israel's premier until 1974, was symptomatic. While nobody attempted to prove that Indian women were liberated by pointing to Indian Premier Indira Gandhi, 'Look at Golda' became the slogan of the myth of Israeli women's liberation. The admi-

ration Golda Meir inspired was largely an expression of the longing for women's liberation, a wishful perception of liberation achieved. In this sense, the myth of Israeli women's liberation is perhaps a creative myth, answering deep-rooted needs among women the world over" (p. 21).

35. Suzanne L. Bunkers, "Midwestern Diaries and Journals," p. 193.
36. Ben Halpern and Jehuda Reinharz, *Zionism and the Creation of a New Society* (Hanover and London: University Press of New England, 2000), p. 323.

The Plough Woman
Identities in the Making

Miriam B. Raider-Roth (Albany, 2002)

> ... perhaps I never made my body whole
> in the blue and quiet gleam
> Of my Kineret! Oh Kineret of my soul,
> Were you once true, or have I dreamed a dream?
> —Rahel Blaustein
> (translated by Maurice Samuel)

I. Introduction

The Plough Woman is a polyphonic narrative that captures the struggles and dreams of more than fifty women who immigrated to Palestine shortly after the turn of the twentieth century. As the women sought to build a new society predicated on the values of Labor Zionism, Judaism, and egalitarianism, they assumed new and complex identities. The most powerful and provocative of these were that of "worker" and "*haverah*" [comrade]. In recounting the assimilation of their new identities, the writers describe critical shifts in their relationships to their community, family, and selves. The women describe these transformations in their discussions of work, gender, liberation, community, and motherhood. The narratives are framed by rich and detailed images of body and physical experience that reveal the women's evolution of identity. This physical imagery not only reflects the nature of life in Palestine at the time but also represents the women's internal landscape.

Written in the early twentieth century, *The Plough Woman* nevertheless raises issues that continue to be central to contemporary feminism. As women assume new identities—new definitions of role, self, and affiliation—how does this transformation affect their relationships with others? How do their understandings of themselves change? In asking these questions, I seek to discern the authors' definitions of their emergent identities and the effect of these new identities on their significant relationships.

In contemporary feminist theory, the questions of identity posed here fall into the domain of "relational psychology." The questions are psychological in that they probe the terrain of the women's "self," paying close attention to the contexts of culture and environment. They are relational in that they seek to understand the interplay between how the women's self-understanding shaped their relationships to the individuals, the communities, and the society around them. A full understanding of *The Plough Woman* demands a psychological method of inquiry that elucidates the women's shifting conceptions of self and their evolving interpersonal relationships. The texts themselves require a method of inquiry that reveals the fundamental tensions embedded in the women's shifting sense of self and relationship.

In this essay, I address these issues by employing the tools of "The Listening Guide," a psychological method designed to uncover the relational complexities embedded in personal narratives (Brown et al., 1988; Brown & Gilligan, 1991; Brown & Gilligan, 1992; Gilligan, 1996; Gilligan, Brown & Rogers, 1990; Rogers, Brown & Tappan, 1993; Taylor, Gilligan & Sullivan, 1995). This method asks the reader to examine the text in three distinct and diverse ways. First, the reader must attend to the narrative and psychological plot of the text. That is, what is the thematic and psychological landscape of the story told? In addition, what issues are silenced, negated, or noticeably absent from the text? Second, the reader listens to the ways in which the author of the narrative speaks of her "self." That is, how is the author's sense of "I"—a narrative representation of self (Brown & Gilligan, 1992)—present and/or absent in the text? Finally, the reader listens to how the author talks about the essential consonances and dissonances within her relationships. These three complementary readings make it possible to hear the women's stories fully, detect the ways in which their new identities affected their primary relationships, and understand how such transformations shaped their evolving sense of self.[1]

II. Becoming a Worker: A Transformation of Body

As the authors of *The Plough Woman* began their lives in Palestine, they quickly assumed new identities as "workers." Whereas their lives in Eastern Europe were filled with domestic work and studies, they came

---

1. Other examples in which the Listening Guide has been used to analyze narrative texts can be found in Gilligan, 1992, and Rogers, 1992.

to Palestine seeking to shed their old identities and become workers of the land in accordance with the prevailing ethos of Labor Zionism. The very title of this volume, *The Plough Woman*, demonstrates the desire to attach the concept of working or ploughing the land to their identities as women.[2]

This new identity involved, first and foremost, a transformation of body. Indeed, one of the most striking characteristics of these essays is the extent to which many of the experiences described are physical in nature; much of the imagery employed refers to the body or physical characteristics. Transforming their bodies (and selves) into workers was a process filled with pain and sometimes horror. They vividly describe how their bodies became weaker or stronger; how they faced famine and starvation; how they battled illnesses such as malaria, tuberculosis and typhoid. The body imagery and descriptions of physical experiences not only reveal how the women's bodies changed but also capture the tensions inherent in the women's understanding of and connection to their work. The language of body that the women use often represents their psychological or interior experiences. By examining this language and imagery, it is possible to view the ways that the physical reveals the psychological.

Dvorah Dayan's essay, "My *Aliyah* to the Land of Israel," for example, describes her acculturation to life in the *kvuzah* [commune] via a physical experience of learning to bake bread. Using highly embodied images, Dayan's story reveals her most potent fears and yearning. In this dramatic and full account, she details the process of becoming of a worker:

And now I must convert theory into practice. A little time passes and my hands begin to tremble with exhaustion. The fingers won't obey orders. I put all my strength into it—but the flour will not turn into dough. I know I oughtn't to do it, but I add more water, and the flour turns into a sticky, sloppy mess. I can't pull my hands out without dragging everything along. I twist them, rub them —no use! My back aches. I am tortured by thirst. The flies settle on my face and I can't drive them away. They crawl over my forehead, into my eyes and mouth. "Bread for fifty people!" I repeat to myself, and attack the mess of flour and water again. I feel all my strength running out of me. I stand on one foot, then on the other. I try to think of other things, but I am haunted by one thought: "I want to add more water." M. passes by and looks at me with pitying eyes.

And now, at last, the first good signs. Something like dough begins to

2. Many thanks to Carol Gilligan for this insight.

emerge. It grows smoother and less clinging, and I can free my hands. I can add water, drink a little myself, and wipe the sweat off my face. The torture changes to pleasure. A stone has fallen from my heart, or I feel as if I had just thrown off my winter mantle and run out with the first sign of spring, over the green meadows.

It seems to me that only yesterday I was a thing torn by doubts and hesitations. In the noisy city, in the great library, in the museum, in the classes, the question would suddenly confront me: Why are you doing these things? Who needs you? Can't they do without you and people like you? And in such moments a paralyzing apathy would creep over me; I wanted to see no one, speak with no one. But now? My *haverim* [comrades] are out in the field, mowing the harvest that we have sown. Close by, I hear the mill grinding out grain. And the flour from the mill comes straight to me, and I bake the bread for all of us. Bread is surely needed. (part I, p. 37)

Employing the lifelike imagery of turning flour and water into dough, Dayan conveys the urgency of her desire to become a competent worker. As the dough begins to take form, she too emerges with a new identity and a burgeoning understanding of her life in the collective. She grasps the fact that her work matters to the group, that her labor is needed and valued, and that her life makes a difference to her community. Dayan's story of becoming a worker in the collective is represented in her experience of learning to bake bread. By isolating the physical images in the narrative, it is possible to identify the ways in which this experience parallels her struggle to assume a new worker identity:

my hands . . . exhaustion . . . fingers won't obey . . . all my strength . . . sticky sloppy mess . . . I can't pull my hands . . . dragging everything . . . twist . . . rub . . . my back aches . . . tortured . . . thirst . . . my face . . . they crawl . . . my forehead . . . my eyes and mouth . . . attack . . . all my strength running out of me . . . one foot . . . the other . . . haunted . . . pitying eyes . . . less clinging . . . free my hands . . . add . . . drink, wipe the sweat off my face . . . torture . . . pleasure . . . stone fallen from my heart . . . thrown off . . . run out.

Describing her work, she highlights the images of pain, exhaustion, and heaviness. Her physical transition from "torture to pleasure" represents her transition from oppression to freedom and is vividly recounted with images that move from twisting, attacking, dragging, draining, and thirsty qualities to those of freedom, quenching, and running. In tracing these words, we can see that in successfully assuming her identity as a worker in the group, she sheds her experience of oppression and transitions to a stance of freedom.

This shift reveals both her physical metamorphosis and the central purpose of her emerging identity as a worker: she successfully becomes a member of the group. In becoming a worker, she locates her place in the group and solidifies her attachment to it. As the "sticky mess" becomes dough and she can free her hands, Dayan articulates the importance of her "comrades" to her own sense of well-being. In redefining her identity, she crafts a relationship with the community that liberates her from the oppression of her Eastern European past.

Dayan's essay palpably communicates the paramount goal of becoming a worker: becoming a comrade and member of the collective. Yet, the assumption of this dual identity often presents new tensions. Whereas the intense identification with work and the group offer the women resources for strength, resilience, and physical survival, it also presents tensions concerning the women's sense of self as individuals. Again, this tension is often expressed in the language of physical experience. For example, Rahel Zisle-Lefkovich rejects the omnipresent worker identity because it threatens her individuality.

In Karkur, I became acquainted with the small *kvuzah* and all its defects. There I also met the [workers] of the Second Aliyah, and the older type of woman worker. I knew what was lacking in this life: will, freedom, effort . . . Work swallows everything and everybody. Bit by bit, the individual becomes smaller and smaller, and suddenly he finds himself outside the ranks of life. The smallness of their life is palpable everywhere; the very air chokes, you feel yourself closed in, you want to run away.

It's true that the work in the small *kvuzah* is more intensive; everyone must carry the burden. But what good is that? The important thing is the person, not the work. It seems to me that it's wrong for a person to become a draft animal . . . (part V, p. 219)

For Zisle-Lefkovich, work overwhelms the individual to such an extent that the individual disconnects from the community and exists "outside the ranks of life." This disconnection threatens her very life, and she experiences it physically by feeling "choked" and "closed in." The only relief is in escape. The transition from feeling "inside" to that of feeling choked off to the outside is amplified by the transformation of the narrative voice. At first Zisle-Lefkovich's narrative is written from a strong first person "I" position, recounting what she knows with an internal authoritative voice: "I became . . . I met . . . I knew." The group and collective life she encounters challenges her individual sense of self. As she describes the individual shrinking in the context of group work, she shifts her narrative stance to a depersonalized (masculine) third-person voice: "the individual becomes smaller . . . he finds himself." The narrative ends with the choking image in a universal second-person "you" voice.

The shifts in authorial voice can be viewed as signposts that demarcate the very phenomenon the narrative describes. Zisle-Lefkovich tells us that the collective work ethic chokes off the individual voice from the community. As she does so, the "I" voice literally drops out of the account, only to be replaced with a more distant narrative voice. Seeking to bring the force of the experience closer to the reader, she shifts to a "you" voice that, though still more remote than the "I" voice, invites the reader to step into the experience she describes.

III. Being a Woman / Being a Worker

The physical imagery in the texts not only illustrates the tension between the individual and collective identities but also captures the complex dynamics inherent in the way women related to themselves as both females and workers. As the women assumed the stance of workers, many felt it necessary to relinquish their female identities. Several authors describe this phenomenon as if the two identities were fundamentally at odds. Batya Brenner, a young immigrant to Palestine who identifies herself in the volume as "B.B.," was especially forthright in her essay "I Become a Worker."

There was a time when I was known as "the dancer." But that was long ago—on the other side. And when I refused to dance at the wedding of my friend, over there, everyone was astonished. But even then it had lost its appeal. My body sought another rhythm now, other motions than those that are made to musical measures. (part I, p. 49)

Brenner describes the kinds of tensions that ensued when women sought to transform their bodies and become workers on the land. Here, the transformation from girlhood to woman worker, from a "pretty girl" to a useful body, is poignantly rendered. Her description paints a sharp divide between the two identities, separated by time ("long ago") and distance ("on the other side"). The identities appear dichotomous—it is an all-or-nothing proposition. Having previously called herself "the dancer," she takes on a new identity that is nondescript, simply a "body" seeking different rhythms and motions. The complete dichotomy between these identities is clear when she recounts a conflict with Hasidah, the dominant woman of the settlement to which she was a newcomer. Watching Brenner's acclimatization, Hasidah comments that she is

just a girl—like all the others. Out there, in the fields, among the boys, she becomes another person. And all the kitchen work falls on me again.

Brenner responds:

I hear her, and I understand her only too well. And I ask myself what this attitude of hers means. What am I to deduce from it? Have I any right to stay on here? She calls me "little girl" but I want to be a worker. I must make up my mind what to do. (part I, p. 58)

In this interchange, Brenner now names this new identity and body "a worker." Both she and Hasidah clearly articulate that being a girl and a worker are two separate identities, as if Brenner "[o]ut there, in the fields, among the boys . . . becomes another person." Brenner is shaken by this conflict. She knows that she wants to be a worker but fears that she is trapped as the "little girl." What right does she have to change, to seek a new identity, when Hasidah is stuck tending the domestic work of the commune (a less respected occupation among the pioneer settlers)? She struggles to understand her obligations to Hasidah, the collective, and her own desires. This struggle paralyzes Brenner, filling her with anxiety and depression, and ultimately forcing her to leave the settlement. She addresses this divide by writing about her dreams and ideology. Articulating her belief in the collective and its centrality in her new life, she finds a way to knit the seemingly disparate identities together. Only then can she emerge from her self-imposed isolation and return to work in the collective.

The merging of gender and work is expressed clearly by the elders or veterans, who articulate a fullness and satisfaction that comes from their capacity to integrate their identities as laborers and as women. They have learned that they do not need to relinquish a part of themselves to survive the treacherous terrain of the Zionist society-in-the-making. In fact, they harness their female identities in order to survive and create their livelihood. In Ziporah Zeid's writing about Sarah Chizhik, one of "the departed," she recognizes that it was Sarah's womanhood that propelled her strength as a defender of the Jewish colonies.

The years of the war weighed heavily on her, as they did on all of us, but with the ending of the war she entered on a new unfolding of life. She was filled with energy and with desire to work. Those who knew her at that time also knew that wherever a Jewish colony was in danger, wherever help was needed, Sarah would be found. It was the woman in her that drove her. (part V, p. 188)

In her diary, Sarah Chizhik articulates her identity using gendered language. She firmly identifies herself as a "daughter" of the Jewish people.

It is the hope to be a daughter of my people which is rejecting the life it has known till now in order to become a people of labor in its own home on its own soil. (part V, p. 191)

Claiming her female identity vis-à-vis membership in the Jewish people, she adds a national, religious, and cultural dimension to her sense of self, thus fusing the notions of gender, labor, and culture. Her strongest hope is for women, including herself, to be fully integrated as daughters of their people, as laborers in their homeland, on their soil. In sum, she claims her rights as an offspring of the Jewish people through gender and labor.

   Chizhik highlights the inextricable link between gender and religious/national identity in her reflections on the *pogroms* in Eastern Europe.

I have heard the "good" news—the *pogroms* in Poland and in the Ukraine. My heart aches for my brothers and sisters; but more for my sisters, because their death is double. They die for being Jewish and for being women. God! What bestiality! What lowness and vileness! (part V, p. 191)

In this wrenching description of the reality of Eastern European Jewry, Chizhik laments the dual oppression of her "sisters" in Poland: their persecution as Jews and as women. It is this dual oppression that prompts her yearning for dual liberation in Palestine. Such liberation, she asserts, can only be achieved for Jewish women through a sense of peoplehood and belonging in their homeland. Key to the creation of this homeland is developing a relationship with the land itself, a relationship of working the soil. The soil is the physical embodiment of their work, the concept of the Land of Israel, and life in the collective.

IV. Liberation: A Marriage of Gender and Work

Chizhik's essay portrays the inherent connections between the women's yearning for liberation and their understandings of themselves as women, as Jews, and as workers. Although the women desire and struggle to connect their identities as Jewish women to their bodies as workers, the obstacles to this connection are immense and often intensified by the pervasive patriarchy they confront in the Jewish colonies. Upon their immigration to Palestine, they paradoxically found themselves relegated to the kitchen, the laundry, and caring for children. Their dreams of full equality were assaulted by the harsh reality they met. Although faced with tremendous disillusionment—made all the more painful owing to the utopian Labor Zionist ideology to which the women so passionately clung—they did not silence their profound disappointment. They did not rationalize the prevailing patriarchal ethos. Rather, the women purposefully abandoned the existing structures and created women's collectives and training farms; they believed that the actualization of their physical experience was the key to their liberation. In the essay "Stages," Rahel Yanait Ben-Zvi identifies the crux of this struggle:

In the thick of that passionate movement toward the land, the women workers suddenly found themselves thrust aside and relegated once more to the ancient tradition of the house and the kitchen. They were amazed and disappointed to see how the cleavage was opening, the men comrades really uniting themselves with the land, but they, though on it, not becoming part of it. The united front was cracking. So that even then a handful of women—all of them very young—set out in a group to build up their own working relationship to the soil. (part III, p. 109)

Like Sarah Chizhik, Yanait Ben-Zvi names the central relationship that is key to sustaining their ideology and idealism—the relationship to the land and the soil. She asserts that her relationship with the soil, not just with the concept of the Land of Israel, requires nurturing and protection. She continues,

But all these things are external compared with the fundamental problem of the woman worker herself, and of her attitude toward the *meshek hapoalot* [women's training farm]. True, the *meshek hapoalot* is a training ground, but it must not be regarded merely as an institution where women come to learn a trade. It is not a trade, it is a sort of personal destiny we teach . . . The woman learns to educate herself, and to awaken from within a deep and permanent relationship to the soil. (part III, pp. 113–114)

Yanait Ben-Zvi teaches that the relationship with the soil is to be drawn from the women. It is organic rather than imposed from the outside.

This inherent part of the women's identity is elicited only through a self-education of working the soil. The purpose of nurturing this aspect of the women's identity is to effect their liberation from traditional domestic roles so that they may actively build their homeland.

While many of the narratives in *The Plough Woman* explore the notion of work as the driving force toward collective liberation—freedom for the Jewish people—the women also closely examine the meaning of work in their own personal liberation as individuals. In "The 'Independent' Woman," for example, Hannah Chizhik, examines how work can help the women redefine their sense of self:

And a new question comes up. We, the women workers of Erez Israel, regard our work as something primary in our lives; through work we will regain our personalities. And yet I must ask myself, what is my authentic inner relationship to my work? (part III, p. 143)

Chizhik argues that through understanding their own relationships with themselves and their work, the women pioneers will locate their "personality" or their sense of selfhood. Indeed, this self-understanding is a central form of psychological freedom.

By closely examining the narrative stance and shifts that are embedded in Chizhik's language, it is possible to view how the collective forum of work yields this individual sense of freedom. By writing in the combined collective "we" voice ("We, the women workers . . . our work . . . our lives . . . we will regain our personalities") and the authoritative personal "I" voice ("I must ask myself . . . my authentic inner relationship . . . my work"), Chizhik highlights the integral relationship between the collective work and the search for selfhood. Her final question concerning her "authentic inner relationship" to work brilliantly illuminates the essence of the worker/woman identity tension. The word "inner" connotes her individual self whereas the word "work," by its very nature in this context, refers to the collective. It is a question of the self in relation to the collective.

V. Motherhood: Negotiating Self, Work and Family

As the women constructed identities as workers, their new sense of self (or these new aspects of their "personalities") inevitably created conflict and tension with other key aspects of their identity. Just as the evolution of the comrade identity challenged the women's sense of individual self, so too did the worker role challenge the women's family relationships—especially their roles as mothers. In "The 'Independent' Woman," Hannah Chizhik expresses this tension forcefully:

It may be that this curious attitude toward our own work has to do with the instinctive knowledge that some day we will have to leave the work because of the child. And therefore—though we do not acknowledge it—we have a different, a lighter relationship to our own work. And this relationship deprives us of what is most important in life—belief in our own forces, respect for our own selves. And we will never know the feeling of harmonious work as long as we do not know a complete inner compulsion to earn our own livelihood.

And when we do find a woman who has complete faith in her own strength, we see her crumbling under the double yoke—her job and her family. (part III, pp. 143–144)

Chizhik reiterates the notion that the women's relationship with work is the guiding force of their self-discovery. Whereas the patriarchy of the settlement organizations posed a major challenge to this self-realization, so too did the women perceive their children and family as a threat to their developing sense of self. This profound tension is evident in the narrative stance Chizhik assumes in the text. By employing the collective "we" and the distant "her" ("we can see her crumbling") in describing the "double yoke" of family and work, Chizhik is able to maintain an up-close collective view of a distant woman. In this dual connected and disconnected stance, she articulates the internal turmoil she experiences in trying to integrate the two aspects of her self. In connecting to her family and children, she feels that she must have a "lighter relationship," or a more remote connection with her work. If she were to feel connected to her self and her family, she would crumble under the weight of these competing demands.

Golda Meyerson (later, Meir) examines this tension in her essay "Borrowed Mothers," in which she describes the ambivalent feelings that arise when her child is cared for by another comrade. Here, she illustrates the sense of disconnection that women experienced when giving their children over to the care of the community so that they themselves could work.

I am not speaking now of the constant worry that haunts the mother's mind that something may have happened. And I need not bring in the feelings of the mother when her child falls sick—the flood of self-reproach and self-accusation. At the best of times, in the best circumstances, there is the perpetual consciousness at the back of the mind that the child lacks the mother's tenderness, misses during the day the mother's kiss. We believe, above all, in education by example; and therefore we must ask ourselves: Whose is the example that is molding the child of the working mother? A "borrowed" mother becomes the model. The clever things the child says reach the mother at second hand. Such a child does not know the magic healing power of a mother's kiss, which takes away the pain of a bruise. And there are times, after a wearying, care-filled day, when the mother looks at her child almost as if she did not recognize it; a feeling of alienation from her nearest and dearest steals into her heart. (part IV, pp. 164–165)

Meyerson's narrative invites the reader to hear her ruminations and internal conversation about her role as mother. In following her narrative position, we can track the tension she describes. She begins in a first person "I" voice that is both present and negated, for example, "I am not speaking"; "I need not bring in." She speaks in the first person and at the same time denies her actions (not speaking, not bring in). In using the immediateness of the "I" voice and the distancing of the negation, she communicates a double meaning embedded in the text: a sense of "living with contradictions," and a sense of struggle in managing two potent forces in her life (Rogers et al., 1999, p. 87; Rogers, 2000).

Describing the alienation she experiences as a mother, Meyerson shifts to a remote third-person voice, in which the mother becomes "she/her" instead of "I." This narrative position communicates a sense of detachment or disconnectedness. Yet, while there is a detachment, the experience is described in immediate physical terms that invite a sensory connection between Meyerson and her reader. Indeed, vivid physical images and body action fill her narrative: "worry," "haunts," "mind," "feelings," "sick," "back of the mind," "tenderness," "kiss," "molding," "second hand," "mother's kiss," "pain of a bruise," "does not recognize," "steals into her heart." The longing, self-reproach, and self-accusation Meyerson experiences vis-à-vis her children are feelings she experiences in her body and soul and at the core of her being. The intensity of maternal physical experience stands in sharp contrast with the detached narrative voice, allowing us to witness and experience the conflict common to the mothers of the collective. While they sustained intense connections and passions for their sons and daughters, the women forced themselves into a remote stance and distant relationship with their children to maintain their connection to work and community.

VI. The Silence of Partners

Although the women are vocal about the tension they experienced in balancing their identities as mothers and workers, they are strikingly quiet about their identities as wives, partners, and lovers. They do not share stories of significance regarding their individual relationships with their husbands and partners. Although there are references to the institution of marriage and the existence of husbands (as seen in Ziporah Bar-Droma's essay "Wife of a *Haver*"), we are privy to little detail about how the women experienced these relationships in the context of the collective. We also do not hear about the existence or possibility of lesbian relationships during this period of women's collective work. In fact, the only renderings of intimate relationships occur between mothers and their children.

When considering the remarkable physicality of the text, it is important to recognize that the relationships that would invite the most physical of experiences are all but edited out of the text. The closest contact readers have with experiences of physical intimacy and sexuality occurs when the women discuss childbirth. Even here, however, the level of detail so evident in numerous descriptions of illness, injury, and death is noticeably absent. Nor do we hear of breast-feeding, except in the most oblique reference to milk. Finally, there is no mention of the physical experience of childbirth.

The reasons for this silence are not discussed in the text or in the various introductions and postscripts written over the years. Perhaps the editors of the collection edited out references to sexuality and sexual relationships. Perhaps the women had explicit instructions not to speak of such personal and noncollective aspects of their lives. Perhaps, there was an internally imposed taboo about speaking of personal, noncollective relationships and of sexuality. While we may never know the cause for this absence, it is important to mark it and to identify the areas in which the women did not choose or feel free to speak.

VII. Entering the Text

Mediating the conversation between self and text is a complex task for readers. As I have journeyed through the records of *The Plough Woman*, I am conscious of the ways in which my own history both informed my capacity to listen and, at times, stopped me cold. I continue to be struck by the women's capacity to name their experiences. They recount with clarity and depth their challenges, struggles, the minutia of collective life, the complexities of their fears that draw us into their immediate experiences, the riveting detail of their physical landscape, and the gripping detail of their psychological geography. As a working mother and former kibbutz member, I am also struck by the relevance and timeliness these essays still hold for women today. In watching the women assume new identities and negotiate the salient relationships in their lives, I too reflect on the identities I have taken on and shed. Their stories prompted me to examine how my evolving sense of self has shaped my relationships with family, community, and work.

Feminist qualitative methods, such as The Listening Guide, can assist readers in navigating the wealth of stories included in *The Plough Woman*. In locating the narrative voices, psychological stances, and embodied images, The Listening Guide helps readers enter the text and develop a unique relationship with the authors and their words. By virtue of the relational quality of this kind of reading, readers are likely to discover themes and voices in the text that are new and not to be found in previous analyses, including the present one. Whereas resonances are bound to surface, dissonances are certain to arise as well. This, indeed, is the essence of relationship. This method of inquiry asks readers to locate their own responses to the text, recognizing where moments of synchrony occur and where episodes of disconnect emerge. These occasions offer readers opportunities to explore the complexity and meanings embedded in the disparate experiences of connectedness and disconnection. In this examination, readers learn as much about the women of these essays as they do about their own stance, sense of self, and relationships.

The rich physical imagery that permeates the text supports readers in this endeavor and offers insight into the women's internal experiences. In addition to these images, the motifs of work, gender, liberation, community, and motherhood guide the reader through the complex territory traversed in this volume. In offering these narrative signposts, *The Plough Woman* offers readers multiple points of entry into the terrain of identity, self, and relationship.

References

Brown, L. M., Argyris, D., Attanucci, J., Bardige, B., Gilligan, C., Johnston, D. K., Miller, B., Osborne, R., Tappan, M., Ward, J., Wiggins, G., & Wilcox, D. (1988). *A guide to reading narratives of conflict and choice for self and relational voice* (monograph no. 1). Cambridge, MA: Project on the Psychology of Women and the Development of Girls, Harvard Graduate School of Education.

Brown, L. M., & Gilligan, C. (1992). *Meeting at the crossroads*. New York: Ballantine Books.

Brown, L. M., & Gilligan, C. (1991). Listening for voice in narratives of relationships. In M. B. Tappan & M. J. Packer (Eds.), *Narrative and storytelling:*

Implications for understanding and moral development, 54 (pp. 43–61). San Francisco: Jossey-Bass Inc.

Gilligan, C. (1992). Response to Melanie: Reflections on Case No. 1. In A. Garrod, L. Smulyan, S. I. Powers, & R. Kilkenny (Eds.), *Adolescent portraits*. New York: Allyn and Bacon.

Gilligan, C. (1996). Centrality of relationship in human development: A puzzle, some evidence, and a theory. In G. Noam & K. Fisher (Eds.), *Development and vulnerability in close relationships* (pp. 237–261). Mahwah, NJ: Lawrence Erlbaum Associates.

Gilligan, C., Brown, L. M., & Rogers, A. (1990). Psyche embedded: A place for body, relationships, and culture in personality theory. In A. I. Rubin & R. Zucker (Eds.), *Studying persons and lives* (pp. 86–147). New York: Springer.

Harding, S. (1987). *Feminism & methodology*. Bloomington and Indianapolis: Indiana University Press.

Reinharz, S. (1992). *Feminist methods in social research*. New York: Oxford University Press.

Rogers, A. (1992). Marguerite Sechehaye and Renee: A feminist reading of two accounts of a treatment. *Qualitative Studies in Education* 5(3), 245–251.

Rogers, A. (2000). When methods matter: Qualitative research issues in psychology. *Harvard Educational Review* 70(1), 75–85.

Rogers, A., Brown, L. M., & Tappan, M. (1993). *Interpreting loss in ego development in girls: Regression or resistance?* San Francisco: Annual Meeting of the American Psychological Association.

Rogers, A., Casey, M., Ekert, J., Holland, J., Nakkula, V., & Sheinberg, N. (1999). An interpretive poetics of languages of the unsayable. *Narrative Study of Lives*, 6, 77–106.

Taylor, J. M., Gilligan, C., & Sullivan, A. M. (1995). *Between voice and silence: Women and girls, race and relationship*. Cambridge, MA: Harvard University Press.

PART I

In the Beginning

The Collective

Manya [Wilbusheviz-]Shohat (Kfar Giladi)

W_HEN_ I _CAME_ to Erez Israel for the first time—I arrived from Berlin on January 2, 1904—I was not yet a Zionist. I had left Russia for Germany as the emissary of a socialist terrorist group[1] that had been organized for the purpose of assassinating the tsarist minister [Vyacheslav Konstantinovich] von Plehve.[2] The money for my journey came from a rich German Jew.[3] To cover my activities I registered in Berlin as a student at the Commercial Academy. I actually studied one-half of the day, and the other half I gave up to the work that had really brought me to Berlin.

My brother, Nahum Wilbusheviz,[4] had gone to Erez Israel one year earlier, that is, in 1903. He was at that time a young engineer, filled with

1. It appears that the group to which Shohat refers is the Social Revolutionary Party. The Social Revolutionaries held ideals expressed by P. G. Zaichnevski in his 1860s publication *Young Russia*. Among these were the overthrow of the tsarist regime and the Romanov family. They also espoused the establishment of an alliance of autonomous agricultural communes as the basis of a new Russian state. The Social Revolutionaries believed in the use of terrorism, but—unlike certain other revolutionary groups—only against the tsarist regime.

2. Vyacheslav Konstantinovich von Plehve was the Minister of the Interior. While still in Russia, Shohat had met with him to plead for help for the Jews in the Pale. Von Plehve had not only rejected her plea but chastised her for having the gall, as a Jew, to make such a request. Following the Kishinev *pogroms*, which began in 1903, Shohat and her co-conspirators decided that von Plehve—and not the notorious antisemite Krushevan, whose inflammatory rhetoric was thought to have inspired the violence— was truly responsible. For this, they decided, he had to be eliminated. Also in 1903, von Plehve met with Theodor Herzl and misled him into believing that Zionism would be permitted in Russia as long as it was confined to the task of resettling Russian Jewry and steered clear of nationalism inside Russia. In reality, however, legal legitimacy was denied the Zionists.

3. According to Rahel Yanait Ben-Zvi, the funds were actually provided by a Lithuanian Jew living in Germany and concerned for fellow East European Jews. See Rahel Yanait Ben-Zvi, *Before Golda: Manya Shohat*, trans. Sandra Shurin (New York: Biblio Press, 1989), p. 34.

4. Nahum (Wilbusheviz) Wilbush (1879–1971), a mechanical engineer, was Manya (Wilbusheviz) Shohat's older brother. He immigrated to Palestine in 1903 and founded Atid [Future], the region's first edible-oil production factory, at first located in Ben Shemen and later in Haifa. He served with the Turkish army during World War I and later participated in the World Zionist Organization's expedition to East Africa to investigate possibilities for Jewish settlement in Uganda.

dreams for the industrial upbuilding of the country. He had already worked out detailed plans, and even prepared a map indicating the chief industrial centers of the future. Nahum was twenty-three years of age; I, a year older.

During my stay in Berlin, a situation of desperate difficulty arose in connection with my work, and by a chain of circumstances it was my brother who helped us out. His assistance to us was bound up with a great spiritual sacrifice on his part. In gratitude to him, I promised him, when he left for Erez Israel, that whenever he felt that he needed me at his side, he had only to call me and I would come.

Meanwhile, my two comrades, the social revolutionaries Nicolai[5] and Sergeii,[6] waited in St. Petersburg, casting about for the means to carry out their terrorist act. Suddenly, I received a cable from my brother informing me that a great misfortune had befallen him and asking me to come out to him. It was only on my arrival in Erez Israel that I learned the truth.[7] Nothing had happened to him. The cable had been a trick to get me away from my dangerous work. I would have left again at once, but the ship had already sailed from Jaffa. Two months later, I learned that Nicolai and Sergeii had been caught by the police and shot. It was only after many years that the truth came out. They had been betrayed by the infamous agent provocateur [Yevno Fishelevich] Azeff.[8]

The news of the fate of my comrades plunged me into a profound depression, and in an attempt to distract my mind from the calamity, my brother invited me to accompany him on a horseback tour through Erez Israel. His purpose was to make a scientific study of the country's resources. Knowing that there was little hope of taking up my old work again, I agreed to go.

Our guide was Mendel [Menahem] Hankin,[9] the brother of Yeho-

5. The identity of Nicolai is unknown.

6. The precise identity of Sergeii is unknown. One of Shohat's acquaintances from the non-aligned movement, he was also affiliated with the militarist faction of the Social Revolutionary party. He formulated a plan to assassinate the tsarist minister Konstantinovich von Plehve (see above) by digging a tunnel to reach the latter's compound.

7. According to Rahel Yanait Ben-Zvi, Shohat had already received a cryptic telegram from Sergeii's "fiancée" stating that he was not well. Shohat correctly interpreted this to mean that something had gone wrong, though she did not yet know that her co-conspirators had been apprehended by the tsarist secret police. She learned of their arrest in a subsequent letter. See Rahel Yanait Ben-Zvi, *Before Golda: Manya Shohat*, p. 34.

8. Yevno Fishelevich Azeff, a Russian revolutionary, was a double agent for the tsarist secret police.

9. Mendel (Menahem) Hankin took the lead in preparing for the journey. Fluent in Arabic, he taught the language to Shohat.

shua Hankin[10]; and the fourth member of the party was a girl, [Sophia] Zvenigorodska[11] by name, who had come to Erez Israel with the orphans of the Kishinev *pogrom*[12] and was helping [Israel] Belkind[13] to organize the orphan school. She was young, beautiful and energetic, and did not seem to know the meaning of fear.[14]

We used to ride ten hours a day, changing horses frequently. In this way, we cut through the entire Arab settlement from Dan to Beersheva. We visited Transjordania,[15] too. The entire trip took us six weeks, and in the course of it there grew up in me a deep and passionate love for the country, a love which filled the brain as well as the heart. It is a love that has lasted through all my life, and its strength seems to be bound up with the renewal of something many centuries old.

10. Yehoshua Hankin (1861–1945) was one of the principal architects of Zionist settlement policy in Palestine. Having emigrated to Palestine in 1882, he developed very close relations with the Arabs, which allowed him to play a central role in the purchase of land on behalf of the Zionist movement. After many years of negotiations, he successfully purchased in 1920 a large tract of land in the Jezreel Valley, on which many Jewish settlements were thereafter established. Henceforth, he was widely known as the Redeemer of the Valley.

11. Sophia Zvenigorodska single-handedly brought many orphans from Kishinev to Shefeyah (also known as Meir Shefeyah), an agricultural school and youth village (named for Mayer Amschel Rothschild) located near Zikhron Yaakov. In 1903, Israel Belkind established a home for orphans of the Kishinev *pogrom* there.

12. In the early twentieth century, Kishinev, the capital of the province of Bessarabia, included a community of nearly 50,000 Jews or 46 percent of the total populace. During Easter, on April 6–7, 1903, brutal violence broke out against the city's Jews. After the *pogrom*, forty-nine Jews were left dead, 500 injured, and 2000 families homeless. 700 houses and 600 businesses were pillaged and robbed. Russians and Rumanians joined in the massacre, and the 5000 Russian police stationed in the area did nothing to stop the mob. The local press, led by the antisemitic journalist Pavolaki Krushevan (see below) and with the tacit consent of the tsarist regime, played a key role in stirring up the trouble. A second *pogrom* broke out in Kishinev on October 19–20, 1905. This time, the damage was less severe—19 killed, 56 injured—in part, due to organized Jewish self-defense. The Kishinev *pogrom* served as a catalyst for the Second Aliyah.

13. Israel Belkind (1861–1929), a founder and leader of the Bilu pioneer movement in Russia, immigrated to Palestine in 1882. He was active in the struggle against the *halukah* [charity] system, particularly its key figure Baron Edmond de Rothschild. As a result, he was expelled from Rishon Lezion and settled in Gederah. In 1889, he established a private school in Jaffa, employing a brand of modern Hebrew advocated by secular Zionists in the diaspora. In 1903, he established a home for orphans of the Kishinev *pogrom* at Shefeyah, to which he personally brought many children. The orphans' home closed in 1906 due to a lack of resources. Like several other Zionist leaders, Belkind spent much of World War I in the United States.

14. According to Rahel Yanait Ben-Zvi, Sophia Zvenigorodska was actually a hindrance to the group, in large part due to her lesser skills and lack of experience. See Rahel Yanait Ben-Zvi, *Before Golda: Manya Shohat*, pp. 37–38.

15. Transjordania was the name given to the area east of the Jordan River, spanning from Mt. Hermon to the Dead Sea, but excluding the Golan Heights and the Bashan Valley.

I had known the Hebrew language from childhood. Both my brothers were Zionists. Until the age of fifteen I had studied the language, Hebrew Bible, and Talmud, and I had read Hebrew freely. And though for years I had been divorced from these things, I found on my arrival in Erez Israel that I had not in reality lost them.

In the spring of 1904 I became acquainted with Hankin's *kvuzah* in Rehovot. I had by that time determined to find out what it was that the country meant to me, as an individual. My plan was to make a tour of the Jewish colonies and to get together such statistics as were available. The task took up a year of my time. I worked out a questionnaire that covered the economic side of colony life. I asked in particular for details of income, and the employment of Arab workers. Few indeed were the colonists who at that time kept statistics of their own. But I became acquainted with the character of our First Aliyah, and I came to a definite conclusion. My *haverim*—the workers—were completely mad! *The way they were working there was absolutely no hope of creating in Erez Israel a Jewish agricultural proletariat!*[16]

The Jewish workers in the colony of Petah Tikvah had accepted the same conditions as the Arabs: their pay was 5 *piastres* [25 cents] a day. They believed that as Zionists they simply had not the right to ask for more. They lived eight in a room—a small room—and their beds were mattresses on the floor. When I told them that they ought to demand houses and public buildings from the colony, they answered proudly that this would be philanthropy . . . They would ask for no help from these sources: it would only be a renewal of the immemorial evil of the *halukah* [allowance].

Finally, the Jewish workers of Petah Tikvah were driven by sheer need to live in a commune. There was no other way out for them. Their commune was the second in Erez Israel, and the first was Hankin's commune in Rehovot.

I had already had some experience with a commune—in Minsk.[17] A group of us wanted to organize the workers without the help of the intelligentsia, and to that end we started a workers' commune. The life was harsh and meager, and the budget was between three and five *kopeks*

16. Emphasis in the original text.
17. At the turn of the nineteenth and twentieth centuries, Minsk, the capital of Belorussia, ranked as the fourth largest Jewish community in the Pale of Settlement. In 1897, the Jews of the Minsk province, which also included the communities of Pinsk, Bobruisk, Slutsk, and other significant towns, reached a total of over 345,000, or approximately 16 percent of the region's population. The city of Minsk, with a Jewish community numbering over 50,000 (52 percent of the population), was a hotbed of Jewish political radicalism, including Bundist and Communist activity. In 1902, the second convention of Russian Zionists was held in Minsk.

[a *kopek* was half a cent] per day per person. All earnings were turned in to the common fund. It was while living with this commune that I learned an important principle: the commune provides the proletariat with the means for its struggle. The Minsk commune[18] prepared me for the collective lifestyle in Erez Israel.

I began on my arrival in Erez Israel with an urban cooperative, for I was more accustomed to city conditions. In Russia, I had learned carpentry in the factory of my brother, Gedaliah Wilbusheviz.[19] I raised a loan in order to start a carpenters' cooperative in Jaffa, and I worked out its rules on the basis of the Russian *artels*[20] [labor groups] which had a communist background. The cooperative existed for three months. When I left for Galilee, internal dissensions broke out and the cooperative fell to pieces.

In the year 1905, Yehoshua Hankin spoke to me about the possibility of buying up the Jezreel Valley [hereafter, *emek*[21]], and it was clear to me that only through such a purchase could a Jewish agricultural class be established in Erez Israel. I was anxious to help Hankin, and I placed before him my plans for collectivist colonization. Meanwhile, Jewish immigration into Erez Israel kept growing.

I then made up my mind to go to Paris and approach the Jewish Colonization Association, founded by Baron [Maurice de] Hirsh[22]—to buy

18. Rahel Yanait Ben-Zvi notes that Shohat and her friends "established a small commune having about a dozen members" around the year 1900. The commune, which lasted only half a year and placed a premium on equality and revolutionary activity, served as a training ground for Shohat's later collectivist efforts in Palestine. See Rahel Yanait Ben-Zvi, *Before Golda: Manya Shohat*, p. 25.

19. Gedaliah Wilbusheviz (1865–1943) was Manya (Wilbusheviz) Shohat's older brother. A Hovevei Zion activist and mechanical engineer, he immigrated to Palestine in 1892. He established a machine and metal-casting factory in Jaffa, the first Jewish enterprise of its kind in the country. He next lived in Berlin temporarily, where he worked to promote investment in Palestine's industrial development. According to Rahel Yanait Ben-Zvi, Shohat lived with her brother while she was in Berlin, raising money for the assassination of von Plehve. He persuaded her of the futility of this plan and convinced her to travel to Palestine instead. (See Rahel Yanait Ben-Zvi, *Before Golda: Manya Shohat*, 34.) During World War I, he served as chief engineer of Jamal Pasha's headquarters in Damascus.

20. The *artels* were groups of laborers or craftsmen in Russia organized on a cooperative and often egalitarian basis.

21. *Emek* is Hebrew for "valley." The Jezreel Valley, with its critical mass of agricultural and pioneering activity, attained a near-mythic status in Zionist circles and was referred to simply as the *emek*.

22. Baron Maurice de Hirsch (1831–1896), a German Jewish banker and rail developer, was a major benefactor of a variety of Jewish agencies including the Alliance Israélite Universelle, the French Jewish aid society; the Baron de Hirsch Fund, established to assist Jewish immigrants in New York City; and the Jewish Colonization Association, established in 1891 to support and coordinate the mass emigration of Russian Jews and to encourage their resettlement in agricultural colonies, particularly in Argentina

land in the *emek* for workers' colonization. I also wanted to do some research in Paris on various attempts that have been made at collectivist colonization. There I came across a cousin of mine, Ivan Wilbusheviz, who was editing the government organ for the French colonies. Through him, I obtained access to the material of the government departments on the colonization in Tunis and Algeria.

I realized soon enough that what I had in mind was not to be found anywhere. Indeed, the experts considered agricultural collectivism ridiculous, and were ready to prove that the agricultural commune had never been able to succeed.

At about that time a Jewish comrade of mine, arriving from Russia, asked me to help him raise money for the Jewish self-defense in that country. I collected two hundred thousand francs for that purpose— fifty thousand of it coming from Baron Edmond de Rothschild—and helped him, further, to smuggle arms into Russia.

I re-entered Russia illegally. During the *pogrom* in Shedliz [1906],[23] I took an active part in the Jewish self-defense. Later, I organized a national group to exact vengeance from the leaders of Russian antisemitism.[24] One of the comrades in the group was Pinhas Dashevsky,[25]

---

and Brazil. He chose the latter because they were relatively unpopulated, conducive to agricultural settlement, and their governments were interested in Jewish immigration. He feared that mass Russian Jewish immigration to the United States would foment widespread antisemitism there.

23. Shedliz (Siedlce), a city in eastern Poland, was home to a Jewish community that grew from approximately 8000 (64 percent) in 1878 to 14,700 (48 percent) in 1921. All the Jewish political parties of the time as well as the Polish Socialist Party were active in Shedliz; however, Zionism won the greatest number of adherents in the decades that spanned the nineteenth and twentieth centuries.

24. It is likely that Shohat is referring here to the tsarist Minister of the Interior Vyacheslav Konstantinovich von Plehve, and Pavolaki Krushevan, an antisemitic journalist. More generally, this is also a reference to the tsarist regime and the secret police. Paradoxically, the head of the latter, Sergeii Vasilevich Zubatov (1864–1917) was sympathetic to the Russian labor movement. Zubatov favored police-sponsored trade unionism and encouraged workers to seek economic and social self-improvement rather than political revolution. He helped arrange for Shohat to meet von Plehve in late 1902. Von Plehve's views were diametrically opposed to those of Zubatov, and in 1903 Zubatov was dishonorably discharged from his position. He committed suicide in 1917 when he learned of the tsar's abdication. See Rahel Yanait Ben-Zvi, *Before Golda: Manya Shohat*, chaps. 3–4.

25. Pinhas Dashevsky (1879–1934), a student Zionist activist and later a chemical engineer, was part of the Jewish self-defense organization in Kiev. He assaulted and wounded the antisemitic publicist Pavolaki Krushevan in St. Petersburg on June 4, 1903. He was subsequently sentenced to five years' hard labor, but was released in 1906. He remained active in Russian Jewish affairs, visited Palestine in 1910, and participated in a Russian Jewish delegation to the United States at the time of the Mendel Beilis affair (1913). Following the Russian Revolution of 1917, he was eventually arrested and died in prison.

who shot[26] the famous antisemite [Pavolaki] Krushevan.[27] The entire group was arrested—with the exception of Dashevsky. Again the traitor was Azeff, who got his information through two socialist revolutionaries who worked with us. The police looked for me in St. Petersburg. I changed my lodgings every day, never sleeping twice in the same place. With clockwork regularity the police always searched, too late, the place I had slept in the night before. My name was unknown to them.

I worked for three months with "The Group of Vengeance."[28] The only Jewish party which supported us were the Territorialists (S.S.).[29] Later, toward the end of 1906, I returned to Erez Israel via Constantinople.

Once again, I turned to my *haverim* with the old idea of a collective. I wanted to go to America to raise money for collective colonization in Transjordania and in the Hauran.[30] I also planned to visit the American collectivist colonies.[31]

26. A conflicting account states that Dashevsky stabbed Krushevan in June 1903. See *Encyclopaedia Judaica*, vol. 5, p. 1310.

27. Pavolaki Krushevan (1860–1909), a Russian journalist and newspaper publisher, used his Kishinev newspaper *Bessarabets* to promote antisemitism. In it, he frequently accused the Jews of subversive revolutionary activity and exploitation of the Russian masses. In a later publication, *Drug*, Krushevan wrote a series of articles promoting the antisemitic fantasy of the blood libel. The series played a central role in inciting the Kishinev *pogrom* of 1903. After surviving the attempt on his life by Pinhas Dashevsky, Krushevan was elected to the Second Duma in 1907. Some of his writings were later incorporated into the antisemitic forgery, *The Protocols of the Elders of Zion*.

28. A curious story omitted here, but related by Rahel Yanait Ben-Zvi, highlights the danger and risks faced by this clandestine group. According to Ben-Zvi, around the year 1900 Shohat was guarding a secret cache of weapons in a house under tsarist police surveillance. One evening, after the police had left, a young Jew asked Shohat for shelter. Alerted by one of his probing questions, Shohat resolved that he was an informant. She shot him, concealed the body, and waited with the corpse until other members of her circle came to dispense with it. Over the decades, this story was embellished and became a part of Zionist lore. For varying accounts, see Rahel Yanait Ben-Zvi, *Before Golda: Manya Shohat*, pp. ix–x; Shabtai Teveth, *Ben-Gurion: The Burning Ground* (Boston: Houghton Mifflin, 1987), p. 56.

29. The reference here is to the *Sionistsko-sotsialisticheskiaia rabochaia partiia* [Zionist Socialist Labor Party], one of the first Russian Jewish revolutionary parties, usually known as the "S.S." On the ideology of the S.S., see Jonathan Frankel, *Prophecy and Politics: Socialism, Nationalism and the Russian Jews, 1862–1917* (Cambridge: Cambridge University Press, 1984), pp. 325–328.

30. Shohat used the term "Hauran," which has strong biblical resonance, to inspire and excite settlers and *shomrim*. See the "Glossary of Places" for more information.

31. The era of mass East European Jewish immigration to the United States witnessed the advent of Jewish agricultural colonies in many regions of the country. At the forefront of this trend was the Am Olam [Eternal People] movement, founded in Odessa in 1881, which promoted the settlement of Jews in the United States in agrarian communes guided by socialist ideals. Several Am Olam communes were established in 1882 in Louisiana, South Dakota, and Oregon, but disbanded soon after due to debt and

Early in 1907, I arrived in America and spent nearly half a year there. I became acquainted with Dr. Judah L. Magnes[32] and with Henrietta Szold.[33] I visited South America, too, taking in the collectivist colonies, and convinced myself at first hand that the agricultural commune could succeed.[34] What we needed was a substitute for the religious enthusiasm that had made these settlements possible, and for this substitute I looked to socialism.

In August 1907, I returned to Erez Israel via Paris. I had one ideal now: the realization of agricultural collectivism. During my absence, the idea had taken somewhat deeper root in Erez Israel. In the colonies of Lower Galilee the Jewish workers lived wretched, disorganized lives. They were housed in stables. Some of them had already lost all faith in the burning ideal of *kibush haavodah*[35] [conquest of labor]. They could

---

other hardships. In subsequent years, the Jewish Agricultural and Industrial Aid Society undertook to create small agricultural settlements in different parts of the country. With the support of the Baron de Hirsch Fund, the Society provided support and administrative guidance to thousands of Yiddish-speaking immigrants, primarily in the northeast and southern New Jersey. A contemporary account that appeared in *The Jewish Encyclopedia* (1906) estimated the number of "Jewish farmers in the United States" to be 12,000. It also emphasized "the fact that only by a combination of farming and local factory employment have the Jewish colonies in southern New Jersey been able to survive." (See *Jewish Encyclopedia* (1906), vol. 1, pp. 256–262; vol. 12, p. 368.) Though numerically insignificant, the colonies served as a training ground for many of the leaders of the American Jewish labor movement.

32. Judah Leon Magnes (1877–1948) was chancellor and president of the Hebrew University of Jerusalem. A native of the United States and an important American Jewish leader, he helped to found the American Jewish Committee and led the New York Kehillah before immigrating to Palestine in 1922. Magnes supported a binational Arab-Jewish state in Palestine, a position that brought him into conflict with other Zionists. He also asserted that support for Jewish settlement in Palestine did not necessarily entail a conviction that all Jews should settle there. Rather, he believed in the strength and vitality of the diaspora and argued that the Jewish national home should serve as the cultural-spiritual center of modern Jewish life.

33. Henrietta Szold (1860–1945), an American educator and social worker, was one of the outstanding leaders of American Zionism. In 1912, she founded Hadassah, the Women's Zionist Organization of America. She settled in Palestine in 1920, where she directed many projects on behalf of Hadassah. With the rise of Hitler to power, she also devoted herself to Youth Aliyah, which sought to facilitate the passage of children and youth from Europe and their resettlement in Palestine.

34. Jewish agricultural colonization in South America was largely confined to Argentina. Starting in 1891, the Jewish Colonization Association of Paris, of which Baron Maurice de Hirsch was virtually the sole stockholder, purchased large tracts of land in various parts of the Argentine Republic. By 1905, over 17,000,000 acres had been acquired, mostly in the provinces of Buenos Aires and Santa Fé.

35. The idea of *kibush haavaodah* [conquest of labor] derives from the philosophy and writings of Aharon David Gordon. This voluntaristic notion, with its layers of unfolding meaning—*avodah*, the Hebrew word for "labor," is also the classical term for worship—tapped an idealistic vein in the radical Zionist milieu of the period. *Kibush haavodah* symbolized the complete transformation of Jewish life.

not become individualist farmers, planters, exploiters of others; their socialist principles forbade it. And they could not continue their competition with Arab.labor, for no European can long subsist on five *piastres* a day. I, for my part, had never believed in *kibush haavodah* through adaptation to the Arab standard of life. At that time, the Jewish National Fund had begun to purchase land as the inalienable property of the Jewish people. The ideal of national territory of this kind had always been close to my heart, for I saw in it the foundation of collectivist colonization. Eliezer Shohat[36] was against my plan. His argument was: "We dare not assume this responsibility. If the particular plan that we adopt for collectivist colonization fails, we shall lose faith in the ideal of colonization as such. The first thing we must learn is to become land workers."

In the farm of the [Jewish Colonization Association] at Sejera, there were *haverim* of ours working under the direction of the agronomist [Eliyahu] Krause.[37] Every year this farm showed a deficit. I said: "Give us a chance to work here on our own responsibility, and we'll manage without a deficit."

The opportunity was given to us. At Sejera, I worked half-days on the books and the other half-days in the cow shed. I told Krause that he ought to admit women to the work, and the first three women workers there were the Shturman sisters: Sarah (Krigser), Shifra (Bezer), and Esther (Becker). They were all very young, and they followed the plough like real peasants.

When we founded the collective, we were eighteen in all who had drifted together gradually toward Sejera. The contract with the agronomist Krause turned over to us the field and dairy work on the same terms as were demanded of an Arab lessee. The owners gave us all the dead and live stock, the inventory, and the seed. In return, we had to turn over one-fifth of the harvest. We were also given sleeping quarters —and very poor ones they were—and a sum of money to carry us

36. Eliezer Shohat (1874–1971) was one of the first members of Poalei Zion in his home region of Grodno, Russia. After arriving in Petah Tikvah in 1904, he worked in agriculture and helped to establish Hapoel Hazair [The Young Worker]. A devoted organizer of workers in the Jewish colonies, he was a founder of Hahoresh [The Plowman], the union of Jewish agricultural workers in the Galilee, and served as a delegate to the Eighth and Ninth World Zionist Congresses. He was also one of the first settlers in Merhavyah, an early proponent of the *moshav ovdim*, and later a founder of Nahalal.

37. Eliyahu Krause (1876–1962) emigrated to Palestine from his native Russia in 1892. An agronomist, he was employed by the Jewish Colonization Association and helped to create an agricultural school near Izmir, Turkey. Without his cooperation, Manya Shohat and her comrades could not have realized their program to establish a collective at Sejera. In 1915, Krause became director of the Mikveh Israel Agricultural School, a position he held until his retirement in 1954.

through the season. When there was not enough work on the farm to go round, the management would employ some of us in the afforestation work.

We worked on our own responsibility. We arranged our own division of labor. Only once a week, when the program was planned, we would have Krause in for a consultation. We also asked him to give regular lectures on agriculture, and no one who lived with us through that time has forgotten those clear and practical expositions.

The workers on the farm did not have a kitchen of their own, and until the coming of the collective they used to eat at a private inn. We organized a communal kitchen, and later on we were even able to feed workers not belonging to our commune.

The name we gave ourselves was, simply, "The Collective." The relations between us and the other workers on the farm were excellent. But they had no faith in our plan and did not believe we would come out without a deficit.

The Sejera collective lasted a year and a half. It ended its work successfully, paid the farm its fifth of the harvest, returned in full the money that had been advanced, and demonstrated once for all that a collective economy was a possibility.

Those First Years

Tehiyah Lieberson (Nahalal)

WHEN I CAME to Petah Tikvah in 1905, some Jewish workers were already there. There were only four [young women] among them: two seamstresses, one stocking knitter, and one who received remittances from her parents. In the season both seamstresses would turn orange packers. But my heart was set on plain labor on the soil. Three days after my arrival, I went out to work with the spade for one *bishlik* [twelve and a half cents] a day. I worked in Gisin's vineyard,[38] and my job was to fill up the holes around the trees.

I used to come home evenings to the colony without any tools, and for a whole month I would leave the regular path and make my way through backyards, so that no one should know that I was working with the men. The workers themselves were against my choice—they were genuinely afraid that I would break down under the labor. They urged me to work with the other [young Jewish women workers] at the orange packing, but I would not listen. I wanted to work with the spade.

It was *haver* S. who first gave me courage to continue. He was the teacher in the colony; and he shifted the school hours so as to be able to come out and take turns with me at the work. In this way, while our [workers] took only one hour's rest during the middle of the day, I took three. S. also talked about me to the owner of the vineyard, who assured him that in time I would become a good worker.

Two weeks later the owner raised my pay by half a *piastre*—making almost four *piastres* a day. I was astonished, and asked him whether he had done this because I was a Jewish youth or because I was really worth it. He answered frankly that I was really worth a great deal more.

And yet for a long time, I was tormented by the question whether I had chosen the right path. The doubts of my fellow workers crept into

---

38. "Gisin's vineyard," located near Petah Tikvah, was owned by the Gisin family, Hovevei Zion members from Belorussia and First Aliyah settlers. Efrayim Gisin (1835–1898) immigrated to Palestine in 1895 to join his three sons and daughters. He became a leader of the plantation farmers and set an important example by welcoming Jewish workers into his vineyard.

me, too, and I needed someone who would give me more faith in my-self and in my own strength.

There worked among us at that time a comrade who was much older than any of us.[39] His good humor and unflagging cheerfulness were a source of strength to all of us. He composed a great many Jewish songs, which we learned to sing together with him. From the beginning I con-ceived a deep affection for this old man—but I had not the courage to seek his advice. Often, seeing me sit apart, completely exhausted, he would call out to me:

"Cheer up! Look at me, an old man, working as hard as the rest, and always happy." But before I could answer him, and pour out my trou-bles, he would be gone.

My work with the spade lasted a month, and after that I passed over to orange picking. During the first two days, I worked for nothing. When my first basket was filled, I submitted it to the overseer, who went through it, orange by orange. He found three that had been touched by the scissors. My heart was in my mouth—I was certain he would send me home. But in the second basket there was only one damaged orange —and from then on I was a perfect orange picker. When my work on this orchard was finished, the overseer sent me to a second. I became known as a skilled orange picker and work was easy to find.

When the season was over, I went to the employment bureau of the colony to look for work. I was told that there were only three colonists who were prepared to take women workers, and none of them had a place for me. For the second time I was seized with despair. I came home and sat down in loneliness, and brooded over the life I had cho-sen for myself. I remembered then the letters that I had received from a well known leader of Hovevei Zion [Lovers of Zion] before I set out for Erez Israel. He had warned me against coming to Erez Israel. "You will find no work there," he wrote. "You will suffer hunger and want, and no one will be any the better for it."

For three days I sought work in vain, and at the end of the third day, when I sat again in my room, beaten, the old man came to me. He in-vited me over to his little shack, and there we talked for many, many hours. He gave me courage to hold out; and in the next few days I found employment, together with him. He became my teacher in the work.

Before long, I was dissatisfied with the simple work. I wanted the more responsible task of grafting trees. A *haver* undertook to teach me. He told me to lay off work with the spade for a couple of days, and to

39. The reference is to Aharon David Gordon.

bring him his meals in the orchard. At that hour the owner was away, and he would then be able to show me how to graft. I fell in with this plan. Two days later, the worker told his boss that I was a skillful grafter, and that I had already been employed for that purpose in other orchards. The owner took me on trial, was satisfied with me, and let me remain.

When I had been working for a year and a half I was told that another female land-worker had appeared in Rehovot—Miriam Zavin.[40] And in 1907 several other women workers came from Russia and went up to Galilee, to work on the farm at Sejera.

I worked in Petah Tikvah for a total of three years, until 1908. Some time before the end of that year, a group of our male workers had gone up to the farm at Kineret. They applied to the director to let me join them—but not in the kitchen, as was the almost invariable rule with women. Up in Kineret, I worked side by side with the men. First, I helped to clear the soil of stones, later I took a hand in the mowing and threshing. There were no houses for the workers in those days. In the summer we slept out in the open. In the winter the woman who worked in the kitchen and I slept in the barn. Raids and attacks by our neighbors were fairly frequent in those days.

With the beginning of the new year, the two of us joined the little *kvuzah* which began to work on its own initiative and responsibility in Um-Djuni.[41] And there at last, I began to feel that I had become a full-fledged worker. The year's work in Um-Djuni ended with a profit, and yet for a variety of reasons the group fell to pieces. A second group came up to the same ground. I was away then, being down for several months with yellow fever. When I recovered I joined the new group—and out of this group grew the present settlement of Dagania.

40. The identity of Miriam Zavin is unknown.
41. Um-Djuni was the original Arabic name of the land that later became Dagania.

In Sejera

Shifra Bezer (Nahalal)

THE FARM OF Sejera has long since been abandoned. But there was a time when it occupied a highly important place in the life of the Jewish workers of Erez Israel. When the first Jewish women workers came to Galilee, it was Sejera that took them in. It was in Sejera that the first Jewish vigil appeared, and it was there that Hashomer [The Watchguard] was founded. In Sejera, too, the first attempt was made to organize the Jewish working class of Erez Israel. Hahoresh [The Plowman] was the name given to that first tiny organization of land workers.

Sejera played a great role in our life. In the few years of its existence, it served as the focal point of the workers in Galilee and exacted a heavy toll of sacrifices.

I came to Sejera in 1907, and found there only four Jewish workers from Europe. The others were Jews from Kurdistan.[42]

When I left the town for the farm, I had not the slightest idea what I was going to do there. No city girl was ever remoter from land work than I. And in those days there was, of course, Hehaluz [The Pioneer] in the diaspora to prepare Jewish youth for life in Erez Israel.

Krause, the manager of the Sejera farm (he has for many years since then been director of the agricultural school of Mikveh Israel) was very friendly toward Jewish labor in general and toward the Jewish woman worker in particular. Every opportunity was given on the farm to the worker who wanted to learn a special branch of agriculture.

On the first day, I was set to sifting barley after the old Arab fashion. My companion in the work was a Kurdistan Jew. But I found this task too monotonous. I wanted something livelier and more significant. In particular, I wanted to go in for dairy work, but I knew absolutely nothing about it. I did not even know how to begin learning something. Without experience, without a plan, I simply went ahead.

42. Most Kurdistan Jews hailed from Iraq. Their language was a *mélange* of Aramaic, Persian, Turkish, Arabic, and Hebrew. Kurdistan Jews first settled in Safed in the sixteenth century, but heightened persecution caused large numbers to immigrate to Palestine in the early twentieth century. They played an important role in the First Aliyah, especially in the building of Zikhron Yaakov and Zikhron Yosef. By 1948, there were approximately 20,000 Kurdistan Jews in Israel.

The first thing I did was to clean out and whitewash the little room in the barn. The dairy vessels were of the most primitive kind. All day long the farm flock, consisting of sheep and goats, pastured in the neighboring woods. A deaf and dumb Arab was the shepherd. Twice a day, he brought me the milk to turn into cheese. Bringing it, he would point to his black mantel if it came from the goats and to his white *kefiyah* [Arab headdress] if it came from the sheep.

I took my first lessons in cheese-making from the womenfolk of the old colonists. And in time I became, as it were, the official dairy worker.

After a while, I was joined in Sejera by my two younger sisters and their two friends. One of the [young women] took over the kitchen work. The other three insisted on going out with the plough. They did not keep up this labor for long, but those first days belonged to a young and happy time.

Later on Manya Shohat came to Sejera, and the first working class collective in Erez Israel was founded. And so, step by step, the Sejera farm expanded into something like a settlement.

The Jewish Guard

Haya-Sarah Hankin (Ein Harod)

T HIS WAS TWENTY years ago in the colony of Kfar Tavor (Meshah) in Galilee. After long negotiations with the council, Hashomer [The Watchguard] took over the guarding of the colony on condition that Jewish labor be introduced.

Up till then the Jewish colonists had employed Arab labor exclusively, and the Arabs, living with their families in the yards of the colonies, knew every corner in the place. It was, therefore, impossible to put a stop to the thefts. The workers inside the colony frequently cooperated with the outside thieves. The colonists knew this well, yet it was no light task to persuade them to take Jewish labor. Finally, a contract was signed, and Jewish workers entered the colony together with the Jewish guards.

According to the agreement, the guards and workers came up into the colony in the month of Elul [September]. The *shomrim* were given, as headquarters, the last house in the village, standing on the last parcel of Jewish soil. The workers were distributed among the colonists and thus provided with lodgings and food. In the course of one year, they were supposed to become skilled laborers.

The first evening of the watch. The patrols are out. Every man has instructions. He knows the extent of his beat. He has learned by heart the whistle signals that carry the alarm from place to place. One of the women workers, S., told a friend that she did not want to work in the kitchen: she loved the silence and the darkness of the night, she loved weapons and horses, and she wanted to join the guard. The young man had confidence in her. He obtained weapons for her, also an *abaya* [Arab cloak] and a whistle. When nightfall came they told no one, but rode out to their posts, and divided the beat between them. In those days, the Jewish colonies in Galilee were ringed in by walls. The young man took the eastern side of the colony; the woman took the western side.

When the first rounds had been finished, it was the custom for the guards to meet and report, and the presence of the woman was discovered. The [young men] were somehow pleased by the idea; all except one, who argued that this sort of thing could not go on. "We must not forget," he said, "that we may have clashes with the Arabs—and particularly with the men who were employed as guards before we came." The man's objections were received in silence—and the woman remained at her post. But it was decided that nobody in the colony other than the *shomrim* should know the secret. And so it was.

With the coming of the Jewish guards and the Jewish workers a new spirit was born in the colony. There was singing and dancing in the evenings. The children of the settler colonists—a handful of youngsters—were drawn toward the Jewish workers. The apathy that had brooded over the place was dispersed, and those colonists who had fought for the Jewish guards felt themselves completely vindicated.

The *shomrim* were at their posts from early evening until six in the morning. All night long, they circled the walls on the *quivive* ["on the alert"] listening for the slightest stirring out in the fields. A whisper, a faint motion, a glimmer somewhere, and the nerves jumped. On the first round, they tried all the gates and doors. On later rounds, they focused their attention on the surrounding fields.

One night, during the second round, the *shomer* noticed that a stall had been opened. He loaded his gun and entered the yard. Suddenly, he perceived in the darkness two Arabs driving animals before them. He shot three times and the Arabs fled. Cases of this kind were frequent before winter came. On one occasion, the thieves were able to get away with a couple of mules. After that, the Hashomer group insisted that Arabs who did not live in the village, but who came there only for the day's work, should not be allowed to stay overnight. So, step by step, the epidemic of thieving was combatted.

The first year of the Hashomer group in Meshah passed peacefully, and the contract was renewed. Hashomer extended its work to the neighboring Jewish colony of Yavniel, and S.'s friend went out on the new patrol.

One night soon after, S. was kept awake until early morning by a strange feeling of oppression. And before daybreak news was brought from Yavniel that there had been a clash. One Arab had been killed, and S.'s friend had been severely wounded. S. saddled her mare, put on her *abaya*, slung her gun over her shoulder, and set out for Yavniel. She forgot, in her anxiety, that Yavniel lay five or six hours away, that in between the two colonies there was not a single Jewish post, and that the road was dangerous. She rode at top speed, obsessed only by one thought: Would she find her friend still alive? Many Arabs pass her on the way. They do not stop her. She only hears them asking each other, as she rides by: "Isn't that a woman?"

One hour still remains between her and Yavniel, and she sees the colony in the distance. And now a well dressed Arab on a richly capari-soned horse comes riding toward her. He stops her and asks:

"Where are you going? Shall I accompany you?"

"No."

The Arab becomes angry.

"Do you want to quarrel with me?" he asks.

He comes closer, spurring his horse forward till it touches hers. Suddenly S. reaches for the man's cloak and pulls him out of his saddle. He tumbles to earth, and she shoots forward. By the time he has re-mounted, she is too far ahead to be followed. They are close to the boundary of the Jewish settlement.

In Yavniel, there was talk of an Arab attack, and the Jews had sent out for help to the neighboring Jewish settlements. Many members of Hashomer responded, but none attracted the same attention as S., in her [Arab] mantle, her gun over her shoulder, her ammunition belt round her. The colonists' daughters in particular were astounded by this woman in arms. That night, S. took an active part in the defense of the colony.

The colony was, in fact, too small to carry a public expense. In the end, the [Jewish Colonization Association] decided to increase its area. Neighboring land was purchased. The *kushans* [deeds] were signed and delivered, but it was impossible to start plowing the purchased land without armed forces. The [Ottoman] regime forbade the Jews the use of arms, but was in no particular hurry to extend its own protection. Every new acquisition of land brought its own sacrifices.

For a long time after the first Yavniel purchases the rains fell, and plowing was out of the question. When the rain stopped, twenty work-ers with ten pairs of mules and with wagons full of ploughs and other implements were sent up to Yavniel. Early one morning, they set out toward the fields in a long row, ready to draw the first furrow. Along with the workers went the Jewish guards. And so while some followed the plough, others on horseback kept circling round the new soil.

Broad daylight came, and the plowers were already far afield, when we saw the entire Arab village coming toward us, men and women, young and old.

We, the women, stood in the yard of the Jewish colony, and watched the whole scene from a distance. The Arab crowd drew nearer and nearer to the workers. At last one of the *shomrim* stopped them. An Arab stepped out from the crowd to argue with him, and after a long talk turned back to consult the others. We watched the crowd advance once more, and once more the riders blocked their path. The workers in the fields, behind the riders, ignored the proceedings. They carried on as if nothing were happening, and the furrows grew longer and longer behind them. At last, the Arab crowd turned back. All day long, without stopping to rest or eat, the Jewish workers ploughed the new fields.

In the evening, they returned. But scarcely had they given fodder to the horses when a runner came from another part of the colony. Arabs had attacked the colonists as they were returning from the fields. Hot on the heels of the runner came a second. The colony was being encircled.

Without waiting, the men set out for the scene of the attack. A strange thing had happened. The Arabs had captured the Jewish workers, undressed them—and left them naked.

For two weeks, the colony lived in a state of siege. Finally the [Ottoman] authorities sent help, and also gave us permission to use our arms. From that time on, life became quieter and more secure.

The Founding of Merhavyah

Esther Becker (Meshek Hapoalot, Shekhunat Borohov)

A LITTLE WHILE AGO I made a journey from Shekhem [Nablus] to Nahalal. Many years had passed since I had been this way. From Shekhem to Jenin[43] everything looked much as it had looked. The chief difference was the smooth road which had replaced the narrow, stony paths, so that Afulah could be reached in four hours instead of in twenty-four. But beyond Jenin, the [Jezreel Valley] [hereafter, *emek*] was absolutely unrecognizable. A host of memories awoke in me as I looked on the Jewish settlements—many of them unknown to me even by name—which were now scattered through the *emek*. And closing my eyes, I could conjure up the *emek* as it once had been, with its solitary Jewish settlement of Merhavyah in the center.

It was in 1909 that Yehoshua Hankin purchased from some rich *effendis* [absentee Arab landlords] the territory of Fuleh.[44] *Fellaheen*[45] [Arab peasants] used to work that soil before "at a fifth"; that is to say, the *effendi* would provide them with seed and with implements, and in payment would take four-fifths of the harvest. The peasant retained the remaining fifth.

To the new settlement that we started in Fuleh, the Jews gave the name of Merhavyah,[46] on account of the broad acres of the *emek* that stretched far and wide on every side of the settlement.

Even before the signing of the *kushans* [deeds], Hankin proposed to Hahoresh [The Plowman], to put together a *kvuzah* to go up to the new ground. The organization began at once, and happy were the few men and women who were permitted to join the *kvuzah*. The territory of Merhavyah was small, and not more than thirty workers were needed for it. It took many meetings and endless debates before the personnel were chosen. A great privilege lay before the group: the preparation of

43. Jenin is an Arab town in Samaria. Its surroundings in the Jezreel Valley are characterized by good farm land and springs. It formed a part of the "dangerous Arab triangle," from which Arabs would attack Jewish settlers.

44. Fuleh is the Arabic name for the area where Afulah was established.

45. *Fellaheen* (sing., *fellah*), Arabic term for tenant farmers.

46. The name Merhavyah derives from from the Hebrew meaning the "expanse of God."

a new Jewish position, the laying of the foundations of a permanent settlement. Twenty-six men and four women went out.

The *haverim* of Hashomer had already discharged the task of preliminary occupation and work in many of the colonies of Galilee. The men and women for Merhavyah were therefore chosen mostly from the ranks of the *shomrim*. The meeting place for the comrades was in Kineret, then the center for the settlements of Galilee. And there they waited for their supplies and for the order.

But things went slowly. The *fellaheen*, who had accepted a heavy money indemnity, refused to leave the soil. Meanwhile, five *haverim* went up to Damascus to purchase implements and returned after a week with carts full of ploughs, saddles, harnesses, straw mats, threshing-sleds, and the rest. Those of us who waited in Kineret were quartered on the farm. We were received with open arms, even though life had been hard enough before our coming. Meals had to be served in three sittings. We slept on straw, either in garrets or in the open yard. But everything seemed good to us; Merhavyah was waiting.

Week after week went by, and still we remained in Kineret, waiting for marching orders which never came. Some of our comrades worked on the Kineret farm, and others were occupied with the work of our group. Our presence became a genuine burden to our hosts. There was not only ourselves; there were the mules, which crowded those of the Kineret farmers. Human beings, we argued, can put up with a great deal—but mules must be taken care of. I myself was not in Kineret with the first, but I became sick of waiting among my chickens in Yavniel. I, too, went up to Kineret. But it was clear by now that we were abusing the friendliness of the Kineret farmers. We made up our minds to relieve our hosts. We "set up house" for ourselves in the open on the shore of Lake Kineret. But the mules had to be left in the stable, for fear of thieves. We did our cooking between two stones under a tree. There we ate, and there we did our washing, waiting with infinite patience for the word of release. And after three months of vagabondage, of gypsy life in the open, we got our orders.

A day of that kind stays in the memory forever. A week before our release, Hankin sent up three men, who spoke Arabic well, to Merhavyah. It was their task to reach an understanding with the Arabs, so that we might occupy our territory in peace. We wanted to avoid quarrels with our neighbors, and we wanted to avoid [Ottoman] government intervention. When the week had passed, word came to us to prepare for the journey. By ten in the morning we were ready with all our worldly goods.

There was joy in Kineret and in all the Jewish colonies around. The workers of Kineret went with us part of the way, and with them many of the colonists from surrounding settlements; and so a great crowd, on foot and on horseback, accompanied the slowly moving wagons when they set out. The procession went singing all the way up the slope to Poriyah; and there we parted, with many benedictions, with songs and with firing of shots, as the custom was in those days.

In the evening, we came to Merhavyah and found the three comrades who had preceded us. And now the grimmer task began. Our first accommodation was in the abandoned, half-ruined Arab huts of clay, which were infested with vermin. But more important than ourselves were the mules. Better quarters had to be found for them. And the sowing had to begin without delay, for with the long waiting at Kineret we had advanced far into the season.

We chose for our public buildings three half-ruined Arab *hushas* [huts], the largest of which was twelve by eighteen feet in size.[47] This one we turned into kitchen and dining hall. There was no furniture. One-half of the floor was nearly two feet higher than the other. So we called the higher half "the table," and the kitchen was set up on the lower half. Round the walls there were clay troughs in which the Arabs used to cover up the fodder for the cattle. These we converted into our stores. Having no stove, we cooked on stones outside. In the two small huts we kept our supplies and our fowl.

There was work in abundance for the women, and no orders were necessary. But two of them were incapacitated, because they were expecting children, and a double burden therefore fell on myself and the fourth. And yet, in spite of the heaviness of our tasks, we could not live entirely without some attempt at "adornment." What irked us most was our "table," even when we covered it with straw matting. True, there was plenty of fun about eating at this table, for there were very few among our comrades who could squat like Arabs, with legs crossed underneath. The others, in spite of their efforts, could never get the hang of it. So either they knelt at table or ate lying on the floor. We whitewashed the inside of the huts, and brought in flowers. And finally, we rose to the dignity of a table: we found a few boards, laid them on a trestle, and achieved equality with all other Jewish settlements in Erez Israel. Around this banqueting board we set empty gasoline cans, and more boards on top of these. We bought white oilcloth in Haifa, and

---

47. At the time, Ottoman law largely prohibited building new structures. As a result, many early Zionist settlements started out by expanding previously existing Arab structures. In general, large rooms and stables were added on to the original buildings and walls were extended so as to define the settlement's perimeter, create an enclosed courtyard for farm animals, and afford a degree of protection.

finally our dining hall took on that appearance which was for so many years characteristic of all the *kvuzot*.

Then came the question of bread. The *kvuzah* was still without its own oven. Fresh bread was brought daily from Haifa, the reason being that there was no bakery big enough to prepare several days' supply. The bread was of poor quality—more like dough than bread—and we saw that we would have to do our own baking. The difficulties were simply incredible. The Arab oven—called a *tuban*—was a primitive contrivance that was kept smoking all night long. In the morning, the *pitot* [pocket bread] were laid on the glowing ashes. Most of the *tubans* in the village were broken. We found one that could still be used, and on this we used to bake.

It was a marvelous sort of business. We could not wait until the *tuban* had stopped smoking, because the bread was needed first thing in the morning, and as soon as the first lot was ready, the second had to be started. So we had to lay out the loaves while the *tuban* was still filled with hot ashes and smoke. After every separate loaf, we had to run out to catch our breath. Squatting inside that oven, we were nearly suffocated. Getting out in time was not easy either, for the interior was black with swirling smoke, and more than once, making a blind rush for the entrance, we cracked our heads against the walls. It was two months before the men could get enough leisure to put up an oven with a chimney.

During those first months of the sowing, our dining hall was jammed. Our own *kvuzah* could not plough and plant the whole stretch, and men had to be brought in from the colonies. There were often as many as fifty mouths to feed—not counting the tourists who used to drop in on us. Between meals we had to find time for the washing of our comrades' clothes. Finally two women joined us: a worker and a *feldsher* [Yiddish, old-fashioned barber-surgeon]; and then the work became easier.

That new district, the great open space of the *emek*, awoke a deep and permanent love in me. More than once I longed to leave the kitchen and join the line of the *haverim* who were driving the first Jewish plough through the *emek*. For it seemed to me that there was no greater happiness than this in all the world.

With the Shomrim *in Galilee*

Ziporah Zeid (Sheikh Abrik[48])

THERE WAS A RULE in Hashomer [The Watchguard] that every *haver* had to remain footloose, ready for duty in any place. It was not unusual for a *shomer* to change his post a dozen times in one year, and wind up where he began. A man had hardly settled in one place before he was sent on to another. On the surface it was an easy life: six gasoline cans and four planks made up the family furniture. Food and lodging were provided by the colony, and there was nothing to worry about. The "home" was a little room, a kitchen or outhouse, large enough for two beds and a table. And since the father was out at night on his post, his bed was taken by his son. But if there was a second child, there was no room for it. Its bed stood outside during the day; and in the night it was somehow jammed in alongside the other two.

Those were nights without sleep for the mother. If she dozed off, she would start up again, to listen for the whistle signal from her husband, which told her where he was.

The *shomer* received all of his pay in kind. Every colonist was pledged to contribute so much grain toward his keep. But there were some that dodged their obligation, and in the interval, before the colony council could straighten out the dispute, the *shomer*'s family went on short rations. In our colony, Meshah, we found a pillar of support during bad days in the teacher [Avraham Albert] Anteby.[49] He turned over to us a little stretch of soil close by the school, which the children were not working. This plot the wives of the *shomrim* turned into a vegetable patch; and what the colonists failed to pay we made up from the soil. We got an excellent harvest of greens, so that we even had some to sell.

Meshah was, for our little group, the last stop after a long life of vagabondage. Hashomer had done its work. Wherever it had once en-

---

48. Sheikh Abrik was founded in 1925 in the Jezreel Valley by members of Hapoel Hamizrahi [The Eastern Worker], the religious labor Zionist party.

49. Avraham (Albert) Anteby (1869–1918), director of education for the Alliance Israélite Universelle in Palestine, immigrated to Jerusalem from Damascus. Educated in Paris, he was an active Zionist and Hebraist leader. He was imprisoned by the Turkish authorities, exiled to Damascus, and died in Constantinople.

tered, only Jewish guards were used. But we did not want to remain professional guards. And so the families Giladi, Seid, Gad-Kurakin,[50] and four unmarried young men—all of them *shomrim* in Meshah—resolved to go up into some place in Upper Galilee, to found there a settlement of their own.

Israel Giladi went out in advance and on his return told us he had spoken with [Hayim Margolis] Kalvariski,[51] who was for several decades the representative of the Jewish Colonization Association for Upper Galilee. Together with the latter, he visited the proposed site and had also been offered a little budget. We could begin to work. One morning in the month of Tishrei [August] in the year 1916, the men saddled their horses—all of our livestock—and rode away to Galilee. The women and children remained behind until the men had found lodgings for them.

Two weeks later, we received the news that room had been found for us in the colony of Metulah, which was not far from our stretch of soil. A colonist would come down to Tiberias to meet us. And when we arrived in Tiberias the colonist's cart was already waiting for us. From Tiberias to Rosh Pinah there was some sort of a road. But beyond this there was only mud, into which the cart frequently sank to the axle. For by now, the winter rains had begun.

On the road, in the midst of the Huleh (the great wild swamp which lies to the north of the Merom spring[52]) my little two-year-old child was suddenly seized with convulsions, and not one of us knew what to do. There was a doctor in Metulah, and another in Rosh Pinah, but we were between these points and could not decide which way to turn.

50. The Kurakin (also Kurakina) family, a Christian family converted to Judaism by Rabbi Isaac Elhanan Spektor of Kaunas (Kovno)—known as the "Kovner Rav"—immigrated to Palestine from Sloniky, Lithuania. Hayim Margolis Kalvariski (see note 51 below) was instrumental in helping to resettle the Kurakins and other families of Jewish converts to colonies in the Galilee. For a time, the Kurakin family lived in Sejera, Mesha, and Beit Gan. One of the Kurakin children, Yafah Kurakin (1895–1919), married Gad Avigdorov, a *shomer* employed by Sejera. They assumed the surname Gad-Kurakin and subsequently settled in Hamarah where, tragically, they lost two children to disease. After Yafah Gad-Kurakin's untimely death, Gad (Avigdorov) Gad-Kurakin married her sister.

51. Hayim Margolis Kalvariski (1868–1947) was a member of Hovevei Zion. From 1896–1900, he taught at Mikveh Israel. He next became chief administrator of the Jewish Colonization Association settlements in the Galilee, in which capacity he purchased new lands and assisted in the founding of Ayelet Hashahar, Mahanayim, Kfar Giladi, and Tel Hai. He was a leader in many Palestine organizations devoted to the improvement of Arab-Jewish relations.

52. The reference is to the freshwater spring (as distinct from the swamp and marsh) that formed part of Lake Huleh, known interchangeably in Hebrew as *yam merom* or *yam huleh*.

So we stopped the cart and began to rub the child almost until it bled. But there were some who said that the child should not be rubbed at all. It should be left in peace.

Arabs came by, inhabitants of the Huleh. One of them drew close and said to us, indignantly: "Don't you see that the child is dead? In the name of God! Leave it in peace!" The other Arabs drew closer, gathered round the child, and repeated, "The child is dead!"

We were a long way from Metulah, and in between there was not a single Jewish settlement.

And as we stood there in despair, now rubbing the child, now letting it lie, a cart appeared in the distance, descending from the Metulah hills. My heart jumped. I was sure help had come. The cart was in a great hurry, but I threw myself across its path and made it stop. In it sat a *ger* [convert], a big healthy fellow with his son.[53] I asked him: "Which is nearer, Metulah or Rosh Pinah?" He said Metulah was nearer. I begged him to unharness his best horse, take my baby, and ride as fast as he could to Metulah. He tried at first to get out of it. But I gave him one and a half pounds in money—all we could scrape together in our group—and promised him more in Metulah. He agreed.

I had given my young, three-week old baby into the arms of an unknown comrade. The *ger* rode away before us with the sick child, and I mounted another horse and followed him. But he went fast, and soon was lost in the distance.

The road was new to me, and the terror that I felt for my child confused my sense of direction. It seemed to me that every tree in the distance was the rider with my child. I urged the horse along what I thought was the right road, and the horse, knowing the path better than I, refused to obey. I became desperate, whipped it, forced it on. And finally it brought me to the edge of a cliff, and stood there sorrowfully, as if to say: "Where are you trying to drive me? Now we'll have to turn back." I gave the horse free rein after that, and he brought me back again to the right road. I hardly knew by this time what I was doing, and I do not know what strength kept me going. But I did go on. And meanwhile I tried to prepare for the worst. I repeated to myself, "The child is dead." Such things had happened to others—why not to me?

I rode into the Arab village of Halsa,[54] and there I asked, "Did a rider pass this way with a baby in his arms?"

Yes, they had seen a rider.

53. The implication here is that the wagon was driven by a European gentile living in Palestine.

54. Halsa is the Arabic name for the area today known in Hebrew as Kiryat Shmonah, located in the Huleh Valley in northern Israel.

"Is the child alive?"

"We don't know. We only saw it in his arms.

"Which is the road to Metulah?"

"*Duqri* [Straight ahead]."

And so I rode onward alone. Suddenly, at the top of the hill, among the eucalyptus trees a red roof peeped out, and my heart jumped. Metulah! Yes, I could see the stone houses. I drew up to the first house, jumped off my horse, and ran over to a group of Arabs squatting on the ground.

"Where did the rider with the child go?"

They opened big eyes. "We saw no rider."

"Where do the Jews live?"

"There are no Jews here."

"Isn't this Metulah?"

"No, this is Talhah." [55]

"And where is Metulah?"

"*Duqri!*"

My strength was ebbing, and the road among the hills tortured me. But suddenly I met, on the road, some of the *harverim* from Meshah [Kfar Tavor]. Yes, they had seen the rider. The child was alive. But I would not believe them, and I implored them to tell me the truth. They repeated: "The child is alive!"

Then I asked them: "What are you doing here on the road?"

They told me they were hiding from the Ottoman government authorities who were looking for men who had run away from military service, and for horses for the army.

"Then you'd better take my horse." I said.

I left the horse with them and ran ahead on foot. I know the Metulah roads well today, but for the life of me I cannot remember by which path I came into the village. I asked the first person I met for the home of the woman doctor, and rushed in. It was Mrs. Ben-Ami, the daughter of the famous writer,[56] and she recognized me at once, for we had

55. Talhah is the Arabic name for the area known in Hebrew as Tel Hai, located on the northwest rim of the Huleh Valley. The Jewish Colonization Associiation built a small farm there in 1906. Tel Hai was later the site of an important battle between Zionist settlers and Arabs revolting against the French mandate in Syria (see part II, note 38).

56. The identity of "Mrs. Ben-Ami" is unknown. However, she appears to be the daughter of Mordecai Rabinovich (pseudonym, Ben-Ami) (1854–1932), a well known Russian Jewish author and journalist who wrote in Russian and Yiddish and was deeply influenced by the Haskalah, Mendele Moykher Sforim, and Perez Smolenskin. Rabinovich was born and raised in the province of Podolia and trained at the University of Odessa. He later helped to organize Jewish self-defense efforts in Odessa when *pogroms* broke out there in 1882. He subsequently became a member of Hovevei Zion and was

worked together in the hospital of Zikhron Yakov (with Dr. Hillel Yaffe[57]).

"Is the child alive?"

"Alive!" she answered. "It's already called for its daddy. Is it your child, Ziporah?"

"Yes!" I answered, "And where is the father?"

"The soldiers took him away last night. He's in Djaida (the army station in Metulah) . . ."

That night the cart with the other women came in. I lived three days with Mrs. Ben-Ami, until my child was well again.

We were quartered in Metulah for a whole year. We kept all our clothes and foodstuffs in common, but our lodgings were widely scattered, and so we could not keep a common kitchen. This was a great drawback in the work.

Our stretch of soil was in a place called Hamarah,[58] by the Hazbani river,[59] a two hours' remove from Metulah. The married men worked the soil of Hamarah, and the unmarried [young men] worked as guards for the Metulah colonists. In the evening, when the workers returned from the fields, they took off their shoes and gave them to the guards; and the guards put them on to wear in the night. In the morning, the guards returned the shoes to the workers. All that winter, not one of the men knew what it was to put on a dry pair of shoes.

In order to reach our fields in time, and get substantial work done, it was necessary to go out with the first glimmer of dawn, and to return by starlight. The wife remained all day long alone with her children. There was no place to go. There was nowhere to buy anything, and, if there had been, there was no money.

When the little sack of wheat was brought home, the woman would

---

a delegate to the First Zionist Congress in 1897. With the outbreak of the Russian Revolution of 1905, he moved to Geneva. In 1923 he immigrated to Palestine. His short stories, children's stories, and travelogues are generally regarded as pious and sentimental. Some of his works were translated into Hebrew by Hayim Nahman Bialik.

57. Hillel Yaffe (1869–1934) was a member of Russian Hovevei Zion and a doctor specializing in the treatment of malaria. He immigrated to Palestine with the First Aliyah, but was regarded as a friend of the Second Aliyah pioneers. In 1903 he helped to initiate a countrywide conference of Hebrew teachers. He was a staunch opponent of the so-called Uganda Plan proposed by Theodor Herzl in 1905.

58. Hamarah, a tract of land in the Upper Galilee purchased by the Jewish National Fund in the early twentieth century, takes its name from a local spring. It was the first location settled by the Hashomer guards, many of whom attempted to stay on as shepherds. Due to the site's physical vulnerability and harsh conditions, it was abandoned in 1920 after the fall of Tel Hai (see part II, note 38). The area was later integrated into the kibbutz settlements of Kfar Giladi and Maayan Barukh on the present-day Israel-Lebanon border.

59. The Hazbani River is the source of the Jordan River, located in upper Galilee.

first sort it, then load it on her back and trudge off to the mill. There she waited some three hours until the slow, old-fashioned millstones had ground the grain into flour. And when she got home at last, she had to start looking for fuel to heat up the oven. We would go out into the fields and gather thorns.

There was no water in Metulah. To do our washing we had to go down with our baskets of laundry to the Harad[60] *wadi* [ravine]. And then we used to return with the baskets of wet wash on our heads. I would get the feeling that my head was being rammed down between my shoulders. The labor of those years used us up early, and left many of us sick.

When the great day of the first harvest came, we all went out, women and children, old and young. We put up a tent in the middle of the field, and left the children there. One mother remained to look after them, and the other women went out with the men to the mowing.

A terrific plague of mosquitoes and other insects tormented us. They seemed to like, more than everything else, the blood of the little ones. In the early morning, there was some relief but evenings the children would return swollen with bites and raw with rubbing.

There was plenty of sickness, too. The woman doctor had left Metulah, and no one had been sent to replace her. So we had to use the doctor of the Christian Arab village of Darmames,[61] who was much thought of by the colonists of Metulah. It was his practice to listen to his patients only when he was drunk; and he always demanded pay in advance—in money and wine. On top of this, he was his own apothecary, and after the official visit to him as a doctor, one had to go to him for the medicine, too.

There lived with us at that time a certain Yafah Kurakina-Gad,[62] the daughter of a family of Russian converts to Judaism in Sejera. She had been brought up in the famous collective of Sejera. Yafah's little child fell sick, and the women took turns in helping to watch it. During the day, Yafah could manage alone, but evenings she was exhausted, and we relieved her.

One night, coming in, I found her in a state of collapse. I told her to go to bed, but she would not, and so we sat together. Early in the morning I went home and sent someone to Darmames for medicine, for the child was in a bad way.

---

60. The location of the Harad *wadi* [ravine], as noted here, is uncertain. This may be a name adapted from Arabic and given to the ravine by the Jewish settlers.

61. Darmames, a Christian Arab village north of Metulah, is located in present-day Lebanon.

62. On Yafah Kurakina-Gad (also known as Gad-Kurakin), see note 50.

When the medicine was brought, I took it to the sick child. Yafah half sat and half lay on her bed, and the child was on her lap. I began to wake them, but it was only Yafah who responded after long efforts. The child could no longer be awakened. And when Yafah came to herself, and perceived the dead child, she broke into a tempest of weeping, and reproached me for having awakened her. "Would to God," she cried, "you had let me sleep forever with the child!" And I knew well why she longed for death. This was the second child she had lost in this life of vagabondage.

We left Metulah and settled for good in the new place, to which we gave the name of Kfar Giladi. We put up a single barrack, for all purposes. The walls we covered with straw matting, and one half of the interior we divided off into five rooms. In the other half, we put the kitchen, the dining room, a section for the children, and a special corner for our social life. Outside, against one of the walls, we put up the cowshed, and against the cowshed, we put up the chicken coop. We had no barn. So we hung boxes from the ceiling of the barrack, and this was our "store room."

In the summer, we lived in tents of straw matting and life was easier then.

One woman was busy with the children, another was occupied in the kitchen, and I had my own special job. I was the colony expert in washing the grain. As a matter of fact, quite a little skill was needed for the *hamarah* [day soil] grain, because it was always mixed with red earth and the washing had to be done down at the lake. An Arab taught me the trick. If you mix the grain with earth, and pour it into a bucket of water, three layers are formed. The bottom layer is earth, the next *taradan* [wild grass seeds], and the top clean wheat.

The wagon that used to take the workers out in the morning would also take me, with all my paraphernalia and my bags of wheat. All day long, I sat alone on the edge of the Tayun[63] stream and washed the grain, laying it to dry on straw matting. In the evening, the wagon came my way again, and took me home with my bundles.

The children would bring me my meals to the water's edge. Their reward was to be allowed to bathe in the clear waters of the stream and to run around naked afterwards. One day a caravan of camels passed by. The children ran out of the water and began to throw stones at the camels. The Arabs were astounded. What were these strange children doing in this place? White! And alone! And at that moment it was hard to tell which were less civilized—the Bedouins or our little ones.

63. The reference is to a stream running in the ravine that stretches from Metulah to Kfar Giladi.

When the Arabs began to look around more closely, they saw the tip of a roof projecting over the distant hill; and there, down by the stream, a woman sat alone, washing wheat. Still more astonished, they came over, and asked me whether I was not afraid to sit there alone.

"That's my bodyguard that attacked you," I answered, pointing to the children.

The Arabs broke into laughter.

The laundry and the baking were also my work. Our comrade Yafah was no longer able to help. She lay sick, and she suffered doubly because she was a burden on us. But it was not given to us to carry that precious burden for long. A few months later she died.

My Aliyah *to the Land of Israel*

Dvorah Dayan (Nahalal)

J UST ON THE DAY when my dreams seemed about to be realized, and a new life was opening before me, my deepest doubts returned, and I asked myself: "Is this the way of my life?"

I was active in those days in the *zemstvo*[64] [village council] in Russia. An important task had been entrusted to me. I was working for the people whom I knew, whose language and whose ways I had absorbed. For this people, I had been trained and educated.

I was the only [Jew] in the entire village—nor did I forget that fact for a single moment of my life. This world to which I had given myself, and which wrapped me around so closely, was not my own. And yet that doubt haunted me. It pursued me from the village into the city, followed me down the corridors of the university, faced me in the brightly lit theater and sat opposite me at the writing desk in my beloved study. Was I choosing the right path?

And on an unforgettable night, I made my decision. There was a happy crowd in my student's room, comrades of mine, chattering joyously. I was the only one who was not at home there. One by one threads within me were tearing. I could not hear what my comrades were saying. I heard instead the desolate howling of the wolves in the nearby zoo, and something in my heart responded. My life, my whole life has been a mistake till now! The people to whom I have dedicated myself till now is not my own: I am a stranger in its midst. And that other people, my own people, is a stranger to me. I know nothing of its life and language. Yes, I know the little tailor, the little shopkeeper—but they are not the people. But among the Russians I know the stevedores on the dock, the peasants who hunger amid their harvests, the lean, staring women and children who stream out evenings from the factory when the bell rings. These are the masses. But where are the masses of my own people? I must begin again, from the very beginning.

One by one my guests leave, wondering at my silence and my sadness, for this is not my wont. When they are gone, I too step outside,

64. The *zemstvo* was a framework of local self-government in tsarist Russia; elected, but with a restricted franchise.

and through the starlit night I still hear, but more clearly than before, the melancholy howling of the wolves. A shiver goes through me. I cannot go on like this.

That night I packed my things, and in the morning left by the first boat for my parents' home in the village.

The warm days of autumn came, and it was strange to be at home instead of in the big city. The folks look at me wonderingly. For hours I wander along the banks of the Dnieper,[65] sunk in thought, and feel the broad autumn winds on my cheeks and hair. On rainy days, I stay at home and pour helplessly over my father's[66] stock of Hebrew books, row upon row of them in a language which I cannot understand. And yet it becomes clear to me that in these books lies the key to my life. The thought ripens in me. I must learn the language of my people— for there is no other way of coming close to them. The months go by and still I wander on the banks of the Dnieper. The sun warms me no longer. A cold wind blows, carrying the first snowflakes, and the beginnings of the winter sleep settle like a blanket on the life of the village. And still I am undecided. I do not know where to begin.

January comes. The village dozes under the thick snow. The family has gone to a neighboring village, and I am at home alone. I sit fingering my father's letters. I know that most of them are from Erez Israel or about Erez Israel, but I cannot read a single word . . . Then suddenly I come across a letter in Russian, from Vladimir Tiomkin. I remember now that my father had told me about this letter long ago, but in those days it had all been alien to me. But now every word of that letter is like a seed in plowed soil. A stronger passion wakes in me with every line, and then suddenly, like a thunderbolt, comes the unalterable resolution: there, in Erez Israel, are the workers of my people! I will go to them, and become one of them. Other thoughts rise, attempt to disturb me, but they are carried away as by a strong wind. I wrap myself up, leave the house, and go down once more to the old friend whose wordless counsel I have always depended on, Grandfather Dnieper. From bank to bank the river is one iron sheet: but underneath I feel the waters moving stormily. I am alone in the white wilderness, and unashamed I shout at the top of my voice: "I am going to Erez Israel!"

.   .   .

65. The Dnieper River, located in western Russia, flows southward to the Black Sea. It is approximately 1400 miles long.

66. Rabbi Yehiel Zeev Zhitlovsky, Dvorah Dayan's father, wrote a history of the Jews of Ukraine. He immigrated to Palestine and is buried in Nahalal.

The ship drives through the storm, and a cold, wet mist clings to the waters and to the ship. My fellow passengers cower together for warmth, but in me there is only a fierce jubilation. I stand alone on the deck, untouched by the cold and darkness. I know nothing of the land I am going to, and there is not a single person there I have ever met. I only know that there are men and women working for their people, and I belong to them.

My fellow-passengers to Erez Israel were two or three wrinkled grey-beards going to spend their last years in the Holy Land, and a woman with a child. The little boy could sing Hebrew songs; and I would sit with him in a corner and listen to his thin, childish treble piping the songs of our country.

Any Palestinian port was the same to me. So I landed at Haifa with the mother and her boy, and went with them to a hotel. I was trusting to Providence . . . Someone would surely turn up who would want to know what I was doing here in Erez Israel. And if it were the right kind of person, then I would know that I had found my path.

I sat at the table in the dining room and listened to the conversation. And the first one to come up to me was a young man with a long beard that made him look much older than he was. He came up with his hands in his pockets, and his head slightly on one side, and before he spoke a word I had already taken a liking to his clever, laughing eyes. I knew I could trust his advice.

Early the next morning, I had changed from my heavy winter clothes into a light summer dress, and, filled with hope, set out with B. for the colony Merhavyah.

Sixteen years have passed since that morning. What was then strange and incomprehensible has now become intimate and simple. Illusions were born and died. There have been hopes that proved false, and others that have been fulfilled; men and women have been close to me, and have drifted away. But as long as I live I will remember those eyes that shone on me in my loneliness with so much brotherly love and understanding.

I am in the *kvuzah* of Dagania. Today, for the first time, I am permitted to bake the bread on my own responsibility. "Bread for fifty people!" I say to myself, and alternately I swell up with pride and shrink with terror. How does a little creature like myself come to undertake this tremendous task, and face a gigantic oven full of loaves? Yes, I know the theory of it perfectly. M., the skillful baker, has taught me everything. She told me exactly how long to knead the dough. She told me when to add the water, and was very emphatic about adding only a little at a time.

She gives me her instructions, and goes out. And now I must convert theory into practice. A little time passes and my hands begin to tremble with exhaustion. The fingers won't obey orders. I put all my strength into it—but the flour will not turn into dough. I know I oughtn't to do it, but I add more water, and the flour turns into a sticky, sloppy mess. I can't pull my hands out without dragging everything along. I twist them, rub them—no use! My back aches. I am tortured by thirst. The flies settle on my face and I can't drive them away. They crawl over my forehead, into my eyes and mouth. "Bread for fifty people!" I repeat to myself, and attack the mess of flour and water again. I feel all my strength running out of me. I stand on one foot, then on the other. I try to think of other things, but I am haunted by one thought: "I want to add more water." M. passes by and looks at me with pitying eyes.

And now, at last, the first good signs. Something like dough begins to emerge. It grows smoother and less clinging, and I can free my hands. I can add water, drink a little myself, and wipe the sweat off my face. The torture changes to pleasure. A stone has fallen from my heart, or I feel as if I had just thrown off my winter mantle and run out with the first sign of spring, over the green meadows.

It seems to me that only yesterday I was a thing torn by doubts and hesitations. In the noisy city, in the great library, in the museum, in the classes, the question would suddenly confront me: Why are you doing these things? Who needs you? Can't they do without you and people like you? And in such moments a paralyzing apathy would creep over me; I wanted to see no one, speak with no one. But now? My *haverim* are out in the field, mowing the harvest that we have sown. Close by, I hear the mill grinding out grain. And the flour from the mill comes straight to me, and I bake the bread for all of us. Bread is surely needed.

With a Kvuzah ~~~~~~~ *herds*

Rivkah Danit (Ein ~~~~~~

I N THE FIRST YEAR of the Great War, there was a severe crisis in Erez Israel, and because of the difficulties of communication the Histadrut was split into two sections, with separate executive committees —one for Judea and one for Galilee.[67] Outside of the four *kvuzot*— Dagania, Kineret, Merhavyah, and Tel Adas, which were settled on the land of the Jewish National Fund and were sure of work and bread— there were some hundred workers in Galilee, all unemployed. The

67. During World War I, British and Turkish forces fought for control of Palestine and the southwestern region of the Ottoman Empire.

For much of the war, the Jewish community of Palestine was virtually cut in two. The southern region, including the Sinai peninsula and most of Judea, was controlled by the British. Meanwhile, the Ottoman regime retained control of the north, including parts of Samaria and the Galilee. The multi-ethnic Turkish army was bolstered by German units and staff officers. There were about 39,000 German-Turkish combat troops stationed in Palestine. A sizable garrison of German troops, under an Ottoman commander, was located in Tiberias. The regime also forced many Zionist settlements, such as Dagania and Merhavyah, to house and supply groups of German pilots and soldiers.

Starting in January 1915, fierce and costly campaigns were waged by the British for control of the Suez Canal, Gaza, Beersheva, Jerusalem, and the coastal plain. During the war, widespread shortages of coal, wood, clothing, and food severely strained the native populations. Moreover, resentment and hostility by the local Arab population toward the Germans, the British, and the Zionists increased steadily. Against this backdrop, the Jewish community in Palestine was placed under virtual house arrest by the Ottoman regime. Jewish immigrants of Russian and Polish ancestry were considered enemy nationals, and the Yishuv was cut off from overseas markets as well as traditional sources of European support. A striking exception in this regard was the role played by American Jewry, which supplied the Yishuv with significant foreign aid and investment.

Between 1914 and 1918, the Yishuv dwindled to approximately 57,000 Jewish inhabitants, roughly a third of its pre-war numbers. Though the community suffered greatly as a whole, it was the "Old Yishuv"—the traditional Jewish centers of Jerusalem, Safed, Hebron, and Tiberias, as well as the Zionist colonists and plantation farmers who arrived before 1905—that was hardest hit. On the other hand, the Second Aliyah pioneers proved to be relatively resilient. Organized in a broad network of cooperative labor ventures and workers' organizations, the Second Aliyah and its leaders gained new prominence and prestige through countrywide relief efforts, self-defense measures, political activities, and economic initiatives such as Hamashbir [The Provisioner], which supplied the general public at reasonable, controlled prices.

By 1918, against the backdrop of Britain's incremental military victories and general air superiority in the Mediterranean theater, there was a virtual breakdown in the regional Ottoman administration of Palestine. As a result, the German-Turkish forces

workers' committee decided, then, that every worker who had parents or relatives in Judea, and who could find food and shelter there, should leave Galilee. For those who had to remain, work was found drying the Jordan Valley swamps and clearing the stones off the hills of Kineret. The swamps, as it happened, needed to be dried, for they were a source of sickness; but we felt that the [Jewish] National Fund was undertaking this only for our sake, and the thought depressed us.

It was known in Galilee that I had a sister in Judea who could take me in, but I had made up my mind to starve rather than leave Kineret.

On the first day of the new arrangement, I went out with *haverim* I had met before to carry stones off the hills. We worked in groups of three, with two baskets to a group for carrying away the stones. In my little group was [Aharon David] Gordon, but I did not know him and had not even heard his name. I only saw an old man who was drawn toward young people, and who labored cheerfully with them, unbowed in body or spirit by his years. And when, on that first day, I felt myself collapsing under labor to which I was unaccustomed and the fierce heat of the Kineret sun—it was Tamuz [August] then—he cheered me. He laughed and repeated (how many have heard him say it!): "Look at me, I am an old man, and I don't lose heart. And you are young and you despair on the first day. Look! Let me show you how to carry a basket full of stones without getting tired."

Three months later, the Histadrut undertook the work on the Tiberias road. The [Turkish] regime had ordered the colonists of Galilee to prepare gravel, and the colonists turned over the work to the Histadrut. It was a contract job and so the first group went out for a week to break stones and to determine at the same time what the price should be. It was with the utmost difficulty that I, a woman, could persuade [them] to take me along. There were all sorts of objections. The work was too much for a girl. It wasn't nice for a Jewish girl to be working on the open road. There was even one *haver* who believed that it would be a national crime! But another girl and I stuck it out for the first week and, in spite of renewed objections, stayed on. At the end of the first month, there was a whole group of women at work on the road.

The work came to an end, and I determined to link up with a *kvuzah* of shepherds who were employed on the herds of the Galilee colonists.

---

deteriorated rapidly. Under these circumstances, the Yishuv gained some measure of relief. The Zionist position was advanced further by the Balfour Declaration (November 1917), the occupation of the north by the British in September 1918, and the immediate postwar situation. For a useful discussion of Palestine and Zionist policy in this period, see Ben Halpern and Jehuda Reinharz, *Zionism and the Creation of a New Society* (Hanover and London: University Press of New England, 2000), pp. 201–207.

These shepherds had an idea all their own. They were going to stay long enough with the colonists to learn the trade and after that they would live like Bedouin [Arabs], wandering the fields of Erez Israel, with sheep and cattle of their own. The idea caught my fancy, and I joined the *kvuzah*. Here again, we worked in threes: two shepherds and myself in one group. They looked after the flocks and I was, so to speak, the housekeeper.

We lived in a room without doors or windowpanes. There was no gasoline for the lamp, and, if there had been, we couldn't have used it because of the wind that always blew through our "room." The pay of the shepherds was not enough to keep them. They were paid in kind— and at that the pay of one was regularly withheld as a possible forfeit against loss of cattle.

We struggled through half the winter, starving much of the time. My *haverim* would go out with the herds into the hills, and take with them, as their day's ration, a piece of dry bread. Before they left, they drank several cups of hot tea with sugar, to warm themselves. I would get up early to boil the water. Then I would go out and drive the herds together, so that they should not wander over the sown fields of the colonists.

A morning came when there was no bread, and my *haverim* went out to the herds without their ration. I cannot forget that day. A fierce rain was driving across the country, and my comrades went to the top of the hill to look for pasture. But as they came downward with the flocks, three of the cows fell into a huge hole and were killed. Hungry, raging, and wet to the skin, they came "home"—and there was not a piece of bread for them in our lovely room. I was unable to get out of bed. They asked nothing of me, nor I of them. We only looked at each other.

At last one of them got up, went down to a colonist, and returned with a loaf of bread fresh from the oven. We tore the warm bread into three parts, and swallowed it. That bread was our meal for the day.

And when the year came to an end, we had a trial on our hands. We had not only not received our pay—we were supposed to make good the lost animals. The worst that could happen did happen: we were fired.

From Judea to Samaria

Yehudit Edelman (Ein Harod)

I

"Excuse me, Gottlieb, aren't you a member of the Workers' Council? I was told to apply to you for work. I want to start tomorrow morning."

"There's no ladies' work."

"I don't want a 'ladies' work. I'll do any kind. They told me workers are needed here; that's why I came."

"I don't know. The colonists don't want girls."

"But you're making a mistake. I'm not looking for girls' work. Are you afraid I won't make good? Give me a chance. If I don't get through the regulation amount, take it off my pay."

"I'll see. Come in tomorrow and I'll have an answer."

Six months later, before the rains set in, Gottlieb said to me: "You know that the heavy work is over. We've got to start in making the 'saucers' (the holes round the trees to catch the rain water). If you like, you can start after Saturday."

We began on Sunday. The sky was gray, the air heavy with moisture. The rain seemed to be suspended about us, and the "saucers" had to be dug in a hurry. Eighteen of us worked in one vineyard, systematically, silently, rhythmically. The spades swung up and down together and the rain seemed to be holding back especially for us. We had passed over into the second half of the vineyard, and had come close to the plowed land beyond, with its wild thorns and grasses. And now the air could no longer contain its burden. The first big drops fell and in a few minutes the flood was all about us. We picked up our spades and dashed back to the colony, wet to the skin and happy.

Saturday morning. The rain beats down steadily. In the little barrack that is our kitchen, the workers stand at the windows, watch the swelling pools outside, and fall into thought. The rain seeps in through the windows and yellow streaks of water crawl down over the white walls. The rain is so heavy that it may wash away the last rows of trees at the other end of the vineyard on the downward slope. The owner is at some distance, in the next colony. If he waits till the rain lets up, it may be too late, and the trees will be torn up by the roots. Suddenly, I put on my raincoat—my good and clever mother, only she could have remembered to make me take a raincoat along—pick up my spade and run through the vineyard. The rain had, in fact, washed away a whole row of shoots. I shovel the earth together swiftly and plant the shoots firmly again. The rain whips my face and holds up the work. The sloppy earth clings to the spade. Two hours of work is enough, and the shoots are saved.

Winter in the kitchen. It's time to clear the tables and wash up the breakfast things. We had tea with raisins instead of sugar, and a salad of oranges with spring onions dipped in oil: two oranges to a person. It's wartime and there's no exportation. So for a few *piastres*, we can buy oranges enough for all the workers. Now we have to sort the beans and peas and soak them, and prepare the meal before the comrades come back from the vineyards. Before nine in the morning we have to go out and gather stocks of *inzhil*—a sort of wild grass—and spread it round the north side of our neighbor's oven. By tomorrow, the *inzhil* will be dry enough to serve as fuel, and then we can bake. We have about enough bread to last us till then. And now it's time to put the pots on the stove constructed of a few cans. Afterwards comes the evening meal, flat cakes that we baked together with the bread. The cakes are dipped in oil and prepared with lots of garlic. They are eaten with the pea soup.

Spring. We are filling up the "saucers" round the trees. Four men are at work in the vineyard: a Yemenite,[68] a Galician,[69] and two Russians.

68. In 1881, Jews began leaving Yemen en masse to escape escalating persecution. In general, the Yemenite immigrants possessed a traditionalist worldview, believing the return of the Jews to Palestine to be the fulfillment of scripture. Many Yemenite Jews originally lived in settlements adjacent to the *moshavot*, where they found steady agricultural employment. Relations between Yemenite and European Jewish immigrants were troubled, largely due to the bigotry of the Ashkenazi settlers. Indeed, the Zionist establishment gave preference to Jews of European descent. In the end, the Yemenite community was compelled to leave the *moshavah* at Kineret owing to the the religious-cultural divide that separated them from the largely secular East European settlers. In 1922, they established their own organization, Hitahdut Hatemanim [Association of Yemenite Jews].

69. Galicia is an area that includes southeast Poland and northwest Ukraine, along with parts of Austria. The region was famous for its many great rabbis, its *yeshivot*, and its high cultural level. The Poalei Zion [Workers of Zion] party was active in the area.

They dig along the length of the vineyard, two rows at a time; and every five minutes they pause and rest. The four men have no language in common. The Yemenite understands Hebrew, but he speaks Arabic; the Galician understands Hebrew and Arabic, but he speaks Yiddish. The Russians know only Russian.

When the work first began, the men wanted to help the girl finish her rows. But it soon became clear that the one who needed help was the Russian boy, because he was behind. On the way back home, one of the boys wants to relieve the girl of her spade. And suddenly it occurs to him that when you are going home after a day's heavy work you don't feel the spade on your shoulder. The hand that was half stretched toward the girl drops again.

II

"Don't go to Samaria," so I was told. "You don't need it at all. There's plenty of work here in Petah Tikvah. Your *kvuzah* is occupied every day. And the colonist P. came into the Workers' Council office yesterday and said he would give you a steady job in his orchard. You won't have to do heavy work. You'll be overseer and you'll have an Arab boy as assistant."

And while I was being told this, the wild man M. growled: "What's the sense of talking to her? She'll listen and then she'll do exactly the opposite."

Rather than submit to *suhra* [forced labor] in Beersheva and in other places which were far from Jewish settlements and were filled with infectious diseases, many of our workers left for Samaria to chop down eucalyptus trees for the [Ottoman] regime. In exchange, they got food and liberation from the [compulsory] military service. When women workers were asked for, to keep house in Samaria, I reported. There were plenty of others to do my work in the orchards of Petah Tikvah.

There were three [young women] in the group from Petah Tikvah that clambered on to the carts which carried wheat from Galilee to Judea. At Tel Kerem [Tul Karm][70] the road divides, one branch leads to Galilee, the other to Samaria; and there we had to get out and wait for a chance conveyance. The railway was being used in those days exclusively by the military, and so we waited at Tel Kerem.

70. Tul Karm, a small Arab town east of present-day Netanyah, grew rapidly in the early twentieth century due to the construction of a highway and a railway line that passed through it. The town also benefited from the planting of citrus groves and the progress of other local farm branches.

We waited till our patience gave out, and finally we slung our packs on our shoulders and went ahead on foot. The packs were nearly as long as ourselves and much broader. They contained our bedding, our laundry, our clothes, and our books. The weight was bad enough, but much worse was the fact that they didn't sit right. The sand was almost as yielding as water, and every footstep was a separate achievement. At last, a cart came along, carrying tree trunks. We flung the packs on board and jumped in after. Life suddenly became tolerable again. In two hours' time, we were in Hederah.

Familiar faces in the workers' home. There's Miriam K. standing over a tubful of wash. I watch her enviously. She works so neatly and effortlessly. Where did she get the trick? Laundry! What a back-breaking torture that was for me, and how long it took me to learn!

On the veranda another familiar face—A., who is something of a public busybody.

"The *merkaz* [central office] sent you?" he asks. "But we don't need new workers. Who told them to send you?"

That was our official reception.

Late afternoon drew on. The two *haverot* who had come along with me collapsed from weariness. But I found a young fellow who was returning that evening [from Hederah] to Hefzibah and I went with him —perhaps there would be work. There was no road, only a wilderness of sand. It was here that I got my first glimpse of the *dzhamus*[71] [water buffalo]. It was evening when we arrived at Hefzibah. My head ached and I wanted to lie down. Some of the *haverim* tried to persuade me to eat something, but I only wanted to lie down. They took my temperature, but they did not tell me till next morning that I had nearly a hundred and six.

This was my first attack of fever—my betrothal to Erez Israel. At Hederah, I had already seen one of the *haverot* lying on the floor with a compress round her head and in the next room, another. It looked like part of a local custom.

We began to work, some of us in the orchards of the Agudat Netaim[72] [Planters' Association] and some in Hefzibah. We used to work immediately before and after the attacks of fever. Soon the following message came from Sarah Lishansky, who was at that time a nurse in

71. The reference is to the water buffalo, the *Bubalus bubalis*, which until the end of the 1940s roamed the Huleh marsh, where the Bedouin Arabs reared it for food.

72. Agudat Netaim [Planters Association] was an association established in 1904 by Aharon Eliyahu Eisenberg (1863–1931) for planting and cultivating orange groves and vineyards in Palestine on behalf of foreign investors. Eisenberg, a Russian Zionist pioneer who immigrated to Palestine in 1886, emerged as a leader of the First Aliyah and later the Yishuv.

Karkur: "You've got a girl down there, among the workers who came from Judea. Her name is Yehudit and she has two long braids down her back. Send her up here, and if she won't come, drag her by the braids." I didn't wait to be dragged. When I arrived I was shoved at once into the kitchen, and I knew that there was no getting away from this place, because there was no other [young woman] to do the work.

We used to get up at three in the morning, when the threshing machine sent its first melancholy whistle over the gray Karkur fields. We went into the kitchen, an old Arab *husha* [hut]; behind it was the well, and opposite was the vegetable patch. We worked and suffered. At ten o'clock the fever would increase suddenly; our limbs trembled, heads ached, and everything fell out of our hands. Twelve o'clock, and it is impossible to go on. I lie down on the bench in the kitchen and wait till the fit passes. Then I get up and work on.[73]

Shortly after my arrival, I made my first acquaintance with a scorpion.

Work was over and we sat outside, waiting for the carts that were returning from Galilee. We knew that our [young men] would not want to spend the night in the desolate wadi [ravine] Arah.[74] Waiting for them, we passed the time chatting and singing.

D. calls out to me, "Yehudit! Come over here, there's a clean place to sit down."

I crossed over, and sat down—and leapt wildly to my feet. It was as if the big toe of my right foot had been shoved against a burning coal.

The *haverim* think it a bit of a joke. "That D. has all the luck," they say. "When he does get a girl to sit down next to him, she's got to be bitten by a scorpion."

D. is terrified. He almost bursts into tears. "How did it happen?" he keeps on stammering. My foot seems to be steeped in a white fire. I must have trodden on the scorpion, it jabbed me so fiercely—a full shot of poison. Already Sarah is working over my foot—of course, she uses boiling water, and the new pain drives out the old.

73. The reference here is to malaria, which was widespread among Zionist pioneers in the Galilee who worked at draining swamps and marshes. As described in the text, malaria commonly manifests itself, first, in an initial chill that may be preceded by a period of malaise or headache. The resulting fever can last from one to eight hours, after which time the infected individual may feel well until the next chill begins. There are several types of malaria. Depending on the variety and severity of the affliction, episodes like those described here may occur as frequently as every four to eight hours. In severe cases, such episodes may last 20 to 36 hours. The episode is known to often begin abruptly every 72 hours.

74. The reference is to the ravine that stretches from Karkur in the northern Sharon Valley to Afulah in the Jezreel Valley.

All night long, as if to make my pain absolutely intolerable, someone keeps disturbing me by shouting angrily: "What's happened there?" But in the morning, I am told that this someone was myself. I had been yelling at the top of my voice till three o'clock. I deny it resolutely—I am always so patient.

And this, too, passes.

The nakedness of the wide fields lies like a burden on the soul. There is not a single full tree to rest the eye. I long once more for the green places of Judea, for the shadows, for the little wood, for the shrubs of a vineyard and an orchard of orange trees. Only far away, on the edge of Karkur, a meager line of eucalyptuses stretches through the desolation. I cannot bear the loneliness of those trees. Sometimes, I feel as if I could rush out there with my spade, and dig and dig, and cover the earth with green. And sometimes, I feel that even the sun is weary of shining on this barrenness, and longs for something living on which to pour out its warmth and affection.

I Become a Worker

B.B.[75] (Ein Harod)

I

Two days I waited for my sister Hemdah[76] to take me down to the workers' club. But she never had the time. And at last I decided to go there alone.

A group of workers stood outside the building. As I drew up, not knowing a soul there, they looked me over curiously, and began to talk about me in friendly mockery:

"Who's this? Pretty, isn't she?"

"And doesn't she know it! Look at the way she holds her head."

I went up boldly and answered: "Suppose I am pretty? What's wrong with that?"

Two young fellows stood apart, looking more impudent than the others. One of them called out: "We can see from your clothes you aren't a worker." I answered in the same tone: "What have my clothes got to do with it? Here—is this the hand of a worker?"

There was a shout of laughter, and voices:

"That's a worker's hand. Big and hefty. Say, how old are you?"

I answered: "I have a friend and she's married."

"And what about you?"

"If you'll be nice boys, I'll marry, too."

At this point my nerve broke down. I blushed and began to stammer. This was my introduction to the club.

When I went inside I felt a strange chill of disappointment. The whitewash was peeling from the walls. The tables were small, without covers. At one table sat some workers drinking soup. The waiter came

---

75. B.B. stands for Batya Brenner. The following essay reveals, in part, Brenner's critique of the labor movement in Palestine and her complex relationship with her brother, the writer Yosef Hayim Brenner. In the narrative, Batya Brenner identifies herself as Amunah, from the Hebrew, meaning "faithful." She also employs pseudonyms (see notes 76 and 77) for her siblings. The other names in the story are probably fictitious.

76. Hemdah, from the Hebrew, meaning "desire" or "precious," is, perhaps, a pseudonym for Ahuvah Brenner, Batya Brenner's sister, who also immigrated to Palestine.

up to one of them, and said sharply: "Listen, you! You've taken two plates of soup and you've given me only one ticket. Where's the second?"

This was beyond me. What were tickets needed for? Didn't they just put the soup on the table and let people eat whatever they wanted?

Someone explained to me: "Every plate has to be paid for separately. You don't think a kitchen can be conducted without some sort of account, do you?"

"But I didn't think you've got to check up on each man, how much he eats."

No, no, this was not what I had expected and I felt a depression coming over me.

The two laughing boys who had been standing outside came up to me.

"Well, how do you like our club?" And without waiting for an answer one of them added: "I suppose you expected a great big hall, with lots of gold framed pictures on the wall."

I answered frankly: "I didn't quite expect gold frames. Only I thought the place would be simple in another kind of way."

"Well, what way?"

"I did expect a big room. And I also expected big long tables. I don't like little tables, it's too much like a saloon. A big table is homier and friendlier—it draws people together. And why can't you have a white tablecloth on the tables? And why can't you have pictures of the first *haluzim* on the walls, the first tillers of the soil?"

"Why, of all things, the pioneers on the soil?"

I answered: "Because we Jews have plenty of city workers everywhere, and there's nothing new in that."

"And what else did you expect?"

"You could have had a few flowerpots in the corners. And if you want to know something more—I thought that the food would be handed out by girls in white pinafores."

"Why don't you come into the club and fix things the way you want?"

"I don't want to work in the kitchen. I want to join a *kvuzah*. I want to learn to work."

"They won't take you into a *kvuzah*. The *kvuzot* aren't for young [women] like you. Besides, you can't speak Hebrew. Forget the *kvuzah* —it's just a dream."

"It's not a dream," I answered proudly. "My brother has friends in a *kvuzah*, and they'll take me in."

"You have a brother here?"

"Yes, and a sister, too."

"Well, well. And who are they?"

"You know them, I think. Their names are Ezra[77] and Hemdah."

"What? Hemdah is your sister? You don't look a bit like her. Listen, if your brother vouches for you, they may let you in. But you might as well know that's just pull."

"No it isn't. My brother is known over there, and he says they can use me. And I hope to start work soon."

"But what do you want a *kvuzah* for?" they started again. "Why don't you join us? We need a girl in the kitchen just now."

"No, I'm going to wait. I want to go to a *kvuzah* if I can."

When I went out of the club that evening the two [young men] went out after me, and for a little while I caught part of their conversation . . . They were wondering whether I would ever become a real worker.

II

I didn't return to the club. I could not understand the lectures, and I could not sing. There was dancing, but something strange had happened to me. There was a time when I was known as "the dancer." But that was long ago—on the other side. And when I refused to dance at the wedding of my friend, over there, everyone was astonished. But even then it had lost its appeal. My body sought another rhythm now, other motions than those that are made to musical measures.

Two long weeks passed, and no answer came from the *kvuzah*. I grew uneasy, and wondered at the reason. Was it true that it was all a matter of pull? Were they ashamed to answer "No" just because my brother had applied for me? Often, in the street, the two young men I had met at the club passed me by. They smoothed down their masses of hair, greeted me with "Shalom," but did not stop to speak to me. What was going to happen with me? Would I have to work in the club after all?

The thought repelled me. I could not picture myself asking a worker for his "ticket." My brother and sister did not worry. When I complained about my idleness they laughed: "Don't worry. You'll get work all right."

At the end of the two weeks, my brother came in one evening and found me in tears. He was startled.

"What's the matter?"

77. Ezra, from the Hebrew, meaning "help," and the biblical story of Ezra the priest (Nehemiah 12:1) who returned to Judah after the Babylonian exile and, with Nehemiah, led the Israelites in rebuilding the country. It is, perhaps, a pseudonym for one of Batya Brenner's brothers, Meir Brenner and Benyamin Brenner, who also immigrated to Palestine.

"I don't understand you," I sobbed. "I'm here two weeks, I can't get into a *kvuzah*, and you take it so calmly—as if I'd come here just so."

My brother looked relieved.

"Is that all? I thought something was really the matter. If that's all you want, well, I've got an answer from the *kvuzah*. They ask you to come."

"Read me the letter."

"They say that one of the [young women] is sick, and there's no one to work in the kitchen. They want you to take the train tomorrow afternoon and at three o'clock they'll meet you at the station."

"Kitchen?" I stammered. "I don't know how to cook. What am I going to do there?"

But this was no time to turn back. I did not sleep that night. At five in the morning I was already up. My sister heard me, and she asked me: "What are you getting up so early for?"

"I want to pack my things over," I said. "I'm ashamed to land there with all this baggage—like a bride getting ready for her wedding. I want to leave out my holiday clothes, and I want to take just a little underwear with me."

"Wait," my sister said. "Don't close up the basket till I've been to the village. I want to give you some money to pack in, just in case."

"In case of what?" I asked. "Do you think I'm going to keep money tied up over there, in the *kvuzah*? You're just making fun of me—I suppose you think I don't know what a *kvuzah* is. I know there's no such thing as 'yours' and 'mine' in a *kvuzah*."

"Well, well," my sister said, ironically. "Even in a *kvuzah* they have 'mine' and 'not-mine.' But I know it's no use arguing with you."

Very hastily, I prepared my basket. Then I made a separate bundle of my bedding. My sister watched me in astonishment.

"What are you making two separate bundles for?"

"I want to see whether I can carry them myself to the station."

"But, listen," my sister said, patiently. "I've ordered a porter to come to the house."

"All right," I said. "He'll carry the basket and I'll carry the bundle. I'm not going to follow him with nothing in my hands, like a countess."

At eleven o'clock that morning, I was down at the station. My brother and sister argued whether I ought to travel alone or not. But Ezra said finally that there was nothing to be afraid of. Besides, now that I was going out into the world, it was better for me to learn independence. I agreed with him—but I turned away so that no one could see the tears in my eyes. Because, after all, suppose no one were to be at the station at the other end?

III

In the train, a woman came up to me and said: "I saw a Jewish child, so I had to come and speak to you. There are only Arabs on the train. Where are you going?"

I wiped away the tears quickly and said: "To a *kvuzah*."

"A *kvuzah*? What is that?"

"It's a kind of group," I said, "where everyone works like everyone else, and they all live together."

"What do you mean, 'they all live together'?"

"Well, they all eat in one kitchen, and they all work together."

"Eating and working together—does that mean living together?"

I began to see that neither this woman nor I knew very clearly what a *kvuzah* was.

"And why must you go and work?" she asked me. "Your parents aren't dead, God forbid?"

"No."

The woman was silent awhile. Then she began again: "You don't look like an ordinary girl to me. I suppose you've been to school. Why can't you be a teacher, or a nurse?"

"I want to work."

"You want to work? Good luck to you. I suppose you're from Russia. My daughter in Jaffa told me that Jews are coming from Russia these days, and building themselves houses on the sands. Some of them have nice clothes, but won't wear them; instead of hats they wear *kefiyahs* [Arab headdresses] and they work on the land. Good luck to them, too. Maybe they'll put an end to the famine."

I remembered now the day I left home, and my mother's parting words: "God be with you, my child. Work! But you are only a child. Don't take on more than you can carry, and don't despise what the world says."

I had always listened to my mother, but I could not understand what those words meant: "Don't despise what the world says." The world says many things. The world says that money is important. If I had taken along what Hemdah wanted to give me, I would not have to worry now. If there was no one at the station to meet me, I could continue with this woman as far as Jerusalem, and there I could write my brother Ezra to come and fetch me. But what would I do now, without a *piastre* in my pocket?

Just before my station, the conductor comes around and takes my ticket from me. My heart begins to beat fast. I try to behave calmly.

I straighten out my two braids, and smooth out my belt. As the train rolls in, I lean out of the window. The long stretch is as empty as a wilderness. Finally I see a little *shtibl* [small house] under some eucalyptus trees. Near the *shtibl* is a group of Arabs, and when I look closely I see among them a tall, dark boy wearing a white shirt, and carrying a whip in his hand.

When the train stops, the tall boy with the whip is already at my window.

I shout: "Is there a Jew here?"

"Are you Amunah?"

"Yes."

"My name's Avraham. I'm a *haver* in the *kvuzah*, and I was sent down to meet you. Let me take your things."

"Not all of them, please."

"Why, what's the matter? You'll get dirty and you'll tear your dress. Here, you hold my whip. I'll take the basket, then I'll come back for the bundle."

"Please, I'll carry the bundle."

The [young man] laughed out loud and stopped arguing with me. Basket and bundle were packed into the middle of the cart. He examined the arrangement thoughtfully, and said: "Well, that won't upset." It was a real task to climb into the cart, for my dress was too tight. He watched me with great solicitude, and felt guilty when something ripped.

We hardly spoke along the journey. All his attention was given to the driving. He watched every stone, every rut, and managed the mules with the utmost care. Before every bump he warned me anxiously to hold tight.

IV

When we crawled into the yard, not a soul was visible. Avraham called out: "Before long it'll be easier to steal things here by day than by night. At night we have the guard, but during the day there's no one around." Then he added, half solicitously, half sarcastically: "I suppose that Shahar, the *shomer yisrael* [guardian of Israel], is sitting all the time at Hasidah's bedside."

Then he turned to me, and his face beamed: "And we didn't upset the cart!"

I went into the house with a beating heart. The first to meet us was Shahar himself. He stood there, book in hand, and said in amazement:

"When did you get here? I didn't hear the creaking of the cart." Then he introduced himself. "My name's Shahar, one of the *haverim* in the *kvuzah*." He looked at me out of watery, colorless eyes, and added: "I suppose you're tired. That road would tire out anybody."

"No," I answered, "In fact, I enjoyed the ride."

"Enjoyed it?" he repeated. He turned to Avraham. "And didn't the cart upset?"

Avraham seemed hurt. "You talk as if I did nothing but upset carts. You're a first-class *shomer*, I must say. Here we come riding into the yard and you don't even hear us."

Angrily Shahar answered: "No, I didn't hear you. I had to change the compress for Hasidah, and I sat with her a while."

"All right, then," Avraham said. "But now will you tell me where the grain measure is? I don't know when you fellows will learn to leave it where it ought to be. I've got to feed the mules. Will you look after that, Shahar? I'm the cook today, and I've got to get supper ready."

"I can't. I've got to be near Hasidah." And then Avraham told me to follow him, so that Hasidah could have a look at me. When we got into the room, he asked the [woman] who was lying down whether she wanted the cold compress changed. Then he added: "Here's the new *haverah*."

Hasidah opened her eyes and, without greeting, she said: "Oh, she's too young, too young. Have you been long in Jaffa?"

"Two weeks," I answered.

"Then why didn't you cut your braids off? They'll be ruined here, anyway."

"Why should I cut them off?" I asked, startled. "My sister has even longer ones, and she manages all right."

"Your sister doesn't work in the field," she answered. "If you want to work, you'll have to cut those braids off."

"Of course I want to work. I'll cut my braids off, if I have to."

"And look at your dress. It's ripped. That isn't the kind of dress to come to work in."

"That's nothing," I said, wretchedly. "I've got other dresses."

She made a motion to Shahar to change the compress, and then she closed her eyes. I went away from this reception with my heart in my shoes. "I'll go to Avraham," I thought. "I feel better near him."

I found him in the kitchen. "Come in," he said, cheerfully. "You'll see what kind of a cook I am. Can you cook?"

"No."

"Doesn't matter. I'll teach you. I'll teach you Hebrew, too."

"Honest?"

"Can you ride a horse?"

"No. I've never been on one."

"You'll learn that, too. We'll go out riding in the fields."

"Can I help you to get supper ready?"

"No, it's all right. I'll be through soon. If you like, you can clean the lamp glass. It hasn't been wiped since Hasidah fell sick."

He gave me a rag, and I, not noticing there was a button in the holder, smashed the glass . . .

Avraham started. "Hey, what's that? What are we going to do now?"

I didn't know the extent of the catastrophe, but I guessed from his tone. I remained standing in a sort of paralysis.

After an awful silence, he began to console me. "Oh, well, we'll get another one tomorrow. But you don't know what a lamp chimney means in a village like this. We've had to sit in the dark for a whole week, sometimes, before we could lay our hands on one of those treasures. Without one you can't do a thing nights—not even read the newspaper."

In the evening they began to return from the fields. The first man in was Aharon, and his first words were, "Well, is the new girl here?"

"Yes."

"Why is it dark? Why don't you light the lamp?"

"Can't. The new girl's already broken the glass."

"She has? That's not so good. Tell me, is she pretty at least?"

"Oh, be quiet. I don't know."

Aharon dashed off, and came back in a moment with the stable lantern, and set it on the table. He looked me over, and then said with a smile, to Avraham: "You've nothing to be angry about."

Somebody else came in, grumbling: "What's the idea of taking the lantern out of the stable? I nearly knocked one of my eyes out."

"Don't get excited. I took it. I wanted to see our new *haverah*, and there's no lamp. So I took the lantern."

"Was it worthwhile, at least?"

"I didn't get a good look, but I guess it was."

V

In the morning, Avraham remained behind to show me my work. The first thing he asked me was whether I could cut onions into small pieces. When I said I could, he went for two barrels of water, and in the meantime told me to keep an eye on the oil which was standing over the fire. I was to take it off as soon as it had warmed up, but I was to be very careful about it because if the oil became too hot the onions would burn when thrown in. He went out, and I remained alone in the kitchen. I was eager to do my best, but in taking off the oil I slopped half of it on the floor. A feeling of despair came over me. In the evening, my great skill was the subject of wide discussion. They asked Avraham whether he would go on teaching me how to cook. He answered angrily: "What makes you all so impatient? Were you born workers? Did you find it so easy to learn?"

The next day things went smoothly. I peeled onions. I washed the bread box. I did everything according to Avraham's instructions and he was happy. "They'll have nothing to grumble about today. Now put the milk on the stove, and for God's sake, watch it closely, and don't let it run over. I've got to get more water, or there'll be no tea for dinner."

"I'll be careful," I said.

I stand watching the milk closely, waiting for the first sign of the rise. And suddenly I hear Hasidah's voice: "Amunah, bring me a glass of water. I don't feel well." I run in, give her water, straighten out the cushions, and ask anxiously: "Is that better?" But suddenly she makes a face, and asks abruptly: "Did you leave the milk on the stove? What's the matter with you?" I dash back. Too late! The milk is running down the sides of the pot, and streaming on to the floor. My heart dies in me. What's going to happen now? How will they be able to eat the gruel? They'll be hungry—and all on my account. But what could I do? Shouldn't I have given the sick woman a glass of water?

When Avraham came in, he turned pale. "Again?" he said.

In an instant, he had fixed everything, added coals, and thrown salt on the stove.

"If you'd at least thrown salt on. The smoke is terrible."

"Thrown salt on what?"

"On the stove, so as to keep the smoke down. I forgot to tell you. I didn't expect this to happen."

He put water on for tea, and went into Hasidah's room.

I wiped the milk off the floor, and began to sweep the room. A cry came from Hasidah: "Shut that door. I'm choking with the dust and smoke."

Avraham came in: "Why don't you sprinkle water on the floor before sweeping? You're not like a girl at all . . . Don't you even know how to sweep?"

"I know how to sweep. I didn't want to use water because you've got to bring it such a distance, and perhaps all of it is needed. And I was frightened to ask you because you looked so angry before."

"Don't you think I ought to be?"

VI

That evening, I was again the subject of discussion. Again they asked Avraham: "Well, are you still going to teach her?"

Avraham lost his temper. "Why do you pick on me? Am I responsible? Did I bring her here?"

Shahar added: "I talked with Hasidah. She said we ought to take her out of the kitchen—we can't stand all that damage. Anyway, she can do some washing. Since Hasidah fell sick, no washing's been done, and we haven't a clean thing to put on for work."

I am asked if I can wash clothes. Sure! I am filled with joy: here's something I can do, at last.

When I got up early next morning, there were already two barrels of water at hand, brought by Avraham. He showed me the three stones that served as a stove and the heap of thorns for fuel. Following Avraham's advice, I poured a lot of washing soda into the hot water, and rubbed the clothes well. But when I got to the dark clothes, I couldn't rub any more, because there was no more skin on my hands. I could neither wash the clothes nor wring them out. Miserable, ashamed, humiliated at my helplessness, I began to cry. It was the first time in my life that things were going against me. And when Avraham came up, I showed him my hands.

He smiled. "You're a real worker," he said, "there's no getting away from that. Leave the clothes in the boiler, with water. You'll finish tomorrow."

I took down the wash, which was dry by now, and went into Hasidah's room. The village nurse was there. As I came in, I heard her say:

"Now that you've got a new girl, things will be easier for you."

"She's not much of a help," Hasidah said. "We've made an unlucky choice. She wants to work, but she doesn't know how. And she's too childish for a *kvuzah*."

The nurse asked me to sew two towels together, and make a compress.

"I can't," I said. "My hands are all raw, and I can't straighten my fingers out."

"Let me see. How did you get them that way?"

"From the wash."

There was a frightened look on her face. "Don't let any water come on your hands for the next few days."

"How can I do that? There's a tubful of laundry outside."

Hasidah smiled. "That's my help. There's something queer about her. The first thing she told me was that she has a lot of clothes, and her sister has even longer braids than she."

And after a pause she added: "It looks as though a long time will have to pass before we have the right kind of people coming to the country."[78]

VII

Those three days without work were misery. Meanwhile, Hasidah got up from her bed, and with her about the house things improved, and the mood improved, too. We had to do the baking now. Hasidah said: "If your hands get better, I'll give you the kneading to do." I would work under her direction, and she would attend to the cooking, because sowing time had come and Avraham could no longer remain at home. Mornings there was a lively feeling of work in the air, and everyone was up with the dawn.

"Amunah, today you'll do the kneading. Are your hands all right?"

I answered resolutely, "Yes." I put a white kerchief round my head, and took a new apron out of my basket, one that I had not yet worn in the country. I was preparing as if for a ritual.

"I'm ready, Hasidah."

She looked me over, "White!" she exclaimed. "From head to foot, like a nurse at the operating table." And when she gave me flour and water, and told me to start kneading, I was as excited as if I was undergoing rather than watching an operation. I kneaded away lustily. From time to time, the dough clung to my hands and was flecked with blood from my half-healed flesh. Without saying a word, I would detach the bloodstained pieces of dough and throw them on the floor. Hasidah called out to me: "Be careful no flies get into the bread."

When the dough was kneaded to her satisfaction, she said: "We've got to heat the oven now."

"I'm frightened. I know I'll spoil something."

"Don't be frightened. I'll watch."

Oh, how much certainty and confidence there was in that "I'll watch"! The bread came out beautifully.

And I thought to myself: Who of my old friends in the *shtetl* back home knows what real happiness is? Who of them has lived through such a joyous day?

Hasidah had magic in her fingers. Whatever she did came out right. By the time the men returned from the field, everything was ready.

78. This statement highlights the tension between veteran members of the Second Aliyah and newcomers.

They asked her anxiously how she felt. There was an atmosphere of solicitude and respect around her. The next morning, Aharon fell sick and there was no one to follow the plough with the seed. Avraham suggested that I be taken along. There was much laughter and yet, in the end, they had to take me because there was no one else. And so I was to go out on the fields! I had no idea of what I would have to do—but I was happy. The boys made room for me at the table, and called out: "Sit next to me, *fellah* [Arab tenant farmer] . . ." All day long, I went after the plough, and dropped the seed. I did not get tired. Around me I heard voices: "Good work." In the evening, I returned on horseback, my hair falling loose over my shoulder. I did not care. I felt well. I was happy. On the porch stood the nurse, together with Hasidah. She had come to attend to Aharon. I rode up to the pair of them and sprang off my horse. I wanted to run to Hasidah, take her aside, pour out all my joy—but her cool look froze the words on my lips.

The nurse exclaimed: "What youth! What health!"

Hasidah answered: "Just a girl—like all the others. Out there, in the fields, among the boys, she becomes another person. And all the kitchen work falls on me again."

I hear her, and I understand her only too well. And I ask myself what this attitude of hers means. What am I to deduce from it? Have I any right to stay on here? She calls me "little girl," but I want to be a worker. I must make up my mind what to do.

That evening, I did not go in to dinner. And when they asked "Where's the *fellah*?" they were told, "in bed." "No wonder," they said, "after that long day in the sun." I did not close my eyes that night, and I could not decide on a course of action. It was impossible to return to Jaffa, to have them say: "Our little worker is back so soon?" And I could not stay on. I had heard enough to make me feel that I was not wanted.

VIII

Early the next morning, the train brought a welcome visitor, Kotik, the secretary.[79] They clustered round him in the dining room, asking for the news, but the first thing he said was: "Where's that [new] *haverah* that just came here? I have a letter for her from her brother Ezra."

I took the letter, and felt myself turning pale. "If you want," Kotik said, "you can send an answer through me. I'm leaving for Jerusalem tomorrow."

79. The reference to Kotik, a comrade who served as *mazkir* [secretary general] of the settlement, is probably fictitious.

Ezra wrote that he had been persuaded to go to Jerusalem, and he was not sorry at all. Things were going well with him and he had a nice room. If I wanted, I could come to him for a little time. Kotik, who was a good friend of his, would advance me the money for the fare. The letter was like the voice of a deliverer! I could leave the *kvuzah* without going back to Jaffa! I was saved!

When breakfast was over, I went up to Kotik, and in a low, timid voice told him that Ezra had asked me to come to him, and that he, Kotik, might lend me the money.

"Why, certainly" he said, with a charming smile.

Then I added: "And, if you won't find it a burden, I'd like to travel together with you."

"Of course," he said, eagerly. "Ezra's little sister . . ."

The *haverim* looked at me in amazement. They began to ask me: "Are you really leaving? Why has your brother sent for you? When are you coming back?" I did not answer. Only Hasidah seemed to be satisfied.

"Well, what did I tell you? A child. Your *fellah*. She's been here a few days and she's off to Jerusalem." And suddenly she became very serious. "Pity she went into the fields yesterday. My room hasn't been cleaned once since I was sick."

"There's still time," I said. "Kotik isn't going till twelve o'clock tomorrow. And if there's no other work for me, I'll start on your room at once."

Hasidah's face lit up. "Will you really? Let's carry the things out, and I'll prepare whitewash for you. And if you'll whitewash the room for me, I'll have something to remember you by."

"What do you mean, 'remember her by'?" Avraham put in. "How long do you think she's going to stay in Jerusalem?"

But no one answered him, and Avraham turned away depressed. I threw myself into the work, and in it almost forgot my hurt and my anger. I did my best to make a straight line of whitewash, to keep it from sprinkling the windows and running down on the floor. When the whitewashing was done I washed all the floors, and in the evening I helped Hasidah carry the things back into her room. Hasidah looked thoughtful. "How clean it is!" Then after a pause, she added: "Suppose you did come back, after all. It wasn't so bad here, was it?"

When the *haverim* returned, they talked in low tones about me. I learned afterwards that they felt guilty. They had not treated me as they should have done. They wanted to persuade me to stay. Or perhaps Hasidah could persuade me to come back after a short stay in Jerusalem.

And sure enough, in the morning, Hasidah said to me: "I forgot to ask you when you're coming back. We were so busy all yesterday that we hadn't time to talk it over."

"I'm not coming back," I said, shortly.

"But why? Do you find the work too hard? Never mind that. Come back. You're too young, I know, but I'll teach you everything, and you'll like it here. And listen, Amunah, I've got a half-pound saved up. I've been thinking a long time of buying myself a pretty dress, and now you're going to Jerusalem, perhaps you'll buy the material for me. You're a good judge, I'll leave it to you."

She went over to her basket and began to rummage in it. From underneath the books she dragged out a brown dress, a heritage of her half-forgotten student days in Russia. But to her horror she found that the mice had eaten away the pocket and the half pound with it. But I had no sympathy for her at that moment, for this was my revenge. She had kept money of her own in the *kvuzah*! How was such a thing possible?

IX

Kotik knocked at my door. "Young lady, it's time to start out. We can't have the wagon today, it's needed for the sowing. We'll have to make the station on foot. Get ready."

All the way to Jerusalem, Kotik did his best to keep me cheerful. He did not care that I could not speak Hebrew. He spoke Yiddish and Russian to me. But I hardly answered a word. I was thinking how I would face my brother Ezra, and what I would say to him.

We knocked a long time at my brother's door, and finally he came out. "I didn't hear you. I was writing letters. Oh, Amunah, so you came! You're not sick, are you? I suppose you came just to see Jerusalem."

I was silent. I felt the tears gathering in my eyes, but my brother's "nice" room was so small that I could not turn away from him.

That day, we hardly spoke. The next morning, when Ezra had gone out, I sat down at the table to write. I did not notice the passing of the time, and it seemed I had scarcely begun before Ezra was back for the noon-day meal.

"Are you writing mother?" he asked.

"No, I'm writing you," I answered. "Every time I want to tell you what happened, I feel like crying. So I'll tell it to you on paper instead." And I handed him what I had written.

He looked through it earnestly, and then he said: "Promise me you won't write any more. Writing makes people old. It throws a shadow over their lives. And you're only a young [woman]. Don't go in for such things. It's better for you to learn how to bake bread and milk cows. That's a lot more important in Erez Israel."

X

A week passed, and there was very little conversation between us. All day Ezra was at work, and I passed most of the time reading the few books he had obtained for me.

Then one evening, we sat down to talk it out. And the first question he asked me was whether I had liked the *haverim* in the *kvuzah*.

"No," I said. "The only one I liked was Avraham. He's a nice boy. He helped me with everything."

"Oh, Avraham is the nice boy, is he? You're still very simple, little sister. You happen to be young, and not downright ugly, and that's why he enjoyed helping you."

"You've such a queer way of talking to me," I said, impatiently. "You remind me of an old schoolteacher who's afraid to say something nice in case it spoils you."

"What did I say now?"

"'Not downright ugly.'"

"Oh, all right. Do you want me to say you're beautiful? Your eyes look quite clever, but you're not too clever at that."

We both burst out laughing.

One evening, we came back from a lecture. My brother put his hands on my shoulders and said: "Confess, Amunah, what's [on] your mind. Aren't you thinking how you'd like to stand on the platform and deliver a lecture like that?"

"You're a million miles out," I said. "I was thinking how I'd like to be able to bake bread and milk cows. That's the only thing I care about— and you've got to help me again. I can't stay here idle any longer. You told me that you've got a friend on the training farm, and that if you wrote him he'd manage to get me in. Write to him now."

My brother shrugged his shoulders. "I'll write," he said. "But don't walk around that way, and don't be on pins and needles till you get your answer. This time, I won't send you out alone."

It was Kotik himself who came with the answer. He walked in early one morning, with a letter. "You don't have to read it," he said, laughing. "I know what's in it. You're going to the village to milk cows! I was present at the meeting where it was decided to take you on. And I'm going to accompany you out there, too, because I'm going back in a couple of days. Only this time, you've got to promise to be a little more cheerful."

My last morning, I had given my brother the manuscript that I had written during my stay with him. He had read it through with deep interest, and now, when I was getting ready to leave, he said: "I honestly don't know how to talk with you. If I talk to you as to a child, you'll be offended. And if I treat you like a grownup, you won't understand me." He tapped the manuscript. "But I'll treat you like a grownup. Your writing lacks style and language. It's not intelligible. And yet there's something in it. If you didn't want to be a worker, it might be worth spending time on it. But as it is—I can't see it."

"If you treat me like a grownup," I said, "I'll answer you like one. You're deliberately belittling my writing. Show me one sentence that isn't intelligible."

My brother looked through the manuscript again. "Here: 'A girl can marry and be happy even at seventeen, as my friend has done; but only a grownup person can be happy in a *kvuzah*.'"

"You didn't understand that?" I asked. I snatched the manuscript from his hand and tore it into scraps. My brother stared at me.

"What did you do that for?"

"I only wanted to show you that my writing means nothing to me. And you may be sure that I shan't lose a single hour of work for the sake of it. But it wasn't necessary for you to belittle it."

Kotik came in hastily without knocking.

"Quick now," he said. "We haven't a minute to lose if we want to make the train."

"I'm ready," I said. "Goodbye, brother."

"Goodbye, sister." And holding my hand, he added: "And so the cows are going to win out?"

"That's my big hope," I answered.

PART II

With the Group

The Kvuzah of Twenty

Yael Gordon (Dagania Alef)

IT WAS A FEARFUL and difficult time—the third year of the World War. The threat of utter ruin hung over the Jewish settlement in Erez Israel. The *haverim* whom we could not employ were taken up by the government for public works, and they labored like slaves for a meager sustenance. But while they at least had enough, or nearly enough, to keep body and soul together, the women had nothing at all. Their condition was one of destitution and desperation. They used to wander from one workers' kitchen to another, from colony to colony, from *kvuzah* to *kvuzah*, seeking work. But there was no work; and they would not eat the bread of charity. And so they covered the country from end to end, hungry and unwanted.

And at last the first victim fell. The young Miriam [Greenfeld] Greenblatt,[1] a quiet, deeply thoughtful girl, took her own life. A shudder ran through the Jewish settlement. The incident was seen as a warning. The long negotiations which had been conducted with various groups and institutions had brought no real results; now it was realized something had to be done at once.

Yosef Busel came forward with a proposition. (Busel was one of the founders of the colony Dagania, a protagonist of the collectivist idea for the workers of Erez Israel. He drowned in Lake Kineret in 1919.) The unemployed women workers of Galilee were to organize themselves

---

1. The original Yiddish and English volumes refer to Miriam Greenblatt; however, this appears to be an error. The young woman in question was actually Miriam *Greenfeld*, a Second Aliyah pioneer who was not accepted by the members of Kvuzat Kineret. Consequently, Greenfeld, like thousands of displaced and homeless pioneers in Palestine during World War I, wandered from one Jewish colony to another seeking work and shelter. (On the situation in Palestine during World War I and the plight of the Yishuv, see part I, note 67.) She eventually returned to the Kineret settlement area, where several hundred destitute Jewish pioneers gathered daily at the local Jewish cemetery to receive a glass of milk and minimal assistance. In despair, Greenfeld committed suicide by drinking a bottle of vinegar. Her story came to symbolize the plight of the young workers in this period and underscored the vulnerability of the labor movement. As noted here, Greenfeld's death prompted the Second Aliyah leadership to take concerted action in behalf of the thousands of homeless and displaced Jewish pioneers during World War I.

into a *kvuzah*. The *kvuzah* of Kineret and the farm school of Hannah Meisel [Shohat] promised the new group a patch of twenty *dunams* [five acres] for a vegetable garden. But the chief income would come from outside work. Some of the women would do the cooking for the men who were draining the Kineret swamps. Others, we hoped, would find seasonal employment in the neighboring *kvuzot* of Kineret and Dagania. There were some women who could sew, and they too hoped to find some sort of employment at their trade. At the instance of Busel, the Zionist bureau in Jaffa advanced to the "unemployed" *kvuzah* sixty pounds for tools and other initial expenses.

We jumped at this plan. Hannah Meisel [Shohat] promised to act as our advisory expert. She put only one condition: she wanted the Women Workers' Council of Galilee to appoint two skilled and experienced *haverot* to take charge of the social life and the work of the new *kvuzah*.[2] But skilled and experienced comrades were exactly what we lacked. After an inner struggle with myself, and against my inclination, I offered myself. I knew what a responsibility I was taking on myself, but the situation was desperate and there was no other way out.

The majority of these unemployed women were strangers to each other; and they became acquainted only as members of the *kvuzah*. There was a wide range of ages, of outlook and of development, a motley of human material bound together for the time by the common misfortune of unemployment. At our first meeting, we discussed the difficult task and the heavy responsibility that we had assumed. In my own speech, I tried to express the genuine fear that I felt. I was not sure that we had in our midst the forces that would enable us to carry out our plans, and establish the *kvuzah* on a permanent foundation. But the meeting was enthusiastic, and a spirit of helpfulness showed itself. We chose there and then the council of the *kvuzah*, consisting of three: Shoshanah Bogen, Hannah Kaznelson, and myself.

The first question was of quarters. Where were we to live? Days passed in fruitless search. The workers did not use tents at that time; these came in only after the war, with the [Third Aliyah]. And new houses were not being built, for the price of materials was prohibitive.

Finally, in the *kvuzah* at Kineret we secured a room adjoining the stables. The windows looked out toward the threshing floor and the highway, and so we got our fill of dust and stable smells. Another, smaller

2. Protests had broken out in 1914 resulting from the absence of a female representative at Hapoel Hahaklai's [Land Workers' Association] fourth conference held in the Galilee. The women workers' movement emerged as a response with the aim of training women for employment. In 1920, it demanded formal recognition of the Moezet Hapoalot from the newly-formed Histadrut.

room was lower down in the colony, on the shore of Lake Kineret. We divided the larger room with a curtain. In one half we worked and ate; here, too, we kept the big box of wheat which we obtained from the Hamashbir [The Provisioner] cooperative. On the other side of the curtain were fourteen very original "beds." A bed consisted of three empty gasoline cans covered with boards and straw matting. The beds stood so close to each other that in the night we would dig elbows into each other. Near the large room there was a tiny cubicle, without flooring and unwhitewashed. We cleaned this out, installed a stove—and we had a kitchen.

From the day when we began to work our garden, the *kvuzah* considered itself as officially established. Every evening the "Council of Three" apportioned the work for the next day, made up the accounts, and gave directives generally.

The work which some of the women had to do was heavy and unpleasant. Other luckier ones were assigned lighter tasks. But the luckiest were those who were privileged to work in our own garden. However, the garden was small, and not more than a couple of women could be employed here at one time.

Let me say that from the outset, in spite of the fact the women had not known each other when they came together, a strong feeling of common responsibility developed at once. They obeyed the orders of the council even when they did not agree with them, and even when they had protested against them at the meetings of the *kvuzah*. The social discipline that was displayed was not the result of force; it sprang spontaneously from a healthy sense of responsibility.

It was only after the war that the *kibbutz* arose in Erez Israel which takes in people who do not know each other.[3] Before that the *kvuzot* consisted always of friends, and new comrades were admitted only after long counsel. In its time, therefore, our *kvuzah* was something of a phenomenon; and, curiously enough, it made a name for itself by reason of the spirit of comradeship that reigned in it.

We were poorly fed, for we budgeted our meals, and would under no circumstances go beyond our resources. We were determined not to get into debt. But when the Kineret summer was added to the burden of our work and undernourishment, we began to [come] down with malaria.[4] The strong and healthy took on double burdens; the weak did

3. The emphasis here highlights the social and ideological tensions among the First, Second, and Third Aliyah settlers.

4. During the summer months, the basin surrounding Lake Kineret reaches high temperatures, often with humidity levels in the extreme. In general, the region was also known in this period for frequent instances of malaria suffered by Jewish pioneers. See also part I, note 73.

what they could. Most of the time they were unfit even for light tasks. They had to lie around hoping that the slender help given them by the Kupat Holim [Workers' Sick Fund], would cure them.

Winter evenings, we ate by the light of a tiny wick dipped in oil; after which we would keep our only kerosene lamp burning for two hours while we read and prepared our lectures. There were three groups living in that yard, the Kineret *kvuzah*, Hannah Meisel [Shohat's] training farm, and [ourselves]. During the week there were scientific courses and language lessons. [On Shabbat] we studied the *Tanakh* [Hebrew Bible]. This yard was the focus of our common spiritual life. We got together a fine choir, and besides the singing there were interesting, comradely talks round the table of the Kineret *kvuzah*. Our group of women participated in everything. In spite of the poverty and privation, this happy little room became a center of attraction; but those who were drawn to us most, and toward whom we reciprocated the feeling, were the swamp workers. There was a special bond between us. They, like us, had been among the unemployed yesterday. And now they were proud of our successful *kvuzah*.

Now there was no shortage of work, for we put our hands to whatever turned up. Our one worry was to pay back as quickly as possible the loan from the [World] Zionist Organization. Our garden flourished, and there were customers for its produce. And if something was left, we used to load it onto donkeys and take it up the hills to Poriyah, where we sold it to some American families and to government officials, or perhaps to the farm workers themselves. Then we would come back singing to our happy "home" next door to the stable. Our patch of soil was so fruitful that we paid off almost the entire debt, and would have paid all of it if not for the merciless *osher* [tithe] which was exacted by the [Ottoman] government.

There were no contractual obligations in our *kvuzah*. If a *haverah* found work elsewhere she was free to go, and we would find someone to replace her. A year passed in this way. By that time, however, our numbers had dwindled to six, for most of the workers had found permanent positions. With my five companions I went over to Merhavyah, and there we founded a new *kvuzah* of women workers, not of the unemployed.

On the Run

Hannah Chizhik (Havurat Hazafon,[5] Tel Aviv)

Two o'clock [in the morning] they made the rounds, and woke all of us. The *haverim* of the *kvuzah* Ahvah[6] [Brotherhood] were to gather for a meeting in the workers' club. A host of refugees had just arrived in Petah Tikvah, and something had to be done. Hassan Bek,[7] the Turkish official, had driven them out of Jaffa and Tel Aviv in order to keep Jews away from the front (Passover eve, 1917).

There were in hiding among us *haverim* from every corner of the country. They were hiding from the agents of the Turkish government, from the periodic searches and seizures. In our house—as in every other—there was not a corner that was not occupied; and I was tired out by the day's heavy work, and by the unceasing tumult around me. Moreover, I was almost broken by the miseries which these expulsions brought in their wake. Yet, when I was called at two in the morning to this meeting, I got up. A great many others had come, too. Yosef Hayim Brenner was among them.

And the subject of the talk was our responsibility toward the homeless. We had an obligation toward them, as toward the whole Yishuv. We could not be content with giving them shelter merely as long as

5. Havurat Hazafon [The Northern Collective] was an association of young Russian Zionist students and pioneers who, in the years following World War I, moved from one Jewish colony to another performing needed agricultural labor. Over time, clusters of the original group, who also retained the name Havurat Hazafon, settled permanently around the country, including Metulah, Hartuv (near Bet Shemesh, southwest of Jerusalem), and Tel Aviv. In 1930, a sizable cohort of Havurat Hazafon members, along with a small group of American Zionist pioneers from Detroit, established Kibbutz Ramat Yohanan; see Mark A. Raider, *The Emergence of American Zionism* (New York and London: New York University Press, 1998), pp. 131–134.

6. Ahvah [Brotherhood] was a collective made up of Zionist pioneers, inspired by the socialist Zionist theoretician Nahman Syrkin (1868–1924), who viewed voluntary Jewish labor as the basis for the new Jewish society being created in Palestine. The *kvuzah* worked in the orange groves of Judea.

7. Hassan Bek, an Arab of Aleppo and military doctor who served as an agent of the Ottoman regime, headed a commission that investigated charges of espionage among the Jews for the British forces during World War I. The investigations were carried out with particular ruthlessness in Zikhron Yaakov, Tel Adas (Tel Adashim), and Kineret.

they stayed with us in Tel Aviv. We had to do more. We had to look after them until they had found some sort of permanent refuge.

The brutality of the [Ottoman] regime grew from day to day, and conditions naturally grew worse. The arrests increased, and among the chief sufferers were the leaders of the Poalei Zion [Workers of Zion] and the *haverim* of Hashomer [The Watchguard]. Then the government issued a last warning, in which it demanded, under threat of the severest repressive measures, that all men of military age should report to headquarters. Among the workers in Petah Tikvah, there were some of Austrian citizenship.[8] In order to make up the tally of the number of men who were expected to report, they decided to give themselves up. They believed that, being the nationals of an allied power, they would be released at once. Three of them died in the Damascus prison. After the war, when a new workers' settlement was formed in Petah Tikvah, we named it Givat Hashloshah[9] [Hill of the Three], a memorial to the three Galician[10] *haverim* who had given their lives for us.

Refugees came daily into Petah Tikvah. The streets were filled with them; and every day an old Sephardic Jew wandered among them, crying in a hoarse, melancholy voice: "God has commanded that you obey the laws of the state.[11] In the next twenty-four hours you must all go to Galilee, and evil will befall him who does not go." (This old man was engaged for this purpose by the Turkish government; he was one of the "public criers" who used to acquaint towns and villages with new decrees.)

At the night meeting which we held in the workers' club, I decided to go with a group of immigrants to Galilee; I wanted to work among

8. Austria was allied with the Ottoman empire during World War I. The Zionist settlers noted here were considered Austrian nationals by the Turkish regime.

9. Givat Hashloshah [Hill of the Three], established in 1925 on a site west of Petah Tikvah, was founded by Third and Fourth Aliyah pioneers. The *kibbutz* initially subsisted on its members' wages as hired laborers in private farms and local industry. The settlement's name commemorates three Jewish laborers employed in the nearby colony of Petah Tikvah who were executed by the Turks during World War I. Among the core leaders of the *kibbutz*, who were associated with Kvuzat Ahvah (see part II, note 6), was Benny Marshak, a disciple of Yizhak Tabenkin (1887–1971), the leading figure of the Kibbutz Hameuhad movement. With the urbanization of the region, the *kibbutz* was moved eastward to a new site in the rural surroundings of Rosh Haayin. The transfer made possible the establishment of two separate *kibbutzim*, each of which, in time, affiliated with a different *kibbutz* movement.

10. On Galician Jewry, see part I, note 69.

11. The reference here is to the halakhic rule that the law of the country is binding —*dina demalkhuta dina* (Aramaic)—and that, in certain instances, it is even to be preferred to Jewish law. This precept stems from the sociopolitical sensibility of medieval rabbinic authorities who, charged with the task of preserving diaspora Jewish life under tenuous and hostile conditions, asserted that Jews were obligated to abide by the statutes of their host societies.

their younger daughters, who were surrounded by particularly great dangers.

I was also charged, at that time, with difficult and responsible tasks for the Poalei Zion party. Often, without realizing how dangerous it was, I would act as liaison between the scattered points, carrying the word from *haver* to *haver*. But however necessary my work in Judea was, I thought that Galilee took precedence over it.

The streams of immigrants turned toward the town of Tiberias, and few of them were to be found in the Galilee colonies. In Tiberias, the hunger grew from day to day. With hunger came infectious diseases, and families began to dwindle. A relief committee was formed, at the head of which was [Meir] Dizengoff,[12] later mayor of Tel Aviv. Dizengoff went up to Damascus, to maintain communications between the Yishuv and world Jewry.[13] To Damascus came the contributions of world Jewry. Yosef Busel was still alive; he was the workers' representative on the committee, and on him fell the difficult responsibility of settling the immigrants in some new location.

All the refugees suffered, but the young women suffered most. They were hungry and idle, and life lost all its savor for them. Tiberias was filled with soldiers, mostly Germans who were then the masters in Erez Israel.[14] Money and provisions were plentiful among them, and a fearful wave of prostitution spread through the starving town. Fearful scenes took place, often among the most pious families, and the greatest sufferers from the calamity were the Sephardic Jews.

When I arrived in Tiberias, and saw the situation for myself, I decided that the first thing to be done was to create a women workers'

12. Meir Dizengoff (1861–1936) came to the Zionist cause while in prison in Russia for revolutionary activities. In 1886, he helped found the Kishinev branch of Hovevei Zion [Lovers of Zion], and, as a chemical engineer, was commissioned by Baron Edmond de Rothschild to open a bottle factory in Palestine. Though the factory failed and Dizengoff went back to Russia, he remained committed to Zionism. He became a member of the Odessa Commitee of Hovevei Zion, and opposed the "Uganda scheme" for large-scale Jewish settlement in East Africa which was proposed to the Sixth Zionist Congress (1906). In 1909, four years after returning to Palestine, he helped found Jaffa's Jewish suburb that was to become Tel Aviv. In 1911, he became chairman of Tel Aviv's council for local self-government. During World War I, the Jews were expelled from Tel Aviv and Dizengoff devoted himself to helping the exiles. After the war, he resumed his chairmanship of the Tel Aviv council. In 1921, when Tel Aviv gained municipal status, he became the city's first mayor and held the post, with the exception of three years, until his death.

13. In this period, the Alliance Israélite Universelle maintained a regional office in Damascus. It served as an important conduit for information and communication between the Yishuv and diaspora Jewry during World War I.

14. On the situation in Palestine during World War I and the plight of the Yishuv, see part I, note 67.

kvuzah for the young immigrants. I worked out the details, prepared a budget, and brought the plan to Yosef and Hiyutah Busel. Both of them were ready to help; they were joined by two other skilled *haverot*, Rahel Rosenfeld[15] and Nehamah Zizer. Busel obtained for us a loan of a hundred francs with which to lease the garden that we were to work. No sooner was the information out, than dozens of young women, the daughters of immigrant families, applied. But the number of free places was limited, and the list was at once filled.

Busel persuaded the relief committee to make special arrangements for the *kvuzah*. Instead of the *rutel* [six and a half pounds] of flour a week which was distributed to every person in the town, the *kvuzah* obtained a loan for three months' provisions. The loan was to be paid back as soon as the vegetable garden began to produce an income.

And now we were ready to dig. But where were we to get seed?

One day, when the heavens were pouring themselves out in rain, I went out of Tiberias to Kineret. It was known in Galilee that I had been one of the lucky ones who had remained in "England" (this was the current name for Judea, which fell into English hands in the fall of 1917, while Galilee remained Turkish until the end of 1918). *Haverim* were amazed at me. Why had I left the happy soil of Judea and thrown myself into the hunger and suffering of Galilee?

In Kineret I went straight to Meir Rotberg,[16] one of the founders of Hamashbir [The Distributor]. I asked him to make a loan to the three members of the Histadrut who were working with the immigrant women workers. The loan was to consist of seed for the garden, and grain for bread. The military forces in the country needed great quantities of vegetables. The German mark was at that time secure; and as soon as the garden produced we would pay back the loan in full.

I returned to Tiberias with seed and grain, and we plunged heartily into the work. We planted cabbages, onions, potatoes, and cucumbers. Everything took well, everything shot up.

Within a short time our little *kvuzah* had become the cultural focus of Tiberias. Teachers among the immigrants lectured in our *kvuzah*, and the Jews of Tiberias [viewed our women with respect], as they went

15. Rahel Rosenfeld received her agricultural training and was active in the *meshek hapoalot* run by Hannah Meisel-Shohat at Kvuzat Kineret. She later joined Kibbutz Ein Harod.

16. Meir Rotberg (1887–1951) immigrated from Ukraine to Palestine in 1905. He was one of the founders of Kvuzat Kineret and a leader of the Second Aliyah. During World War I, Rotberg, together with Berl Kaznelson (1887–1944), proposed the establishment of a network of consumer cooperatives that led to the establishment of Hamashbir. Rotberg was later a founder of the Haganah, and he lived and worked as a labor leader in Haifa.

through the streets early in the morning and late in the evening with their spades on their shoulders.

The two loans, from the committee and from Hamashbir were not enough to see us through. And just when supplies gave out, the most exacting work began—the digging. Starvation stared us in the face. Among the *haverot*, there were some who even had to share their daily ration with their families. More than once, I saw one of the *haverot* leave the line, tear up some grass from the field, and try to still the pangs of hunger. There were times when we thought it impossible to go on.

The vegetables began to ripen, and it was necessary to set a watch in the night against thieves. We could not pay a watchman, and therefore we became guards, too. I was the first to go on sentry duty.

It was a Saturday night. I had made the round of the garden once, and was just returning to my post when I stumbled against something that loomed black in the darkness. An Arab wrapped in a black *abaya* [cloak] got up out of the onion patch. I uttered such a wild scream that I almost frightened the life out of myself.

The garden lay outside the town. No one heard me, and no one came to help me. I remained in the place until morning, and next day we decided to set two guards. We trembled most of all for our onions, because they had come up beautifully. When we finally began to take in some money for our produce, life in the *kvuzah* became more tolerable. And when the potatoes ripened, and they had to be guarded in turn, we were able to engage [an Arab] watchman. But in a few days we had to dismiss him, because apparently the thieves and he ignored each other! We returned to guard duty ourselves.

I remember particularly a certain Friday night. I had gone out with two *haverot* on the watch. We spread ourselves a mat in the middle of the garden, and sat there talking quietly. From time to time we got up and made the rounds. The first half of the night passed peacefully. In the second half we were suddenly aware of the noise of a multitude approaching: hordes of Turkish soldiers were passing along the road by the garden.

It was shortly before Passover. Apparently preparations were being made in the night for a new offensive. All of us were seized with the same thought: the hungry Turkish soldiers might break into the garden in search of food and find—us! I signaled to the other two women to remain absolutely silent. I tried to appear calm, but I was trembling from head to foot. At every instant, I expected to hear the closer tread of approaching feet. Only with the dawn, when the Arab guards in the neighboring gardens left their posts, we got up from our places and went home, exhausted and broken.

The happy time arrived at last. Big military trucks came rolling toward our garden. The yield was a rich one, the prices were steady, and we made money. Then we decided to begin paying back the loans to the committee and Hamashbir.

That first day was a day of triumph and victory. All of us gathered in the little room, and with much ceremony we deposited the first payment in the safe—which consisted of an old tea can. We even drew lots to fix on the lucky person who would have the privilege of taking the first payment to the committee. Hasidah[17] was the one to draw the winning number. She put on holiday dress and danced rather than walked into town.

We paid all our debts and still had something left. Every *haverah* in the kvuzah got a bonus—a franc for every working day. And even to the watchmen, who had worked a few nights for us, we sent their extra share.

17. The identity of Hasidah is unknown.

In the Days of Hassan Bek[18]

Frieda [Kaznelson] (Herzliyah[19])

I T WAS IN KINERET in the month of Heshvan (October) 1917. The days were still hot, and the nights magically clear. Every day, new stories reached us of the sufferings of the Jews in Judea, Jerusalem, and Samaria at the hands of the Turks. A systematic search for military evaders was being conducted. Our men were taken away to forced labor with the Turkish military; most of them were in the transport, driving heavy loads from Beersheva in the south to Metulah in the north. We heard that the Turks were making special efforts to locate arms. They had already searched Merhavyah and Tel Adas. In particular, they were looking for the *haverim* of Hashomer. At that time, I knew nothing about the espionage story, or about the English arms in our possession.

In the summer nights there would be raids of bandits. We, the women, used to sleep on the roof, and we were frequently awakened by the shooting. Sometimes the men would go out, and be absent for hours in the hills, driving off the raiders.

The Turks came to us in Kineret, too. "The Commission," as we called it, came early one morning. I remember how the news reached me. I was told that the men had been called out for an examination— every male in the colony, including the old and sick. They had been taken away, but we believed that they would soon return. But hours passed, and there was no sign of them. Reports began to spread that they had been taken onto the bridge across the Jordan, and were being beaten unmercifully. The women who were bringing them food were caught, and were being whipped. I went down to the bridge, and among the prisoners huddled together there, I saw also Yosef Baraz[20]—the only man who had been taken from the colony of Dagania.

18. On Hassan Bek, see note 7 in this section. On the situation in Palestine during World War I and the plight of the Yishuv, see part I, note 67 and part V, note 5.
19. Herzliyah, a town north of Tel Aviv, was founded in 1924 on land bought by the American Zion Commonwealth. The settlers were generally second-generation farmers.
20. Yosef Baraz (1890–1968) immigrated Palestine in 1906, already having been active in Zionism in his native Kishinev. He was an agricultural worker in Hederah and Kineret and helped found Dagania, where he subsequently resided. Baraz was involved in labor politics, first as a member of Hapoel Hazair [The Young Worker] and later as

As often as I tried to pass over to the prisoners, the guards approached me offensively. I had to exert all my will power in order not to spit in their faces; but I knew that in their hands lay the fate of our men. Within a few days we had managed to accustom ourselves to the new, strange conditions. The women in the colony took over all the work, and did double duty in the barns and the fields. They supplied the soldiers who came for food and fodder. One moment I remember, when I was sweeping the stables. M. was outside—he had not been arrested and he was watering the animals. He strolled casually up to the window and winked at me: there was so much courage and hope and endurance in that wink of his that I felt myself strengthened . . .

The Turkish officers beat our men and threatened that, if they did not reveal where the weapons were, they would plough up all our fields. Actually, they did nothing. They did not even set up a guard in the yard of the *kvuzah*.

The men had slipped the information to me where the weapons were concealed, and Aharon Sher[21] (who was killed afterwards in Tel Hai) explained to me the difference between English and Turkish guns. I understood that the first things to be gotten rid of were the English guns, though I didn't quite see why they were more dangerous than the Turkish. I looked through the stable loft and found the boxes of English guns under a huge mound of hay; with them were several packages of English guns and cartridges. In the night we determined to move the supplies from this dangerous place. We lowered the packages of ammunition into the toilet cans; we were sure that no one would look there. While we worked we heard suddenly the creaking of wheels outside— and we stood still, as if paralyzed. The creaking passed and we went on with our work. We decided to get the guns down to Lake Kineret, and throw them in. We took them out, and by moonlight stole down the water's edge, the guns slung on our shoulders. There we skirted the water till we found a deep place, and let the guns down. Several times we made the journey back and forth. One of the women on this job was the mother of a small child. Until this day, I shudder and wonder at our marvelous luck in not being caught. But there was not a soul to be seen; it was as if the earth had swallowed the Turkish soldiers. When the task was done, there was a sort of freshness in the air around, and in our

a member of the Mapai party. He served as a Histadrut emissary to the United States in 1921. On the subject of Dagania, he wrote a memoir entitled *A Village by the Jordan* (New York: Sharon Books, 1957.)

21. Aharon Sher (1900–1920) came to Palestine during the Second Aliyah. While living at Kineret, he volunteered to help defend Tel Hai and Kfar Giladi from Arab attacks and was subsequently killed in fighting there. On the battle at Tel Hai, see part I, note 55 and note 38 in this section.

hearts, too. The next morning the soldiers turned up to arrest all of us. Sher pretended to be sick. When he tried to get out of his bed he acted so realistically that I was terrified. But soon I understood that he really wanted someone to bring him a glass of water. When I gave it to him he whispered that this night we would have to place three guns and packages of cartridges under the date tree at the foot of Kerak hill.[22] I did not know the meaning of this, but I felt that it had to be done. It was with the utmost difficulty that I persuaded two women to help me. I told them, as I remember, that on this depended our lives and the lives of our men. I spoke so earnestly, so wildly, that they agreed it was almost as if I had hypnotized them. And that night, we put on black shawls and hid the guns under them. We had agreed that we were "going out to find a black cow that had got lost." And instead of walking stealthily, we went out into the darkness calling "Hey, Blackie, Blackie, where are you?" In this way we managed to place the guns and cartridges in the appointed place. When I got back I collapsed on my bed, seized with a horrible cramp; nothing was wrong with me—only my nerves had given way.

During the days that followed I could not eat. I would go up to the table and put a black olive in my mouth, but it would not go down. The women worked like draft animals; all the burden of the *kvuzah* had fallen on them. But I could do nothing. Nor did they ask me to do my share. I was reserved for something else: I received secret instructions and obeyed them. I asked no questions. I did what I was told to do.

I learned before long the purpose for which the three guns had been hidden under the date tree. Sher, A.Z.,[23] and F. pretended to give way under the *bastinado* [beating] and confessed that they were the three shepherds of Kineret, and they had hidden their weapons under the tree. They believed that in this way they would relieve the whole colony. And I think I saw them in the night being led away by a convoy, their heads down, the guns carried by soldiers.

In a few days Ben-Zion[24] was set free, and the first ray of hope shone on us. The same night I, together with Ben-Zion and young Mikhael[25]

22. Kerak is the Arabic name of a hill located near Bet Yerah in the Jordan Valley, where the Jordan River issues from Lake Kineret. The site is mentioned in Josephus' chronicle of the Roman conquest of the Galilee in 67–68 C.E. by Vespasian (c. 9–79 C.E.), the future emperor of Rome. In the late nineteenth century, the area was purchased by the Zionist movement and designated to be the site of a modern Jewish garden city. Instead, it became the cemetery of the Kineret settlement area and the Labor Zionist movement.

23. The initials here apparently stand for Alexander Zeid.

24. Ben-Zion Mashevich, a founder of Hashomer [The Watchguard], was killed by Arab attackers in 1921.

25. The identity of Mikhael is unknown, but he appears to have been an associate of the prominent Second Aliyah leader Alexander Zeid (see note 23 above).

(a fine, lovable boy who was wounded later in Upper Galilee and died in horrible anguish in the hospital of Tiberias) carried out of the buildings the rest of the guns. We hid them in the gulch that cuts across our fields. That night we were crazy with joy, like people who had escaped from death and were now going to rescue their *haverim*.

A few days later the other men were transferred to the prison in Tiberias. I followed, took a room in a hotel nearby and brought them food every day. I trembled that the food might not reach them, that some of them might be transferred where I could not look after them or that something worse might happen—hanging was not impossible. In particular we were uncertain about the lives of the three, Sher, A.Z., and F. And there was no news of them. It only seemed to me that sometimes, when I went to the prison, I would catch sight of a familiar face.

I remember trying to chum up with the wives of some of the arrested planter colonists. These women spoke French, and might be able to find out something. But they shied away from me. Those days brought friends closer together than ever before, but they also widened the gulf between strangers.

One evening, when I returned to my hotel, afraid as always of bad news, I was told that Sher and A.Z. had called during the day, on their way back to Kineret! They were at home now, and our rejoicing was all the deeper because secretly we had scarcely dared to hope that we would ever see them again. The next day I returned once more to Tiberias. There I learned that the other prisoners had been sent on to Nazareth, and there was no more reason for me to stay on.

Twenty-four Hours

Nehamah Zizer (Tel Aviv)

AFTER A DAY'S WORK in the kitchen, hungry and exhausted, I lay down to sleep. My "home" was a little hut on the shore of Lake Kineret; it had three rooms—a kitchen, a living room, and a cubicle which was storeroom and pantry.

I had taken up half the storeroom for my "bed"—the usual bed of those days, planks on empty gasoline cans. But for a long time I could not sleep. The mice would not let me. They squeaked and fought around me, jumping in and out of the empty pea and bean cans.

And lying there, I ask myself: What will happen tomorrow? There's not enough in the house to feed a puppy. If we look long enough, we may scrape up a glassful of peas, but suppose I have got soup enough for twenty men—what about the next meal? These men come home from the fields hungry. And what shall I give them with the tea? It's so long since we've seen sugar that we've forgotten what it looks like. The raisin supply is a memory. Food is scarce and money even scarcer—in fact, there is none . . . It's no good thinking; better try to sleep. I draw the sheet over my head, scared that the mice will start playing with my two long braids.

Suddenly, a knock at the window. I answer out of my sleep: "Who's there?"

"It's me."

I recognize the voice of a *haver*. "What is it?" I ask.

"Open the window, and take this."

I look up at the window, and make out a rifle, a belt, and a bag of loose cartridges.

"What shall I do with it?"

"Hide it in a safe place."

I go to the window and take gun, belt, and cartridges. He adds: "We don't know what'll happen tomorrow. We just had a meeting. The decisions are secret."

"All right," I say. "You don't have to tell. Shalom!" I close the window and lie down again. Secret decisions . . . dangers . . . no one must know . . . My thoughts will not rest. Of late, the *haverim* have been behaving queerly at their work; things are not going smoothly. I know nothing, understand nothing. A secret decision is a secret decision. Again I cover myself. There's a heavy day ahead of me, I must rest. I must sleep. I must sleep. And at last I fall into a doze.

Again a knock at the window. "Nehamah, are you still sleeping? Nehamah!"

I start up. "Get up, Nehamah. The shepherds have been arrested." And she names my two friends. "The colonists have been arrested, too. No one's safe."

I go to the window again. Dawn has come. The sun is just lying level on Lake Kineret. The picture rises again before me—but I understand nothing; the words of the Sephardic girl convey nothing.

She goes on: "Everyone's been arrested. Look! Police everywhere." I look out. Near my door stands a policeman, and the meaning of it all becomes clear to me. I begin to storm.

"Listen," I said to the girl. "I can't speak Arabic. Tell him [women] are sleeping in here. Tell him to get out."

She tells him, and he does take himself off, but not far. He stops at a little distance from the house.

I work hastily, and pack into the bed everything that was handed over to me. Then I cover it all up, so that it looks as though someone were sleeping there. Then I slip out to see what has happened.

I go down to the colony. The [women] are going about their work, and they will not speak. In the *kvuzah* yard, again, only [women]. The men have been taken away. I meet Ziporah,[26] a relative of *haver* A. Passing by, she tells me in staccato whispers: "Listen! Careful—the police are watching! A.'s house is just full of that stuff. We've got to get it out of the way before the search starts. Can you do it?"

That was all I needed. We passed each other, and understood without further parley that we were to meet as soon as possible in A.'s house.

I go down the slope. The house is surrounded by police. I ignore them and pass right into the house. A.'s parents are there, in a panic. I soothe them. They themselves do not know what dangerous stuff there is in the house, but they feel blindly that some disaster is impending. In a few minutes Ziporah turned up, and we began to feel better.

As the police kept away, we set to work at once. We placed the guns in baskets, and heaped loaves of bread and tomatoes on top. When I was through, I told Ziporah that I was going out to work in Hannah Meisel's garden, and I went out with a basket.

Hannah Meisel's garden was surrounded by a barbed wire fence and

26. The identity of Ziporah is unknown.

with yellow acacia, so closely grown that it was impossible to take a short cut through. When I got round to the gate I saw that all the [women] were outside—a white flood poured over the green, square-cut patches.

And here, too, all round the field, a chain of policemen.

"*Hevreh, hevreh!*" I shout. "Come eat!"

In an instant the [women] had surrounded me and began to empty the basket. Meanwhile, I pretended to do some work with the spade, and a few minutes later I returned to A.'s house. In this way I smuggled through basket after basket. And just when I left with the last basket, I heard carriage bells on the road. "The Commission" had arrived to look for weapons, and the first point they made for was A.'s house.

All's well. The house has been cleared—but here I am with the last basket in my hand. No sense in running—they'd stop me at once. I walk slowly, the spade over my shoulder, the basket in my hand. I sing loudly and cheerfully: "*Uru ahim, al tanumu, laavodathem uru, kumu*" [Hebrew: Wake brothers, do not slumber; to your labor, brothers, rise][27] and singing I pass through the field, into the farm. There everything has been looked after.

Enough for one day. And then, like a flame leaping up in me, I remember the "goods" I had left lying around in my room. It is noon. I have had neither bite nor sup, and I am exhausted. "The Commission" is in A.'s house, two doors away from my room.

I turn back, and make for my room. Every second counts now. The police are masters everywhere. But they won't get a word out of us women. They surround us on every side, but we'll see who's quicker-witted. Too late to save the men—they're arrested. But we'll stand by this place.

I pass through a police cordon. I hear them say; "*Hadi shatre! kul yum bistril*" [Arabic: A real gem of a girl; she's been at it since early morning]. So I am not suspected yet. I take out bread and tomatoes to eat—and I have my plan! I'll pretend to get the oven ready, and meanwhile I can smuggle the gun and the other stuff out. And when "the Commission" turns its back, I can really shove them into the stove.

27. This Hebrew phrase derives from a folk song, penned by Noah Shapira, entitled "*Shir haavodah*" [Song of Labor]. Popular during the Second and Third Aliyah, the song imitates an Arab melody, especially the chorus (*yah-ha-li-li-hah*), and illustrates the Zionist pioneers' fascination with indigenous Palestinian culture. Meanwhile, the song's verses transvalue traditional Jewish notions of piety and emphasize the cause of the Zionist pioneers: "Wake brothers, do not slumber; to your labor, brothers, rise / The world stands on *avodah* [Hebrew for 'worship' and 'labor']; rise up, sing a song of thanks / *Avodah* is our entire life; it will deliver us from all our misfortunes." See N. Shapira, "*Shir haavodah*" in *Elef zemer veod zemer*, eds. Telma Aligon and Rafi Pesahzon, Vol. 2 (Tel Aviv: Kineret, 1983), p. 115.

I put the ammunition into the bucket, and went to fetch water; I put three cartridges into the Browning[28] and slipped it on. I had made up my mind: one cartridge was for the man who tried to stop me. Two were for myself.

"The Commission" had left A.'s house and paid no attention to me. It returned to Tiberias, leaving word that this same night the infamous Hassan Bek[29] in person would visit our colony, that multiple murderer who would take things out of the hands of the police, and lash and torture his victims himself.

Now I have a little respite. I sit half-dead on the doorstep of my house. Everything has been done. But then I remember—A. must be told that his house has been cleaned out. I go over to the colony; all the prisoners are jammed into one small room.

I knock at the window and ask for *haver* A. He makes his way through to me.

"Shalom!"

"Shalom!" I answer. Then quickly: "The house is cleared. The guests found nothing." I raise my voice, and say in Arabic: "And what shall I do now, sir?"

"We're terribly thirsty in here," he said. "Bring us a jug of water— but a large one."

"I understand, sir," I answer. I went into the house of a colonist, asked for a big jug, filled it with water, took a glass, and returned to the prison. The guards would not let me go inside, but they let me pass the jug and glass through the window. In two minutes A. passed the jug back. It was considerably heavier than before. I went into the fields and emptied it.

After a time I returned to the prisoners for news. A. appeared at the window, white as chalk. He said: "P. got the *bastinado* [beating]. It's more than an hour since they tortured him, and he can't utter a word yet. It's better to be killed. I'm afraid they're going to start on you women now. Be strong, and show what you can do."

The men had determined among themselves that if they heard the scream of a woman they would burst the room open and rush to our help, come what might. Evening came, and we sat in the *kvuzah* with ears strained. We heard them at last—Hassan Bek and his escort. He would find no weapons with us—that much was certain now. But he would not be satisfied. His murderer's blood needed a victim—the more so, in fact, because he would find nothing.

28. The reference here is to a .30 caliber semiautomatic rifle used during World War I. Called the "Browning," it was named after its creator, the American firearms inventor John Moses Browning.

29. On Hassan Bek, see note 7 in this section.

And we on our side had also made a decision. We would gather, all of us, on the second floor of Hannah Meisel's house, and defend ourselves against dishonor. I came armed; and, though this had not been agreed upon, the other women came armed, too.

Hannah's house, lifted high above the terrace of trees and flowers, looked down toward Lake Kineret. Downstairs, on the ground floor, was the big kitchen and dining room. Upstairs was the dormitory and a huge veranda which was always flooded nights with moonlight or starlight. I remembered that it was on this veranda that they laid me once, when I was stricken down with malaria. Now I was here again. Three women were watching with me. We lay and listened for the sound of approaching feet. No one came.

It is night. From time to time we send someone out to inquire what has happened to the arrested men. *Haverot* meet women with various instructions and messages, each one doing her work silently and efficiently. That night several of the Kineret colonists were put to the torture. We heard from our room the screaming and shouting that came out of the prison—a ghastly noise in the wide, still night. But no weapons were given up.

Late in the night I stole out to the prison and looked in at the window. There was not room enough for the men to stretch out. They squatted on the ground, and they sang. One of their songs was in Russian:

> The stormy days carry us, each day is a wave.
> Driving us nearer the shore of the grave . . .[30]

My heart seemed to pour out of me. Darkness all around. Not one light burned in the colony. I returned to our group, and we sat and waited interminably for developments.

The torture was resumed that same night, before the prisoners were taken to Damascus for trial. Hassan Bek did not appear, but his minions did their work well. Finally, one of the prisoners broke down under the torment, and involuntarily cried out that two of the women knew where the weapons were.

In the midst of that web of police spies, our own work was conducted swiftly. Word was brought to Ziporah and myself that it was time to get out. And before dawn we stole out of Kineret, and ran up the hills to Poriyah.

30. The reference here is to a popular Russian folk song. Following is a more precise rendering of the original Russian verse: "Stormy, like the waves, are the days of our lives / Every day our path to the grave becomes shorter."

With A. D. Gordon

Hannah Kaznelson (Jerusalem)

THEY HAD DIVIDED us off, that night in Kineret, into two rooms—one was the prison room; the other was the torture chamber. From time to time, they came in for the next victim; from time to time, they brought in new prisoners. Seated in the prison room we could hear the blows of the *bastinado* [beating] on the other side of the wall, and sometimes the screaming of the tortured man. We held our breath; the fate of the colony was in the balance.

[Aharon David] Gordon turns up among the arrested. We do not know whether he has been caught or whether he has given himself up. But we do know that soon he will be taken into the next room—it is their habit, or their plan, to choose always the oldest and the most important.

Suddenly the old man gets up from his seat and stretches out his hands as if he were about to start dancing. He thrusts everyone aside, to clear a space for himself, snaps his fingers, and breaks into impromptu singing:

> Let my foes torment and flay me,
> Let them drain me, drop by drop;
> There's a merry song within me
> Pain can never stop.

As if glued to our places we sit there, we, the young ones, listening to the singing of the "old" man. A shudder runs through all of us.

A Word to the Legionnaires

R.K. [Rahel Kaznelson-Shazar]

[Author's note from original Yiddish text:] An address delivered at the farewell conference of the agricultural cultural workers' organization and the Erez Israel volunteers when the latter departed with the Jewish Legion, August, 1918.

THE ONE THING, which has prevented me from adopting an attitude of respect toward the [Jewish] Legion, has been the question of murder.

But I have answered myself: Can it be shown by anyone that Moses, or Garibaldi,[31] men who poured out oceans of blood, were less moral than the opponents of war? It seems to me that opposition to war springs from culture and from humanity, but not specifically from morality. And now I perceive that the real sin, the real evil, lies in the alien spirit that has been introduced in our midst ever since the Legion movement began.

At the conference of the women workers one *haver* said, "Our graves will be sign-posts, pointing out the road of life and work to those who will come after us." And there were women there who found it in their hearts to applaud the speaker. How deeply it hurts me that such an attitude toward death should have developed among us. Wherever people applaud the mention of death, the ugliness of life has begun.

And I ask myself: Has anyone ever had the insolence to speak the following words to a Jewish worker of Erez Israel: "When you are following the plough, when you are doing guard duty at night, always remember, if a man falls on you and kills you, your name will be written into the memorials of your people, and these memorials will be translated into all the languages of mankind, and they will be read in every Jewish home"? Yet why do people dare to say to the worker now: "If you fall in battle, there will be a marble memorial for you on Mount Zion,[32] and your name will be engraved in our books forever"? And

---

31. Giuseppe Garibaldi (1807–1882) used guerrilla tactics to liberate most of Italy and bring about its unification in 1870. He also advocated European unity and was famous for his idealism and political efforts on behalf of the common man.

32. Mount Zion is a hill and fortress in Jerusalem where King David's tomb is located.

why do the Jewish workers of Erez Israel accept these words calmly, as if their spirit were not alien to them? Is not this a new form of assimilation? I know that in the big world, outside there, such words carry great weight; they are forever on the lips of generals, but what have they to do with us?

It seems to me that such words are fitting only for those who have protected their lives at all costs, and with every means. But we, we who have given our lives away . . .

Such an attitude toward life benefits the inhabitants of cities, who live far from nature. But how can a land-worker applaud when he sees the grasshopper coming up to destroy the wheat that he has sown? And we who have been brought up on the idea of life, how can we applaud words of death?

When have we ever arranged magnificent funerals for our dead? When Dagania buried the slain *haver* Moshe Barski,[33] it did not even call the neighbors of Kineret to the funeral. Over the grave of Yosef Salzman,[34] [Aharon David] Gordon said a simple *kadish*[35] [prayer of mourning] and no one else dared to speak a word.

Nor is it a Jewish custom to glorify death. The pure, true Jewish outlook, the outlook of those Jewish land-workers that wrote the Bible, is that death is a misfortune and nothing more.

It is difficult for me to speak now of [Vladimir] Jabotinsky.[36] He is

33. Moshe Barski (1896–1913) was a Second Aliyah pioneer and one of the founders of Kibbutz Dagania. He was attacked and killed by Bedouin Arabs while en route to deliver medication to the Jewish colony of Milhamiyah (see part V, note 30). The members of Dagania wrote a letter to Barski's parents in Russia informing them of his death, to which his parents responded by sending another son to Palestine and subsequently immigrating as a family. Barski was the first Zionist pioneer to be buried at what became the Kineret cemetery on Kerak hill (see note 22 in this section). He was the namesake of Moshe Dayan (1915–1984), the Israeli military commander and hero of the Six-Day War (June 1967) who later served as Israel's Defense Minister.

34. Yosef Salzman (d. 1913), a Second Aliyah pioneer who immigrated to Palestine from Russia in 1907, was a close associate of the socialist Zionist leader Yizhak Tabenkin (1887–1971). In 1912 he joined the founders of Kvuzat Kineret. A year later, he was attacked and killed by Bedouin Arabs.

35. The *kadish* [sanctification] is an ancient Aramaic prayer recited by mourners.

36. Vladimir (Zeev) Jabotinsky (1880–1940) became a Zionist after the 1903 Odessa *pogrom*, during which he helped to organize Jewish self-defense. A charismatic Zionist leader as well as a brilliant orator, writer, and translator, Jabotinsky was a central figure in the Jewish public arena in the decades leading up to the establishment of the State of Israel. He led the campaign for the creation of the Jewish Legion during World War I. (On the situation in Palestine during the war, see part I, note 67 and part V, note 5.) In 1920, foreseeing the imminent riots in Jerusalem, he formed clandestine Jewish self-defense units and led them into action without the permission of the British authorities. For this offense, he was sentenced to fifteen years hard labor, but he was granted amnesty within a year, in part due to the international outcry following his imprisonment. He served on the Zionist Executive, founded the right-wing Betar youth movement in 1923,

dear to us because, like us, he has been reborn. He is near to us because he left the language and literature of strangers, learned Hebrew, and has the same feeling for poetry as we have. But he is alien to us in the matter of his outlook on work; he does not understand the affirmative values that are created by work. And it is hard for us when such as he bring this alien spirit among us. It is even hard to speak of it.

A few days ago there was a meeting in Jaffa. Jabotinsky spoke there, and he told the audience that once, when a superior officer had insulted him unjustly, he had answered: "Yes, sir." [37] I went away from that meeting and heard young boys repeating, with blind enthusiasm: "Yes, sir!" I felt that these strange words were bringing poison into our blood.

Was it necessary to talk like that to grown-up, developed men before they went into the Legion? Would it not have been proper to speak in an absolutely contrary spirit—to say: "You are entering the Legion to do things that outrage your conscience, that will debase your soul; you will know that this is a sin, but you must take this sin upon yourself, together with all that is good, together with all the anguish that it will bring you"?

"Yes, sir" is darkness out of which light will never be born.

And yet there are things that may fire the soul of the Jewish worker when he enters the Legion.

We are going out to conquer men in order that we may bring them into liberating work which will teach them responsibility, consciousness of duty, and tolerance—work which makes them understand the meaning of reward and punishment, which replaces blind instinct with clear vision.

We are going out to create the Hebrew language, which shall take root in the hearts and mouths of our people, as it deserves to do.

We are going out to create a united Erez Israel.

You are going now to Galilee. You know from your studies of history that Galilee has never found its right place in the life of our people. You know that the prophets came from Judea and Samaria, and in the days when the Jews lived in Erez Israel Galilee was known as "Galilee of the gentiles"—for the Jews there were in a minority and suffered at the hands of the majority.

Even today, when we walk out the outskirts of Migdal, there rise be-

---

and served as the head of the World Union of Revisionist Zionists. Jabotinsky later supported "illegal" immigration and was commander of the Irgun Zvai Leumi [National Military Organization]. He vigorously opposed the Labor Zionist movement throughout his career, believing that socialism was secondary to Jewish nationalist concerns, and argued against the partition of Palestine.

37. The original Yiddish text includes this English locution.

fore our eyes, out of the waters of Lake Kineret, the shadows of Jesus and his followers, the Jewish fisherman who carried the [Christian gospel] to the peoples of the world. But for the Jewish people, Galilee has not yet said its word; only now has it begun to speak.

Kineret! Home of the soul! How often, in uttering its name, we are tempted to say, "Kineret the Holy."

What is it that has spread this sanctity over Kineret? Is it Lake Kineret and the Jordan River? Is it the grand old man [A. D. Gordon], who has lived there? Is it the [young] Jewish [woman] who first began to plant and sow in its garden? Galilee has not yet spoken its word, but that word will yet be spoken.

Here in our midst a new organization is being formed—and it came into being at the same time as the Legion. It is the Histadrut. That organization will fight for labor, for our language, and for our land— for labor which educates, for the language which unifies, and for the Galilee of the future.

Behind the Front

Yehudit Brontman (Nahalal)

It was the oppressive year of Tel Hai, when [Yosef] Trumpeldor[38] and his companions fell at their northern outpost. It was my lot to begin my work then—not up there in northern Galilee, in the danger zone—but behind the front, in Dagania.

We seem to have forgotten what the colony Dagania, on the Jordan, did in that year. But I will remember it as long as I live. For with me it was the time of life when a person must learn to suffer and sacrifice for the good of the whole.

Dagania was the last Jewish settlement on the eastern frontier of the country. Close to it began the stretches of the Bedouin country of Trans-jordania. And, whenever the Bedouins [Arab nomads] took it into their minds to make a descent for plunder, the two Daganias (Dagania Alef and Dagania Bet) had to encounter the first attacks. Dagania Alef was a fixed *kvuzah* but Dagania Bet was still in transition; it was a "*kvuzah* of

---

38. Yosef Trumpeldor (1880–1920) first distinguished himself in the Russian army during the Russo-Japanese War. He believed that demonstrating Jewish loyalty and bravery in battle would dissuade antisemites of their negative attitudes to the Jews. In spite of repeated disillusionment, he continued to serve in the Russian imperial army, even after losing an arm. He was a staunch believer in Zionism and the Tolstoyan ideal of agricultural communism. As a prisoner of war in a Japanese camp, Trumpeldor set up a Zionist immigration group. Following his release and his study of law, he developed an idea for the creation of a network of socialist Zionist communes. In 1911, he immigrated to Palestine, where he sought to realize his plan. As a Russian national, he was expelled from Palestine by the Turks during World War I. (On the situation in Palestine during the war, see part I, note 67.) He fled to Alexandria, where he met Vladimir Jabotinsky (see note 36 in this section) and helped to organize the Jewish Legion. While Jabotinsky rebuffed the British offer of auxiliary duties for Jewish soldiers, Trumpeldor led his Zion Mule Corps to serve at Gallipoli. Although the corps was well respected, it was dis-banded after Gallipoli, and Trumpeldor returned to Russia to try to win approval for a Jewish military force there. His efforts in this regard did not bear fruit. Remaining in Russia, he organized a Jewish self-defense organization, for which he was arrested, and after his release, he worked as a leader of Hehaluz [The Pioneer]. In 1919, he returned to Palestine to carry out work for the movement but was distracted by the tense situation in the Upper Galilee settlements. He assumed command of Tel Hai (see part I, note 55) and was killed in the Arab attacks of 1920. In death, Trumpeldor attained a mythic and heroic status unequalled by any of his pioneering contemporaries. His apocryphal last testament—"it is good to die for our country"—inspired countless *haluzim* and Zionist activists of subsequent generations.

occupation"—a group holding on to a Jewish position, preparing it for later permanent settlement. The *haverim* of Dagania Bet still lived in rough, hastily constructed barracks that were perfectly useless in an attack. Behind Dagania Bet stood Dagania Alef, with its two massive stone houses, and its stables and barns of stone. Dagania Alef was therefore considered the extreme eastern outpost of Erez Israel. For months, moreover, Dagania was the passageway for the *haverim* who came from all parts of Erez Israel up to northern Galilee to help defend Tel Hai and Kfar Giladi.

The land was just beginning to breathe again after the sufferings and privations of the war years. The *haverim* of Dagania were anxious to put an end to all the improvisations and irregularities which had crept into their system during the uncertain time of the war, and to begin a new economic and social life. According to the plan only eleven families were to remain in Dagania, a total of about thirty persons. And the *kvuzah* had begun to adapt itself to the new life. Then came the incidents of Tel Hai and upset everything once more.

Many of our *haverim* left for Galilee, and, when they came home, they used to tell us of the fearful time through which those two remote points of the north, Tel Hai and Kfar Giladi, were passing.

And meanwhile a rumor spread that the two Daganias were in line for a regular Bedouin assault. We went on with our work, lived in the usual routine, but we were without inner peace. Until one morning black dots began to move on the far-off horizon. These were the Bedouin horsemen; and true to our forebodings, they made first for the wooden barracks of Dagania Bet. Trenches had been dug round these barracks, but it was thought better to withdraw the men to Dagania Alef. From the distance we saw our *haverim* setting fire to their barracks before they withdrew.

In Dagania Alef the safest place was the second floor of the big house. That was the center of our system of defense. There we kept our children and the children of Dagania Bet. In the night no one undressed. The house, the kitchen, and the stables lost their ordinary character, and became strategic units. Every unit was in the charge of some responsible *haver*.

I and another *haverah* had to be in the second house, which contained the dining room, the kitchen, and the bakery. We also had there a small pharmacy with the most essential medicines. We set up our watch in the bakery. The most important point in our building was the kitchen. The dining room was too exposed—it had windows on three sides; and therefore the best center of defense was the kitchen.

I do not remember how many days we passed there in the bakery.

But I do remember that the element of fear was completely absent. Only one woman, who had come to Erez Israel only a short time before the events of that year, left Dagania. None of the other women thought of leaving the place, or of sending away their little ones.

We lived for some time in this state of siege, and then slowly things began to quiet down around us.

Detachments of Jewish soldiers were distributed throughout our district. We were, after all, under the protection of England, and did not that mean security?

When the Dagania section had quieted down, there was still Galilee to be taken care of, and ours was a sort of station for the men who went up there. There were times when we had dozens of men quartered with us. We had to look after them, and help them to continue their journey to the posts of danger. We never knew at the beginning of the day how many mouths we would be cooking for; and besides the problem of food, there was always the laundry of the strangers to be washed and mended, and even their sick to be tended.

For not one of these transients failed to get at least one day's meals and one night's lodgings and, if he fell sick, the comradely care which he needed.

The Workers' Club[39]

D.A.[40] (Tel Aviv)

M**Y FIRST WELCOME** to Erez Israel was a long affair; it lasted no less than three months, for that was the time that it took me to find my first job. At last I was able to get into the kitchen of the workers' club of Jaffa (Tel Aviv did not exist yet) as a cook. In the yard of the club there was a sort of ruin which could by courtesy be called a room. Because I had children to look after, I was accorded the privilege of making our home in that ruin.

Before coming to Erez Israel I had belonged to a political party which knew of only two "races": the workers and their oppressors. When I was in Erez Israel my *haverim* abroad still used to send me literature to my new address—I lived in Yosef Hayim Brenner's house. He would bring the packages in to me without saying a word. Before long I had accumulated quite a little library of anarchist pamphlets: *The A.B.C. of Anarchism*, *The Lie of Religion*, etc.

But after I had lived some months in Erez Israel I began to revise my views on nationalism. I could not bring myself to distribute the literature that was being sent. The ideas it propagated had been dear to me, but my heart said to me, "This is not the place for such propaganda," and I obeyed my heart.

The well-bound packages lay untouched in my basket, and the heap kept growing. I hadn't the courage to write my [former] comrades not to send any more; likewise I had not the time to sit down to a long letter of explanation. Once I had begun work in the kitchen, I was busy night and day—for besides the kitchen, there were my children, who went through a good deal of sickness.

One day Brenner came into town from his colony. He found me looking and feeling well, in spite of the work and the hard life; and it

---

39. The Palestinian labor movement sustained a complex web of social, economic, and political entities. One such unit, the *moadon poalim* [workers' club], was a fixture of urban life and served as a hub of the workers' cultural and intellectual life in the early decades of the twentieth century.

40. The apparent writer of this essay is Dvorah (Abramovich) Avrahamit, a Second Aliyah pioneer who was active in Moezet Hapoalot. She contributed two pieces to the original Yiddish volume (1931). The details of her biography are unknown.

made him happy. After some preliminary conversation he cast a glance at the packages in the basket and asked suddenly: "What are you doing with those books?"

"Till now I've done nothing."

"Are they going to keep on sending them to you?"

"I don't know. I haven't even acknowledged the receipt of the first batch."

"Are you thinking of distributing them?"

I could not answer . . . Brenner understood me, and with a smile he said:

"You'd better write them to stop sending books."

"And what about these?" I asked him.

"Oh," he said, in the same tone, "these have to be read, of course."

"But they'll drive me out of Erez Israel."

"Nonsense!"

Late in the evening, after Brenner was gone, I unpacked some pamphlets and laid them out on the reading table in the club. The next day the club was blazing about the "uninvited guests."

"Find the fellow, teach him a lesson, and drive him out of Erez Israel." These were the comments. But I observed that these same wild men waited for their opportunity and slipped the forbidden literature into their pockets. Brenner came in that evening. He sat at the long table and watched old [Mikhael] Halpern[41] who was fanning the air with one of the pamphlets and shouting: "Don't worry; this man will belong to us yet; he came to Erez Israel an anarchist, and he'll finish up in harness with us."

41. Mikhael Halpern (1860–1919), originally a member of the Social Revolutionary party in Russia, was converted to Zionism in the wake of the *pogroms* of 1881–82. He immigrated to Palestine in 1886, where he helped to establish the first workers' organization in Rishon Lezion. Active in Poalei Zion [Workers of Zion] and Agudat Poalim [Workers' Association], he swiftly emerged as one of the Palestine labor movement's key personalities. He worked for fifteen years as a laborer and *shomer* in Judea and Galilee. He also led an unsuccessful effort to recruit Ethiopian Jews for a "People's Legion."

The Strike in Akko

Malkah[42] (Havurat Hapoalot, Ramat Gan[43])

THERE WAS A GROUP of us, new *haluzot* who had just landed in Erez Israel. Before we had had time to acclimatize ourselves, and get used to the life, we found work in the old citadel town of Akko.

Two facts were in our favor: we were new to the country and we were not yet members of the Histadrut. The owners of the Nur [Light] match factory[44] in Akko always preferred unorganized women workers.

The working conditions in the factory were ghastly. Many of the women received between five and ten *piastres* (twenty-five to fifty cents) a day. Sanitary conditions were unspeakable. There were no Jewish doctors. We could not make use of the Kupat Holim [Workers' Sick Fund], because the bosses did not recognize the labor organization. Among the Arabs there were children of six and eight who were employed in the most dangerous part of the work.

There were no experienced workers among us to teach us methods of organization. Our location cut us off from easy contact with the center of the labor movement; but this separation also served to draw us, the workers, closer to each other; and in this closeness one ideal was nourished: we were going to build up a new Jewish settlement in this remote and abandoned town of Akko; we were going to create a new, decent life for the workers, and we were going to bring a new spirit into the lives of the Arabs in the factory. In the ancient garrison town of Akko a new kind of war now began, and blood was shed in a cause that had been unknown till our coming.

The strike broke out February 16, 1927. The strikers made the following demands: improvement of sanitary conditions; hiring of a Jewish doctor; some sort of payment during sickness; a fifty per cent increase in wages for workers now earning from five to ten *piastres* a day; an increase

42. The identity of Malkah is unknown.

43. Ramat Gan is a city adjacent to Tel Aviv, originally founded by the Ir Ganim [City of Gardens] corporation, which endeavored to create a "garden suburb" with many parks and playgrounds.

44. The Nur [Light] match factory was established in Akko at the height of the Fourth Aliyah (1924–28), when there was a sharp rise in the immigration of middle-class Polish Jews, many of whom were shopkeepers and artisans.

of twenty-five per cent to those getting ten to twenty *piastres* a day; children were not to be put to dangerous work. There were sixty Jewish and forty Arab strikers. The strike lasted for four months and twelve days.

I want to describe just one incident in that strike; we had put up pickets round the factory, to prevent strike-breakers from entering. One Friday, when the last picket was about to leave, we—a group of us who had already been relieved from our posts—received a message to come back at once to the factory. Without thinking much, we set off at a run, choosing different streets so that no panic would arise among the Arabs of the city. In front of the factory we found what looked like a battle array: policemen on horseback and a huge throng round them. The workers massed themselves together, and extended in chain formation across the street. At a given signal the horsemen rushed the crowd and scattered it, leaving only the workers. These were arrested, handcuffed and led away. Only the women were left on the spot. The employer waited for the arrival of the Irish-British police to deal with these.

We were tired, so we sat down on the ground to rest. In a little while we heard the noise of automobiles—the Irish police! The officers sprang out, approached the boss, and asked him what was to be done. He told them that he was sick and tired of having us around. He wanted us removed.

We heard a whistle of command. In an instant the soldiers were let loose on us. The street became a battlefield. We were thrown to the ground and murderously beaten. Blood stains began to show on the earth. And when we had been beaten into submission we were thrust into the automobiles. A few women remained where they were—they had fainted.

We were taken to the prison, and there we found the men who had been arrested before us. The sight of us, with hair wildly disarranged, with blood stains on our clothes, froze them in horror. One of our *haverim* could not contain himself, and began to curse the [British] government. An English soldier dashed at him and struck him. The [women] screamed and tried to throw themselves between the two. The noise brought officers to the scene. They ordered that we be removed from the room, and so we were separated from our *haverim*.

We were thrust in through a low, iron door which banged [shut] behind us; we heard the lock being turned. We looked at each other in a sort of stupefaction, our very faces strange to us. And sitting there, we began to sing at last the beautiful, cheering "Fisher March" of the Ohel[45] [Tent] theater company.

45. The Ohel [Tent] theater company, originally known as the workers' theater of Palestine, was established in 1925 by Moshe Halevy (1895–1974), a veteran of the

The police returned, ordered us out of this room, and marched us down a long corridor, on either side of which were little cubicles. We were concentrated in one of these. There we waited, wondering what was going to be done with us. Meanwhile the police walked up and down, and kept looking in on us; it was a curious sight to them—Jewish [women] in prison!

The little room became darker and darker; the sun was setting on the other side of the walls. *Haverim* from the outside were admitted to us; they brought us food and told us that the Jewish population of Akko had organized a protest meeting. While they were still speaking, we heard suddenly the ringing sound of a smack—and our *haverim* vanished. For a while their voices carried to us from the outside. Silently we sat down on the floor, around the lantern.

Russian Jewish stage and former assistant director of Habimah in Moscow. The company was sharply criticized in the 1930s for emphasizing proletarian over national themes, but its performances were generally well received by a variety of Jewish and Zionist quarters. In 1934, the company made a highly successful European tour. In 1958, the Histadrut rescinded its support of the theater and the company disbanded. The theater enjoyed a brief revival after 1961 until its closure in 1969.

The Strike in Zikhron Yaakov

Carmelah[46] (Kineret, Kibbutz Hashomer Hazair from S.S.R.[47])

IT IS TWO o'clock in the afternoon. Since early morning the women workers have been standing at the gate of the orchard and have stopped the strike-breakers, the Arab women, and Yemenites brought down by the PICA [Palestine Jewish Colonization Association]. Yesterday a resolution was passed in the workers' club to declare a strike against the PICA for having reduced the pay of the women workers from fifteen to ten *piastres* a day.

Twice we drove away the local police from the gate of the orchard. Now we are told that the next train is bringing British *gendarmerie* from Haifa.

Voices are heard. "Let's go away. They'll drive us off anyway. It's three o'clock. Tomorrow morning we'll come back early."

But opposing voices are louder: "No! No! We'll not go away of our own free will. The moment we go, the strike-breakers will get in. Let's stay."

The strikers' committee is in session. Messages fly back and forth between the meeting and the group of women at the orchard gate. We wait for the decision of the committee.

The decision is: Stay on!

Here they come—the British soldiers with an officer at their head. The conversation with the officer was a waste of time. He tried to argue with the women picketers at the gate, and with the men workers who stood at a distance. (They, not being directly involved, had to stand to one side, as "onlookers.")

We were given fifteen minutes to think the matter over. But we only closed our ranks, one behind the other, to guard the gate. The fifteen minutes passed, and then the soldiers, who had been standing woodenly at attention, advanced on the workers and began to strike them with the butts of their rifles. The women screamed—but they stood

46. The identity of Carmelah is unknown.

47. Kibbutz Hashomer Hazair was the name a Marxist Zionist youth collective, affiliated with the Hashomer Hazair youth movement, that hailed from the Soviet Socialist Republic (S.S.R.) and temporarily resided at Kineret.

still closer together. Who were these assailants? British soldiers in Erez Israel, called out by the Palestine Jewish Colonization Association against women who were struggling for a bare means of subsistence! The first row of the women held out in front, near the men who had come to their help. The last row of women clung firm about the gate.

How long can a group of unarmed men and women hold out against English soldiers? The first line shuddered and began to yield. The rifles flashed up and down, broke the strikers, pursued them.

Our turn next—our last row of women. I hear a trembling voice near me.

"I'm frightened."

"If you're frightened, leave! Leave at once! We don't want to be told that we were scared of English soldiers."

"Don't talk like that to me! Give me strength." Again the officer came up.

"Wouldn't you do better to submit this whole matter to the [British] High Commissioner?"[48] The answer comes from the group.

"We won't leave this gate."

In spite of that determined answer, the officer still gives us five minutes in which to think it over. He stands in front of us and waits. But in our minds there is only one question: Will we have the courage and the strength to put up a fight, not to run when they advance on us? It is the first time that we clash with the police. It is not the orchard gate we are defending, and not only our crust of bread—we are defending our pride! If only these five minutes would pass! We press each other's hands feverishly; we jam ourselves closer about the gate. And now the line of soldiers comes at us—civilized Englishmen with guns in their hands, setting on women! There is a smile on their faces, as though the whole incident were something of unusual interest. And it is this smile which burns deeper than anything else. They try to break through, to open the gate, they pull savagely at the women—but we hold firm. Their comrades come to their help.

I find myself suddenly hanging in the air between Englishmen and *haverot*. Two soldiers are pulling at me, and cannot get me loose. A third joins them. I have only one prayer in my heart—not to let go. A feeling of hatred wells up in me for those blue-green eyes and that blue-green uniform.

48. The High Commissioner was the chief executive in Palestine under the British Mandate. The one referred to here is Herbert Samuel (1870–1963). Samuel, who was sympathetic to Zionism, was the first openly Jewish cabinet member in Britain and served as president of the Royal Institute of Philosophy from 1931–56. He held the position of High Commissioner during the years 1920–25. After Samuel drastically curtailed Third Aliyah immigration, he lost a good deal of popularity among Palestine Jews and Zionists.

But in the end they smashed through, and I was flung to one side, to be surrounded by the local police. I got up and tried to return to the struggling mass at the gate. Again I was seized and flung back. The officer was no better than his men—they belong to one level of culture . . . Behind the guard stand the arrested men, tied to each other in one long chain. Out of the struggle we smile at them—the smile of friendship and encouragement shining across a sea of hatred and rage.

At last the gate was opened. The arrested men were led off to Zikhron Yaakov, and the women workers dragged after them. That night we ran through the streets of the colony, crying: "Liberate them! Liberate them!" We bloodied our hands beating on the door of the temporary prison in which our *haverim* were locked. We sacked the office of the PICA, and left it turned upside down. And we quieted down only when our *haverim* were set free.

Fighting for Work in Petah Tikvah

Rivkah [Broizman] (Havurat Hapoalot, Petah Tikvah)

THIS IS THE first day of our imprisonment here.[49]

I remember well how they lifted us, bound hand and foot, into the automobiles. We managed to gasp out words of farewell to our *haverim* who remained there on the "battlefield"—and then everything disappeared.

My side ached. My face was burning, and there were tears in my eyes—but they were tears of rage.

We did not know where the automobiles were taking us, to the colony or to the prison in Jaffa. We were not accustomed to being bound like that, and as the machines rolled on we tried now and again to move our limbs. Yet we could not help laughing through our tears. Automobiles and groups of workers passed us on the road, and we saluted them by shaking the manacles on our hands.

The passersby stared at us in fright—they could not understand what had happened. We passed through Tel Aviv, and were recognized by acquaintances. They called to us: "Where are they taking you?" One of the women in our car shouted back: "For a stroll on the seashore." And she was almost right! Here we were driving through the narrow streets of Jaffa and the sea burst in on our view.

The automobile drives into the police yard: we are taken out and forced into a small room, and from there we issue again into the yard. High walls surround us. On a rug sits a Yemenite woman, and three Arab women near her. The woman guard and the others are anxious to find out why we have been brought here. We answer that we wanted work, and [here is what we got]—we show them the blood spots on our dresses. We ask the Yemenite woman why the Arabs are here. She answers: "For stealing."

The day passes, and we sit there on rugs, feeling as though our limbs have been smashed. The police come in, leisurely, at ease. They take our names and go away. They have plenty of time.

49. In the winter of 1927, the Jewish workers of Petah Tikvah put up a fierce struggle for their right to be employed in the orange harvest. In the course of the struggle there was a clash between strikers and police, and many of the former were injured and imprisoned. (This note is translated from the Yiddish text.)

It grows dark. We are led back into the prison—a tiny, whitewashed room, with a tile floor and an electric lamp—a charming home! We lay the rugs and blankets on the floor, and lie down close to each other, tired out as if after a day's work. The woman guard brings food for the prisoners, a gruel in a tin cup, and a loaf of black bread. For us she has white bread, eggs, and oranges.

"Where's this from?"

"Your *haverim* brought it."

Who was it? The [Histadrut]? We had not expected it; we had forgotten that we were bound up with an entire world which was following our fate closely.

We woke up the next morning realizing for the first time that we were really in prison. And yet, in spite of the prohibition, we got the newspapers. When the woman guard went out, we fell on those papers like hungry wolves on meat. We read wildly, too impatient to follow the text sentence by sentence. We want to get all the news at one glance.

We learn now that the entire labor body of the country stands with us. We seem to have done something! If it brings no results here and now, there is hope that results will follow. In any case, we have focused the attention of the country on our case. Oh, it was worthwhile! We can hardly remember another moment of such joy and satisfaction.

They brought us mail to the prison, and I received a postal card from my home, back in Europe. My father wrote that one sister had been sent to Siberia for being a "counter revolutionary." And here I was in prison for being too revolutionary! Another sister, so my father wrote, "lives in loneliness among gentiles."

I read and read and repeat the words.

"To be a daughter of the Jewish people means, to be faithful far away among strangers, and to be a stranger at home among one's own."

Destruction of the Havurah in Haifa

Sarah Malkin (Havurat Hapoalot, near Haifa)
WRITTEN DURING THE ARAB RIOTS OF AUGUST 1929

I T WAS ON Friday evening, August 23, 1929, that the *haverim* came back from the [Yagur-Nesher] [Eagle] cement factory[50] outside Haifa to guard our settlement, that we learned what had happened in Jerusalem.[51]

The night passed peacefully. When the sun rose the next morning we somehow felt more lighthearted. The *haverim* returned to the Nesher factory and we went out into the fields.

A few hours later our watchman, the *haver* Eliezer Hurwiz,[52] was called to Haifa to the workers' council. They told him that we would have to leave the place because it was rumored that the [Arab] riots were going to spread from Jerusalem over the entire country. Our place was far from town, closed in by the hills, and near by was an Arab village which was known to be a center of [unrest]; it would be hard to afford us protection. After a long conference we decided not to leave the place, for we knew that, once it was abandoned, it would be completely destroyed.

We explained this to our *haverim* of [the] Nesher [factory], who stood guard with us the second night, too. They pleaded with us to give up our decision; the situation throughout the whole country was dangerous and, empty-handed as they were, it would be impossible for them to defend our settlement in case of attack.

Sunday morning the same thing—again the demand from Haifa that we abandon the position; again we reply, "Send help so that we can defend the place." Meanwhile we make what preparation we can. On

50. The original Yiddish text uses the hyphenation "Yagur-Nesher." Yagur refers to a Gdud Avodah [Labor Legion] settlement located in the Zevulun Valley (11 km. southeast of Haifa) that was founded in 1922 by Zionist pioneers of the Third Aliyah (1919–23); it later became a *kibbutz*. The Nesher [Eagle] cement factory was established in this period as well. The factory employed groups of Third Aliyah workers, many of whom resided temporarily at Yagur. During the Third Aliyah, the introduction of industry into Palestine became a central feature of the emergent Jewish economy.

51. The reference here is to the Arab riots of 1929, which resulted in the massacre of Jews in Hebron and other places, and dramatically changed the Yishuv's internal debate over the issues of Jewish sovereignty and security.

52. The precise details of Eliezer Hurwiz's biography are unknown.

the distant road we see the automobiles of the Arabs flying back and forth. There are rumors of an impending attack in Haifa.

At five o'clock two automobiles come from [the] Nesher [factory], and now the men speak determinedly: "The place has to be abandoned." We feel now that argument is useless. With heavy hearts, we begin to pack things into the automobiles. I go into the shed to get the cow, and there stands one of my *haverot*; she and I lower our eyes, and the thought goes through us simultaneously: "So much labor we put into this place, so much suffering—and now everything is to go up in smoke."

We caught the chickens, bound them, and placed them in the machines. A couple of packages contained our clothes. Meanwhile the men stood impatiently by and urged us on, "Faster!" Darkness begins to creep up. The haste, the tumult, the screaming of the fowl—everything confuses us and runs into a pandemonium. We are ready now, the automobiles are about to start, and something new turns up. The watchman refuses to get in! "I don't leave this place," he says, obstinately. "It's my job to stay here and see it isn't destroyed." The moment we hear these words, we make an effort to clamber out of the cars, saying: "If he stays, we stay." But it's too late. The *haverim* give the signal to the [driver] and the [vehicles] are off.

It was a fearful night that we passed in Haifa. We could scarcely wait for the dawn. As soon as it was light we got into the first automobile we could commandeer and drove back at top speed to the settlement. When we saw, in the distance, the watchman standing at the door of the dining room, a load fell off our hearts.

Once we were at the settlement, we were also without news from Haifa, for Jewish automobiles no longer passed up the road. For the same reason, we could not return to [the] Nesher [factory]. We settled down to the usual routine of work. At eight in the morning we observed a crowd of Arab men and women, numbering between thirty and forty, approaching us. They were armed with clubs. At the hedge they came to a halt and, after a pause, began to make for the gate. But they did not seem to be united. There seemed to be quarreling among them; we saw the Arab women trying to pull the men away from the gate. And indeed, the crowd retired a little from the hedge and stood there, yelling and pointing at us. Before long three Arab automobiles arrived. One of them turned toward the Arab village, the other went on to Haifa, and the third stopped with the crowd.

And now our watchman perceived that things were getting bad and that we would have done better to stay in Haifa. He was beside himself with remorse, but it was too late. There was nowhere to run to! To go out upon the road would be to deliver ourselves up. And once again the watchman became obstinate—but this time at the other extreme. "It's my fault that you came back here!" he exclaimed. "I'm going out of here! I'll find my way to [the] Nesher [factory] and have them send an automobile." We implored him not to jeopardize his life, but he paid no attention to us. He saddled the horse and set out at a gallop. We saw him disappear, and our hearts told us that we would not see him alive again. When the Arabs saw him ride off, they drew closer and began to yell: "Clear out of this place! If you don't, you'll be cut to pieces."

Twenty minutes of horror passed. We locked ourselves in the dining room, the only building with stone walls, and waited there, pale, helpless. And we read in each other's eyes the question which had no answer: "How will we defend ourselves? What with?"

It seemed to us that hours, unusually long hours, had passed since the watchman had set out. And then, at last, we heard the shrill, liberating whistle—the *haverim* of [the] Nesher [factory] had arrived in an automobile.

We still had to pass through the Arab village, and we wondered if we would be able to get through. The road passed by the *sheikh's*[53] house. In front of it, the whole village had gathered, and the *sheikh* sat on a white horse, delivering an address. A crowd of young people had detached itself, and was waiting for our car, and as we flew by, a hail of stones came crashing round the automobile. We got through safely. In [the] Nesher [factory], they received us as if we had been dragged back alive from the grave.

Two airplanes circled above the village, firing at random to disperse the Arabs.

The guards were doubled in [the] Nesher [factory]. The women were now installed for the night. We could not rest. We kept staring in the direction of our home, waiting for the inevitable—for the flames and smoke.

Nothing was observed in the night. At noon of the next day, however, a column of smoke rises from that corner of the horizon. From the roof of the factory we can just make out that the Arabs have set fire to the hayrick. The barracks are intact. The hayrick blazes, and we begin to hope that this will be the sum total of the damage.

But at midnight a wild blaze colored all that part of the sky. [They are burning down] the barracks . . .

We become frantic. We implore the *haverim*: "Quick: let's go back. Perhaps we can put the fire out." Always we get the same answer.

53. *Sheikh* is Arabic for the "leader" of a family or village. The *sheikh* is also often the local religious authority.

"Can't do a thing. We have no weapons. And we have to guard [the] Nesher [factory] first."

We stand there paralyzed, and watch the blaze. So much labor, so much love and sacrifice! All of it going up in the flames.

An automobile with English soldiers comes rushing up to the factory. They tell us in detail what has happened at the farm, what is burning and what has been destroyed. But they cannot take us there.

Early in the morning, we asked the four Englishmen who had been sent to defend [the] Nesher [factory] to take us over to the farm. They agreed. We arrived in the midst of a deathly silence, a desolation that appalled us. This has been our home for the last three years! Nothing at all is left of the barracks; only the ribs of the iron beds stick out gruesomely from the ruin. The store room is empty; fragments of the smashed incubator lie scattered on the ground. We take a look at the tree nursery. Everything is green and fresh and undisturbed. We breathe once more. The ruffians[54] did not understand at all that for us the nursery means everything, that it is more important than the barracks.

The English soldiers grow impatient. We must leave. But how hard it is to tear ourselves away from here.

And, sitting in the automobiles, we begin to make plans for getting back the same day in order to water the young trees.

54. The Yiddish text refers to the Arab attackers as "robbers."

PART III

At Work

Stages

Rahel Yanait [Ben-Zvi] (Meshek Hapoalot, Jerusalem)

Fʀᴏᴍ ᴛʜᴇ ʙᴇɢɪɴɴɪɴɢ of her appearance in the country twenty-
five years ago, the woman worker has been closely bound up with the
general labor movement; and yet the ways of the women workers are
peculiar to themselves.

Even at the outset, when workers took their first grip on the land,
in the days of the first *kvuzot*—Sejera, Dagania, Kineret, and Merhavyah—days of triumph for the workers' ideals, even in those days, some
of the women workers had already separated off into a special women's
kvuzah . . . a *kvuzah* without a home, a wandering *kvuzah* which had
neither soil nor plan nor budget.

What brought this thing about?

In the thick of that passionate movement toward the land, the women
workers suddenly found themselves thrust aside and relegated once
more to the ancient tradition of the house and the kitchen. They were
amazed and disappointed to see how the cleavage was opening, the men
comrades really uniting themselves with the land, but they, though on
it, not becoming part of it. The united front was cracking. So that even
then a handful of women—all of them very young—set out in a group
to build up their own working relationship to the soil.

And quickly enough there began to spring up those early *kvuzot* of
women workers—on the shores of Lake Kineret, in the Jezreel Valley,
and on the sands of Judea. And if the *kvuzah* subsisted only for one year,
and if the land it worked was only hired—who cared? For the principle
issue was not the farm, the economic unit, but the *kvuzah* as such.[1] Nor

1. The ideal of *kibush haavodah* [conquest of labor], which is implicit here, was most
fully developed and articulated by A. D. Gordon, the philosopher of the Second Aliyah.
Gordon asserted that the redemption of the individual would be accomplished through
physical labor, and that the individual's welfare and happiness was linked to the elevation
of the collective and society as a whole. In an open letter to the members of Dagania
written in 1921, Gordon asserted:

the basic idea of the *kvuzah* is to arrange its communal life through the strength
of the communal idea, and through communal work so that the members will be
interdependent and will influence each other along their positive qualities . . . The
kvuzah, for instance, can and must work on two fronts. One one side—that of work
and nature—man must free himself, man must reform himself through work and

did they find it so hard to break in the naked soil of the wilderness, if thereby they could slake their thirst for work on the land, and satisfy their passion for a partnership with mother earth.

There was much joking about those early *kvuzot*. No one believed in the success of our idea. But the deep, burning enthusiasm which had caught us up enabled us to ignore the doubts of others. Yes, it is quite clear now to everyone that the temporary *kvuzah* was economically senseless. But in those days it had a deep sense, and because of this it emerged whole from the difficult war period.

Shortly before the close of [World War I], the dream of a Jewish Legion ripened into realization. The woman worker was caught up in that rush of sacrifice not less than the man; what the *kvuzah* had not been able to satisfy in her, she sought to fulfill in this new phenomenon. It is not easy to write about those sacrificial days. Were the women really caught up in a military emotion or were they merely imitating the men comrades? No, no. That spirit was absent on both sides. We were enslaved by one idea; one well of feeling sent up its deep, turbulent forces in both of us; the idea was not war, but liberation. But for the men there was the front—and for the women, again, disappointment. There were hundreds of women who reported for duty with the [Jewish] Legion, just like men. Of course, they were not taken. That rebuff left us flat and wearied; we were not to participate in that great moment. This incident deserves a place of its own in the history of the women workers' movement.

The year after the war those [young women's *kvuzot*] disappeared; it was something sudden, as if a sponge had wiped them off the slate. Nor was there any struggle about it. The women felt that this form had outlived itself; something new had to answer the spirit of the changed times. Yes, we could no longer form our associations so easily, wander from place to place, take root and uproot every year. The time had come for the permanent settlement, stable, rooted in its own soil.

After the wandering *kvuzah* came, as its natural inheritor, the *meshek hapoalot*; after group vagabondage came the planned, sensible and stabilized unit.

And so the women's farm was created in Petah Tikvah, the tree nursery in Jerusalem, and the collectives in Nahlat Yehudah and Shekhunat Borohov.

---

nature . . . On the other front, there is the life of the family in the *kvuzah*. The *kvuzah* must serve as a family in the finest meaning of the term. It must develop its members through the strength of their mutual, positive influence . . . (*A. D. Gordon: Selected Essays*, trans. Frances Burnce [New York: League for Labor Palestine, 1938], pp. 281–282).

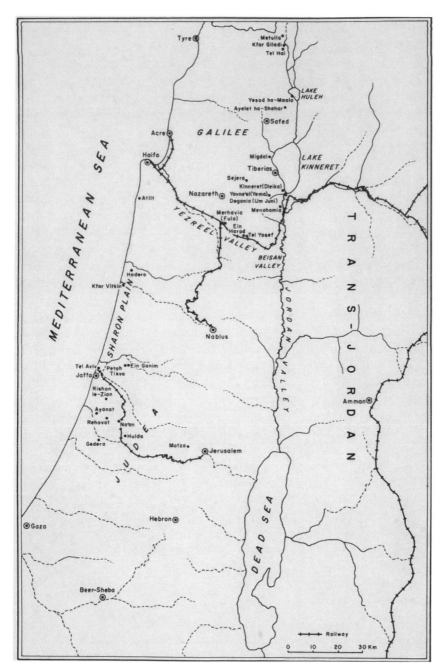

FIGURE I. Map of Palestine.

FIGURE 2. Kfar Giladi.

FIGURE 3. Dagania at its founding (1910).

FIGURE 4. Dagania (c. 1931).

FIGURE 5. Children's home of Ein Harod (August 1929).

FIGURE 6. Women's training farm in Jerusalem.

FIGURE 7. Women and children in Nahalal.

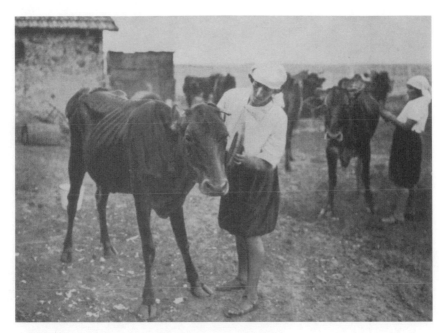

FIGURE 8. Women's training farm in Nahlat Yehuda.

FIGURE 9. Harnessing a mule.

FIGURE 10. Paving a road.

FIGURE 11. Children swimming in Lake Kineret.

FIGURE 12. Children of Ein Harod on an outing.

FIGURE 13. Children's home of Moezet Hapoalot in Tel Aviv (1928).

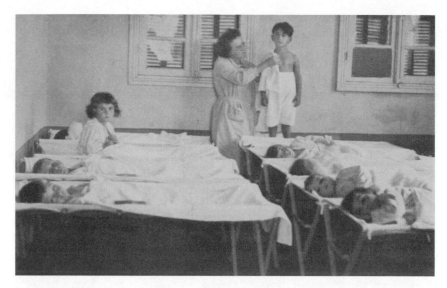

FIGURE 14. Children's home of Moezet Hapoalot in Hederah (1930).

FIGURE 15. Shoshanah Bogen, before immigrating to Palestine (c. 1913).

FIGURE 16. Dvorah Drakhler, before immigrating to Palestine (c. 1913).

FIGURE 17. Sarah Chizhik (1919).

FIGURE 18. Pessie Abramson (1914).

FIGURE 19. Sarah Lishansky,
before immigrating to
Palestine (1907).

FIGURE 20. Rahel Zisle-Lefkovich in Ein Harod (c. 1925).

FIGURE 21. Rahel Blaustein (c. 1925).

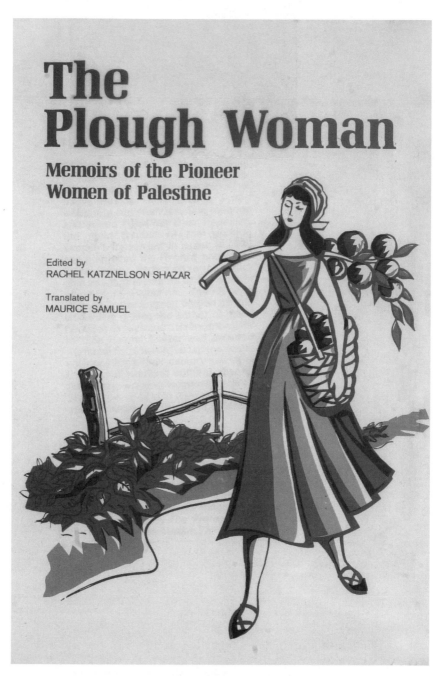

The
Plough Woman

Memoirs of the Pioneer
Women of Palestine

Edited by
RACHEL KATZNELSON SHAZAR

Translated by
MAURICE SAMUEL

FIGURE 22. Dust jacket, from the second English edition (1975).

This was in 1921, the time of the big expansion in agricultural work, when the Jezreel Valley was bought and new forms of land units sprang up, [namely] the large *kvuzot* and the *moshav ovdim*. In every place, the woman worker had her own important role to play.

It does not matter what the exact forces were which brought about the result, whether it was through the pressure of the original women's farms, or through the actual necessities of the life on the land—but as a worker the woman found her role to be richer, fuller, and more variegated than ever before. Her place was definite: the vegetable gardening system, the dairy work, chicken raising, and tree-planting. She was gradually relieved from the exclusive claim of the kitchen and laundry; the men learned to give her a hand there. But once she broke into the fuller life of the system, the woman began to understand how much she lacked in training and independent preparation.

A new and complicated question emerged: the question of mother and child in the workers' collectives. The woman began anxiously to seek a way to unite care of the child with productive labor on the soil. And out of this search arose new life-forms in the field of child-rearing. If we have been enriched by many values in this field, we must thank the woman worker on the land.

Another period came: the time when thousands of Palestinian Jews were taken up with the road-building which was a feature of certain after-war years. Among these road-laborers were women, too, participating, but often at a loss as to the meaning of this participation, doubtful of themselves and of their new role.

The body of workers in Erez Israel grew constantly, and the number of women workers with it; but most of these were still employed in their own separate settlements or else were wage workers in the villages. The mother in the worker's farm and the daughter in the farm settlement of women workers still have more in common than the mother in the village and the daughter in the town—the land-work is a bond. And this question of the relation between mother and child plays as important a part in our conferences and our conversations as the questions of work and of immigration into Erez Israel.

The *meshek hapoalot* has a distinct purpose: to prepare the woman worker for the general *meshek* [farm settlement]. But at first it had an additional purpose: it was a larger school life. There was an educational value in the dividing up of the work, the sharing of responsibility and the adaptation of the individual to the group life. The *meshek* had to be self-supporting; and therefore the *haverot* in it had to take up all its economic problems. In such surroundings the character of the *haverah* set firm; she developed the necessary independence and initiative. We were amazed sometimes to see the difference which one year made in a woman. Helpless at first, she was at the end of this period an intelligent cooperator, participating in the management and showing a thorough understanding of the complicated economic and administrative problems of the settlement.

Work in the settlement was a joy. Steeped as we were in our labors, the hours of the long day slipped by uncounted and unnoticed. But the purest and most supreme joy was in the tree nurseries—our pioneer contribution to the country.

In old Europe and in new America, which possess such magnificent agricultural institutions, and even in California with its nurseries which number their shoots by the millions, it is always the man who directs. Managers, gardeners, workers—all men—are the creative and responsible elements. The woman worker is hardly to be seen. Here and there I found a few women wage workers, or office-workers—in brief, they were given the inferior or mechanical work, which dulls the individual. Not one single tree nursery did I find created by women.

With our own hands we raised, on our soil, tens and hundreds of thousands of shoots, and a kind of bond was created between our fruitful little corners and the wild, bare hills around us. We were participants in the great task of re-afforesting the country.

But we share in something more than in the forestry. We play a role in gardening, chicken-raising, and dairy work. It is true that these activities have not yet taken deep, organic root among us. They still lack something; here we are short of a breed cow, there the barn is not completed; elsewhere we lack buildings, or soil—or even water; and nearly everywhere we are short of quarters for the workers. The universal trouble is that the settlement has not yet established itself on its own feet.

The critical years 1926–27 came upon us.[2] Everywhere, unemployment, hunger, and suffering—and most of all among the women workers. The *mishkei hapoalot* knew all the bitterness of those years. So many women workers came knocking at our doors and there was no way of admitting them. The settlements were still small, their absorptive capacity was limited. Two hundred women in the settlements had food

2. The economic boom and inflated land prices that characterized the years following World War I artificially raised costs associated with Jewish land acquisition and resettlement in Palestine. In this period, the speculative private land market grew to include urban and suburban plots as well as outlying tracts of agricultural land. The subsequent collapse of the market in 1925–26 caused Jewish investment in land holdings to decline abruptly. Against this backdrop, the Jewish National Fund emerged as virtually the sole agency responsible for Jewish land purchases. Large-scale unemployment became pervasive in the Yishuv and many recent settlers re-emigrated.

and genuine creative work; two thousand outside of them were hungry and without employment. And among the latter one heard dark, bitter remarks about the *meshek hapoalot*—the darling women's institution, which picks and chooses and accords its privileges according to its own rules . . .

Out of this suffering came creation. The *meshek hapoalot* gave birth to the *havurah*. The idea was born among the *haverot* in the *meshek hapoalot*, and they transformed it into a reality.

The *meshek hapoalot* is still young—and it has its special needs. There is, for instance, the tree nursery. How much labor, how much attention, must be put into that enterprise, year in, year out, creating and re-creating! The worry about water, the care which must be given to every individual plant and sapling! And then the worries of selling them . . . The *meshek hapoalot* absorbs the woman worker wholly, body and soul. But if the woman feels herself fitted for this work she gives herself up gladly and unreflectingly.

But the heaviest strain on the *meshek hapoalot* is the constant round of women who come and go. So much effort must be expended before the new *haverah* gets into harness, and before she adapts herself to the group life. And when the two years have passed, and the "course" is completed —she goes, and the *meshek hapoalot* begins all over again with another newcomer. This in itself, apart from the agricultural, the "real" work, is an exacting task, and it is little wonder that the years plough so deeply into the faces of the women who direct the settlements.

And then new changes come up in the realities of Erez Israel. Factories and workshops rise in these towns. Thousands of women pour into the cities and go into the factory or into private homes; and during those same years, 1926–28, the country is closed to Jewish immigration.[3]

Just yesterday there were hundreds knocking at the door of the *mishkei hapoalot* and suddenly we are short of hands! And those women whose lives have been sunk in these institutions feel as if a blow had struck at them. Something must be done. Out of the new needs come new ideals: the *meshek hapoalot* must give more. It must be perfected from within. Every one of its agricultural enterprises must become a model. It is, after all, an institution that educates and trains. And then other problems must be settled, worked out to better ends: markets, the inner form of life in the institution, improvements in the theory and practice of teaching. But all these things are external compared with

---

3. Arab outbreaks against Jewish settlers in 1920 and 1921 were followed by British restrictions on Jewish immigration. Thereafter, Jewish immigration was increasingly viewed by the Mandatory as a potential threat to the rights and position of the indigenous Arab population.

the fundamental problem of the woman worker herself, and of her attitude toward the *meshek hapoalot*. True, the *meshek hapoalot* is a training ground, but it must not be regarded merely as an institution where women come to learn a trade. It is not a trade, it is a sort of personal destiny we teach . . . The woman learns to educate herself, and to awaken from within a deep and permanent relationship to the soil.

The development of the *meshek hapoalot* was naturally influenced by the general conditions in the labor movement.

We, the women of the *meshek hapoalot*, are particularly proud of one fact: our accepted and accredited public workers also take up the physical labor and are swallowed up by it. As soon as they go on the soil they forget their public or communal occupation and become one with the actual labor itself. And many of them are now spread through the collectives of the [Jezreel Valley], the Jordan [Valley], and Kineret, in the women's settlements and at many another point. This characteristic of so many women leaders, their ability to sink their public careers in sheer physical work, is often pointed to with pride among us, as a sign of a certain superiority over men. But it is possible that the ability is rooted in passivity, in an absence of courage and a weaker taste for public work.

In fact, how else can we explain the fact that we have achieved so little among the women workers in the city?

Hundreds and thousands of women belonging to the [Old Yishuv], women of all classes and ages, are pouring into factories, toward the sewing machine and loom, and even into domestic service—and at what wretched pay! And so many of them are not at all organized, have no membership in the Histadrut.

The basements in the side streets of the towns swarm with workers' families. In Jerusalem—and principally there—the worker families live mostly among the [Sephardic] Jews [of the Old Yishuv]. The family suffers as a whole, but it is the working class mother that suffers most. And if any child needs the upbringing that is found in the collectives, it is that city child of the worker. What joy it would be for that mother, what a blessing for the child, if a workers' settlement could be founded for them somewhere outside the city, a little patch of earth begging to be worked. Why is it then that no movement has been started among the women workers for such settlements?

And one point more, about wage work in the colonies. However difficult it is for the men to find jobs, insecure as these jobs are—yet they have made a place for themselves in every branch of agriculture, in the plantations and fields. But the woman still has to fight out the problem of her right to work in the colony, in the orchard and vineyard; and not merely at the picking of oranges. And how few women get a man's pay for doing a man's work!

Out of this rises doubt, dissatisfaction, and inadequacy; in the *kvuzah* and the *moshav ovdim*, everywhere the woman feels the same. In no form of Palestinian life does the woman play her proper role economically, culturally, and spiritually.

The road that lies before the women in Erez Israel is still a long one, but its direction already seems to be clear: however strong our desire to broaden the basis of woman's life in village and town, so as to make it all-inclusive, the directive principle is and must remain, for the entire women workers' movement, agricultural.

To leave out agriculture is to leave out the most vital part of the labor movement in Erez Israel; to take away the *meshek hapoalot* is to take away from the women's labor movement its chief and characteristic productivity.

In the Kvuzah

Liliyah Basevich (Ein Harod)

I N REGARD TO the *kvuzah* we have developed an attitude which is
altogether too much like that of the nagging mother toward her children—an attitude of unceasing criticism. There seems to be no limit to
the demands that we make on the group and on the individual—as if
the *kvuzah* were already the perfected form of life in a perfected social
system of the future. From the individual we demand that he be a good
worker, disciplined, devoted, filled with a sense of responsibility, open
and accessible to his *haverim*. From the *kvuzah* we demand that it shall
satisfy all the material and spiritual needs of the individual.

We forget that in the existing order of things, with its competitive
character, men and women are brought up to be enemies. We who have
gone into the *kvuzot* have taken a leap into the future; we have refused
to wait, but must incorporate the best that is to come in our own lives.
But we cannot leap out of our skins; and we cannot cast off with one
gesture all the heritage of our early training and be reborn. We are still
the same persons. And the many *haverim* who yield to despair because
we are not perfect are only the victims of an exaggerated idealism.

Why are we so prone to pass over the good element in our life? We
have so much to say about its shortcomings—is there nothing to be
said for its achievements? There are enough good points in our own
life (and how many more in the life of our children!) to justify a little
praise, a corrective to the monotonously one-sided and misleading self-
criticism in which we indulge.

We were very young when we came into the country. We knew nothing about life, and nothing of the prosaic side of men and women. Our
group contacts had always been festive: we saw each other during visits,
during outings, and on those occasions when the youth movement
brought us together. We were friends and *haverim*, and each of us worried for the others. Little wonder that in those days we thought that all
human beings were good.

But it is otherwise in the actual life of the *kvuzah*. Here we come
into intimate contact (I will not say that our knowledge of each other is
intimate) and it is inevitable that we should also learn of each other's

shortcomings—human shortcomings which are even apt to eclipse the greatest virtues.

There is a special feature in *kvuzah* life that goes under the heading of "being good." To "be good" means, with us, to be faithful and responsible in the work. In the one case, it may be the heart that supplies the impulse; in the other, it may be a highly developed sense of duty. The result is, however, the same. Such a person is "a good worker." Not that the phrase is frequently used; more often than not we simply accept it as something natural and self-understood. That is what we are here for.

And in the same way we are actually unconscious of the concept "mutual help" because we work together all day long, and the process itself is one of mutual help. We fail to remember, in our fits of self-criticism, even those cases of exceptional and generous mutual help that occur in our life.

Here is one instance. There are few things that make a new mother more unhappy than the failure of her own supply of milk for her baby. In the *kvuzah* it is a simple and accepted custom, in such cases, that one mother shall help another, and mothers feed the children of others with the same devotion as their own. If one who is capable of doing this should show signs of discontent—let alone refuse!—she would never be forgiven. On one occasion, I remember, a woman happened to forget to feed a *haverah*'s baby, and, when she recollected suddenly, she ran through rain and mud down the long road to the children's house. But we say nothing about such things. We find them natural; and in any case we see no reason to make any particular fuss about decent moral behavior.

Our "peasant," who gets up in seeding time at four o'clock in the morning, and does not return till late in the evening—is he less devoted than the man who tills a field which is his own? The woman who cooks for dozens, or for hundreds of men—is she less concerned, less thoughtful, than if she were cooking for her own family? And have we not ourselves admitted that there is something wonderful about our women who work in our nurseries, our children's houses, and make themselves one with their charges? Is there not in all this an influence which lifts the individual above those meaner concepts of "advancement," of "getting on in the world" on which he has been brought up? As for those of our *haverim* who are taken up with the public work, and who know no rest night or day—do we treat them with the respect which is their due? And if we do not, does that prevent them from carrying on?

We complain sometimes of the lack of friendliness; we fail to visit, let us say, a sick *haver*. The truth is that we are usually so exhausted that we are unable to summon up energy for an evening with friends. Apart from this, we are with the crowd all day long, and in the evenings we feel the longing to withdraw a little into ourselves, to rest, to read.

In life at large, the most typical sin of the individual is his attitude of carelessness toward public property. In organized society the utmost ingenuity is needed, on the part of a state or city government, to protect its possessions. It seems to be almost instinctive in the individual to be prodigal with public property, even when he gets no benefit himself. I remember how, in Russia, there was, during [World War I], a great shortage of electricity. But you could not persuade the people to conserve. Lights would be left burning all night—what's the difference? This blind destructiveness of "anonymous" values lives in almost every human being. Can this be said of us? And is it not true that even in the last few years there has been a great advance in this respect among all our groups?

There are some who complain that our children are "dry," "formal" —"they lack the softness and gentleheartedness that we used to have as children." These people forget the virtues which our children have, and which we lacked as children: the being accustomed to work, the discipline with regard to the group, the sense of responsibility with regard to tasks, the strong love of nature, a strong, authentic love, without the sentimentalism of the past.

We simply do not know how fortunate we are in our children, We hear the complaint, "The children are too cheeky!" But do we pause to distinguish between spiritual freedom, forthrightness, and strength, on the one hand, and "cheek" on the other? Are not some of our concepts a trifle conservative?

And there are others who find fault even with the affirmative side of our communal-rearing of children. They complain that we actually give up too much time to the children. The collective life gives the parents a certain amount of time each day to devote exclusively to their children. The child thus feels that the parents are concerned only with him; he is never "in the way." And this, too, is a bad thing!

Of course it would be absurd to say that in the *kvuzah* everything is good. But what is at fault is not the *kvuzah* as a form of life, but certain indirect factors. It is our poverty that is at fault, and our constant exhaustion. We are poor; we are unable to meet even the minimum demands of the individual, and this is the source of our discontent.

Our ideal is that everyone shall get according to his needs. Actually, because of the perpetual shortage, this essential equality is transformed into a formal, external equality. For instance: we serve out food in equal portions! The boy and the girl, the worker in the field and the light worker, all get the same. And when shall we be able to get rid of this formal equality? Only when we shall have got rid of our poverty.

Our poverty oppresses the individual, makes it impossible for him to satisfy his personal needs in accordance with his own appetite and taste. The heavy work, the constant tiredness, the blazing heat, the poor food, the life in tents and barracks, the impossibility of taking one decent rest in the course of the year, to refresh oneself with a sight of the world—these are the real causes of our dark moods and our bitterness.

But life will not always be like this for us. Houses will be built, our returns will improve, the work will become easier—and life will be easier, too.

Let us therefore be cautious in our criticisms. Our lives are too difficult, too complicated. There are many shortcomings to be overcome, many shadows to be removed—but let us understand the good things, too, and appreciate them.

The *Woman in the* Moshav Ovdim

Shoshanah Rekhthant-Yafeh (Nahalal)

I T WAS IN 1921 that there appeared in Erez Israel the form of settle-ment called the *moshav ovdim*—the individualist cooperative settlement, where the worker owned his own land, but could not exploit the labor of others, and where a high degree of cooperation developed. At this time of writing (1928) it is hard to say: What has the *moshav ovdim* meant for the woman? Only a few observations can be made.

The woman and her husband enter the *moshav ovdim*, and the work divides itself automatically between them. The man works in the field, far from the home, and directs the entire business; she works in and around the house. This is not a strict division. When the wife is not tied to little children, she often works by the side of her husband in the fields; and, per contra, he is sometimes to be found "at home" in the vegetable garden and round the chicken coop. But, on the whole, the direction of the home is in the woman's hands. It appears to me that this division is natural and right; and it is only when either the man or woman is con-stantly overworked, and the yield is not enough to keep the family, that suffering appears. But this question of increasing the productivity of agriculture in Erez Israel, so that it shall exact fewer human sacrifices, is a national, and not a woman's question.

As long as the woman in the *moshav* is a mother of young children, she can do very little for the farm. At best she can look after the few chickens, and attend to the tiny vegetable plot. But I have noticed that even when I have not the time to do the actual work, I feel I must at least take one look every day at the garden, if only to see whether the shoots I planted a while ago are already coming up.

A woman must be exceptionally talented to be able to grasp clearly all the problems of a large farm; but on the little family farm the ordi-nary woman can feel herself quite at home. And for me the principal advantage of the *moshav* is, that it gives the woman a chance to feel free and to live her own life. More than this, the *moshav* forces a certain independence on the woman. It brings the woman directly face to face with life itself, and there is nothing to shield her from the contact with hard reality.

It is true that the woman in the *moshav* pays heavily for her independence. Her burden is heavy—but we ought to understand that the carrying of a life-burden does not necessarily mean oppression, any more than comfort necessarily means freedom.

The source of our suffering is this: that the yield is not yet proportionate to our labor. Although we have over-strained ourselves—and perhaps because of it—we still cannot satisfy the most essential needs. It is true that part of the explanation lies in the conditions which have reigned and still reign in the country; but part of it lies, perhaps, in our own lack of skill and experience. For we are the first generation of Jewish land workers here. And if it were possible to work only eight or ten hours a day, like our *haverim* in the towns, that alone might make the life of the woman in the *moshav* tolerable.

But, of course, not all women face the same circumstances. Where the children are a little older, and already attend school, the woman can go peacefully about more specific and more systematic work. A certain fine calm pervades the home life, and it can be said simply that there are families in the *moshav* which would provide an artist with an authentic idyll of the Jewish village. But where the woman must still tend little ones, there life is hard. She does not know a moment's freedom during the day, and she is never permitted to sleep the night through. She gets up at dawn, and does not know where to begin first—to feed the children or the chickens. In the majority of cases, there is not money enough in hand to lay in a stock of provisions, either for the family, or for the chickens and cattle; and so every other day the woman must go to the cooperative store, and take her turn in the line. And sometimes she must go to the clinic with her child, and there again is a line ahead of her.

Perhaps the morning passes this way; noon arrives and the noonday meal is not yet ready. And if the husband stays in the fields through the day, the woman still has to milk the cow and carry the milk away to the cooperative dairy. Sometimes she has to make a choice: if she gives her children the attention they need, she must neglect the garden and the cows—and the economy suffers; and if she attends to the economy, it is her children who must suffer.

When we first entered the *moshav*, we imagined it would make things easier if the youngest children were brought up together. But after living seven years in the *moshav* we have come to the conclusion that for us it is an impossible plan. In the *kvuzah* the children are under the care of a *haverah*; we, however, would have to employ a trained teacher, for it is obvious that no woman could be asked to separate herself from her own farm and do the child work. In the *kvuzah* the payment consists largely of the produce which is grown on the spot; in addition there is a little money expense for other necessities. But in the *moshav* the pay would have to be in cash, on the scale fixed by the Histadrut. This additional expense would be beyond the means of the woman in the *moshav*, and what she would gain in being liberated from the upbringing of the little ones, she would perhaps more than lose in additional labor.

Something else must be borne in mind. At the outset, when the farm is just being established, the woman in the *moshav* gets hardly any directly productive work. As long as the irrigation system is not installed, and the chicken coops are not built, there is, naturally plenty of work, hard work for the woman; but she earns next to nothing. And when the years have passed, and the farm has developed somewhat, and the woman adapts herself to the new life, then she suddenly perceives that the general group expenses are very high; and most of the *haverim* in the *moshav* are in debt to the [local] council for taxes. And this being the case, the group education of the little ones, expensive as it is, becomes a mere dream. Moreover, there are many women on the *moshav* who are opposed on principle to the group education of the very young.

The conditions under which the woman in the *moshav* works are exceptionally hard. No one would dream of telling a man to work the fields without a plough or to set up a dairy without a shed. But a woman is expected to raise chickens when she has neither a chicken yard nor a coop. How much energy is lost that way? The woman goes out to feed the chickens—but first she must search them out in neighboring yards. She sows and plants in a yard without a fence, and chicken and cattle trample the beds, and undo all her work. She washes her laundry under a burning sun, without a roof above her and without the proper vessels. She bakes the bread in a primitive oven. How much useless suffering we could spare her if we understood that the economy of the home is entitled to the same systematization as the economy of the field.

What becomes of the woman in such circumstances? She is perpetually enslaved, perpetually under the heavy yoke: she has no time to enjoy a book—no time even for the workers' newspaper *Davar* [The Word].[4] It is true, too, that the men in the *moshav* cannot indulge themselves in the luxury of sitting down to a book; they too are in constant harness. But men have had a better education in their boyhood, and

4. *Davar* (The Word), the labor daily, was founded by the Histadrut in 1925 as a means of addressing the Jewish worker and creating a public forum for the Palestine labor movement. Founded and edited by Berl Kaznelson (1887–1944), Palestine's preeminent Labor Zionist ideologue, *Davar* played a crucial role in the cultural, intellectual, and political affairs of the Yishuv. When in 1933 Labor assumed control of the World Zionist Organization and the Jewish Agency, *Davar* unofficially assumed executive responsibilities.

this helps to carry them through the later years. Most of our *haverim* learned the Hebrew language and its literature in their childhood, and when they arrived in Erez Israel felt themselves at home in the new culture.

But in the case of the woman her ignorance in this field not only hinders her from adapting herself to the life of Erez Israel, it also overshadows her relation to her children. She is not simply "occupied" with her children, she is completely sunk in them. The man, however faithful he be to his children and his farm, has only to shake them off in order to be free, and then he can easily take up public or cultural interests. He reunites himself with them as if he had never known the physical slavery of his farm.

And in this respect there is, I think, little difference between the woman in the *moshav* and the woman in the *kvuzah*. Whether she brings up her children herself, or sends them into the group under the care of the teacher, she is still a woman and a mother. But I sometimes believe that if a woman entered her own family life with a richer spiritual and educational equipment she would not, later, as a mother, feel herself so completely sundered from the world at large.

One more point I want to touch on: mutual help among the women of the *moshav*. I have observed that it is the women with little children who soon become used up. When such women are compelled to go away to a hospital, or a rest home, the problem arises: Who will take care of the children? As a rule our mutual aid consists in the fact that when a woman is ill, the neighbors will take turns looking after the children. But when it is a question of a protracted illness, this sort of help is inadequate. Then the mutual aid committee is compelled to hire, at its own expense, an outside person. But this is not the right way out [of the dilemma]. In the first place, the children suffer under this arrangement; in the second, we are averse to using hired help.

For cases of this kind a common children's house would be the right thing. Such a house should be constructed by the central workers' hospital in the [Jezreel Valley],[5] and the various committees of mutual aid in the *moshavim* should contribute to its support. It is up to the Moezet Hapoalot to work out the plan for this institution and to place it before interested circles.

The years will pass, our children will grow up, the farms will develop — and then life will be easier. Out of our sons and daughters will be built the Jewish family, rooted deep in its own soil. And then many of those problems that leave us helpless today will be answered of themselves.

---

5. The workers' hospital in Afulah was operated by the Histadrut.

In Nahalal

Dvorah Dayan (Nahalal)

W<small>HEN</small> I <small>LOOK BACK</small> on these last seven years—the years of my life in the settlement of Nahalal—I am aware of no striking or outstanding incident; the only thing that has happened is that human labor has made something out of nothing. I remember the sand dunes used to grow along the lake at home—hillock added to hillock. So my life has grown here, one hillock of labor after another, an economy with its own form and content, a family with its own tradition. Perhaps we all exaggerate when we speak about our past, yet I must say that in these seven years in Nahalal I did not for one moment forget that I was a wife, a mother, and the director of a household, an economic unit.

Nahalal is founded on the family; this is the inner being of the place. It may seem fantastic that people should be erecting a new structure on a foundation that is already shaky. And yet the life of Nahalal does not swallow up the personality of the woman; on the contrary, it strengthens and confirms it.

The form of our village is that of a circle around a center and the form is symbolic of our life. The center is the focus of our public life; meetings are held there, committees sit, problems are discussed, solutions found. One special committee sat long in continuous, earnest session to work out the new form of Jewish village life; in this difficult, intensive work the woman had no part.

At that time, all the families lived in wooden barracks of uniform pattern. Between barracks, a space of twenty meters; in each barrack a family—husband, wife, little children. This was the hardest time in our life. The men worked together; they ploughed the fields in common, for these were not yet divided out. In common, they also did the magnificent job of draining all the swamps in the Nahalal region.

Not a cow had yet been bought. Gardens were without hedges and without water. The produce was divided among families on a per capita basis, and there was barely enough to keep life going. Oil and kerosene were measured almost with a dropper. Collecting her day's supplies, feeding the children, gathering branches for fuel, cooking, washing the children and putting them to sleep, stopping up the holes and cracks in the walls—this took every instant of a woman's time.

And, later, lying in bed, I used to think: "Tomorrow—the same round." One thought tormented me: "What power compels me to stand such close, daily guard over my petty private interests?" What cord bound me, and could that cord never be broken?

That time did not last long: but it sticks in the memory like an intolerable day of *hamsin*[6] [heat spell] in the Jordan Valley.

The first productive work given to women in Nahalal was tending geese. Why geese, of all things, I don't remember; but I do remember that we all went at it with vast enthusiasm. At that, we did not have much joy of our work; I least of all. Geese are too libertarian; they like freedom, disorder, and company. It was a regular, troublesome job, every evening, to gather one's geese, separate them out from one's neighbor's, and drive them home. But at other times, when I stepped into the night, and I saw those white patches on the dark field, and heard the quack-quack of their conversations, it seemed to me that this was the authentic voice of the young colony, and then a happy warmth poured through my heart.

That first period passed without satisfaction and without creativity; and then the first money came for the upbuilding of the settlement. We bought cows—but they were Arab cows, which [produced little] milk. [Editors' note: see fig. 8.] Still, they were cows. Their voices came to us from the stalls—and sometimes the milk pail would have something in it.

We began to plant orchards and vineyards, to keep chickens and turkeys, to plant and water vegetables. The place began to hum. Hands and heads were busy all day long; the work took everything, body and mind.

Then came the years of growth. The children grew; the numbers of the cattle grew; the coops became more crowded, the summits of the fruit trees reached higher, the stocks in the vineyard spread out their nets.

The great, free world of creative work opened its gates to the woman.

---

6. *Hamsin* [heat spell] is the Arabic word for a dry hot wind that comes from the east.

The Meshek Hapoalot *in Nahlat Yehudah*

Miriam Shlimovich (Ein Harod)

W<small>E, THE</small> *haluzot* of the Third Aliyah (1919–23), found it hard to understand the women workers' movement of Erez Israel. We had been brought up in and by the Russian Revolution, at a time when women were occupying important economic and cultural positions. We believed that the wall which divided man's work from woman's had fallen forever. I, at least, was therefore astonished to find in Erez Israel separate women workers' institutions. If the enterprises to be found in the *mishkei hapoalot* are also to be found in the general farms, why the separate farms? But before long the realities of Palestinian life taught me to approach the women's question in quite another way.

Soon after my arrival I went to work in one of the *kvuzot* in Galilee. I was bitterly disappointed when I perceived how small the role was which the women played, how weak their influence on the common system. And doubt awoke in me. It was possible that the *haverah* did not earn her own keep, brought in less than she used up! Would it therefore not be better for me to return to my earlier work, and be a teacher again? There at least I would be sure of doing creative work, and of feeling no difference between myself and the *haverim*. I was offered the post of teacher in a large *kvuzah* that had a school; I promised to give my answer shortly, and meanwhile set out for the town of Tel Aviv.

On the way I made a detour to the *meshek hapoalot* at Nahlat Yehudah. The work of the women there made a tremendous impression on me. Here were women carrying on without help, on their own initiative and responsibility, and doing as well as the men. I made up my mind to try once more for land work. Hannah Chizhik, who directed the place, proposed that I work half-days on the farm, and in the evenings teach the women Hebrew. I accepted.

We worked under difficult conditions. The farm got its water from the colony of Nahlat Yehudah. We had no cistern or pipes of our own. I and another woman were busy all day long lugging cans of water from the barrels while another *haverah* had to run every so often to the colony council to plead for more water. And as soon as there was a quarrel between ourselves and the council, they threatened to cut off the water.

And there were actually days when we had to bring our water from Rishon Lezion, if we did not want the shoots in the nursery to wither and die, or let the cattle and fowl go thirsty. The summer was embittered by this situation and only in the rainy winter season did we breathe freely.

But, in spite of all the hardships and suffering, the work had life and content. The colonists who came to see "the work of the *haluzot*" had nothing but praise. It was a joy to look at the tree nursery. Before long our settlement had made a name for itself as a model farm. The women believed in themselves and in the path they were indicating for the women workers of Erez Israel.

I worked, as a matter of fact, all day long, and evenings I taught the [young women]. Teaching was a sort of continuation of the day's occupation; the lessons in Hebrew and in working class literature were echoes of our daily experience.

In the winter we sold the nursery, and the colony balance sheet showed a profit. This was triumph! It showed that the *meshek hapoalot* could stand on its own feet.

The settlement lacked not only water, but land. The Jewish National Fund had given us twenty-five *dunams* [approximately six acres]—but there was a neighboring plot of sixty *dunams* that the Jewish National Fund was supposed to buy for us. In the meantime, however, we used to rent land either from Arabs or from the Jewish colonists of Rishon Lezion. The story of how we bought the additional land for the women's farm of Nahlat Yehudah is long and complicated, but it is probably without a parallel in the history of the workers' movement in Erez Israel.

I shall give it in brief. Ever since this settlement was founded, in 1922, negotiations had been going on for that extra patch of sixty *dunams*. In the meantime the economic condition of the colony of Nahlat Yehudah went from bad to worse. The consequence was much quarreling between the colonists, and a perpetual bitterness of which we were frequently the victims.

When we saw that the perpetual threat of cutting off the water supply was endangering our tree nursery, which was the hub of our economy, we sent two women to the central office of Hapoel Hahaklai [Land Workers' Association] in Jerusalem,[7] and to the Zionist Executive.[8] We demanded a cistern for ourselves. This time we got it. As a rule we would fill the cistern in the evening, when the colony was not

---

7. Hapoel Hahaklai [Land Workers' Association] was among the earliest groups of organized workers of the Second Aliyah. It later became Merkaz Hahaklai [Central Farmers' Association].

8. The reference is to the executive body of the World Zionist Organization.

drawing water, and the supply would last us two or three days. It made things easier.

That had nothing to do, of course, with the fundamental problem of more land. Negotiations continued—and the owners suddenly doubled their price. The Jewish National Fund refused to pay the new high price; and we almost talked our hearts out, almost wore ourselves to nothing, before we managed to bring about an agreement.[9] But it was bought in the end, and we looked forward with longing for the summer when the deep plough would pass over the land, and the new land would be added in part to the vegetable garden and in part to the nursery. We also planned to have a vineyard and a patch to be sown with grass for the fowl and the cattle.

How easy it was to work after the new land was bought—it was as if we had become winged beings. We did not feel at all that we were working here temporarily, that the day would come when we would have to pack up, and find, each one for herself, a permanent place. The work was the main thing, and aside from it nothing mattered, neither our past nor our future. But I was aware of an obscure fear that on the general farms I would be swallowed up again by the powerful traditions of our feminine past, and I would no longer know the joy of independent, self-supporting work.

And now the big moment approached. We were expecting the tractor that was to do the deep ploughing, when suddenly there was a change of heart in the colony. A few men called the others together and persuaded them to prevent the ploughing. They, too, were in need of land. No one was worrying about their plight, and so in protest they would prevent us from ploughing our new land until land was bought for them, too! The tractor came. The colonists stood by their resolution, and no ploughing was done. We tried to argue with them, we threatened and pleaded in vain. The tractor stood idle for a few days, and finally returned. A profound depression settled on our farm—all our hopes were dashed to the ground.

And only a year later did we see the land ploughed. Part of it was turned over to the colonists and part of it to us. We began at last to carry out the complete plans of the settlement.

9. See Rahel Yanait Ben-Zvi's entry "Stages" in this section, note 2.

The Tobacco Kvuzah

Tovah Yafeh[10] (Dagania Bet)

W HEN OUR LITTLE *kvuzah* of women building trade workers [from Tel Aviv, who were known as "Dvorah" (Bee)] had finished putting up the house of *haver* M., it found itself confronted by the major problem of "to be, or not to be." We were holding the last position that women had won for themselves in the building trade, and it was hard to give this up. But employment at building was getting scarcer and scarcer, while within our hearts the longing for agriculture was growing stronger and stronger. In the end, we were approached with a plan to transform ourselves into a women workers' *kvuzah* for [planting] tobacco. The place was to be Kfar Tavor (Meshah). We accepted the offer of the Merkaz Hahaklai [Central Farmers' Association] [of the Histadrut] and were sent to Kfar Tavor. We had by that time, become scattered throughout the country; and it was no easy job getting us together again. But finally we arrived, some on foot, others in carts, at our new home. This was toward the end of Kislev [December] 1923.

The plan of the Merkaz Hahaklai was to create a women's working and training *kvuzah* on the plan of the *mishkei hapoalot* already existing in Judea: vegetables, dairy farming, and chicken raising. The difference would be that, instead of occupying ourselves with tree culture we would work on tobacco. There were to be twenty women in the group. The planting of the nursery for the tobacco shoots was to begin only in the spring. In the meantime, the colonists would employ us at tobacco packing. This was the agreement between the Merkaz Hahaklai and the Union of Galilee Colonists.[11] Also we were to live in a big wooden barrack. The barrack, we were told before setting out, was already on the spot. We would only have to put it up. Land had been rented for us from the colonists. We were to be initiated into the tobacco work by an expert. Other details would become clear in time.

The beginning of the enterprise did not augur very well. On arriving, we found that employment at binding tobacco was very hard to

10. The details of Tovah Yafeh's biography are unknown.
11. The Union of Galilee Colonists, a regional non-party association of Jewish settlers, was organized during World War I.

get. Even those workers who had long been on the spot could not find jobs. The barrack "already on the spot" was a myth. The rains began and we had not yet found a suitable piece of ground for our settlement: the actual plot that had been rented lay at a considerable distance from the colony, and within the colony there were no empty plots. It began to look as though the whole idea was absolutely chimerical. We only wondered what on earth we had been sent up here for . . .

Then the *haverim* came up from the Merkaz Hahaklai office. They got down to details, in regard to work and the budget. Money was appropriated for cows and chickens: a certain sum was fixed for each one of us to keep us going—a pound and a half per month. The total budget, an advance on our tobacco earnings, consisted of fifty [British] pounds for the barrack and twelve pounds per *haverah*, the latter provided by the Zionist Executive. This was the plan. Unfortunately it just did not work out.

We were supposed to earn our keep during the winter at tobacco packing, but it soon became clear that only a few of us would find work there. We therefore began to look for work elsewhere, and this naturally brought us into conflict with the other workers, who had been here before our coming and were now out of jobs. We were looked upon, by these workers, as spoiled and pampered persons; the Merkaz Hahaklai and the Zionist Executive were looking after us, while they depended on their daily earnings. The upshot of it all was that by the end of the winter our *kvuzah* had a big deficit.

Just before Passover, four of our members went to Tiberias to bake *mazot* [unleavened bread]. We thought that, with their pay, we would cover the winter loss. But this too turned out to be a dream—the pay was too low. And we could not get rid of the job for the simple reason that the responsibility for its execution had been assumed by the Labor [Bureau][12] in Tiberias. So our *haverim* had to work to the bitter end and come back empty-handed.

These were the "side-incomes" we earned! We were always compelled to do record jobs for the lowest pay. And meanwhile our own little farm began to clamor for our attention—just at the moment, naturally, when side-work was becoming more plentiful.

The greatest part of our time and energy was absorbed by the nursery for the tobacco. But it was worthwhile. It became the finest nursery in the colony. It ripened in time and gave us healthy shoots that took at once in the field. The colonists prophesied that we were going to become rich. "Experts" estimated that we had enough shoots to cover one

12. The reference here is to the headquarters of the Gdud Avodah [Labor Legion], which was located in Tiberias.

hundred *dunams* of soil. But here, too, we were doomed to disappointment. We had barely enough for fifty *dunams*. Instead of dropping the grain by handfuls, we planted it in rows, and two-thirds of the plot was wasted.[13]

The winter garden gave us little joy at first, which is usual with gardens that are cultivated extensively on grain land. Besides, we were late. When the rains began we had not yet got our seed for cabbages and cauliflower; the few beds of carrots and radishes were not successful, and when the potatoes became ripe they were systematically stolen.

We lost considerably on that garden. Not only did we fail to pay back the cost of the ploughing (I am leaving our own work out of the account); we barely got enough of an income to cover the seed and the fertilizer.

But for all that, the work in the garden was good. At the worst times the beets and tomatoes helped us out a little. Moreover, we were learning—and this meant a great deal for the women who had never worked on the land before.

The barrack was a continual pest. We planned to bring it over before the rains began, and put it up when the rains were on and there was plenty of free time. The exact opposite happened. The barrack was bought in the nearby Arab town of Jenin[14]—but not before mid-winter. To bring it to Kfar Tavor through the mud and rain would have cost too much; so we got it in the early spring when there was plenty of work to do among the colonists. We just about managed to put the barrack up on the public place in the colony before the time for tobacco planting came. The women themselves laid the foundations and did all the inside construction work. From the wood that was left over we managed to put up two more buildings: a coop for the chickens which had hatched, and a stall for the cows. In fact our *kvuzah*, which had originally belonged to the building trade, managed somehow to exercise its old craft till the last day of our stay in Kfar Tavor.

We were more fortunate with our hens. Looking after chickens does not come under the heading of "light work"—especially when the chickens are being kept as "lodgers" in someone else's yard. But our chickens responded magnificently. Ten hens gave us seventy chicks. We did not eat many of the eggs. At first we left them to be hatched, and

13. The settlers often resented the presence of seemingly patronizing experts; the trend began with the reluctance of the First Aliyah pioneers to heed the counsel of French administrators sent by Rothschild to save the failing *moshavot*.

14. Jenin is an Arab town in Samaria, located in the southern corner of the Jezreel Valley, near the junction of the roads leading to Haifa, Afulah, Nazareth, and Nablus (Shekhem). The population of Jenin was approximately 1,000 at the turn of the nineteenth and twentieth centuries.

later we fed them to the chicks. After that the hens stopped laying. But if not for the few eggs we did get, and if not for the young chicks, God knows what would have happened to many of our members, who, during that summer, went almost into a conspiracy of sickness.

The buying of the cows for our colony was handed over to one of the expert colonists. He did not trust the local product, and made a journey, therefore, to the Golan [Heights][15] in Transjordania among the Bedouin [Arab nomads], and came back with two cows and two calves, magnificent animals, wild and healthy as the land they were born in. One of the cows had a massive head almost like an ox, and the mere sight of her was terrifying.

The cows were brought before the barrack was ready; they, too, were therefore "lodged out." They were difficult animals to handle, and it was not always possible to milk them. It took us a month to break them in. Then the pasture gave out and the maize was not yet ready; other food was hard to get. And when the girl who looked after the cows fell sick, and another girl began to milk them, they seemed to fall to pieces. They stopped giving milk and turned so wild again that it was dangerous to go near them.

It almost came to a catastrophe. One day the girl went to milk the cows, and found herself caught between the two animals, and could not extricate herself from the narrow stall. The animals went wild and began to take revenge on her for their sufferings. After this incident, we had no alternative but to sell the wilder of the two animals, with its calf, to the colonist who had brought them. The other cow, which we also stopped milking shortly after, stood there in the yard like a fifth wheel on a cart. Unfortunately this "wheel" had to be fed, and not until the end of the year did we get rid of it.

When the *kvuzah* was ultimately dissolved, and each of us went her own way, the last darling calf, to which we had given the affectionate name of Hayim-Yankel, also went his way—to wit, on the long journey from which no Palestinian or any other calf ever returns.

But to resume the story. The tobacco, as I have said, was our principal occupation, and was supposed to make good all the losses we had incurred elsewhere.

We worked hard at the picking of the leaves, staying in the fields from dawn to evening. Our food was poor. We went out without having had even a cup of tea, and only at ten o'clock almost after a day's work

15. The Golan Heights is a mountainous and sparsely populated region northeast of Galilee. The cease-fire lines following Israel's War of Independence in 1948 placed the Golan in Syrian territory. The region became a major strategic liability for Israel, which captured it, suffering heavy losses, in the Six-Day War of 1967.

—did we get our first bite. Our strength began to give way. The numbers that went out every morning decreased, and with them decreased, naturally enough, the work turned out.

At the end of the summer we fell victims to a new epidemic, [plain] "weakness."[16] The women crawled rather than walked around, with low temperatures, their legs giving way under them, their heads always aching. It was impossible to send these women to the hospital, and the doctor's advice sounded like a poor joke: "Plenty of good food, eggs, milk, etc. . . . ."

The bad food prevented us from getting better. By the month of Elul [September] we had no one fit to work in the kitchen. As soon as a girl tried, she collapsed. Our barrack looked like a hospital.

When we first came to Kfar Tavor we were quite certain of success; we were going to make money. And the shopkeepers and colonists must have felt the same way, because they gave us all the credit we wanted. A few months later the pressure of the debts began to make itself felt. We begrudged ourselves even our meager meals, and every extra penny had to go to the shopkeepers. Whenever we got an order on the cooperative supply of the Galilee colonists,[17] part of it was deducted on account of the debts. And when our *kvuzah* began to buy direct in Tiberias, we had to pay out part of our purchases. On top of our general distress, we had the uncomfortable feeling that our creditors were in the right.

The little debts tormented us more than the big ones. There were certain things that we simply could not do without: milk for the sick, wheat, straw for the animals, cotton thread, etc.—and all this we could not get for cash; we had to have credit. There were two sources of loss—in the buying and in the selling. We became experts in exchanging goods; some of the women were so skilled that without them our whole machinery would have stopped working. And the time, the energy, the labor we expended on all this! It seems to me that only for the sake of a *kvuzah* would people put up with this sort of thing. But that daily struggle with pettiness degraded the ideal which had brought us all to the [settlement].

So far I have said nothing about the extraordinary qualities which became evident among the members of our group during those hard times. The responsibility was carried by all of us, and we were bound together by our love of the work, and during the darkest days this love

16. The reference here is to malaria; see part I, note 73.

17. During World War I, Palestine was virtually cut off from outside markets. As a result, foodstuffs and resources were generally supplied to the Jewish colonies by Hamashbir [The Provisioner]. On the situation in Palestine during the war and the plight of the Yishuv, see part I, note 67 and part V, note 5.

was our one reservoir of strength, our one consoling possession. We looked upon the belongings of the *kvuzah* as something sacred, and guarded the common store from the smallest loss. The women were considerate of each other in the division of the work. Above all, no complaints were heard even in the most difficult hours. When new *haverot* came up they were inducted into the work and in a short time they were on the same footing as the old.

But we had gone off the beaten track into a place where the labor element was lacking, and a cultural life was impossible. Those women who could have helped us in this respect were too taken up with their physical tasks. We hadn't the money for books, or even for a subscription to a newspaper; and the continuous, draining labor, together with the unprescribed hours, prevented us from concentrating on cultural work. Once or twice we exerted ourselves and started something, but we had to let it fall.

It was only when the final decision came to dissolve the *kvuzah* that we flung ourselves on books. A few of our *haverot* began to read the works of [Aharon David] Gordon; we knew that our sufferings had not yet come to an end—but we wanted at least to understand what we were suffering for.

The Birth of the Havurah

M.S.[18] (Ein Harod)

THE BIG CRISIS began in Erez Israel in the year 1925, and its first and hardest blows fell on the women workers.[19] In the labor councils of the towns it was not understood that special methods must be applied to the problem of the women in the crisis, and even the most thoughtful leaders seemed to believe that there was no way of combating women's unemployment.

A mood of despair seized the *haverot* in the cities. All ways seemed to be closed. There were new women pioneers who had been preparing for years before they entered the country, loyal and steadfast spirits; and even they began to fall under the influence of the enemies of the Histadrut and of the working class. The small group of Communists[20] exploited, at all town meetings, this mood of despair, and a feeling of resentment began to rise against the Histadrut which was accused of "sacrificing the women workers."

The few *mishkei poalot* which then existed could absorb a few dozen more *haverot*; and the handful of women who entered the *kibbutzim* remained idle. When the men workers began to feel the crisis, the women had already been suffering for some time. The Moezet Hapoalot tried to introduce women into the building trade, but without real success. One by one the women left the new trade, and only a few obstinate spirits remained. The situation became steadily worse. The [Central]

18. The writer of this essay appears to be Miriam Shlimovich; however, details of her biography are unknown.

19. See note 2 in this section.

20. The first Communist organization in Palestine was Mifleget Poalim Sozialistim [Socialist Workers' Party], founded largely by former members of Poalei Zion [Workers of Zion] who opposed unification with Ahdut Avodah [Unity of Labor] in 1919. The group, which was extremely anti-Zionist, became the Palestine Communist Party (PCP) in 1921. Most of the members were Jewish, but it was oriented largely towards the Arab *fellahin*. Meanwhile, although communism was technically illegal in Palestine until 1941, the PCP was able to recruit members from a variety of sources. Young people seeking excitement in covert and revolutionary movements were targeted as well as disillusioned *haluzim* and people who had come to Palestine for reasons other than Zionism. In 1924, the Histadrut expelled the PCP members for siding with Arabs against the Jewish settlers. Many PCP members returned to the Soviet Union, where a large portion were later killed in Stalin's purges.

Women's Committee of the Vaad Hapoel of the Histadrut looked in vain for a solution.

It was then—in the winter of 1926—that Hannah Chizhik suggested the formation of the *havurah* form of commune in the towns and in the colonies. In the *meshek hapoalot*, women work on a communal basis while they learn agriculture; agriculture is, however, their main occupation and purpose. In the *havurah*, there would be some agriculture, too, but the main support would be the wages earned by members at outside employment, in factories or in farms. The capacity of the *meshek hapoalot* was limited to the needs of the settlement and its economy. But the *havurah* could always expand. In the *havurah* the land work would be intensive—an inner support; outside work would be taken wherever it could be found. Evenings, the outside worker would return to the *havurah*. She would have a home. The organization would help her to fight her battles, and would relieve her, too, of the dreadful loneliness of her own life. The purpose of the *havurah* was therefore manifold, and it aimed at nothing less than the transformation of the life of the individual woman worker, and its integration with a collective life in new surroundings. The inner, agricultural work of the *havurah*, beside supporting the institution, would also give it a character of permanence, binding the *haverim* to the place and to each other.

This new proposal was placed before the Central Women's Committee, and it was so timely that it was accepted at once. On its side, the Labor Department of the [World Zionist Organization] set aside a certain sum for the founding of the *havurot*.

During the crisis, most of the men workers and a great many of the women received the famous *siyuah* [aid],[21] but the women workers' movement conquered its own despair and broke for itself the demoralizing influence of this reluctantly accepted form of help. Hundreds of workless women preferred to join the *havurot*, and most of the members of the Moezet Hapoalot occupied themselves with the direction of this new form of labor collective. It should be mentioned that at this time another effort was made to relieve the distress of the women work-

---

21. The *siyuah* [aid] was a sum of money added to the salaries of groups of laborers and individual pioneers who performed itinerant agricultural work for the World Zionist Organization during Palestine's economic recession in the mid-1920s. (See Rahel Yanait Ben-Zvi's entry "Stages" in this section, note 2.) The subsidy was intended especially for the large numbers of pioneers who required training and did not have permanent homes. Following Palestine's economic recovery, the *siyuah* was cancelled and roughly a third of the intentional communal groups it had spawned disbanded. The organization of various *kibbutzim* into distinct *kibbutz* movements at this juncture was brought about, in part, as a result of this episode.

ers. Thanks to the efforts of the Tel Aviv labor council large numbers of women were admitted to the factories in Tel Aviv.

The first *havurot* to be organized were those of Tel Aviv—one in the center of the town, the other to the north. They took in sixty members. It may be said without exaggeration that today these two *havurot* are the finest institutions which the labor movement of Tel Aviv can boast. They created, in a short space of time, a model farm, and began to exert a profound influence—by their mere existence—on the women workers of the city.

In the spring of 1926 was held the third conference of the women workers, which accepted formally the plan of the *havurot*. Moezet Hapoalot proposed to the Zionist Executive that *havurot* be founded in different parts of the country; and so ready was the time for this work that, even before the Zionist Executive had accepted the plan, *havurot* began to spring up of their own accord. Moezet Hapoalot was unable to concentrate and guide the creative energies which the proposal had released. Nor did the budget of the Moezet Hapoalot anywhere near meet the needs of the new institutions—the less so since part of the budget had to be spent directly on the unemployed.

But fortune was with the *havurot*. At the critical moment, the newly founded Pioneer Women's Organization in America[22] forwarded the sums needed for the organization of the new units.

The new *havurot* opened to the women workers doors that had been firmly closed to them until then. They began to play a significant role in the life of the Histadrut and created a new cultural element in the worker's movement. Dozens of women received in the *havurah* their first knowledge of land-work, and later spread this knowledge throughout the country.

22. See Mark A. Raider, "Pioneer Women's Organization," *Jewish Women in America: An Historical Encyclopedia*, ed. by Paula Hyman and Deborah Dash Moore (New York: Routledge, 1997), vol. 2, pp. 1071–1077.

The Havurah *of Petah Tikvah*

Rivkah Broizman (Havurat Hapoalot, Petah Tikvah)

W<small>HEN</small>, <small>IN THE MONTH</small> of Elul [September] in 1926, a group of us decided to found a *havurah* in Petah Tikvah, we had not received any promise of help. We simply went at it. From one of the *kvuzot* we managed to get three old tents, and we set them up on the narrow lot opposite the Workers' Club in Petah Tikvah—much to the astonishment of the passers-by.

The morning after we had set up the tents, we went out to look for work. Meanwhile, a grocer promised us food on credit until the first wages came in. We were five in number at the outset, and two weeks later our number had swelled by an additional seven, all new arrivals in Erez Israel. They came to our *havurah* because they were out of work; they had heard about us, but what a *havurah* was, and what life in general meant in Erez Israel, they scarcely understood. Only yesterday these youngsters had left their parents' homes in Europe; their bodies had not yet been broken in to physical work. And evenings we all sat in the tents silent, depressed, our minds filled with memories of home.

Winter was approaching, and the doubts grew with the nights: Would we succeed? Would we hold together and found a permanent *havurah*? Would these new *haverot* stand up under the strain? Would we ultimately get a piece of land of our own, like the other *kvuzot* in the colony? And would we be able to build a barrack before the rains came upon us?

What we longed for most was a piece of land of our own, so that we might create a little farm for ourselves. We knew, of course, that we were a *havurah*, and not a *meshek hapoalot*; farming and land-work would therefore never be our main occupation; but all of us felt the same desire to see the first green things starting up on our patch of soil. After much effort the Merkaz Hahaklai [Central Farmers' Association] obtained a piece of land for us in the colony, and we moved to our new quarters. New *haverot* came to us every day, and we had to put up a new tent. And then the winter came.

We were afraid of the first rain; the tents stood on an elevation and were not protected from the wind. And then the clouds opened suddenly, and a shout of laughter and happiness went through the tents.

Every new burst of rain evoked in those young hearts a new burst of joy. On the morning after the first rain we broke the ground for our vegetable garden.

The struggle for work was long and cruel. The majority of the women, whether individual or belonging to the *kibbutzim*, were content with minor jobs, the kind of thing that was considered suitable for women. The *havurah* was the first institution in the colony to drop the distinction, and to demand work of any kind. The only measure was the physical strength of the worker. Our example was followed by the other women in the colony. Our group soon became famous among the colonists.

Evenings, the *haverot* came home from the work which it had been so difficult to find. The table was narrow, the food meager, but the conversation eager and comradely. There were always new things to tell. And after supper we went off to the colony to a meeting or a lecture. Frequently enough, there were reports read in our own group. Our folk had worked themselves into the life of the colony; and if they were absent from some occasion, it was noticed at once.

The barrack for the kitchen and dining room was not finished until well on in the rainy season. We had no incubator of our own, and we did not wish to lose a whole year. So for the first period, we brought forth our chicks in the *havurah* in north Tel Aviv. And when we had the chicks, we crowded a little closer together and made room for them in a section of the barracks. We still slept in tents, of course. After the chicks we brought in beehives.

Winter was raging now. Every day another tent would go over in the wind, and every day new [young women] came to join the *havurah*. The *havurah* grew steadily, and the new *haverot*, as they came along, absorbed its spirit readily and threw themselves heartily into the work.

Our little daily worries and triumphs made the time pass quickly; here was the winter gone, and we were still in tents. The whole institution—chickens, nursery, beehives—had grown and thriven. The "new" *haverot* had become part of our life, and felt themselves bound to the world of the worker and its ideals. The first year passed and we could say with a calm certainty that we had been successful. We had founded a new economic unit of workers.

Women Build Houses

Tehiyah [Lieberson]

THE TOWN OF Tel Aviv was in the full swing of expansion. For the first time, thousands of Jews had entered the building trade and had mastered it. And the Jewish woman worker began to batter at the doors of the trade. But it was not so easy to get in.

The men had quite a number of reasons for keeping us out. Some said the work was too strenuous for women. Others argued that if women were admitted into the building trade communes, which contracted for work as a group, the output would decrease and the pay with it. The women were not very sure of themselves—but they pressed hard for admission. The fight went on for quite a time, and finally the workers' council of Tel Aviv decided that every building trade *kvuzah* had to admit two women.

This was the way I was admitted to one of the *kvuzot*. I knew that I was being received not spontaneously, but under orders. The whole struggle seemed to me a fantastic thing. I asked myself: Have the men forgotten the time—it was only yesterday—when they, too, were unskilled, and their contracts resulted in deficits? And aren't there, among men, too, the strong and the weak, the efficient and the inefficient. Why this hostile attitude, from the outset, to the *haverah*?

I remembered, too, that before setting out for Erez Israel I had worked everywhere in the Hehaluz [training centers] on a footing of absolute equality with the men. In time, I used to think, we will establish the same equality in Erez Israel. But when I got here I could not stand the amused irony, the patronizing, superior attitude of the stronger toward the weaker. I wanted, therefore, to give up my right to enter the building *kvuzah*; but friends of mine in Moezet Hapoalot persuaded me to hold on; just because the men looked at it as they did, it was my duty to go in, and to try and create a new relationship.

Without any particular liking for it, I reported to the tent which housed the council of the *kvuzah*. The place was jammed with noisy, arguing men, and the moment I entered I was aware of a reaction of astonishment. One of the men made a silly joke about "our suffragettes," but the man in charge turned out to be friendly. He told me what kind of work I was to do, and when I would start. I went out of the tent encouraged.

I knew that the first days would be the hardest. In every group of men, you are sure to find some who like to make a newcomer the butt of their jokes—and woe to the newcomer if he doesn't know how to take it. I also knew that there was a great difference between the land-work in Hehaluz or the "black labor" (our Palestinian name for heavy, unskilled work) which I had been doing till now, and the cement work which I would begin tomorrow.

At five o'clock I reported. The leader of the group showed every one his place; mine was with the cement workers.

A couple of workers rolled up a barrel of cement, and emptied it on a heap of sand and stones. I stood by and poured on water while the men mixed. The mixture, when ready, was carried over to the building place in buckets or on planks.

They worked slowly at first, yesterday's weariness still being in their limbs. Gradually, the work livened up. Gradually, I, too, was caught up in the rhythm of it. One of the men began to sing, the others joined in, all in time with the work. Everything became light and easy and joyous.

But in comparison with the tasks of the men, mine was a trifling one, and I felt the slight. "Is this going to be my day's work?" I asked.

One of the men answered my question with another: "What other kind of work can we give a woman?"

"Well, who used to pour the water before I came?"

"We used to take turns."

I said I would take turns too. I was not going to pour water all day long.

So I changed off with one of the men, and began to carry cement. The *haver* who loaded the cement on to the plank said: "That's all right. Let her lift this a couple of times—she'll be asking for something easier."

And I must confess that the load nearly made me stagger. But I called up all my willpower, and walked with steady steps, as if this was the most usual thing for me. I knew a dozen pair of eyes were watching me slyly, and if I faltered once there would be a shout of laughter.

Later I noticed that the *haver* who did the loading was putting more on my plank than on anyone else's. I understood—and said nothing. After a while I stood still, and looked at him with a smile. He became confused. The *haver* who carried the plank with me kept complaining that it was too heavy. He wondered how on earth I could lift my end, and became angry with the loader. But I asked him to keep quiet and wait. I was right. The next time the load was considerably lighter, and the loader got his share of abuse from the others.

The same story was repeated when it came to filling in the foundations. And in this way a fight went on between me and a couple of the men, all day long, until I forced them to give way. The next day they confessed that instead of getting a laugh at my expense, they had learned to respect me.

My reputation as a good worker was soon established, and I was looked upon as one of the best. When the elections came round for the council of the building workers, my name was put up.

There isn't very much to this story. I only tell it to help make clear the struggle that the women workers of Erez Israel had to wage when trying to break into a new field.

The "Independent" Woman

Hannah [Chizhik] (Tel Aviv)

THE WORKING WOMAN has one ideal: she wants to work and earn on a footing of equality with her husband. And in order to do this she has to employ a girl to look after the house. And at once a "class-contrast" is created, and little conflicts become unavoidable. I come home evenings after a heavy day's work, and I find the house not done. It angers me. Isn't it the duty of the [female aid] to keep the house clean and in order? But this [aid] is a *haverah* of mine, and she surely didn't come to Erez Israel for the purpose of dusting the rooms in my house. She surely left her home over there after a bitter struggle with her parents because she couldn't stand the old family life and the old family work; now she is trapped in the same round, and with strangers!

But what about me, her "employer"? When I get home after a full day's work, another day's work begins for me, because in her eight working hours she can't get through. So when I do get a free moment, I can't keep my eyes open. What, then, has happened with our struggle for a fixed working day?

And for us women of the towns, I see only two alternatives and both of them lead us away from our goal. The first is to leave our trades and become old-fashioned housewives once more, supported by our husbands; the second is to be both worker and housewife . . .

And a new question comes up. We, the women workers of Erez Israel, regard our work as something primary in our lives; through work we will regain our personalities. And yet I must ask myself, what is my authentic inner relationship to my work? Why did I feel so utterly wretched when my husband was unemployed? Would I have felt so bad about it if he had been working, and *I* had been unemployed?[23] I am compelled to answer, "No!" The despair of the woman when her husband is not earning is grounded in something more than mere economics, for that attitude is unchanged even if she is earning enough to keep the entire household going.

It may be that this curious attitude toward our own work has to do

23. The emphasis appears in the original English text.

with the instinctive knowledge that some day we will have to leave the work because of the child. And therefore—though we do not acknowledge it—we have a different, a lighter relationship to our own work. And this relationship deprives us of what is most important in life—belief in our own forces, respect for our own selves. And we will never know the feeling of harmonious work as long as we do not know a complete inner compulsion to earn our own livelihood.

And when we do find a woman who has complete faith in her own strength, we see her crumbling under the double yoke—her job and her family.

And of course we rebel against the intolerable yoke which such a woman carries. And is nothing left but that my *haverah*, whom I take into the house, shall assume the burden of the family that I myself am not willing to bear?

Wife of a Haver

Ziporah Bar-Droma[24] (Tel Aviv)

In Erez Israel there came a parting of the ways. Over there, in the Russian exile, *haverim* and *haverot* had been equal comrades in the movement. We worked together, suffered together in the prisons and in the remote countries to which we were expelled:[25] the moment the first pioneer certificates[26] reached us, admitting us into Erez Israel, we were divided into the two classes: *haverim* and *haverot*.

The very first instructions we got from Erez Israel hinted at this inequality, and when we landed we were actually separated into two groups. In the one group were those who were "building the country"; in the other were those who would take care, in everyday matters, of "the builders of the country." And always we hear the same formula: "This piece of work will need so many men, and the men will employ so many women . . ."

Over there, in the exile, we had [*together*] passed through a common preparation, in the schools and in the movement. *Here* the women workers have organized themselves into a *separate* labor movement.[27] In the exile, we felt ourselves to be adult participants in the social process; here our education begins again in the kindergarten.

We found here hardly any bond or relationship between the unmarried working girl, who feels that she is a full-fledged member of the Histadrut, and the working woman who is married. It was not a change of status in the life of the same women—it was a division into two worlds. And this explains the unnaturalness of the women workers' movement and the inner struggles and contradictions in the soul of the *haverot*.

When a *haver* chooses a trade, he enters into a permanent relationship with his professional union. But the woman feels within herself—and others are there to remind her—that she is only a guest, a tempo-

---

24. The details of Ziporah Bar-Droma's biography are unknown.

25. The reference is to Siberia and Central Asia.

26. Following World War I, the Jewish Agency, acting in behalf of the British Mandatory, distributed a limited number of certificates to would-be immigrants to Palestine. The certificates were awarded on a selective basis and East European *haluzim* often received preferential treatment.

27. The emphasis here appears in the original Yiddish text.

rary member, in the trade organization. And when she marries, she has not even the right to the professional status of "houseworker"—no, not though she meets completely the statutory demand of the Histadrut, which says that those are entitled to membership who live solely by their own physical or mental labor, without employing someone else. No, she is admitted into the Histadrut as "that *haver*'s wife."

It is true that the housewife has the legal right to her own member-ship card in the Histadrut; but as the dues are obligatory only in the case of the bread winners of the family, few women have availed themselves of their privilege, and they remain on the roll as "wives of *haverim*."

And perhaps that invidious title, "the wife of a *haver*," does belong properly to such women as come into the labor movement only through their husbands. But does it fit those women who were brought up in the Erez Israel labor movement, and who did their duty by it for many years?

And who of us has not seen "the worker's wife" working in other people's houses, or doing other people's laundry, while her children run around neglected, or cared for by her out-of-work husband? Who has not seen those unhappy women who, without any help from the His-tadrut, carry the full burden of their little children and of a chronically sick husband? Are not these women entitled to a place in the Histadrut as full-fledged members, and not merely as the "wives of *haverim*"?

This transition from *haverah* to "*haver*'s wife" influences the whole of our social life. Even at the women workers' conferences, the married members occupy a separate "professional" rubric—the rubric of "work-ers' wives."

We forget too often that the "*haver*'s wife" is a mother who must bring up a new generation in the tradition of the Histadrut. The women workers' movement has sinned against labor in not having provided such women with a special role, special duties and functions. Had this not happened we would not now be faced by the fact that not only is the woman a temporary member of the Histadrut, but actually a temporary member in the labor movement! We should not have to be witnesses of a situation in which the home of the *haver* is gradually weaned away, in spirit, from the ideals of the Histadrut.

The "*haver*'s wife" has little share in social life: she is seldom to be found even at those gatherings which are occupied with her personal problems, such as parents' meetings in the schools, in the trade organi-zation to which her husband belongs, at the conferences of the workers' quarters in which her family is inscribed—not even though, later on, she will have to obey all the resolutions that are passed there. The work-ing class mother is so sunk in her daily work and worries, and so exhausted by them, that she becomes separated from her own class, and is wholly isolated from the world.

And is there no way out of the impasse? In the *moshav ovdim*, there is a system of mutual help among the women not less than among the men. And though it is true that the labor class is more scattered in the towns, and is likewise less strongly unified, it is not impossible to institute a system of mutual help. We need good children's homes, communal kitchens, playgrounds which should be open several hours a day, and on holidays and the Sabbath as well. We also need a separate sick fund, so that we can substitute for the sick mother in the house and in looking after the children. As things are now, the sick housewife must either go on working until she collapses and her children are simply thrown on the street, or else she must get "cheap" help. All this could be avoided if the bond between the working class mother and her kind were not allowed to break, if the women workers' movement would not treat us like an alienated branch of the organization—if, in brief, our problem were considered everyone's problem.

The path that lies before the working class mother is not an easy one, nor has it yet been marked out. It is one that uses up the person, leaving scars forever on the soul; and much of this suffering is due to the unjust attitude adopted toward us by society.

PART IV

With Children

Fundamental Problems

Nina Rikhter (Bet Alfa[1])

I want to speak here about the group upbringing—as distinguished from the home upbringing—of children, about the place of this problem in our life, and about my work in it.

First: What impelled the *kvuzah* and the *kibbutz*—the two forms of workers' communes—to abandon home for group upbringing?

The idea springs originally from the will to deepen the relationship and strengthen the bond between the individuals in the group. To this end, we are ready to relinquish what is dearest to us into the hands of the collective whole. We know that the future of the group as such depends on the spirit in which our children are brought up. There is an additional motive: we want to make women free in social and family life.

This group upbringing of children already has a history in Erez Israel, and a tradition has slowly been created. Unfortunately, we are so absorbed and used up by the daily grind that we cannot go into the root principles of the question, though this would clarify many problems for us, and release new energies. At the present, every *kvuzah* and *kibbutz* has followed its own path; group upbringing is an established principle; but no general principle of method, and no general formulation of the problem, have yet been reached.

Is it possible, at this stage of our history, to sum up the results of this group upbringing, and state what it has given us? Can we say that the *kvuzah* really feels itself to be the *baal habayit* [householder] of its own children? Have the parents been freed from the special worry of their own—and of nobody else's—children? And has the woman really been liberated?

It is not easy to answer the first two questions. From the outside it does look as though the children today belong to the *kvuzah*. In the actualities of life the thing has not gone so far by any means. The *kvuzah* does try to see to it that its children shall lack nothing, either materially or spiritually. But what we consider of importance is the inner attitude

1. Bet Alfa, founded in 1922 at the base of Mt. Gilboa, served as the first settlement for Hashomer Hazair and an eastern outpost for the central valleys.

of the group and of every individual *haver* toward the children and the inner feeling of responsibility toward every newborn child.

The situation differs from *kvuzah* to *kvuzah*. The readiness to assume the cares of the upbringing of the children depends on the inner condition of the *kvuzah*, on the tone and spirit of the common life. And just as we have nowhere worked out fully a final and harmoniously interwoven living-together of the *haverim*, so we have not reached the final stage in which the children belong to the group as a whole.

And how is it with the parents? To us the act looks simple and natural enough: but it is not easy for the mother to relinquish her newborn child to the children's home.[2]

There is much to be said about the general influence of the collective form of life on the family, but I want to consider only the fact that among us the child grows up away from the parents' home. In our form of life it is not easy, even in a general way, to create close and narrow bonds between parents and children. The hours of labor which we have to put in every day leave the father little time for his children, especially when the latter have a separate home, and have their own regulations. Sometimes the parents may be free but cannot visit the children because this would create disorder. In a family that lives its own separate life, it is the mother who creates the living relationship between father and child.

In our case, however, it is not the mother who feeds and tends the child, for the child enters into its own social life, and has its own group interests. Yet, in spite of this, our children always long for their parents and look forward eagerly to every meeting with them. The child suffers if the parents do not come when they are expected, and often the relationship between them is tense and nervous.

The real solution of the problem regarding the relation of the family to the communal group, and of the communal group to the child depends on two factors. First, will the collective be able to create that human atmosphere in which parents will give up their children to the group without fear or regret? Second, will the *haverim* who have no children of their own be prepared to share to the full the burden of the upbringing of the children, with its joy and suffering?

One thing we have achieved by our method of child upbringing, and that is the liberation of the mother in the group. For this we may be

2. In the *kvuzot* and *kibbutzim* of the pre-state period, children were raised communally and lived in baby houses and children's houses. Their parents generally occupied a separate room of their own, equivalent to a small apartment. As the functions of child care were institutionalized, group child care became a regular feature of the collective's work roster, and the concepts of "group upbringing," "the educational group," and the *metapelet* [child care worker] were established.

grateful. We see now that it is only by the method of group upbringing for the children that the mother can be a free member of the social structure. Once relieved of this heavy yoke, certain that everything will be done, physically and spiritually, for the good of her child, the mother can devote herself to the work that she has chosen. The very possibility of choosing her work gives the woman a footing of equality in the family and makes possible a free, unforced relationship between husband and wife.

In the whole complex of practical questions raised by our methods, the most important is this: does our children's home create for the young ones a separate and isolated little world, or is it part of the world of the grownups? In the small *kvuzah* this question is not altogether actual, for there the number of the children is small, and the whole place, with all its workings, is perpetually present to the child. Hence, in the small *kvuzah*, the approach to the child is easy and simple. But in the large settlements there is a danger that the children will be, as it were, locked up within the walls of their children's home. This is something which must not be permitted to happen if we want the child to remain bound to the group, to the *kibbutz* and its economy, to the work and to everything that we hold dear. To achieve the desired aim, the *kibbutz* must be constantly aware of what is going on in the children's home, and the life of the young ones must constitute a matter of deep daily interest.

And now let us turn to the personnel occupying the key posts in the process—those who are set over the child during this crucial formative period. We must face the truth that this important function in the organism of the *kibbutz* is entrusted too frequently to individuals with little knowledge and experience. For the number of our children keeps growing, and we have not concentrated on the problem of the children's home those energies and that devotion to which it is entitled.

The question of the right [woman worker] in the children's home is one of the most important in the settlement. She is responsible not only for the physical and mental condition of the young, but also for the general atmosphere that dominates the home and, in large measure, for the attitude of the group toward the home. We have few working women specialists in this line. In the course of time, the woman in charge learns much from the actual work, but there is, meanwhile, a constant and heavy drain on her strength and her nerves.

We shall establish our children's homes on true and firm foundations only when we shall have prepared the right number of skilled and devoted *haverot* who will know how to engage the interest of the entire settlement in their work. First, we must make things lighter for the woman in the children's home by improving her working conditions. The working hours must be shortened. (In some of the *kvuzot* the educator works ten and twelve hours a day.) The woman in charge of young ones must have a clear head, and must always be in the right mood. Further, the *haverim* must understand and appreciate the work of the educator; and the latter, after a time, must be given the opportunity to finish her training, either in Erez Israel or abroad.

A series of problems is raised by the kindergarten teacher. With children up to two years of age even the unskilled teacher may be used, for she hopes that her healthy, natural mother instinct will help her out, and that she will learn from the work itself. But it is otherwise with children between the ages of three and six, and none of our *haverot* would dare to accept the responsibility without the requisite training. And therefore, the trained kindergarten teacher must be looked for outside of the commune, and this creates special difficulties.

In most cases, the education of these [young women] is unsuited to our life and our form of community, and it is not easy to transplant them into the soil of a *kibbutz* [in Erez Israel]. The [young woman] herself is assailed by a thousand doubts, and often the *kibbutz* itself cannot help her; and it is the children who pay, in the end, for all these experiments. Often enough, this situation simply has to be accepted. But the ultimate solution will be found when the *kibbutzim* choose the right persons and then give them an opportunity to get the proper training.

And now something regarding the mother in her relation to our institutions, particularly the baby house.

The woman who has lived for some years in the *kibbutz*, and knows our institutions, certainly believes in this group upbringing as the best. And yet she suffers from a deep inner division. Nearly every woman wants to feed and tend her own little one. She wants to look at it every now and then, watch its daily development, particularly during that wonderful period of the first year. And if our mothers must surrender all this they suffer and long. Besides this, a mother trembles much more about the care of a newborn baby than about an older child, and with justice, because the first year of a child's life is the most important and the most dangerous. These denied emotions are responsible for the atmosphere of tension often to be found round our baby houses. It is true that in most cases the mother has perfect confidence in the devotion of the women who work in the baby house; and that confidence grows from year to year, it becomes mutual and is accompanied by understanding. And yet these difficult elements cannot be eliminated. They come most vividly to the fore when the child is sick. However strongly the mother controls herself, she still loses her peace of mind and her feeling of security. Her confidence in the *haverah* in charge weakens. She begins to make demands which, objectively seen, are inadmissible, and the two women cease to understand each other. At such moments, we perceive the genuine difficulty of group upbringing for children, and we see ourselves lacking in self-training and self-control.

The struggle between intelligence and instinct emerges clearly in another case—when one mother comes to the help of another who can no longer give her baby milk. The possibility of this form of mutual aid is one of the strongest points in favor of our baby houses. And the practice is a usual and accepted one. But sometimes it occurs that the child of the second mother needs more milk, and then it is very difficult for the first mother to ration her own child.

These are the details that make clear what goes on in the heart and mind of a mother who gives up her child to the group. It is unreasonable always to expect complete self-control; and we do wrong to accuse a mother of all sorts of weaknesses when this struggle is going on within her. This, indeed, is the moment for the most intimate kind of understanding.

The economic side of our children's homes has been the subject of much discussion, for this is the foundation of the whole system of group upbringing. Why is the cost so high for each child, and why do we need so many workers in the homes?

The majority of our group institutions are in the *kvuzot* and the *kibbutzim* of the Jezreel and Jordan Valleys, and this is one of the reasons for the high cost of upbringing.

Babies cannot be given cheap care in a climate which is hard even on grownups. The heat and the dryness are a strain on the children. In the summer months, they lose their appetite, they vomit and run temperatures. Naturally not all of them suffer alike. Our climate bears hardest on babies that have just been weaned—that is, on babies between eight and eighteen months of age. The "older" ones, from two years on, gradually acclimatize themselves. When a child has been weakened by the great heat, it needs the special attention of a nurse if its later development is not to suffer.

There is another factor making for high costs. When a large number of children live in the same house, the danger from infectious sicknesses increases. To combat this danger, we have instituted a rigid system of hygiene, and this system, again, means money and personnel. And it is well to notice at this point that in times of epidemics in the country the children in our *kibbutzim* suffer less than all others. Official statistics also show that the infant mortality is lower in the group homes than among children brought up in individual families; they show further that our mortality rate compares well with that of the most developed countries in the world.

We are naturally doing what we can to reduce the costs and, in many of the *kvuzot*, they are considerably lower than they were a few years ago. But here again the possibility of advance depends in large measure on the creation of a number of skilled and permanent child specialists. It is only through such workers that we shall improve our system: and it is up to all the comrades in the *kvuzot* and the *kibbutzim* to help along. The collectivist workers' movement as a whole must create a common scientific institution for the solution of the problems of group upbringing for children.

Group Upbringing and the Child

Eva Tabenkin (Ein Harod)

I T WAS BEFORE our marriages that we, the first *haverot* in the *kvuzot*, decided in advance that our children would be brought up in the group; not because we considered it a necessity of our life in the *kvuzah*, but because we regarded it as a high ideal. Later, having become mothers, we still clung to this view.

We were proud and happy in the first trials of our strength and faith, in Dagania, Kineret, and Tel Adas. Calmly, and in full consciousness of what we were doing, we chose the ablest of our *haverot* for the task, and were prepared to entrust our children to her care while we went about our own work. Those first years exacted heavy sacrifices from us—of all the trials we underwent in the country and in the *kvuzah*, this was the hardest and most important. It will always remain so, for with every mother the old story begins anew.

Now, after these ten years of experience let us make an accounting and let us choose one standard of evaluation—the physical and mental development and well-being of the child.

It has become clear to us that for school children the richest and most harmonious form of upbringing is the children's home as it exists in our midst—not an isolated little world, but a children's community integrated with our own, growing with us, nourished with the spirit of our soil, lovingly cared for and watched over not only by the parents, but by the *kvuzah* as a whole.

We have never thought of finding a substitute for parental love. We only wanted to add to it the love of the community, so that the child might never feel that when it steps out of its own home it is among strangers, needing protection. How much the first mothers in the *kvuzot* suffered because of the false idea that parents must actually be alienated from their children! But, as the number of children and of parents grows among us, the old errors die out.

Even in the *kvuzah* the child without parents suffers, though it is known and felt in the children's home—from the comrade in charge down to the youngest one—that such a child must be treated with more tenderness than any other. Externally that child lacks nothing.

But watch such an orphan closely! See him waiting eagerly for someone to come to him specially, and you will understand the pain which loneliness means even in the group form of upbringing.

For there are no bounds to the love which a child must have, so that its warmth may serve it through all the heavy after-life. And these children of ours, who will certainly inherit some of our burdens, do not look forward to an easy life.

Love and compassion alone can give us the strength needed to stand constant guard over the lives of our children, to listen with utmost patience to their needs and demands, to understand them without speech as long as they cannot speak for themselves.

And because among the comrades in charge, the nurses and educators, there are "many who are called, few who are chosen," difficulties must arise between them and the parents. We must bear in mind that the mother instinct of itself makes the mother a "chosen one" in respect to her child.

But this deep mother instinct no longer suffices to fill our lives, as it once sufficed for our mothers. I do not know whether it is good that this should be so, but so it is. The child does not, by itself, satisfy our life needs, does not answer all the demands which we make of ourselves.

And I also know that there is no road leading back to the one-time mother and one-time wife. Each of us women must now tread her own path, and even the child cannot hold us back. And if one of us should become weary, and should want to turn back—she will find it impossible. Those of us who still carry in their hearts the beautiful idyll of the past, lose it when they have the chance to observe closely what has become of family life in the cities today . . .

And this consciousness that there is no road back, makes the road before us all the harder.

And yet . . .

The hardest time in the life of the child, the period that calls for the maximum care and worry in the mother, is in the first three years. And when, a few days after the birth, the mother must relinquish her child into other hands, and cannot herself tend to all its needs, her sufferings begin. For all these little cares and attentions are so important. The newborn child changes from day to day, and the progress is observed in all of these trifles, when the child is being bathed, when it wakes from sleep, when it smiles for the first time, and when the first glimmer of consciousness lightens in its eyes—in every movement, in every note of its voice, it reveals itself anew.

And in the baby house, even when it is developed to the highest point, no one will wait for these little events with the same eagerness and tenderness as a mother does.

But, on the other hand, it is impossible to estimate the significance of the help which the baby house gives the mother when, ignorant, helpless and weak, she leaves the hospital after her confinement. It is seldom that a young mother in Erez Israel can fall back on a family with generations of tradition and experience to help her in her new role. What substitute has this young mother? The book of instructions? Not every woman has the time and the opportunity to read books; besides which, do we not know how much help there is in a book when we have to face realities—with a crying baby in our arms? Only those who have seen for themselves what the lonely working-class mother must suffer, in the towns, or in the *moshav ovdim*, when her first child is born, can estimate the worth of the baby house for mother and child, can appreciate the value of its accumulated experience.

The baby house does not grope blindly through its problems, as even the educated and able mother often must. Under the direction of the children-doctors and the devoted nurses they go forward with certain steps. But we are worried constantly by one thought: how can we bring into the life of the child which is being cared for in the home, the bright glance and the loving smile of the mother—for which even the tiniest creature instinctively longs?

It will be observed that when we compare the condition of the children in the *kvuzah* with that of other working-class children in Erez Israel and elsewhere, or even with the condition of the children of other classes, we are perhaps demanding too much of the group method of upbringing. But we cannot forget what was in our minds when we approached the whole problem at the beginning—what ideals and wishes we had regarding life in Erez Israel generally and our own lives in particular. For it is only as part of a high cultural life that the group upbringing of children has meaning, and only in the larger setting of a general ideal will we find the strength to continue seeking, through this form, a loftier and finer life for ourselves and for our children.

Children's House and Parents' Room

E.T.[3] (Ein Harod)

IF THERE WERE someone among us here, in the commune of Ein Harod, who could describe adequately what we have achieved in the way of group upbringing, it would afford much encouragement to those who are only just starting out on this road. Bit by bit, our women workers in the children's homes have ceased to be an isolated group working out its own salvation without the help of the other *haverim*. Today the entire *kibbutz* follows with interest the progress of the children's homes. And bit by bit, too, we are establishing a harmony in the relations of our children to the group home and to the room of their parents.[4]

The theory has been advanced that, in order to concentrate the impressions of the child, we must provide the children's home with so many comforts and attractions that the child will never feel the need of the room which is the home of its parents. But even if we had the means to carry out this theory to the limit, we should be doing wrong if we did not make possible outside contacts between children and their parents. Let our child get everything it needs from the specialists in the children's homes; let it spend the whole day there; but we must not put a check on the intimate meeting betwen child and parent. What these meetings mean in the life of the three—father, mother and child—must depend on their mutual relations. If we could turn our children's homes into palaces, I still would not relinquish that quiet, peaceful hour which I spend with my child in my own room, after the day's work, for the noisy public contact in the children's homes, in the presence of dozens of other fathers and mothers.

We have been convinced by observation that the more the child loves the room of its father and mother, the more it is satisfied by the life of the children's home. For after the exciting, strenuous day in the latter, the child finds by the side of its parents a deep tranquility that is almost unknown to those children who grow up in private families.

But this restful evening visit raises another painful question. Is it

3. The author of this essay is Eva Tabenkin.
4. See note 2 in this section.

right, after this hour of peace, to make the child return for the night to the children's home, to say goodnight to it and send it back to sleep among the fifteen or twenty others? This parting from the child before sleep is so unjust! In the morning that separation is natural. The sun shines, the child is bright and lively, it wants to run to its *haverim*, play with them, walk with them, work with them. As to the objection that it is bad for the child to sleep in the same room with its parents—can we not see to it that every family shall have two little rooms? Do we not, on the contrary, also know the dangers that beset children who sleep together in groups?[5] A child sleeping at home is certainly sheltered from these dangers.

The women on the night watch in the children's homes take turns and turn about. And when my turn comes to "go on guard" I feel my heart contract every time a child calls out in the night—sometimes out of its sleep, not knowing what it is calling—"*nakht-vakhtern! nakht-vakhtern!*" [Yiddish: "Night-keeper! Night-keeper!"]. What is taking place in the soul of the child in that moment, between sleeping and waking? And who knows what is more important for the child, the conscious life of the day or the unconscious life of the night?

5. The reference is to communicable illness.

Mother's Talk

Hasia [Kuperminz-Drori] (Kfar Yehezkel)[6]

Tнis is тне day of judgment, when everyone is weighed in the balance—by "everyone," however, I mean only the children. The mothers stand in line outside the drugstore [of the *moshav ovdim*], waiting for their turn to use the scales. And waiting, they talk of all the homely details of their children's lives.

A mother comes out of the drugstore with shining face, her baby on her arms. Before she can say a word she is surrounded and overwhelmed with the question:

"How much?"

"Two hundred grams for the week!"

A few minutes later another comes out, her eyes darkened by sadness. Her four-month old daughter is in her arms. We feel the pain in her heart, and we think it best to ask nothing. It is she who begins to speak.

"Three weeks my little girl hasn't gained a gram. And I'm to blame because I have to work in the garden and neglect the child. And I don't know—maybe I'm short of milk. I don't drink as much as I'm supposed to."

She goes on with her bitter self-criticism. The others comfort her. "You don't always have to blame yourself. You know that there are whole periods, in the summer, when the little ones just don't go forward. Even in the children's homes in the *kvuzot* you have such cases. We're too impatient, and we get frightened too easily . . ."

When the mother has gone, a hot debate sets in.

"Well, is it any better when the child goes to the kindergarten? We're not as scared about it—but we know it's already been spoiled at home. We always give way; we don't want the child to eat its heart out—and we haven't got the time to fight it out properly. And then we blame ourselves because we spoiled the child."

"And then the new worries, when the child begins to go to school. Will he grow up to follow in our footsteps? Will he have the courage

6. Kfar Yehezkel, founded in 1921, was one of the first *moshavim* in the Harod Valley.

and strength of will to continue our work. If at least he isn't any weaker than we are . . ."

Other doubts crop up in the conversation. Ought we to give the child some work only when it asks for it, or ought we to demand its help, so that it may learn the duties of work early in life?

And another question: "Should we follow the old, traditional ways of our fathers and grandfathers and bring up our daughters differently from our sons? Or should we do the opposite? Perhaps it's all wrong to let the girl devote herself entirely to housework."

There is no clear answer to all these questions. We only know one thing. We, the older people, must observe scrupulously all the social rules and obligations that we have assumed in the *moshav*, so that the children may profit by example. However hard it is to leave the garden, the house, and the little ones in order to live up to our standards of mutual help, it has to be done.

Things are hard today. Better times are coming, the children will be older, and beside the joy they bring us, they will also take a hand in the work.

Borrowed Mothers

G.M.[7] (Tel Aviv)

Taken as a whole, the inner struggles and the despairs of the mother who goes to work are without parallel in human experience. But within that whole there are many shades and variations. There are some mothers who work only when they are forced to; the husband is sick or unemployed, or else the family has in some other way gone off the track of a normal life. In such cases, the mother feels her course of action justified by compulsion—her children would not be fed otherwise. But there are mothers who cannot remain at home for other reasons. In spite of the place which the children and the family as a whole take up in her life, her nature and being demand something more; she cannot divorce herself from the larger social life. She cannot let her children narrow down her horizon. And for such a woman there is no rest.

Theoretically it looks straightforward enough. The woman who replaces her with the children is devoted, loves the children, is reliable and suited to the work; the children are fully looked after. And there are even pedagogic theorists who say that it is actually better for the children not to have the mother constantly near them. As for the mother who is occupied outside the house—she of course has the great advantage of being able to develop. In any case, the ancient danger of retrogression is lessened; and therefore she can bring more to her children than if she were to remain at home. Everything looks all right. But one look of reproach from the little one when the mother goes away, and leaves it with the stranger, is enough to throw down the whole structure of vindication. That look, that plea to the mother to stay, can be withstood only by an almost superhuman effort of the will.

I am not speaking now of the constant worry that haunts the mother's mind that something may have happened. And I need not bring in the feelings of the mother when her child falls sick—the flood of self-reproach and self-accusation. At the best of times, in the best circumstances, there is the perpetual consciousness at the back of the mind

---

7. The author of this essay is Golda Meyerson (later, Meir).

that the child lacks the mother's tenderness, misses during the day the mother's kiss. We believe, above all, in education by example; and therefore we must ask ourselves: Whose is the example that is molding the child of the working mother? A "borrowed" mother becomes the model. The clever things the child says reach the mother at second hand. Such a child does not know the magic healing power of a mother's kiss, which takes away the pain of a bruise. And there are times, after a wearying, care-filled day, when the mother looks at her child almost as if she did not recognize it; a feeling of alienation from her nearest and dearest steals into her heart.

And having admitted all this, we ask: Can the mother of today remain with her children? Can she compel herself to be other than she is because she has become a mother? That feeling of alienation between mother and child can occur, and does often occur in an even more serious form, when the mother always remains at home and cannot grow with her children. And the modern woman asks herself: Is there something wrong with me if my children don't fill up my life? Am I at fault if, after giving them, and the one more person nearest to me, a place in my heart, there is something left over which has to be filled by things outside the family and the home? Can we today measure devotion to husband and children by our indifference to everything else? Is it not often true that the woman who has given up all the external world for her husband and her children has done it not out of a sense of duty, out of devotion and love, but out of incapacity, because her soul is not able to take into itself the manysidedness of life, with its sufferings but also with its joys? And if a woman does remain with her children, and gives herself to nothing else, does that really prove that she is more devoted than the other kind of mother? And if a wife has no intimate friends, does that prove that she has a greater love for her husband?

But the mother also suffers in the very work she has taken up. Always she has the feeling that her work is not as productive as that of a man, or even of an unmarried woman. The children too, always demand her, in health and even more in sickness. And this eternal inner division, this double pull, this alternating feeling of unfulfilled duty today—toward her family, the next day toward her work—this is the burden of the working mother.

PART V

The Departed

Shoshanah Bogen

R.[1]

Sнosнаnaн Bogen was born in 1898 in the *shtetl* Petrikov,[2] province of Minsk, Russia. She came of a numerous and wealthy family and was the youngest child of her parents. Shoshanah's father died while she was a child, and the big family business was conducted by her clever and energetic mother. Occupied though she was by her affairs, the mother did not neglect the education of her children. Her home was the Zionist home of the *shtetl*, and she did not forget her Zionism even when she talked business with a merchant or went over a bill. A famous man in the *shtetl* was Shoshanah's grandfather, her mother's father, a proud Jew of severe religious principles. "The grandfather's little one" was the nickname they gave Shoshanah.

Shoshanah received her first education in a modernized *heder* [traditional Jewish primary school] then she passed to the Russian public folk school. She did not finish her course at the latter. She left one day when she heard the Russian children making fun of the Jews. She was twelve years old when she began her social activities. She was steeped in Zionist thought, and she took part in the youth movement in the *shtetl*. But she did not find this enough. She began to beg her family to send her to Erez Israel. It was not an easy thing for the family to let the youngest child leave, but in the year 1913, at the age of fifteen, Shoshanah was already in Erez Israel.

She came to Petah Tikvah, where she found a number of *haverim* from her *shtetl*, all of them older than she; and at first she lived together with them, working in the orange plantation *bahariyah*[3] [packing shed] and showing herself a capable and devoted worker. But within a year she drifted away from the group of *haverim*, left their common quarters, and went off to live by herself. She had already become known among the workers of Petah Tikvah, and was listened to with respect

1. The identity of R. is uncertain.
2. Petrikov was an administrative city located in the Minsk province, Belorussia. In tsarist Russia, the Minsk province was one of the "western" provinces of the Pale of Settlement.
3. The Hebrew term *bahariyah* refers to the physical site, probably a large shed, to which the oranges were delivered during the harvest and sorted for marketing and export.

when she spoke at their meetings. In particular she became friendly with the Yemenite Jews, visited among them, spoke a great deal with them, and became familiar with their condition.

After two years of intensive living Shoshanah fell sick; she suffered from pains in the legs. And it was then, finding it impossible on many days to go to work, that she took to writing. Then she became better, and left for Kineret, where she joined the group of the unemployed women—the well known "*kvuzah* of twenty."[4] Here she was appreciated at her worth, and was chosen one of the directing committee of three. It was a heavy task, and a severe responsibility for a young woman of seventeen.

In Kineret, she studied *Tanakh* [Hebrew Bible] with a small group of *haverim*. The influence of the *Tanakh* is very strong in the little writing she has left behind her. Working in the fields, she used to learn chapters of the *Tanakh* by heart, like someone who learns by heart the verses of a beloved poet. She attended the workers' conference and listened eagerly to the proceedings. And in Kineret she also found her "grown-up" friends—people who were many years older than she.

She began to suffer again from her old pains, and so she returned to Petah Tikvah to take a rest with her relatives. This was in the period 1917–18. The English had conquered Judea and the movement for a Jewish Legion began.[5] In the tense and charged enthusiasm of those days, Shoshanah passed through a profound inner development. It was as if everything within her were only just awakening. She was tor-

4. The reference here is to the *kvuzah* of women pioneers who farmed a vegetable garden, equivalent to twenty *dunams* (five acres), on land provided by the *kvuzah* at Kineret and supervised by Hannah Meisel-Shohat. See Yael Gordon's essay, "The *Kvuzah* of Twenty," in part II.

5. During World War I, the British government came to the conclusion that British control of the entire area of Palestine would best serve its interests in Egypt and Mesopotamia. This realization gave added impetus to London's wartime plans for the conquest of Palestine by British forces alone. On October 31, 1917, the British opened up an unexpected offensive and took Beersheva, going on to Gaza (November 7, 1917) and Jaffa (November 16, 1917). When this was achieved, the administration installed in "Occupied Enemy Territory South" (i.e., Palestine) was purely British, and it controlled the areas between Hebron and Tiberias, as provided for in the Sykes-Picot Agreement of 1916, and also the Safed and Beersheva districts. The conquest of the south territory, referred to here by R. as "Judea," coincided with the proclamation of the Balfour Declaration on November 2, 1917, by the British government. The declaration expressed of "sympathy with Jewish Zionist aspirations" in Palestine. When General Edmund H. H. Allenby, commander of Britain's Egyptian Expeditionary Forces, entered Jerusalem in December 1917, four hundred years of Ottoman rule over the Holy Land abruptly ended. The British advance spared the Yishuv from increasing Turkish persecution and saved it from starvation and disease. A small section of the Jewish community—the inhabitants of Samaria and Galilee—were to endure nine more months of Turkish rule, until the north was occupied by the British in September 1918. Against this backdrop, Vladimir Zeev Jabotinsky led the campaign for the establishment of the Jewish Legion.

mented by the problems of the individual, of society, and of the Jewish people. Besides, there were personal experiences, relationships to others. Shoshanah sought the answer to her problems among young and older friends alike—but she found none. When the women workers' *kvuzah* of Mikveh Israel[6] was formed, Shoshanah joined it; afterwards, she came to stay in Ben Shemen.[7]

There, lonely and unhappy, she wrestled with her destiny until she took her own life on the first day of Elul [August] 1918, being then twenty years of age.

6. Mikveh Israel, from the Hebrew meaning "Israel's hope" (Jeremiah 14:8 and 17:13), was established as an agricultural school in 1870 by Charles Netter (1826–1882) of the Alliance Israélite Universelle. The school, which Netter directed until 1873, was envisioned as the start of a future network of Jewish villages. It introduced into Palestine numerous species of fruit and forest trees. It also experimented with new crops and possibilities for improving local farming methods. In 1882, the Bilu pioneers found work and were trained at Mikveh Israel; they subsequently founded the colony of Rishon Lezion. In 1898, Theodor Herzl (see note 12 of this section) greeted Kaiser Wilhelm II at the entrance to Mikveh Israel. The agronomist Eliyahu Krause (see part I, note 37) directed the school from 1914 to 1955. Starting in the 1930s, the school became an important center of Youth Aliyah.

7. Ben Shemen, located southeast of Tel Aviv, was built on land bought by the Anglo-Palestine bank in 1904 for a *moshav* and a youth village. In 1906, Israel Belkind established Kiryat Sefer there for orphans of the Kishinev *pogroms* (1903–05) and in 1908 a training farm was created. Ben Shemen was abandoned during World War I because it was located on the battlefield. It was resettled in 1921, when a new *moshav* was founded there, and an agricultural school followed in 1927.

Fragments

From the Letters and Notebooks
of Shoshanah Bogen

M<small>Y DREAM</small>. When I was eight years old God showed himself to me. We had been learning the *Humash* [Pentateuch] during the day, and were told how God had tried Abraham, telling him to sacrifice his son Isaac. This was my dream in the night:

I am walking on the shore of the lake, and God reveals himself to me in a great flame. And these are his words: "I am the God of Abraham, Isaac, and Jacob.[8] Go wherever I shall send you.[9] Here is the lake in front of you; walk through it."

With joy and love I go forward through the lake. I am in the midst of it and I do not drown. And I ask: "God, my God, why does not the water come up to drown me?" And God answers:

"Because you have obeyed me and have done what I commanded. Now rise and come up to me."

Ropes were let down and angels drew me up, into the heavens. I saw a table, and at the head of it sat an old man with a long beard, and around him many angels. They made me sit down among them and I was given wine to drink. And I drank the wine thirstily.

Suddenly I was let down on to the earth again, and I was near our store.

My heart cried out against the return to earth . . . At my feet lay a sack of gold, a dress, and a silver comb. I took the dress and the comb to give to my best friends; the gold I carried into the store.

The next day I came to the *heder*, but told my dream to no one. I was afraid no one would believe that I had really seen God.

. . .

8. This phrase is derived from Exodus 3:6 in which God appears to Moses as a burning bush and identifies himself as "the God of Abraham, the God of Isaac, and the God of Jacob."

9. The phraseology here appears to be modeled after the famous biblical injunction "*Lekh lekha*" [go for thyself] that appears in Genesis 12:1–2: "Now the Lord said unto Abram: 'Get thee out of they country, and from thy kindred, and from thy father's house, unto the land that I will show thee.'"

A CHILD. A village. A house in the *shtetl*, and high on the roof of the house an attic, from which all the *shtetl* and its people can be seen.

A little girl stood there, in pain. She looked on the people running around below, weighed down by heavy baskets and heavy sacks. But she saw that the heaviest burden was in their hearts.

And she was in pain because she could not help these people by making their burdens lighter. And she was more in pain because least of all could she help them with the burdens that were within them.

And the little girl uttered a great cry against all this oppression and pain—a cry that made everyone stand still suddenly.

And she stood there, waiting—but she heard nothing. In that moment was born in her the longing to go to Erez Israel. For she hoped that there the people would carry only the burdens which were outside, and none of the burdens which were within.

Half a year she lived in the country, slaved and labored with all her *haverim*, danced and sang joyously with all her *haverim*. But suddenly she perceived that she was mistaken; she was aware of that secret inner burden, that pain that is not seen. And she trembled, and wanted to die, and feared she would lose her mind.

In her great pain she became silent, for she had heard suddenly the cry she had been waiting for, the thunder of cannons, the cry of the beast which is in the human heart. And her soul was appeased. Others, seeing her joy, were angry with her, and they asked: "What is this? In this storm thousands of human beings are perishing, and you find joy in it?"

But her heart would not obey them. In the night she would stand with others waiting for the thunder of the cannon, and drinking in the storm.

TO R.K.[10] I always had to believe in life. So I will go on believing that there are people who can play on the violins of their own souls and play on the violins of others at the same time.

Once the violin in me began to sing because yours was playing.

Do you remember? We were reading the Psalms, the chapter "By the waters of Babylon."[11] You interrupted the reading and began to talk with us at length about your relationship to music. And you said: "If you were a musician, you would utter your wildest cry, out of the depth of your pain—in silence."

How true that was for my violin.

10. The identity of R.K. is uncertain, though it is probably Rahel Kaznelson-Shazar.
11. This phrase dervies from Psalm 137:1.

Many have played on the violin of my soul, but none played as well on it as [Theodor] Herzl.[12]

THE RAIN. The first shower comes, the first kiss of nature.

I am working; and in a stab of memory I think of my satchel, with the pencil and paper inside. I tremble—but I go on working.

But nature is good and loves me. That is why she sent the rain. And I yield and sit under the tree with pencil and paper.

The rain stops; I am angry and wounded, but I have to return to work.

But again a message comes—the second angel of the rain bearing it to me. I run quickly to my place under the tree, to change a word here, a letter there. Again the rain stops and again I get up to work.

And then the angel comes for the third time—and the third time is a sign and symbol, and now with joy I run to my pencil and paper. It is worth half a day's pay.

Oh, how good, how good!

. . .

12. Theodor Herzl (1860–1904), father of modern political Zionism and founder of the World Zionist Organization, was originally a highly acculturated Jew with few attachments to Judaism and Jewish life. In many ways, Herzl's trajectory exemplified the experience of modern European Jewry. Caught between the twin promise of liberalism and emancipation on the one hand and the rise of antisemitism and anti-Jewish violence on the other, Herzl was shocked to the core by the Dreyfus Affair in 1894. The affair centered on Captain Alfred Dreyfus (1859–1936), an assimilated Jew and career officer, who was falsely accused of espionage. The affair became a *cause célèbre* virtually over night and a watershed in the history of antisemitism; it stunned many and the confidence of the Jews in the liberal order was severely shaken. In the event, Herzl, who covered the affair as the Paris correspondent of the *Neue Freie Presse* of Vienna, was prompted to conclude that the only solution to the Jewish problem was a mass exodus of the Jews from their host societies and resettlement in a land of their own. He spelled out this idea in a treatise entitled *Der Judenstaat: Versuch einer modernen Loesung der juedischen Frage* [The Jews' State: An Attempt at a Modern Solution of the Jewish Question] (Vienna: M. Breitenstein, 1896). Herzl was responsible for convening the first World Zionist Congress in 1897 and the establishment of the movement's main instruments, the World Zionist Organization, the Jewish Colonial Trust, and *Die Welt* [The World], a Zionist weekly. In 1902, he published *Altneuland* [Old-New Land], a utopian depiction of the Jewish society he envisioned. Although he failed to reach lasting agreements with European leaders or convince wealthy Jewish benefactors to fund his plans, Herzl's tireless leadership paved the way for much of subsequent Zionist political activity. At the Sixth Zionist Congress (August 1903), one year prior to his death, Herzl clashed with East European Zionist groups who rejected his "Uganda scheme," a proposal for temporary Jewish resettlement in East Africa, in favor of an unwavering commitment to Jewish settlement in the Land of Israel. Notwithstanding this clash and differences in cultural orientation, Herzl was generally regarded by an adoring East European Jewish public as "King of the Jews."

HERZL. From childhood onward I always thought of Herzl as beautiful. I heard, too, that kings loved him. Once I read in the newspaper of the love that was poured out at his funeral. But there was no comparison between the printed pictures of him and the face that I saw in imagination.

Always in my desire to go to Erez Israel, the beauty of Herzl stood before me. And a little while before I went, I approached his picture and talked with him.

He answered: "Go."

I buried Herzl in my heart and began to serve his body; in all the changings and strivings in Erez Israel I looked for him in my heart. But he was not there.

Several times I went to Herzl memorial meetings, and heard orators speak of him, and I laughed out of my great pain. I had hoped to meet Herzl in the *bet midrash*—but not even his picture was there. Only words: "Herzl is dead—Herzl is alive." Dullness and weariness! Not one true word was in their mouths.

And I, whenever I remembered Herzl, I trembled suddenly out of love for him.

And once, during a memorial meeting, I heard a joyous voice. A choir was singing the *"El maleh rahamim"*[13] [God full of compassion], and I ran close to the singers to catch a sight of their inmost joy. But soon I went away from them, silent.

I remember another such service—the last that was held in Kineret. I knew surely this time that I would not hear the words for which I longed; and, therefore, I wrote down my own words on paper, intending to read them. But I mastered myself.

And now the old [Aharon David] Gordon went up on the platform. I was certain he would say something dear and close to me, and it was so.

"The anniversary of Herzl's death is a day of inmost reckoning for all of us; and each of us must ask himself whether he is really fulfilling the duties which he has taken on himself."

Young people who had come within the last five years and who were looking for "the new word" smiled to hear these old things from Gordon. But the smile of their mockery was a defense; they were frightened because Gordon had looked too closely into their souls.

. . . We serve the body of Herzl in our work, in our language, and the

13. *"El maleh rahamim"* [God full of compassion], is a prayer for the dead recited at funeral services, on the anniversary of a death, on visiting graves of relatives, or after a mourner has been called up to the reading of the Torah. *"El maleh rahamim"* dates back to the medieval period, when it was originally recited for Jewish martyrs.

upbuilding of the country. But we forget that he who wrote *Tel Aviv*[14] for our land carried a richer Tel Aviv in his heart.

THE LIBERATION OF WOMAN.   When she arrived in the country they tried to make her understand she was a girl. She answered: "But do I not know it? And have I ever even longed to be a boy?" And again life sang to her the cradle song of the loving mother who smothers her child with kisses. "Why should you suffer and labor? You were born for an easier life; somewhere, someone is already born who will worry for you."

Filled with pain, she worked harder than before, and was silent; till the moment of revolt came, and an answer was found not only for her, but for those who kissed her and smothered their own lives in the darkness. And if one of them spoke to her about the "woman problem," she would look at him with a smile and say quietly: "Poor boy! You are so busy with my liberation that you have not noticed that I have already liberated myself, while you have still remained in your slavery."

WINGS.   Of what avail is it to tell me that I do not spread out my wings, when you should first have said these words to yourself? My soul could not bear your weakness, but I loved you greatly, and I loved the pain that was in you. And that was why my wings remained unspread.

Now your kisses are healthier and your fear is a healthier one, and this gives me strength to spread my wings.

Until now I have always needed people, and looked for advice. Now I will follow no advice, not that of good friends, and not even yours. I will obey only myself.

Will you be able to calm yourself now, walking in the fields?

Within myself I am sure that I will not fall. And suppose I fall after all—will that not prove that I had to fall?

TWO ENCOUNTERS.   Adam meets Eve in fierce bodily love, and soon the shadow descends on them. The encounter eats up their strength, and to

14. Editorial note: Although the English translation of *The Plough Woman* (1932) uses the title *Old-New Land*, we have reinserted the title *Tel Aviv* in the present version of the text, as this is how it appears in the Yiddish volume (1931). Indeed, *Tel Aviv* was the Hebraized title given to Theodor Herzl's utopian novel, *Altneuland* [Old-New Land]. Herzl wrote the latter between 1899 and 1902. In it, he illustrated his Zionist vision of the Jews' future. The novel also sought to refute the charge that Zionism was impractical. See Theodor Herzl, *Old-New Land*, trans. Lotta Levensohn, reprint (New York: Markus Wiener Publishing and Herzl Press, 1987).

calm themselves they think up ideals: the Jewish people, vegetarianism, kindness to animals, labor, children. Darkness and blackness. Moods. Pain. Tears. A worm gnaws inside, a hellish jealousy burns continuously. The poison of their jealousy is passed on to their child. Their love and their darkness are reflected in it.

From Zion shall go forth this law: love yourself with so strong a love that it shall be reflected in every man whom you meet by the way.

Adam and Eve will meet in a deep, quiet love, in the love of a good mother to her only son.

Heart will hear heart, without speech. Body and spirit will be happy in their common creation—the son.

And the son will begin to lay strong foundations for Adam and Eve, and he will roll away the reproach of the family life of his people.

And if it be a daughter? She shall change the prayer: "Blessed art Thou who has not made me a woman"[15] into "Blessed art Thou who hast made me a woman."

And out of this encounter will stream forth a love without bounds toward all human beings because they are human beings.

THREE DAYS. When I began to work in the orchard I wrote, in thought, three letters—one to B.K., one to Y-li, and one to A.I.[16]

And, so thinking, I suddenly saw God; not in a flame, but God Himself. Not Him who touches and vanishes, but God who shines out of me with His great light.

But while I was in the midst of my thoughts, I did not know that this was God speaking. My tears fell, and I was seized with fear because of the task laid on me.

And God said to me:

"Three days have passed over you. The first day, labor; the second, light and life; the third, sanctification to Me."

And He said further:

"A child is in your spirit, a daughter three days old. Take care, she is still tender."

I asked: "Shall I therefore not live?"

15. This benediction comes from *birkot hashahar* [morning benedictions], which constitute the first part of the traditional Jewish morning prayer service. After a number of preliminary hymns and blessings, there follows a series of 15 benedictions. Historically, the female alternative to the fourth benediction ("Blessed art Thou who has not made me a woman") was "Blessed art Thou who has made me according to Thy will." Shoshanah Bogen's unapologetic feminist assertion is a significant departure from the tradition.

16. The identities of these individuals are unknown.

"Live and suffer, think and despair."

I asked again: "Shall I therefore not live as I have lived till now?"

"Live, but do not think that this is life. True life comes in silence, not in storm; else it is not life."

Suddenly I heard the voice of God with greater strength:

"Shoshanah, do you want to live already? Have you forgotten that life brings death? Remember this! It is the madhouse that waits for you."

I wept bitterly for my fate. And I said: "God, if you send me on the mission for which you have appointed your chosen ones, I go in happiness."

And still weeping I prayed silently: "And I am so weak. I tremble with fear, and my greatest fear is this, that I am not certain that this is indeed my destiny."

But it had been so decreed. God said: "Take!" and I took.

A deeper prayer broke out from my heart's depth: "Almighty God, help me!"

Out of the darkness of my terror came a great light, a boundless flood of light.

"Shoshanah, you were born to two names: Shoshanah Hayah. With your name Shoshanah [a rose] you have lived twenty years; but in your body there was death. Because the flower has withered and the body carried you. Twenty years more I give you with your name Hayah [life] but you shall not throw away Shoshanah, as you have not wholly thrown away till now Hayah. Pluck the rose and carry it with you."

Peace and quiet came into my spirit.

And again God said to me:"Who has permitted you to sacrifice life to death? Seek! Perhaps you will not need to pluck the rose. For I do not delight in sacrifice. I ask for the fruit that is not sacrifice.

"In the days of your death-in-life you saw sin and trembled. But the sins were not so heavy; they were heavy only because you sinned them; for then the smallest sin becomes a great one.

"All men sin with the body, because they are weak; but you have sinned with the spirit because you were not weak. From this day on, lift up your eyes to life. Go higher! Seek! If you find life, good. If not, look straightway to the earth. Such a death is rich and filled with light."

THE DEATH OF YOSEF. This was the child that came to Erez Israel five years ago; in his shining face and sparkling eyes spoke infinite life. He rejoiced in his work, and was happy in poverty, because his aim was realized: he lived in the land and in his work. But slowly a shadow gathered over him. Beside the land and the work he needed friends, and this it was not easy to find. For a year he suffered, choking his life back within him, and then he began to find himself and his place. He made friendships with some of the [young women]. He grew, and his needs grew, and he was drawn toward the friendship of the men. They took him into their midst and he shared their life with them. He became happy again in this intimacy. He was satisfied for a time. But he was like a child among grownup people. His heart began to draw him toward Galilee; perhaps he would find there what he sought. He came to Kineret, to that quiet, modest retreat, whose modesty has the power to still all inner struggles.

The Kineret group, with its heavy and severe demands, weighed too much on him. Filled with sadness and irony he came to Petah Tikvah, in Judea.

But after a few days, without a coin in his pocket, having only a piece of dry bread for the journey, he returned once more to Kineret. A change came over him. His life blossomed, chiefly among the [young women]. Love and joy filled his life. In the fullness of that blossom he was so young, so fresh! And again the worm began to eat within him. He sank deep into thought, into problems to which there was no answer. The loveliest landscapes of our country opened before him, but he had no joy in them. The life of the group repelled him. It seems that among other questions, the darkest of all tormented him: "What for?" His life turned inward, gathered bitterly in a sea of despair. He looked everywhere for comfort, began to study—but everywhere he found death.

After a few days they found his body on the threshing floor.

It was a night of thunder and lightning. A comrade had gone out for straw, and he stumbled on a body. Terrified, he called to it, and received no answer. He came back to the living room, and told them all that someone was lying on the threshing floor, sick or dead.

They went out with the big lantern, and stood in a stony circle round the blossom that was dead.

Silently they brought him back into the yard. Then they took a ladder, and covered it with boards, and carried him into one of the rooms. No one spoke; but now and again someone would utter a cry; now and again someone would fall fainting.

In the dead silence [some young men] went out and dug the grave on the hill. In dead silence they lowered the body into it. And for three days the big red stain was left in the room, as if they meant it to remain.

Some say that suicide is weakness; others that it is heroic. There are deep and inmost forces that look for a foothold in life, and cannot find it. Nor can they burn themselves out within. When they have risen to the rim, the vessel bursts.

If the men and women around understand in time, they can still save the life. But in our social life the only help is—to bring the last solution closer—death.

It is neither weakness nor heroism, only compulsion. So dying, a man expresses his truth and the lie of society. For he is unwilling to go on with the life around him, and unable to realize the life within him.

If society did not, because of its terror, see in suicide either weakness or heroism, but a simple fact, perhaps many of us would not choose to leave this world. For one thing is clear: if a person must submit to the tyranny of little things, death is finer and stronger.

There are two ways to victory. From the trial of life very few emerge victorious. They are the rare and chosen ones, and for them life becomes a song of happiness. The second victory is given through death.

All spiritual agonies begin with the sins of the parents, and continue through the sins of society. If the parents have eaten sour fruit, the teeth of the children need not be set on edge. The sins of the parents are on their own heads, and the children are clean. If they are cleansed by death, it is not an evil thing. The evil thing is if they continue in their life of falseness. This is the life of blind worms who want to forget that they had souls, who seek comfort in pleasures and call them nature and freedom. These are the signs of death in the midst of life itself. A healthy person cannot bear them; either his wholeness of character fights them down, and he remains alive or else knowing himself defeated he dies; and this, too, is a victory. Happy is he who dies in victory; happier is he who lives in victory.

On the Last Words of Shoshanah

Rahel Kaznelson [Shazar] (Tel Aviv)

IN THE LABOR ANTHOLOGY *Baavodah*[17] [At Labor], the last words
are those of Shoshanah who took her life a few days before the book
appeared. And she ended with: "Happy is he who dies in victory; happier is he who lives in victory."

After the event, we, the survivors, looked on each other with different eyes.

"Hail, Caesar! We, who are about to die, salute thee!"[18]

The power of these words, making us tremble, is born of their ultimate affirmation of life. Reading the last words of Shoshanah, our lives
too gained new affirmation.

"Kingdom of life! One who is going among the dead, salutes thee!"[19]

Is it right of us to reprint the words of Shoshanah?

> The storm in the poet, an ocean of rage
> Lies hidden and hushed on the silent page.[20]
> Uri Nissan Gnessin[21]

17. *Baavodah* [At Labor], edited by the socialist Zionist ideologue Berl Kaznelson
(1887–1944), is an anthology of writings by Zionist pioneers published in 1918 by the
Agricultural Workers' Union.

18. A translation of the Latin statement, "*morituri te salutamus*" [We, about to die,
salute thee!], uttered by the Roman gladiators to the emperor.

19. This is a translation of the Latin statement, "*Regnum vitae! Te moriturus saluto!*"

20. The precise provenance of this quotation is uncertain, though it likely derives
from one of Uri Nissan Gnessin's (see following note) early novels.

21. The Hebrew writer Uri Nissan Gnessin (1881–1913), a native of Ukraine, published his first works at age fifteen. As a youth, Gnessin and Yosef Hayim Brenner
founded two literary journals for a small circle of friends. The Zionist leader Nahum
Sokolow (1859–1936) later invited Gnessin to join the editorial staff of *Hazfirah* [The
Dawn] in Warsaw. Gnessin subsequently wrote poems, short stories, and literary criticisms. In 1904, he published *Zlilei hahayim* [The Shadows of Life]. Thereafter, Gnessin
entered a period of wandering, restlessness, and depressed isolation. He fought violently
with Brenner over the short-lived London-based periodical *Hameorer* [The Awakening],
which they co-edited. After a brief sojourn in Palestine, where he proved unable to
adjust, Gnessin returned to Russia permanently. His prose introduced new literary tech-
niques to Hebrew literature such as the psychological monologue and explored the
themes of alienation and uprootedness. Among his works, four stories are considered
most important: *Hazidah* [Aside], 1905; *Beintayim* [Meanwhile], 1906; *Beterem* [Before],
1909; and *Ezel* [By], 1913.

We are too tired to reconstruct those passions.

Intimate friends will perhaps penetrate beyond the hush of the silent lines, enter into their secret, and follow back the thread of her life, perhaps into her childhood. Who knows what they will uncover?

But these, the friends, are the real guardians of her traces whose magic spreads bit by bit to the circles close around them. It is the memory of common years and hours that wakens to life what is hidden and hushed in the printed lines, and for a few people a living reality will exist in her memory.

When these few are no more, no one will understand the magic of the picture. For a time the flame which should have shone authentically from her will be reflected through others. And in time the last shimmer too will be extinguished.

Dvorah Drakhler

Haya[22] and Eliezer [Kroll] (Kfar Giladi)

SHE WAS BORN in a village in the province of Podolia,[23] Russia, of parents of the middle class. Her education was typical of the Jews of the village. She had little formal schooling. Only her brother, who was a Hebrew teacher, would be home a few times a month and give her lessons in Hebrew and Russian. Dvorah loved this village life.

Dvorah's older brother and sisters had already been drawn into the Zionist youth movement, and so from earliest childhood she herself was steeped in Zionist ideals. This influence on the one side, and the actual village life on the other, became synthesized in her into the idea of Jewish village life in Erez Israel—something that she would help to build up.

This dream became conscious in her when she was about twelve years old. The occasion was the departure of her older sister for Erez Israel in the year 1908. And when the older sister returned once on a visit, she found Dvorah a grown person, with a clear will and determination to go to Erez Israel.

By the time of the World War she had carried out her wish. Her joy was without bounds. She went straight to the *kvuzah* of Tel Adas [Tel Adashim], where her sister and brother-in-law were working. The *kvuzah* was composed of *haverim* of Hashomer, and they had settled in the new place only a year before.

Dvorah threw herself into the work with all her young strength and enthusiasm. She was seventeen years old, and already carried on her

22. The details of Hayah (Drakhler) Kroll's biography are unknown. She was Dvorah Drakhler's sister.

23. Podolia, a tsarist Russian province located in southwest Ukraine, sustained a sizable Jewish population. In 1881, the Jewish community of Podolia was estimated at 418,450. After *pogroms* erupted in the region in 1882, there was a large exodus of Jews from the province. By 1897, the Jewish population of Podolia had decreased to 370,600 (12.3 percent of the total populace). During the Russian civil war (1918–21), Podolia suffered severely and there were widespread *pogroms* throughout the region. Jewish life in Podolia continued to deteriorate under the Soviet regime. In the 1920s young Jews in Podolia organized clandestine cells of Hehaluz [The Pioneer] and other Zionist youth groups. The Jewish community in the region was ultimately destroyed by the Nazis during World War II.

shoulders that burden of life which belongs to Erez Israel. She always asked for tasks which would absorb her completely and take up all her strength and devotion. She wanted great responsibilities. And in the year 1917, when the Turkish government, through its representative, Hassan Bek,[24] began the persecution of the Yishuv generally and of the labor class and Hashomer more particularly, the real time began for Dvorah.

As is well known, great numbers of workers were arrested in those days—including as many of the *haverim* of Hashomer as did not go into hiding. The arrested men were sent to be tried by the military court in Damascus. The conditions in the prison were ghastly; and on top of the hunger, the dirt and the cold, there came an epidemic of typhoid to which many of our *haverim* succumbed. We needed at that time devoted *haverim* and *haverot* to stay in Damascus, to wash and cook for the prisoners, to bring them their food into the prison and to smuggle in whatever else they needed.

When this situation arose, Dvorah responded at once. Her comrades tried to dissuade her, pointing out that she was new to the country, that she did not yet know the language and the ways of the Arabs, that Damascus was a big city filled with soldiers, and that her main outside contacts would have to be with the military. Dvorah listened to everything, and answered with her quiet smile: "No matter. I'll go, and you'll see that the work will be well done."

Even the journey to Damascus was, in those days, filled with danger. There were hardly any civilians on the trains. A special permit was needed for the journey. And Dvorah actually traveled on a military train, on to which she was smuggled with the help of *baksheesh* [a bribe].

Those months in Damascus were months of suffering for her. Often when she used to go through the streets with food for the prisoners, it was snatched out of her hands by hungry Arabs. Her contacts with the prison exposed her to the typhoid that raged within. But neither fear nor suffering could deter her. She stayed on, doing her work until the time of the trial; and then returned [home to Tel Adas] with the handful of *haverim* whom typhoid and the court had spared.

Back in Tel Adas, she resumed her work with the old energy; but she was not destined to work for long. In the year 1919 came the events in Upper Galilee. Bedouins [Arab nomads] and Arab peasants were stirred up into a war against the French; and three Jewish settlements, Metulah, Kfar Giladi, and Tel Hai, lay on the borders of French territory.[25]

24. On Hassan Bek, see part II, note 7.
25. The end of World War I was followed by significant Arab nationalist agitation in Palestine. After the Huleh Valley was marked for inclusion in the French Mandate terri-

Bands of roving Bedouins began to attack the Jewish villages. Metulah did not hold out long—it was abandoned by the colonists. But the two labor settlements of Kfar Giladi and Tel Hai decided to hold on at all costs. The *haverim* of these two places sent the children and their mothers to Tel Adas. Help was needed—not only men, but women to look after the defenders.

Again Dvorah begged to be sent. She was by this time one of the few *haverot* who had been accepted into Hashomer. The road from Tel Adas to the settlements was beset with danger; there was only one way to travel—in the night, during a rainfall and armed . . . Dvorah knew this well, but she kept on pleading with [Manya Shohat], and though the latter pretended to be angry, it was clear that she was pleased to have a *haverah* of this caliber. Once, as if in a rage, she exclaimed: "Are you absolutely determined to die?" And Dvorah answered, with that constant smile of hers: "No, I want to live. But I want to help our *haverim*."

In the end she went, of course, and began to work in Tel Hai.

The attacks increased from day to day and conditions became intolerable. Some of the *haverim* began to waver, and a meeting was called to decide whether they should go or remain. Dvorah was of the majority that voted that they should remain.

The eleventh of Adar [5680] [March 1, 1920] came, and the attack against Tel Hai was renewed. After much shooting on both sides an armistice was called, and messengers from both sides met. The Arabs contended that French soldiers were hiding in the yard of the settlement; they demanded that a search be permitted, and, if there were no French hidden there, they would retire from the place. [Yosef] Trumpeldor[26] gave the command to admit some of the Arabs, and Kamil Effendi[27] came in, with a few of his aides. The orders were for every man to stand at his post. Kamil and his escort searched the yard, and finally went up to the top floor of the house. There were, in that room, six of our people, Dvorah, Sarah Chizhik, and four men. When Kamil and his men went up into the room, Trumpeldor, who had accompanied them, remained standing at the foot of the stairs. Suddenly, Kamil began to demand the arms of the six people in the room, and, being refused, tried to employ force. Dvorah suddenly appeared at the door

tory of Syria, Arabs revolting against the French attacked the cluster of small Jewish settlements in the north, particularly Metulah, Kfar Giladi, and Tel Hai. The decision whether the colonies should be fortified or abandoned was hotly debated by the Zionist leadership of the Yishuv. In the event, Yosef Trumpeldor (see part II, note 38) and his followers determined to defend the settlements.

26. On Yosef Trumpeldor see part II, note 38.

27. The term *effendi* [sir], used as title of respect in Turkey, came to denote an Arab official or landowner in Palestine.

of the room, crying "They are trying to take our weapons!" and then she flew back to help her *haverim*. Before Trumpeldor had a chance to reach the top of the stairs, he was shot by Kamil in the stomach and fell. From the room upstairs the sound of an exploding bomb was heard, followed by a few shots, and then silence. The *haverim* standing at their posts did not know what had happened, and when Kamil and his aides came down, they were allowed to pass through—those were Trumpeldor's orders.

Later, when the other *haverim* ran up, they found the six in a heap, two wounded and four dead, torn by bombs. Among the dead was Dvorah.

Sarah Chizhik

Ziporah Zeid (Tel Aviv)

DEATH IS AT its cruelest when it lies in wait for one who is struggling through an inner crisis—and, when he emerges successfully, stands ready to enter the battle, and feels within himself a secret force urging him on to create, strikes him down. It was at this point in her life that Sarah Chizhik was killed [at Tel Hai].

Outwardly Sarah was tranquil and had little to say. Inwardly she was a thing of storm. As a child she already hated the dull routine of a woman's housework. Her pleasure was working in the garden or among the chickens. I remember how overjoyed she was—and Sarah seldom showed great joy—when [Hayim Nahman] Bialik[28] came to Dagania, and she prepared for him a bouquet of twenty kinds of flowers, all of them grown in our little garden. "Let him see what we can do," she said.

She seemed to be remote from the daily life and ways of the village; she seemed to be seeking something, as if she felt this was not her right place. In her free time she used to study. The *Tanakh* [Hebrew Bible] was her intimate friend, and reading it she would dream of another world, far from ours. She knew the books of the Prophets by heart.

From her earliest days on she could not bear the sight of injustice. She passed through one of the darkest crises of her life when one of our teachers, whom we had considered an ideal kind of man, committed a base act. She then resolved that if such a man could fall so low, it was best to leave home and find new surroundings to live among. And she believed that if there was such a thing as right left in the world, it would

28. Hayim Nahman Bialik (1873–1934), considered the poet laureate of modern Hebrew, hailed from the Pale of Settlement where he received a traditional Jewish upbringing. At age 18, he broke with orthodox Judaism and devoted himself to secular, modern Jewish culture. He joined Hibbat Zion [Lovers of Zion] and became a teacher and a writer of Hebrew poetry. A Zionist who considered Theodor Herzl's diplomatic efforts too compromising, he identified with the Zionist pioneers in Palestine and became enchanted with the Palestine labor movement. Bialik's poetry generally dealt with a broad range of subjects. In 1903, he was sent to Kishinev to help investigate the aftermath of the Kishinev *pogrom* (1903) and prepare a report on its impact. The experience prompted Bialik to write one of his most famous poems, "The City of Slaughter," which was to become a symbol of the Zionist revolt against Jewish complacency and vulnerability in the diaspora. He immigrated to Palestine in 1924.

be found among the workers. Work became her religion, and every patch that she planted brought forth the blossom of her true, believing soul. Perhaps she loved this garden work because she believed that the truest people were our land workers.

She left home and went to work in a *kvuzah*; and with that a change came over her. She became another person—for I remember how she told me once, coming from Hederah, with what joy she worked in the kitchen, and cooked for many workers. She boasted that her cooking was liked best—Sarah, who had always hated kitchen work!

The years of the war weighed heavily on her, as they did on all of us,[29] but with the ending of the war she entered on a new unfolding of life. She was filled with energy and with desire to work. Those who knew her at that time also knew that wherever a Jewish colony was in danger, wherever help was needed, Sarah would be found. It was the woman in her that drove her. In those days there were very few women among the workers; and in the places where life was uncertain, and danger hung low like a cloud, the comforting, sisterly hands of a devoted woman were needed most. And Sarah went up to Tel Hai to meet her death. The journey from Tel Aviv to Tel Hai was the happiest moment of her life.

29. On World War I and the plight of the Yishuv, see note 5 in this section and part I, note 67.

Fragments

From the Letters and Diaries of Sarah Chizhik

MILHAMIYAH,[30] ADAR 5675 [MARCH 1915] — FROM HER DIARY.

On the fifth of Adar we got up very early—my father, two brothers, a sister and myself—and packed food for the whole day. We got into the cart of a colonist who was going to Dagania, past our field. A quarter of an hour beyond the colony, the Jordan showed itself, transparent and still. But that stillness was only on the surface, because the heart of the Jordan is an angry one. We began to pass across, struggling with the swift waters, which tore at the sides of the cart and forced their way in.

Our field is a broad meadow on the east bank of the Jordan. We begin to uproot the weeds. Around us—peace and silence. Now and again we hear the croaking of a frog, or the sudden trill of birds.

We are alone here, alone in a sea of waving wheat. Most of the fields are Arab, a few of them Jewish. When we stand up straight and look toward the east, we see the lovely, broad meadows stretching far away to the foot of the Transjordan hills; and our hearts beat faster when we think—each one of us to himself—how many Jewish colonies could be planted on this empty space! And when we turn round and look westward all the colonies look back at us—especially our own Milhamiyah, with its roofs and green orchards twinkling in the sunlight. There among the hills, westward from Lake Kineret, shines Poriyah, which rich Americans have bought lately; and on the southern shore of the Kineret is Dagania, which belongs to the Jewish National Fund. And somewhat to the west, on the same shore, you see the colony Kineret.

30. Milhamiyah, southwest of Lake Kineret, is the Arabic name of the site where the *moshavah* Menahemiyah was established in 1902 by Jewish Colonization Association. The *moshavah* was part of a plan to establish a network of Jewish settlements in Galilee based on grain production. The colony developed slowly and suffered from attacks by Bedouin Arabs. In the 1920s a local gypsum quarry provided employment and supplied the Nesher [Eagle] cement works (see part II, note 50). The name Menahemiyah is based on the original Arabic name of the site and the first name of the British High Commissioner Herbert Samuel's father.

EKRON,[31] 27 OF SHEVAT 5680 [FEBRUARY 1919] —
FROM A LETTER TO A FRIEND.

[Rivkah!] It is eight o'clock in the evening, and I am sitting in the house. Some of the [young women] have gone to bed, others are reading in their rooms. Our [hut] is a small one, and stands outside the colony. In front it is guarded by eucalyptus trees, and behind is a little flower garden. A true village house, especially from the outside.

Rivkah! You write me that what I need is a place where one can live as well as work. But I already feel myself bound to the fields and to land work, and I cannot do without them. Now, having learned a little about the town, I have begun to appreciate the work in the village! But it is very doubtful whether I will ever find a place where everything will satisfy me. I only let myself dream that there will be a *kvuzah* where I—or rather we, you and Hayah and myself will work together. If it would only come true!

I feel well. All day long your sister Yehudit and I dug beet roots and radishes. That's easy and pleasant work. We are proud of our beet roots (I can say *our* beet roots, can't I?); the beans are blossoming, the peas and onions are coming out beautifully. We are sowing summer vegetables and have planted tomatoes. The landscape round Ekron is lovely. To the south the horizon lies far, far away, level; to the south are the hills of Judea, which have a habit of changing distances. This *Shabbat* [Sabbath] we will have an outing among the hills.

EKRON, 27 SHEVAT 5680 [FEBRUARY 1919] — TO A *HAVERAH*.

My darling Haya! I am always dreaming that a time will come when you and I and other friends will work and live in one group. I know that we will easily fit together. How happy we shall be, and how well the work will be divided. It is going to be a big enterprise, with many branches. And Hayah! I am sure that we won't keep accounts with each other about the work; our lives will be an example of equality. We shall give much to our work, and we shall take much from it.

FROM THE DIARY — 5680 [1919].

I am twenty-one years old! That means that I have lived twenty-one years. How easily that is said! No, I have not lived all these years—for a long time I only breathed.

31. Ekron (also known as Mazkeret Batyah [Memory of Batyah]), a *moshavah* southeast of Rehovot, was founded at the initiative of Baron Edmond de Rothschild (1845–1934). The name Ekron was given out of the desire to link the settlement with the nearby biblical site of Ekron, which (according to 1 Samuel 7:14) was part of a region restored to ancient Israel by Samuel, the Israelite judge and prophet who lived in the eleventh century B.C.E.

I was once very naive—perhaps I still am. I used to be beside myself when I saw all the bad things that are done in the world. Why is it that good and honest people have not the power over wicked people? And what hurts and angers me most is that the wicked are always proclaimed as the good and honest, while the really honest must suffer in silence. I am not speaking just so; I have seen these things in actual life. And more than once I have felt that all is vanity,[32] and life is loathsome.

One hope and only one is left me. What if that should also be extinguished?

It is the hope to be a daughter of my people which is rejecting the life it has known till now in order to become a people of labor in its own home on its own soil.

I want to believe that this time, in spite of everything, right will triumph; I want to see the triumph and rejoice in it myself . . .

FROM THE DIARY — 5680 [1919].

I have heard the "good" news—the *pogroms* in Poland and in the Ukraine.[33] My heart aches for my brothers and sisters; but more for my sisters, because their death is double. They die for being Jewish and for being women. God! What bestiality! What lowness and vileness!

I often say to myself that I do not yet know life. But I do know what human beings are; they are something unworthy of their name.

KFAR GILADI, 11 ADAR 5680 [MARCH 1919] — TO A *HAVERAH*.
Shalom, Rivkah!

This is to tell you that we made the journey safely. I'll give you all the details.

Before we left Ayelet Hashahar, I felt bad—I don't know why. But as soon as we got on to the road, and we got the word, "Keep moving

---

32. In the Yiddish text, Sarah Chizhik inserts the Hebrew phrase "*havel havalim*" [all is vanity], a quote from Ecclesiastes I:2.

33. The *pogroms* referred to here were part of the third wave of anti-Jewish riots that swept through Eastern Europe between 1917–21 during the Russian civil war. Red Army units attacked Ukrainian villages while retreating from the Germans. Among the worst massacres were the *pogroms* in Novgorod Severski and Glukhov. Nonetheless, it was the Red Army that was seen as helpful by the Jews, and its official policy prescribed stiff penalties for soldiers involved in *pogroms*. The White Army, on the other hand, operated under the official slogan "Strike at the Jews and save Russia." Every zone that the White Army occupied during its retreat from the Red Army in the Ukraine and Poland became a *pogrom* site, and it was the aim of the former not only to inflict hurt but to wipe out the Jewish presence entirely. By the end of the third wave, which included 887 major and 349 minor pogroms, about 60,000 Jews were killed. Only the defeat of the White Army prevented the total destruction of Jewish life in the area. The *pogroms* and resulting mass devastation prompted a sense of Jewish partiality to the Red Army and the Communists and a surge of Zionist sentiment.

and keep quiet," I began to feel better. A little way out we met the others. They made a queer impression, sitting on the ground with their weapons in their hands and a sort of dreadful silence reigning over everything. They saw us and got up. We went on further. I took the revolver from K. and marched on firmly. I thought of that night in Petah Tikvah when the Turks came back unexpectedly, and all night long we went around silently and gave orders silently. But this time, as we went striding through the night, we felt a certain strength. After an hour's marching, we came to a [stream]. It was safe to talk now—and after the silence the men began to joke. Some wanted to walk through the [water] as they were, shoes and everything. But we decided it would be best to take those off and wade through with naked feet. It did look queer, afterwards, thirty-five men sitting on the ground putting on their shoes again, in a silent night . . . Now and again we heard the barking of a dog far away; and sometimes, in the distance, we caught the glimmer of the Huleh swamp.[34]

At dawn we reached the slope of a hill, and after a rest began to climb. And as we went upward the slight of dawn increased. The scenery was glorious, especially Mount Hermon[35] in the distance. All morning we climbed and crawled over hills and rocks, and at about one o'clock we got to Kfar Giladi. The most difficult part of the journey was coming down the abrupt slope . . .

The surroundings here are beautiful. The group makes a good impression; the dangerous situation doesn't seem to affect them at all. Everyone is cheerful, and there is a good deal of singing.

I shall be going up soon to Metulah, with the nurse. We shall fix up a hospital and a kitchen.

Your Yehudit is well; she is working in the kitchen, and feels fine and cheerful. Yes, in this place everyone must feel fine.

Shalom, shalom to all of you.

With labor's greetings, your Sarah.

34. On the Huleh swamp, see the entry "Huleh Valley" in the Glossary of Places.

35. Mount Hermon, a mountain range on the northwest border of Transjordan (present-day Israel, Lebanon, and Syria), dominates its surroundings. The peak of Mount Hermon is visible from a distance of more than 60 miles. The mountain is mentioned in Psalm 89:12 and Song of Solomon 4:8. It is called *Jebel al-Sheikh* [the chief mountain] in Arabic.

Pessie Abramson

Yael Gordon (Dagania Alef)

PESSIE ABRAMSON came with her parents to Erez Israel after the *pogroms* of 1905. The family settled in the colony of Rishon Lezion, and Pessie went to elementary school there. At that time the teacher in Rishon Lezion was Yosef Vitkin[36]—one of the leaders and teachers of the Second Aliyah. Years after she had left school, Pessie would speak of this man with love and reverence, and would tell of his friendship with his pupils and his influence over them.

Three years later, the family moved to Kineret and Pessie worked with the family; but as soon as Hannah Meisel [Shohat] opened her farm school, Pessie applied and was one of the first to be admitted.

It was at the farm that I first met her; and I can still see her—a healthy, happy, joking girl, with a firmly built body—all life and joy. But Pessie was just then between childhood and womanhood, and she had her thoughtful moments, too. But in her work she was already splendid.

In 1914, Pessie joined the workers' *kvuzah* that had taken over the responsibility for the dairy, the garden, and the kitchen on the Merhavyah "cooperative."[37] From then on her responsible work began.

Pessie became a model worker, the wonder of her companions. Whatever tools she took up, she handled them like a daughter of peasants, like one who had inherited generations of land tradition. But more than this, she was one who revolted instinctively and fiercely against any shadow of injustice that was cast in life around her. She stood bravely for the independence of woman. In her soul there was a fine synthesis of the woman, the mother, and the *haver*; but that harmony

36. Yosef Vitkin (1876–1912), a native of Mogilev, Belorussia, immigrated to Palestine in 1897. He initially obtained work as a laborer in the First Aliyah colonies. Later he became a teacher and served as headmaster of schools in Gederah, Rishon Lezion, and Kfar Tavor. He was known as a leading education reformer and advocated a curriculum of natural sciences, agriculture, physical training, and biblical study for moral and cultural purposes. Regarded as a precursor of the Second Aliyah, his influential pamphlet *Kol kore el zeirei yisrael asher libam leamam ulezion* [A Call to the Youth of Israel whose Hearts are with their People and Zion] (1905) was widely distributed by Hovevei Zion [Lovers of Zion] and helped to inspire the Second Aliyah.

37. The quotation marks here appear in the original Yiddish text.

did not bring her inner peace. There was a constant struggle in her between the demands of the woman, and the duties of the person responsible for and to the group. But after dark moments of suffering she emerged abruptly and unexpectedly into a joyous, contagious mood.

From Merhavyah, Pessie passed over to Tel Adas [Tel Adashim], where she joined the *kvuzah* of Hashomer. But she did not remain long there, being sent soon after her arrival to Petah Tikvah, with a *kvuzah* of women workers from Galilee. This was in 1916, the most difficult year of the war.[38] The achievements of the Galilee *kvuzah* among the workers of Judea make up a separate story.

It was a law with Pessie never to evade a responsibility, and this time she accepted the heaviest responsibility of all—the management of the workers' kitchen. The workers of Petah Tikvah were starving. The colonists could not give them their wages in cash, and gave them notes instead, and on these notes the workers borrowed. The loans they got just about sufficed for bread. But those who had no work had not even this much.

In that ghastly time, Pessie took on the direction of the kitchen, and became so to speak the center of all that need and misery. When she was not in the kitchen, she could be seen running through the colony, trying to get something for her charges. She could not do much. She worked beyond her strength, in the kitchen, in the garden, wherever she was needed. Her own food she cut down to the minimum. The inevitable came, and she collapsed. The doctors directed that she be sent back to her parents in Galilee, but even there, lying sick, she could not forget her hungry comrades in Petah Tikvah, in comparison with whom the [field] workers in Galilee were leading peaceful and contented lives.

Pessie was strongly bound to her family. In Erez Israel her parents became workers and remained workers all their lives. Her relationship to her mother was fine, enthusiastic and comradely. Most of all she loved her little sister, and did her best to educate the child in the ideals of the Erez Israel labor class. She was happy when, in the letters of the young girl, she felt that her influence had not been in vain.

When Pessie recovered, she was sent by the Merkaz Hahaklai [Central Farmers' Association] to Hederah. There were many workers in this colony, and Pessie undertook, with a few *haverot*, to institute a workers' kitchen after the model of the kitchen in Petah Tikvah.

In 1918, toward the close of the war, Pessie returned to Tel Adas, which she had visited once, briefly. Here, however, she could not manage to fit in. With all her motherly devotion, with all her hard work, she

38. On the situation in Palestine during World War I and the plight of the Yishuv, see part I, note 67 and note 5 in this section.

was so sensitive to the slightest wrong that was done a *haver*, so unwilling to accept any compromise, that she found herself in conflict with the others. After a harsh inner struggle, she left Tel Adas and went to the women workers' *kvuzah* of Merhavyah.

Here she suffered from something else—a constant faultfinding with herself. And although [the *kvuzah* was] happy with her work, she herself always felt that she was not fulfilling her duty. And yet whatever she touched prospered in the kitchen, the house and the field. There was a holiday mood [there] when Pessie worked in the kitchen, and the workers came to their meals as if visiting their mother.

She spoke little. She became silent and self-contained. It was only in rare, serious talks that she revealed the deep pain that awakened in her because of the hard life in the country. To all other difficulties were added the evils of the reign of Hassan Bek;[39] and the multiplicity of miseries crushed her soul.

She did not remain long in Merhavyah either. She was called to Yavniel to direct a group of young women workers—the daughters of families driven out of Judea. Here she was director, teacher, and inspirer. Again she overworked. The old, energetic, healthy peasant girl was reduced to a shadow of herself. She began to suffer pains in the legs, and the doctors demanded that she leave off work for a long time.

At the end of 1918, the English took Galilee,[40] and Pessie went with [Meyer] Spektor,[41] whom she had met in the commune at Tel

39. On Hassan Bek, see part II, note 7.

40. The British military advance on the Galilee took place in mid-September 1918. For this campaign, General Edmund H. H. Allenby, commander of Britain's Egyptian Expeditionary Forces, prepared by massing his troops from the Jordan River westward to the Mediterranean Sea. The British assault opened on September 19 with artillery bombardments of German-Turkish positions situated in the coastal plain, aided by the British air force and the advance of infantry, including English, Scottish, Welsh, Irish, and various Indian and French regiments. By midnight of September 19, the Arab town of Tul Karm was under British control. Nablus was captured on September 21. Meanwhile, three divisions of the British cavalry had advanced through the coastal plain northward with sweeping success. These last movements, combined with the steady progress of the British artillery and infantry from Nablus, enveloped and destroyed a significant portion of the retreating German-Turkish forces. As a result, the British captured many thousands of prisoners and secured a number of fords and bridges across the Jordan River. On September 23, the British gained control of Akko and Haifa. Two days later, after a fierce battle, the British captured Zemakh on the southern tip of Lake Kineret and Tiberias and its environs, immediately thereafter, in the face of little resistance. In the event, Allenby's conquest of the Galilee and the approaches to it from south, east, and north was complete. See also part I, note 67 and part V, note 5.

41. Meyer Spektor (1893–1955), a Second Aliyah pioneer, was born in Russia. In 1910, he immigrated to Palestine at the age of seventeen and shortly thereafter joined the ranks of Hashomer. He was initially active in the guarding of Hederah and later moved to the Lower Galilee, where Hashomer guarded the Kineret settlement area. From 1911–14, he worked as a *shomer* in Rehovot and Rishon Lezion. In 1914, he helped

Adas,[42] to Tiberias. Here she took the warm baths, and here, too, her first child was born. The birth of the child produced a tremendous effect on her. She was utterly absorbed by her new duties, her new joys and worries; and at the same time she ate out her heart because she had "escaped" from our common labor.

At that time, Spektor joined the group of mounted guards[43] who protected the Galilee settlements against sporadic attacks. He lived constantly on his horse, and was seldom at home. And, deprived of him, Pessie felt more deeply than ever her loneliness, and her separation from the old groups. At last, she could no longer bear it, and with her little family joined the group of *haverim* who were returning to Upper Galilee to rebuild the colonies which had been laid waste—Tel Hai and Kfar Giladi. Pessie lived a year and a half in Kfar Giladi. After the birth of her second child she became very weak, and in the social life of the [community] there was still much that displeased her. She made several attempts to work, but the strength for it was no longer there. She became more silent than ever, kept her own counsel and, unsuspected by the most intimate among [her comrades], reached her last, dreadful decision.

She had been lying in bed for several days. She rose, made the bed, fixed the tent, and wrote a short note. On the tent pole there always hung an English rifle. The tents stood at a distance from the yard, and no one heard either the shot or her dying groans. This was on Thursday, the twentieth of Iyar 5682 [May 1922]. Three months afterwards, died her younger child, Uri; both have been laid to rest on the little hill between Tel Hai and Kfar Giladi.

---

to establish the colony of Tel Adashim. When the British captured the Galilee in 1918, he was inducted into the Jewish police unit of Tiberias. It was around this time that he and Pessie Abramson produced a son named Yizhak. In 1920, he moved his family to Kfar Giladi and became active in the smuggling of munitions into the Yishuv from Vienna and Berlin via Beirut. In 1922, Pessie Abramson gave birth to their second son, Uri. During the Arab riots of 1929, he played a key role in the defense Jewish settlements in the southern part of the country. In the riots of 1936, he was an important figure in the defense of Tel Mond. He was among the founders of the Israel Defense Forces.

42. This phrase ("whom she had met in the commune at Tel Adas") does not appear in the original Yiddish text.

43. The reference here is to Hashomer.

Letters of Pessie Abramson

PETAH TIKVAH, 5676 [1916/17] — TO HER *HAVEROT*.

MY DEAREST SISTERS! What news? How is the work going and what kind of spirits are you in? What are the workers doing? Are any of them sick? I want to know everything about you and about everybody in my beloved Galilee.

It's so good to remember that somewhere there is a clean corner of the earth where people love each other; and it's best of all to remember that there my dearest friends live. Working over here, I remember each one of you in turn, and the feeling of it is so good—just as if I was working with you. Does this read silly to you? Well then, laugh at me, and I wish I could hear your laughter.

The work over here is going along so-so. We feel like exiles; we are waiting for the day when we can return to Galilee.

The summer vegetables have caught on well. How is it over in your garden? And what are we going to hear from your [women] workers' conference? Complaints against others, or self-accusations?

It's been a hard year, but it has given us a lot. It has taught us a great deal about life. And at least every one who is with us has learned to work—isn't it so?

I'm homesick for the singing we used to have two years ago, for E.'s songs, and Y.'s voice. I want to listen to the hills again. I want to hear S. reading us a new book, and I want to see G. prancing around on his horse like a hero. All of my poor brothers, struggling with their bit of soil—all of them are before my eyes: they, and the families of Ha-shomer, with the darling children.

Here I don't seem to live. All of me is with you. My heart has become like a sponge which draws in all the bitterness and pain of life, and I can't breathe. Don't think I'm sick. Physically, I am in perfect condition, and work all through the day. It's good so.

PORIYAH, 5677 [1917/18] — TO [MEYER SPEKTOR].[44]
N. let me read the letters he wrote you. I think you should give heed to what he says and do what he asks. As for me, Meyer, I shall not stand

44. The original Yiddish text identifies the addressee as "M.S." in this letter as well as those that follow.

in your way at all. Whether you remain in Tel Adas [Tel Adashim] or not, I shan't return there. I want to make it clear that I shall remain in Yavniel.[45] I feel I can't work alone, far from you—but I'll agree even to that. You must not take me into account. I'll always manage.

YAVNIEL, 5677 [1917/18] — TO [MEYER SPEKTOR].
You write that you are frightened by my letters. I won't write any more. Can you be afraid of what you have to be told? What can I say to you? No, I can't write more. Do as you think proper; you are wholly free.

Only one thing: it interests me to be a spectator, to watch life and people. That draws me. And work draws me. When a piece of work first begins, there's so much to learn from it.

I feel ashamed—and my shame grows greater and greater—when I hear that they haven't finished with the work in Tel Adas, and the barley is still standing in the field. Why, this alone should be a reason for staying on. And people aren't ashamed to leave a place right in the middle of the work! And you are one of them!

YAVNIEL, 5677 [1917/18] — TO [MEYER SPEKTOR].
I was exhausted yesterday, and could not answer. I went on an outing this Saturday. Haya-Sarah [Hankin] and I visited all the gardens of Yavniel; we inspected them, saw the mistakes which had been made, and then went up to the cemetery. We sat down there, and Haya Sarah began to tell me about her life, and about Yehezkel [Hankin], who was among the first *shomrim*. Those stories exhausted me.

Later N. came up to me, angry with everybody, complaining about things. She said: "I've been working for thirteen years, and this year I'll be left without a place. Others, who've been working less than a year get all sorts of offers from the *kvuzot*. I suppose I'll have to go and be a servant girl somewhere." I was terribly distressed by her words, and suddenly I had an idea. She ought to be given five *dunams* of land, and let her work for herself, on her own responsibility. I suggested this to her, and she was very happy. But I suppose there will be plenty of opposition [to it]. We'll see.

I didn't take on the work of clearing off the stones that was offered us by the colony. The price was too low. I'm letting the [young women] do something else—something that really has no meaning—I'm letting them work the ground again, though this isn't the right time. But I'd rather lose any amount than accept a price that is going to force down the rate of wages in the colony, because that would be the greatest loss of all.

45. At this time, there was a *kvuzah* of women workers in Yavniel.

Everything is hard, especially in the beginning. Our cucumbers have gone sick; now we have to tear them up and start all over again.

YAVNIEL, 5677 [1917/18] — TO [MEYER SPEKTOR].
I'm writing you again about the little things that turn up in my life. A little while ago a [young woman] came to my room and said: "I hear that you're Pessie. Take me in and I'll work like the other [young women]. My [householder] won't let me—but I want a different kind of life." (A charming dark [young woman], very appealing). I promised to give her work, but I warned her: "We work, but we have to provide our own food. We have no [householder] to look after us." And she answered, "I'm ready for anything."

Then, when I was on my way to work, I heard a group of women, sitting outside a house, talking about me; from what I caught, they are going to complain about me to the colony council: I spoil their [young women], and they have to pay higher wages.

It's no use, I suppose; everybody is chattering about me, and that's the one thing I hate. There's no help for it.

5678 [1918] — TO [MEYER SPEKTOR], WHEN HE AND
HIS [*HAVERIM* JOINED] THE JEWISH LEGION.
[*Mazel tov*] [good luck] to all of you, Meyer, and my blessings, which come from the inmost depths of my heart. I haven't the words to express my feelings.

TIBERIAS, 5679 [1919] — TO HEMDAH HURWIZ.[46]
You will think it curious if I tell you now, that once I wanted to see you without your knowing it. I thought that if such a thing were possible I would feel easier. Hemdah, you would not believe your own eyes if you saw me in my present condition. But in my heart nothing has changed —I feel that I shall never be able to be a mother . . .

Hemdah, you musn't think that here I work less than I used to when I had the kitchen, the garden, and the yard to look after. There are days when I can't take a moment's rest! And my heart is not at peace—I suffer, and I can't tell anyone. There are whole days when the only people I see are the storekeepers, and all I hear is what they tell me. Sometimes, alone, I grind my teeth—but outwardly I show nothing. As for writing, this is the first letter I've written, and I've no one to write to but you. What have I achieved this year? If I could only live as I lived once, if I could only be free. It makes me wretched to think that I am

46. Hemdah Hurwiz, a Second Aliyah pioneer, was among the founders of the *meshek hapoalot* in Kineret.

living [off] someone else, and even though I work all the time, there's no satisfaction in the work.

TIBERIAS, 5679 [1919]—TO SARAH MALKIN [WRITTEN ON THE LETTERHEAD OF HAPOEL HAHAKLAI] [LAND WORKERS' ASSOCIATION].[47]

I suppose you're angry with me because I'm still using the letterhead of [Hapoel Hahaklai], though I've left the work which I loved so. Believe me, Sarah, that I know everything you're thinking about me. You don't want to see me, and that tells me a lot.

People ask me: "Where are your *haverot*?" But I understand you. People point at me, saying, "Look how lonely she's been left. As long as she had strength and energy to give, she had friends [and *haverim*]." Well, Sarah, I oughtn't to say how bad I feel. I am lying in the hospital, and, Sarah, if you could see my child, you would forgive me everything. He is so sweet. He comforts me, and helps me to forget my longing for what used to be.

TIBERIAS, 5680 [1920]—TO M[EYER SPEKTOR].

Our little Yizhak is a blessing. I can't tell you what a darling he is. You should have seen: I was getting him ready for his bath and he was lying naked on the bed when the Arab brought me a letter from you. And I said: "Listen, Yizhak, little one, here's a letter from Daddy!" And I looked at him, and he looked at me, and both of us were happy. Meyer! I've got someone to share my happiness and my longing!

That's our little one. Every time I pass his bed, I thank God that we have such a lovely child.

From Hamarah[48]—no news. *Haverim* came from Mahanayim and told us they could hear heavy firing in the distance for the last three days. Yesterday Y.L. and Y.N. left in that direction to reconnoiter. But they haven't come back. Perhaps they are in Ayelet Hashahar and can't get any further.

I'm getting better steadily. My body moves more lightly, and it's easier to work. I baked bread today, and it came out perfect. Little Yizhak interrupts me; it's his meal time.

KFAR GILADI, 5681 [1921]—TO ZIPORAH.

It's such a long time since I saw you and heard you. There are times when I want to run away from everything. But where can I run, and what can I look for? Every place has its faults and failings, and what will be next year I don't know.

47. On Hapoel Hahaklai [Land Workers' Association], see part III, note 7.
48. On Hamarah, see part I, note 58.

Ziporah, believe me when I say that sometimes it looks as though there's no place for me in life. Everyone treads the old paths. Once I saw them looking for new paths, and I was drawn to them. It seemed to me that everything was being renewed, and a new life was about to begin. And now everything is in a rut; they have looked and (so they say) they have found! Yes, Ziporah, they did find something: a life which is worse than the old one.

SAFED, 5682 [1922] — TO [MEYER] SPEKTOR.

[The child] (Uri) cries all day long. I am all in a muddle. If the child were only better, I'd go home.

I haven't the peace and quiet that I had before [he] was born. There are two others in my room, and the place is a bedlam. All day long they chatter and joke, and it's so hard for me to hear them now.

It's half past twelve at night. I'm used to getting up at this hour to give baby the breast. But he's sleeping now, so I go on writing. Meyer! It seems that I can't live like other people. I've already written you that if in the next half a year things don't go the way I expect, I shall leave Kfar Giladi. The Histadrut will help me to find work and I'll live for the children's sake.

You write me nothing about yourself, you only want news of me. Are you satisfied in Kfar Giladi? Are you happy there? You mustn't think I shall be angry if you're happy up there; no, no, I shall be happy if you've found something.

Sometimes I think: children and work! How I once longed to have both in my life. But I didn't think I'd find it so hard.

Meyer, send me my pistol to the town. I may need it if there are riots. I am alone here with the child.

SAFAD, 5682 [1922] — TO [MEYER SPEKTOR].

I can almost walk around. I've only got a bit of pain and I'm still weak. The child grows more beautiful from day to day. Everyone talks about him in the hospital.

I won't under any circumstances go back to father and mother with two little children who won't give them any peace. And you know how I would feel there. You mention the suffering in Kfar Giladi. But I can't do what you suggest: I can't go away from a place in the hope that some day I'll return. Nor is there any hope that in half a year's time things will be better in Kfar Giladi. Is it possible that you don't understand me yet? Even before I had little Yizhak, it wasn't a good thing to keep changing places and people. And if I have to go on living in Kfar Giladi later, I oughtn't to abandon the place now. If I do go, it has to be for good.

No, Meyer, the time has not come for me to leave Kfar Giladi. They've got to divide up the work so that I can go on living there. And after I've had a talk with the doctor, I'll start work again.

A kiss for dear little Yizhak.

TIBERIAS, 5682 [1922] — TO [MEYER SPEKTOR].
I'm sitting and writing, and the little one lies there and watches me, as if he was asking me to send his love to his father and his older brother. So I send it . . .

Uri is a darling baby. He's already begun to cry: "Daddy! Daddy!" It's sweet to hear.

In two days he'll be six months old. And how is it with my big son? There's a woman here taking the warm baths; she has a son who's the living image of Yizhak. I always go to the baths at the same time as she does, so as to look at her child.

I hear that Yizhak never mentions me, that he's forgotten me completely. Do you know that when I heard it, I was horrified? Write me if it's true. I must know. I've asked you several times to bring him to me, but now you can't because there's a lot of sickness around.

You've probably heard about S. Today I read in the paper that he was out in his accounts and killed himself. He leaves behind a little girl.

Sarah Lishansky

Yizhak Ben-Zvi (Jerusalem)

Sarah was born in the year 1882,[49] in the *shtetl* of Malin, province of Kiev.[50] She was descended, on both sides, from distinguished families of *hasidim* [pious ones].[51] Her mother came from the famous *zadikim* [Hasidic rabbis] of Chernobyl[52] and having, as an orphan, been brought up in a high Jewish tradition by her grandfather, transmitted that tradition to her own children.

It was a tradition of wide hospitality, scholarship and piety. While the old man was alive, the house was filled, weekdays, on *Shabbat* [Sabbath] and holidays, with Jews who came from far and near, relatives, friends and just plain *hasidim*. They sat at his table and they said prayers with him in the large hall in which stood an *aron kodesh* [ark of the Torah scroll].

Like most of the girls of her time and age, Sarah went first to the regular *heder*, where she learned to read Hebrew and to translate the [Hebrew Bible]. Afterwards, a wandering teacher gave her the rudiments of arithmetic and Russian. The first books she read were Yiddish folk books, the stories of [Jacob] Dineson[53] and the legends of the

49. Another source indicates that Sarah Lishansky was born in 1884. See *Enziklopediyah lehaluzei hayishuv uvonav* (1947), ed. David Tidhar, vol. 2, 701.

50. Malin, a town west of Kiev and northeast of Zhitomir, is located in the north-central region of Ukraine. It was also the birthplace of Samuel A. Horodezky (1871–1957), one of the early historians of Hasidism.

51. *Hasidim* [pious ones] is the Hebrew term for the followers of Hasidism, the Jewish religious and mystical revival movement founded by Israel Baal Shem Tov (1669–1761) (see part VI, note 79) in the Ukrainian regions of Volhynia (see note 73 in this section) and Podolia. Hasidism swiftly spread to other parts of Eastern Europe.

52. Chernobyl, located on the Pripet River in Ukraine, was the site of an old Jewish community dating back to the late seventeenth century. The Jewish community possessed a great deal of prestige as a center of Hasidism, owing to the dynasty of *zadikim* [Hasidic rabbis] in the town begun by Menahem Nahum, a disciple of the Baal Shem Tov (see part VI, note 79). By 1897, the town's 5,526 Jews made up 59.4 percent of its total population.

53. Jacob Dineson (1856–1919), the Yiddish publicist and pioneer of the sentimental Yiddish novel, played a leading role in the modernization of East European Jewish elementary education by advocating secular curricula. Such schools were often called "Dineson schools." He was a close associate and friend of Isaac Leib Perez (see following note).

hasidim. Later she turned to [Isaac Leib] Perez[54] and the new Yiddish literature; and it was only after many years that she reached the Russian classics. But when she came in contact with them, they exerted a profound influence on her which lasted for the rest of her life.

Even as a child Sarah showed a strong leaning toward "public" affairs, and with her [young] friends founded a benevolent society to help the poor of the town.

At the age of sixteen, Sarah passed through a fearful crisis, the result of a *shidukh* [marriage arrangement] that her parents wanted to force on her. It was only in later years that she managed to shake off the effects of this experience.

At that time—1900—the Jewish labor movement was just beginning in southern Russia. Sarah was not a woman given to mere theorizing. When she joined a social movement it was with heart and soul, and no sooner was she drawn into the ranks of labor than she began to organize a group for herself and to open a school for children. In the midst of her work, she decided to become economically independent, and to earn her own livelihood, and she therefore left Malin and went to study in Kiev, where she joined the "S.S." socialist Zionist party.[55] There, in 1905, she lived through the three ghastly days of the *pogrom*, and took an active part in the organization of the Jewish self-defense. Two years later, she graduated as nurse and returned to her native town.

In Sarah, the social instinct was bound up with a sisterly personal need to help those in suffering. Living at home, in Malin, she once more became the center of the youth and labor movement. Finally, getting into trouble with the local police, she left Malin and moved to Vilna in the year 1907.

Here, in the Jerusalem of Lithuania,[56] with its ancient Jewish tradi-

54. Isaac Leib Perez (1852–1915) was a premier Yiddish writer of the *fin-de-siècle*. Along with Mendele Mokher Sforim (Shalom Jacob Abramovich, 1835–1917) and Shalom Aleikhem (Shalom Rabinovich, 1859–1916), he was also an important figure in Hebrew literature. He generally favored Jewish socialism and Zionism, but never affiliated with any political party or organization. His home in Warsaw was a center for Yiddish writers and aspiring authors. In his work, he adapted older genres and introduced new literary forms (e.g., the short story and symbolic drama) into Yiddish and Hebrew literatures. His published work focused on the lives of the *hasidim*, the common people, and the oppressed.

55. On the "S.S." socialist Zionist party, see part I, note 29.

56. Starting in the modern period, Vilna became known as "*Yerushalayim delita*" ["the Jerusalem of Lithuania"], owing to its preeminence in rabbinic, spiritual, and communal East European Jewish affairs. It was home to several important rabbis, including Elijah ben Solomon Zalman (1720–1797), known as the Vilna Gaon [genius], the widely acclaimed Talmudic scholar and leader of Lithuanian Jewry. The Vilna Gaon championed the so-called *mitnagdim* [opponents of Hasidism] and attracted numerous disciples. His spiritual leadership had a lasting impact on East European Jewish society.

tions and its new Jewish socialist movement, Sarah's spirit ripened to maturity. And later, going to St. Petersburg, she rounded out her education in a living center of Russian culture.

Once again, in 1908, Sarah returned to Malin. Adult, able, she concentrated in her hands the leadership of the professional societies, the Jewish home, the Jewish self-defense, the party propaganda. In addition she worked day and night at her profession of nurse and medical assistant.

In 1909, Sarah's family left for Erez Israel. The ties between her and her own were very strong, and she decided to break the bonds which held her to Russia, and to follow. In Erez Israel, she was lonely for a time, but before long she had found her own way in the new country—the way of the nurse and the *haverah* of the worker. At first, she worked in a Jewish hospital in Jerusalem. Then the war broke out and she was transferred to a [Turkish] government hospital. After that, she went to the *kvuzot* of Karkur and Tel Adas [Tel Adashim]. When she worked in this district, Bedouins would flock to her clinic, and she did not withhold her help from anyone.

Her great idea was to place the Kupat Holim [Sick Fund] of the Histadrut on the highest possible level. She opened a clinic in Tel Aviv and for years gave it all the devotion she was capable of. In spite of her instinctive dislike of publicity, she was repeatedly chosen on the most important committees and public bodies; and she was a deputy in the first Vaad Leumi [National Assembly] of Erez Israel,[57] a member of the Workers' Council of Tel Aviv, and a delegate to the Workers' Conference.

In the midst of her strenuous labors, Sarah became ill. For a year and a half she suffered, and then, in a last effort to find a cure, went to Berlin and Vienna. In the latter city occurred, at that time, the World Conference of the Poalei Zion party and the Thirteenth World Zionist Congress. Feeling herself almost beyond hope of recovery, Sarah attended all the sessions, and took an active part in them, forgetting in her devotion to the cause her own sufferings. Returning to Erez Israel, she felt a certain improvement, and resumed her beloved work with Kupat Holim. But before long she collapsed again under the same

57. The Vaad Leumi [National Assembly] of Palestine functioned as the executive body of the official Jewish community in Palestine. Legitimated by the British Mandate as the central governing body of the Yishuv, it was comprised of diverse political parties and groups representing the broad social-political spectrum of Jewish life in Palestine. Every four years, the Vaad Leumi published the *Register of Adult Jews*, a list of members whose voluntary association was optional, entailing responsibilities as well as benefits. The Vaad Leumi remained in operation until Israel's independence on May 14, 1948, at which time a provisional council took over its duties.

deadly sickness—cancer. She lingered for a few months with her family in Jerusalem, and until the end did not cease to interest herself in the workers' movement in Erez Israel and all the enterprises she had labored in. She died in the month of Av 5684 [August 1924].

The memory of this extraordinary woman will remain one of the inspirations of our movement—a symbol of its power to lift and perpetuate those who are bound up with its ideals.

Sarah's Shtetl

Zalman Rubashov [Shazar]

THEY TELL ME that the Ukrainian *shtetl* of Malin,[58] where I once spent two summers together with Sarah Lishansky, is utterly changed. On the eve of the World War, a fire devastated a great part of it. Then, after the war and the [Russian] revolution, the antisemitic bandits of [Simon] Petlyura[59] descended on it. Today, the Russian Jewish Communist paper, *Der shtern*[60] [The Star] boasts that the Yevsekzia[61] has managed to "finish off" the counter-revolutionary Zionist youth group Hashomer Hazair [The Young Guard], which hid itself in the little nearby forest. They boast further that "the enemy has been destroyed" and the town of Malin is in the hands of the Jewish Communists.

All this may be true. But the Malin which is firmly set in my mind is the *shtetl* I knew some twenty odd years ago, in the summers of 1908 and 1909, soon after the collapse of the first Russian Revolution,[62]

58. On Malin, see note 50 in this section.

59. Simon Petlyura (1879–1926), a Ukrainian leader who organized soldiers into nationalist battalions, is generally regarded as instrumental in perpetuating the widespread anti-Jewish violence that overran Ukraine in 1919–20. When the Red Army forced Petlyura's units to retreat, his followers assembled into gangs and instigated *pogroms* against the Jews in Zhitomir, Proskurov, and other towns and villages in Ukraine. Petlyura himself subsequently fled to Poland and then France, where he headed the Ukrainian anti-Soviet movement. On May 26, 1926, he was assassinated by a Jew named Shalom Schwartzbard. In 1927, following a dramatic Paris show trial, Schwartzbard was acquitted by the court.

60. *Der shtern* [The Star], a Yiddish Communist daily newspaper published in Kharkov, Ukraine by the Yevsekzia (see following note) between 1925 and 1941.

61. The Yevsekzia was the Jewish section of the propaganda department of the Russian Communist Party from 1918 to 1930. It virulently opposed Zionism and supported the assimilation of the Yiddish-speaking masses into the broader Russian proletariat and emergent Soviet Union. With the backing of the police and other governmental authorities, the Yevsekzia dismantled synagogues, Hebrew schools, libraries, and *yeshivot* and aimed to destroy or seize control of Zionist organizations. At the same time, the Yevsekzia attempted to create a Jewish Communist culture with new schools, theaters, and other projects. Additionally, the Yevsekzia published three influential Yiddish Communist organs: *Der shtern* [The Star] in Kharkov (see previous note), *Der emes* [The Truth] in Moscow, and *Oktyabr* [October] in Minsk. In 1930, the Soviet regime disbanded the Yevsekzia following the latter's 1926 decision to moderate its anti-Zionist and antinationalist policies. The institutions created by the Yevsekzia were gradually liquidated by the Soviet regime in the 1940s.

62. The reference here is to the failed liberal Russian revolution of 1905.

and before the new stream of Jewish immigration started for Erez Israel.[63]

Even then, of course, Malin was no longer rock-firm in the ancient ways of its life. It is true that the rabbinate was occupied by the two young cousins who had inherited their place from their uncle, the "old rav" [rabbi], according to the ruling of the powerful rabbi of Chernobyl.[64] It is also true that from time to time the great rabbi of Chernobyl would himself visit the *shtetl*, and then a holiday would occur in the middle of the week. Likewise, is it true that every morning through the year—but more markedly on Saturday nights—there would drift from the *shtetl*'s many *batei midrashim* [houses of worship] the ancient, unforgettable and yearning chant of the psalms. And on the eve of the Tisha Beav [Ninth of Av],[65] a deep, gentle sorrow descended on the whole *shtetl*, and lay brooding over it from the confines of the woods of Mishevka[66] to the woods of Mikhaelovka.[67]

And yet the town was not what it once had been; something had stirred in it.

Scattered through the town were the homes where young people were already reading the forbidden books of modern knowledge—in Hebrew, it is true, but forbidden modern knowledge just the same. Here and there Zionist groups had risen and had disappeared, leaving their trace, chiefly in the modernization of the *heder*.

And another change. Behind the town, a paper factory had been built by a rich Jew of Berdichev,[68] and here a hundred Jewish [young

63. The reference here appears to be to the immigrants of the Fourth Aliyah (1924–1928) and the start of the Fifth Aliyah (1929–1939).

64. On Chernobyl, see note 52 in this section.

65. Tisha Beav [the Ninth of Av] is the traditional day of mourning for the destruction of the Holy Temples in Jerusalem. The explusion of the Jews from Spain is also said to have occurred on the ninth of Av. Over time, the date became a symbol for all the misfortunes and persecutions that have befallen the Jewish people, including the loss of Jewish national independence in late antiquity and the Crusades of the medieval period.

66. Mishevka (Mashevka) is a village located halfway between Poltava and Karlovka, southwest of Kharkov, in the eastern Ukraine. The nearby town of Karlovka included a significant Jewish population, whose origins dated back to 1794. The Nazis destroyed the Jewish community there during World War II.

67. There were many small Ukrainian towns and villages named Mikhaelovka. The *shtetl* noted here is probably a small town by that name located northeast of Odessa and Kherson in southeast Ukraine.

68. Berdichev, located in the Volhynia region, is a town in Ukraine. In 1861, it was the second largest Jewish community in tsarist Russia, with a population of 46,683. Shortly thereafter, the numbers began to decline, and in 1897 Berdichev had 41,617 Jewish residents (80 percent of the total population). In 1919, a *pogrom* instigated by the Ukrainian army severely impacted Berdichev's Jewish community. By 1926, its 30,812 Jews made up 55.6 percent of the population. Berdichev became one of the foremost centers of the Bund (see note 69). The local Jewish community was ultimately destroyed in the Holocaust.

women] worked, daughters of families that had once been well-to-do.
Among these workers came and went the local [Jewish] socialists—
members of the Bund[69]—and the handful of [S.S.] socialist Zionists.[70]
Every year, after the *yamim noraim* [days of awe],[71] half a dozen [young
men and women] would leave the town to attend the high schools and
universities of Kiev and Odessa. In the month of May, they would return to the *shtetl*, a happy, laughing crowd, bringing with them, like
some strange, psychic epidemic, a nameless, unexpressed longing for
new things. Somewhere, on a little side street, a group of enthusiastic
[young men and women] would gather the children of the working
classes every morning, and teach them reading, writing, arithmetic and
even some geography in pure Yiddish. And the youthful teachers were
astounded at their own daring, at the impudence of this enterprise at
once so dear them—and so vague and obscure. In the evening, this
same group of [young men and women] would meet with friends and
sympathizers to rehearse the drama *Yevrai* [The Jews] by [Yevgeni]
Chirikov[72] so that by giving a public performance in Russian they
might cover the expenses of their Jewish school.

In a little room on the edge of the *shtetl*, near the woods, lived the
teacher, an extern student, who taught the youth of the town and prepared them for high school. He spread not only formal education but
ideas, too; he tore ancient threads and wove new ones, weaving a world
of thought and song and dream. This man, Russian teacher and Hebrew poet, was the focus of all that was finest and most rebellious in the
youth of the town. The circle that gathered round him was permeated
with the belief that life has a purpose, and that something must be done

69. The Bund is an acronym for the Algemeyner Arbeter Bund in Poyln un Rusland
[General Jewish Worker's Union in Poland, Russia, and Lithuania], a Jewish socialist
party founded in Russia in 1897. The Bund sought to mobilize the Yiddish-speaking
masses of the Russian empire and fought violently with other Jewish political parties.
After the split between the Bolsheviks and the Mensheviks in 1912, the Bund affiliated
itself with the liberal-leaning Mensheviks. The Bund played a vital role in East European Jewish life throughout the 1920s and 1930s. Over time, it gradually succumbed
to the hostility of the Soviet government, declined, and was dismantled.

70. On the "S.S." socialist Zionist party, see part I, note 29.

71. The reference here is to the Jewish high holidays of Rosh Hashanah [New Year]
and Yom Kippur [Day of Atonement].

72. Yevgeni Chirikov's (1860–1936) play *Yevrei* [The Jews] (1904), simultaneously
published in German as *Die Juden* [The Jews], was a spirited attack on Russian antisemitism. Chirikov's play is best understood against the backdrop of the rise of antisemitism in tsarist empire during the second half of the nineteenth century. Indeed, the
pogroms and the Dreyfus Affair prompted several important Russian writers to defend
the Jews. Most of the defenders were moderates, liberals, and leftists, such as Anton
Chekov (1860–1904), Maxim Gorki (1868–1936), and Vladimir Korolenko (1853–
1921), each of whom produced sympathetic portrayals of the Jews and warmly championed their plight.

with it, something great, pure, true, and liberating, a deed which demanded every sacrifice, and for which every sacrifice could be made in joy. But for this deed much preparation was needed; for its sake the individual must break with his home. By comparison with it, the individual counted for nothing, for in it the real meaning of existence could be found. And yet no one in that circle knew exactly the character of this deed, and of this dedication; no one could say where this mysterious altar was located.

The young [women] in that circle were more characteristically seized by that mood than were the [men]. They believed more deeply in the importance and the sanctity of that altar; but they were also more uncertain about the roads that led to it.

The fascination and temptation of assimilation in Russian life had passed its full bloom. Even in Lithuania, the [young] Jewish [women] no longer threw themselves with the same self-forgetful enthusiasm into Russian literature and the Russian revolutionary movement. But in Volhynia,[73] this tide had never run very strongly, and least of all in Malin. The first [young women] to master the Russian literature—and Sarah was among these—wanted to do so within their identity as Jews and their will to be Jewish. For in this interval of the first Russian Revolution [of 1905], the Jewish labor movement had acquired a charm and attraction of its own; and after the revolution there had come a series of *pogroms*. At the same time, too, there began a Jewish folk movement and an awakening toward Jewish literature. That hidden altar would have to be looked for among the Jews themselves.

And when this became evident, the utter and tragic helplessness of the Jewish [young woman] first became evident.

At first, when the broad road led for everyone in the direction of socialism—in the early years of *Iskra*[74] [The Spark], the S.R.'s[75] [So-

73. Volhynia, a Russian province in northwest Ukraine, was a center of East European Jewish life, dating back to the fifteenth century. In 1897, there were 395,782 Jews living in Volhynia, comprising 13.2 percent of the total population. Hasidism exerted a strong influence over the area's Jewish communities. By the turn of the nineteenth and twentieth centuries, however, both the Zionist movement and the Bund were firmly established in the region. The *pogroms* in Russia during the 1880s and in 1905–06 only indirectly affected Volhynia's Jewish population. However, during World War I and the Russian civil war, numerous *pogroms* afflicted the region. Many thousands of Jews were killed in this period. The misfortunes of the Jewish community of Vohynia impelled large numbers of young people to immigrate to Palestine.

74. *Iskra* [The Spark], founded by Vladimir Lenin (1870–1924) and his associates in 1900, was the organ of the Russian Social Democratic Labor Party.

75. The S.R.'s [Socialist Revolutionaries] were members of the Party of Socialist Revolutionaries (P.S.R.) which was founded in 1902. The PSR proclaimed itself the heir to the Narodnaya Volya [People's Will] party. The latter espoused an agrarian Russian society and advocated the use of terrorism in the struggle to the overthrow of the tsarist regime and reorganize the state.

cialist Revolutionaries], and even the Bund—young Jewish men and women had traveled together as equals, the woman as certain, as self-confident and as critical as the man. The road was equally new to both of them, and both of them were equally equipped to travel along it. But when the road began to lead back, when Jewish socialism demanded an approach to the Jewish masses, the man was better equipped than the woman—and the woman followed uncertainly and sadly.

The devotion of the woman [to traditional Judaism] was deeper than that of the man. She had absorbed more intimately the living tradition of the *shtetl*, its quiet dreariness, its mournful chants, its melodious speech, and the whole of its dark life; and this bond of the soul she still retained even when she went into the rich and tempting Russian world. But what she possessed in the way of emotional devotion, she lacked—in some measure, at least—in clarity of understanding. What was the meaning of those things—themselves outward manifestations—to which she was so passionately attached? What was the deeper content of those melodies that she guarded so faithfully, and which awakened in her a quiet fear? What in them was important and what was unimportant? And how was one to make a decision if these values contradicted one another? This was not at all clear to her. The echoes of the fierce debates among the men only confused her the more, and served to accentuate her alienation. She was at the same time deeply attached and strangely alien, and in her helplessness she looked for some surer approach.

Foremost among the women of that town who suffered from this division—and they appear one by one in my memory—was Sarah Lishansky.

The help that she sought and surely merited was given to her in small measure. The great and cruel friend, to whom her heart appealed, did not lead. He was a Hebrew lyricist, an enthusiast and skeptic in one, filled with destructive criticism and biting irony. Bitterly, he mocked both her socialism and her Jewish school, and close as he was to her, he turned cold looks on her enthusiasms and did not reveal any path to her. She brought the burden of her sufferings to him and he, the friend who felt finely and deeply, but who was sated with sorrows, was afraid to stretch out his hand to her lest he make her burden heavier.

As to the other young people in her circle, their help could mean very little to her. They did not stand at the center of her life; they were not even within the inner circle.

Till at last she found her true support, the sure rock of firm support she had sought so long in vain; and it came from the most unexpected quarter.

When her younger sister wrote from Erez Israel, asking her to join her there, Sarah was in great doubt. She was afraid of the Hebrew language, which she did not know; she was afraid of a country that was strange to her. But she came, and she made contact with the workers here, and all at once the long-sought road was revealed to her. She suddenly found the people who knew what that great deed of liberation was, and where the altar was to be found. And it was as she had dreamed; it was a deed that demanded all, and gave all. And with all the pent-up enthusiasm of her untapped youth, she threw herself into her new mission. The emotions and longings that had been gathering in her for years overflowed from her, an inexhaustible flood of devotion and heroism. Her personal asceticism was sublimated into a fanaticism of service to others; and in place of a love that despaired there was a mild compassion for all. From that time on, her happiness was evident in the tenderness and gentleness of her smile—for her sacrifice had been accepted.

Rahel Zisle[-Levkovich]

Lo-Nuham[76] (Shekhunat Borokhov)

R̲AHEL WAS THE CHILD of a generation which, out of its pain, wove the dream of a new life and became the pioneer of its realization.

She was born in Yanova, a *shtetl* in Lithuania, near Kovno.[77] Her upbringing was that of the usual daughter in a pious, Jewish middle-class home. She went to the Russian elementary school, and from time to time she took Hebrew lessons from the teachers who came to the *shtetl*.

She was a clever, lively [individual], but the life of the *shtetl* gave her little opportunity for development. In her childhood, her ideal was the student type, which appeared now and again in the *shtetl*, speaking Russian fluently.

The war years came, with their expulsions, horrors, and wanderings. Finally, the family returned to its *shtetl*, which was now occupied by the Germans, and was therefore more than ever cut off from the rest of the world, and from the big Jewish centers. The heroes and the leaders of fashion were now the German lieutenants. They ruled by the right of victory, and still more by the right "of a higher culture and a nobler race." The *shtetl* became slavish in spirit; the older people always took their hats off in the street to every non-commissioned officer, and the younger people tried to speak German and to make contacts among the mighty. Rahel, sixteen years old, was among the first to rebel against this spirit, among the first to assert her self-respect; and round her she

76. The identity of Lo-Nuham is unknown. The pseudonym derives from the Hebrew meaning "not comforted."

77. Kovno, a Lithuanian city located at the juncture of the Viliya and Neman rivers, was a center of Jewish cultural activity. In 1897, there were 25,441 Jews in Kovno (30 percent of the total population); there were 32,628 in 1908 (40 percent of the population). The Jewish community of Kovno produced numerous important religious figures, scholars, and literaturs and was home to several significant Jewish schools, libraries, and Yiddish newspapers. The Jews of Kovno suffered severely during World War I, and in May 1915 the tsarist regime expelled the Jews from the entire province. When the region was later occupied by the Germans, local Jewish communal life was revived. Kovno next grew in importance after it became the capital of independent Lithuania. In 1923, there were 25,044 Jews living in Kovno (25 percent of the total population). Zionist associations took root in the region at the turn of the nineteenth and twentieth centuries, and Hehaluz [The Pioneer] was particularly active. The Jewish community of Kovno was completely destroyed during World War II.

gathered a small group which gave itself to the study of Jewish questions. She learned Hebrew rapidly, took up Jewish history and the newest Jewish movements, and before long became a Zionist. The group expanded until it included most of the Jewish youth of the *shtetl*, and a new spirit entered Yanova. Hebrew was being studied and spoken. Evenings were arranged for national-cultural purposes, and gradually a spiritual atmosphere was created.

For Rahel, with her searching soul, with her hidden energies, this was far from enough. She looked for more vivid means of self-expression. She left the *shtetl* and entered the German Jewish gymnasium of Kovno. Here educational standards were high, and Rahel was eager to learn; but the atmosphere of the place was demoralizing. The director and most of the teachers were rabbis of the Frankfort school,[78] and their fantastic pietism and severity alienated the youth. There was constant conflict between the teachers and the older pupils. This situation disenchanted Rahel and she longed for a quieter atmosphere.

Historic events came, the revolution in Russia, the awakening of the masses in Germany, the anticipations of liberation in the Jewish people. Hopes and promises filled the air with brightness. Rahel understood and felt all the human significance of the revolution. She saw the possibility of beginning life anew, the opportunity to live in accordance with the dictates of her own conscience and the full expression of her personal energies. Together with a group of *haverim* she decided that all her dreams could be fulfilled in a [comradely life of togetherness among] workers in Erez Israel. With her to dream was to act—and the leap was made at once. The group found work in a Lithuanian farm [in Mariampol[79]] and created the commune. This became the first organized group

78. The reference here is to a Jewish high school based on German Orthodoxy. Modern Neo-Orthodoxy emerged in Frankfort am Main, where the first stirrings of a markedly secular and assimilationist program gave rise to Wissenschaft des Judentums [Science of Judaism] and Reform Judaism. The traditionalist opponents of Wissenschaft and Reform Judaism, led by Rabbi Samson Raphael Hirsch (1808–1888), created a German brand of halakhic Judaism in harmony with the modern world. The latter, especially its pattern of life and educational institutions, became the dominant paradigm of German Orthodoxy.

79. Mariampol, a city in southern Lithuania, had a significant Jewish community dating back to the early nineteenth century. In 1897, there were 3,268 Jews in Mariampol, comprising 49 percent of the total population. On the eve of World War I, roughly 5000 Jews lived there. Many local Jewish youth attended Russian secondary schools. The local Jewish economy was based on small industry and trading in agricultural produce. In this period, Jewish cultural life in Mariampol was vibrant and included a Hebrew secondary school, nationalist political activities, and a training farm for Zionist pioneers. During World War I, many Jews were expelled from Mariampol. The number of Jews in the city subsequently dropped to 2,545 (21 percent of the total population). The Nazi regime established a ghetto in Mariampol during World War II and the local Jewish community was massacred in September 1941.

of *haluzim* in Lithuania:[80] the Ahvah [brotherhood] group. Shortly before the time for her graduation, Rahel left the gymnasium and joined the group.

She threw herself into the work with the energy of a person who had sought an outlet for years and found it at last. She conquered all the difficulties of the transition to physical labor, and became a good worker. Her high general and womanly qualities made her one of the natural leaders, one of those whose influence molds the style and character of comradely relationships. New forces unfolded in her, enriching the life around her. Her love and devotion shone from her; and she understood the meaning of little things, too. She was the embodiment of energy, motion, and healthy understanding. And in all, she observed to extremes the manner of her new life; she went barefoot, even on visits to town, clothed herself very simply, ate no meat, and was plain and forthright in her dealings with people.[81]

Most characteristic of her forthrightness and honesty was her relationship to her family. She would not relinquish one jot of the implications of her new life, and in this she grieved her parents greatly. And yet her relationship to them became so tender, so loving, that she healed the wounds which she had been compelled to inflict. And when she came to Erez Israel, she did not rest until she had brought her parents over, too.

After half a year's work in the commune, she fell sick with kidney trouble, and her life was in danger. And when she was cured, she remained weak for a long time because she was too eager to return to her work, and because, in her fanatical vegetarianism and in her rigid simplicity of clothing, she retarded her full recovery.

The winter of that year, the *haverim* of the commune scattered through Germany, Belgium, and France, working in the coal mines and waiting for the immigration into Erez Israel to begin. Rahel remained

---

80. Hehaluz [The Pioneer] in Lithuania was established after World War I and based itself initially on cooperative societies in carpentry, tailoring, etc. Due to a lack of capital and experience, the societies did not last long. They were replaced by agricultural training groups and a central training farm known as Kibush [Conquest]. Lithuanian Hehaluz, numbering 1000–1500 members, also organized urban cooperatives in Kovno and other cities.

81. The sensibility noted here is akin to the asceticism practiced by the Zionist philosopher Aharon David Gordon (1852–1922), who believed that salvation for the Jewish people could come about only through the efforts of the individual to change him/herself. Gordon's worldview is rooted in the conviction that the cosmos has unity, that nature and humanity are one, and that all living things are organic parts of the cosmos. He lived simply and was a strict vegetarian. On Gordon's philosophy of vegetarianism, see *A. D. Gordon: Selected Essays*, trans. Frances Burnce (New York: League for Labor Palestine, 1938), pp. 274–278.

in Kovno to earn the money for the journey. She still retained the style of life of the commune, guarding herself, above all, from the exploitation of others. Sometimes she would astonish a porter by giving him twice what he would ask for, saying that she earned a great deal more for a great deal less work.

The long awaited moment came, and Rahel left for Erez Israel, together with the whole *kvuzah*. Immediately on her arrival she separated from the group, and went to Hederah, there to learn for herself the ways of Palestinian life. In the orchards of Hefzibah she made her first living contacts with the earth, and from that time on her ideal was working the land and nothing else.

From Hederah she went to a *kvuzah* in Karkur. Here she came to believe in the idea of the large *kibbutz*, and became a member of the Gdud Avodah [Labor Legion] in Migdal. She was given work in the hospital, which at that time was housed in tents and where the conditions were primitive and difficult. The work was suited to her capacities and character, especially to her sensitivity to the sufferings of others and to her powers of devotion. But she lived too intently in her work. She reacted too violently to the life around her, and even her abounding energies began to fail. She was forced to change her work. She went back to her original Lithuanian *kvuzah*, which was sent to build the houses of Kfar Giladi.

When the Jewish National Fund had bought the Nuris bloc of land,[82] in the Jezreel Valley, Rahel joined the big commune of Ein Harod. Here she remained a full eight years, until the last day of her life. Here it was that she met and married Shlomo Lefkovich [Lavi], and here her three children were born.

She had two little corners of her own in Ein Harod—the tree nursery and the children. It was the same instinct that drew her to both, the desire to nourish and to mold form and character. She had been blessed with an extraordinary tenderness toward all organic things. This instinct was an expansive, devoted motherliness, which flowed out beyond her

---

82. The Nuris bloc of land, whose name derives from an ancient village in the vicinity of the Harod spring (known in Arabic as Ain Jalud) at the base of Mt. Gilboa, was the scene of a battle between the Philistines and Saul in c. 1190 B.C.E. The Israelites were supposed to have encamped at the Harod spring prior to the battle (1 Samuel 29:1). Shortly after World War I, the Jewish National Fund purchased a large tract of land in the area that was covered by malarial swamps. In 1921, pioneers of the Gdud Avodah [Labor Legion] set up tent camps there and started to drain the swamps. The location soon became the hub of a lively debate in the socialist Zionist movement over the idea of the "large kibbutz"—the notion of a countrywide commune of separate economic units. With the decline of the Gdud Avodah, many former members banded together to establish Kibbutz Ein Harod, which became a center of the emergent Kibbutz Hameuhad movement. In 1929, the community of Ein Harod was moved to a new physical site (see note 83).

own children toward the children of others, toward all human beings, and toward all living things.

In the latter years of her life she was active in the social work of the *kibbutz*. She was a member of the comrades' court, the housing committee, and the educational committee. She was particularly concerned with the direction of the *mashtelah* [plant nursery], which absorbs some fifteen to twenty *haverot* in Ein Harod and is one of the most important branches of the economy.

In the fall of 1930, Ein Harod stood on the threshold of a new epoch. After eight difficult years in barracks, erected in a malaria-infested district, the *kibbutz* was to pass over to the new houses built in Kumi.[83] The future was full of promise. But during the transitional period, the shortage of housing accommodation became acute, and the winter approached, with its harsh winds and capricious weather. One half of the *haverim* took sick with grippe, and the other half had to work double shifts to keep the place going. The epidemic made its way into the children's home, and Rahel put forth a superhuman effort to meet the emergency. During the day, she was busy with the children; at night, she sat in committees or did other social work. The strain was obvious and she fell sick. It soon became clear that her body, weakened by over-exertion, and by much malaria, would not be able to fight off the disease.

She herself did not expect to die. An hour before the end, she was still worrying about the children; she fell asleep, and in her sleep passed peacefully away—her face retaining in death the tranquillity of a person who lies down to rest with all her tasks fulfilled and her conscience clear.

On Friday, November 7, 1930, the five hundred comrades of Ein Harod and Tel Yosef accompanied her silently to her last resting place. Above the grave, they planted young trees which she had cared for herself. The following spring, they dug up the soil not far from the cemetery for a big orchard, to be named "Pardes Rahel" [the orchard of Rahel].

Our movement, whose highest ideal is the creation of the new individual, found in her its purest personification.

---

83. Kumi is the Arabic name of the Zevaim Ridge, which is located on the northern rim of Harod Valley. In 1929, the Ein Harod settlement group transferred from the area near the Harod Spring to the slope of the Zevaim Ridge.

Letters of Rahel Zisle-Levkovich

I

THIS EVENING, I'm going to devote to you. I've decided not to go to the meeting; instead I'll tell you everything that's happened in me in all this time.

I've been nineteen months in the country, and I've tried all sorts of occupations. I've worked in orchards (in Hederah and Hefzibah), at vegetables (in Karkur), in the hospital (in Migdal), at building (in Kfar Giladi), in the secretariat of the Gdud Avodah, in the kitchen, in the *mashtelah* [plant nursery], and then again in the orchard (in Ein Harod). And I'll tell you how it all came to pass, and you can think what you like of me.

When I first got here, I wanted neither [a small *kvuzah* nor a large *kibbutz*]. I wanted to go and work for some colonist planter. I thought the colonist would provide me with a living and in the evenings I would have enough time to look around and find out about the different *kvuzot*, the life on the land, and so on; afterwards I would be able to choose what I was best fitted for.

I wanted to live alone, because that way I could think better. And so I thought that in the colonist's house I would find the loneliness I needed. My first idea was to work in the stalls, the vegetable garden, and the chicken coop. But I was mistaken. I found out that if a colonist agrees to take a Jewish woman worker, he wants her to be a servant in the house. I thanked him and went off with a group [of *haverim*] to Hederah.

But the desire to live alone still haunted me, so I fixed myself up in Hefzibah. Three or four people were employed there in tree planting, and the work gave me much more than I expected. The man in charge, an expert in his line, uncovered the world of botany to me. I began to understand and—what is more important—to feel the life of every plant and tree. I began to be observant of every little change in their lives. The work became very dear to me, and I was wholly absorbed by it and by books on it. I learned how to graft oranges, and became very fond of that work.

But soon the rains began, and because of the mud I could not go every day to Hefzibah. My *haverim* went away to Migdal, with the Gdud Avodah, and wrote me long letters from there; enthusiastic letters, which made me think well of the Gdud. But I was scared by the bigness of the group, so I remained in Hederah.

Life in Hederah was hard. The rain was heavy that season, and we had no lodgings; besides which we had to suffer a great deal from the overseer. The relations with him were very nasty and tense, and it didn't look as though there would be any change for the better. Well, I was invited to Karkur, went there, and stayed. I was sinking more and more into the Palestinian life. In Karkur, I became acquainted with the small *kvuzah* and all its defects. There I also met the [workers] of the Second Aliyah and the older type of woman worker. I knew what was lacking in this life: will, freedom, effort. There was lacking the energy of earlier days. And the smallness of the *kvuzah* separates them from the center of things, because there is so little coming and going. Nothing new appears to make life brighter. Work swallows everything and everybody. Bit by bit, the individual becomes smaller and smaller, and suddenly he finds himself outside the ranks of life. The smallness of their life is palpable everywhere; the very air chokes, you feel yourself closed in, you want to run away.

It's true that the work in the small *kvuzah* is more intensive; everyone must carry the burden. But what good is that? The important thing is the person, not the work.[84] It seems to me that it's wrong for a person to become a draft animal. In the [large] *kibbutz*, the work can be distributed more evenly; I know that there the standard of work isn't as high, but that is because we haven't got men with a big outlook and wide imagination. I am sure that the work itself will in time produce such men. In Karkur, I had a good opportunity to study the [shortcomings] of the small *kvuzah*, and I became a firm believer in the large *kibbutz*. Afterward, when I came to the Gdud Avodah, I was surprised by the accuracy of my forecast, even down to details.

My job in Karkur was very much to my liking. I worked on the farm

84. The attitude expressed here is reminiscent of the concept of *kibush haavodah* [the conquest of labor] attributed to the Zionist philosopher A. D. Gordon, who asserted the paramount importance of intrapersonal relations among the new social forms in Palestine. For example, in an open letter written in 1921 to the members of Dagania, Gordon explained: "I did not say that a *kvuzah* requires nobler men than does a *moshav ovdim*. I held that no matter what form of settlement is employed, the important factor is men and not form. The more one emphasizes form, the less one attends to the human side. I not only do not demand a chosen few for the *kvuzah*, but on the contrary, I should like to see all kinds of people participating and becoming finer, more important individuals." *A. D. Gordon: Selected Essays*, trans. Frances Burnce (New York: League for Labor Palestine, 1938), p. 281. See also part III, note 1.

of an English Jew. The farm had only just been begun. I planted a eucalyptus grove. (Just recently, I went back to the place and found the trees
between four and five feet high. Can you imagine my pleasure?)

And then I learned that Aharon[85] was sick with typhoid.

I went to him, and reached him when he was practically over the
sickness and ready to leave the hospital. We went together to Migdal,
to the Gdud Avodah, and I spent a week there. I observed their life and
felt myself drawn to it. Really, in comparison with Karkur, Migdal was
full of life and freshness. At that time [Yosef Hayim] Brenner was living
there, and the evenings just hummed with social and cultural activities.
How they used to swallow the lectures, and even the incidental remarks
of Brenner! Besides Brenner's lectures, we had language courses, a botany class, and a class on Erez Israel. All this filled me with enthusiasm.

When I returned to Karkur, I kept dreaming of the Gdud Avodah.
The one thing that scared me there was the work [of the *haverot*]—only
in the kitchen! I felt that I could never change from the field and the
garden to the housework, which had no content for me. Nor did I quite
grasp the ideology of the Gdud Avodah, though I was given to understand that its particular philosophy had crystallized. However, I joined
up and, to avoid kitchen work, I went into the hospital. There was a lot
of typhoid going around, and this opened up a new field of work and
initiative. The doctors were satisfied with me and asked me to stay.

I got much out of the work in the hospital. I learned to feel the sufferings of others. I got to know the human being in sickness, and the
doctor at his work of healing. I learned the value of devotion, and I
tried to give everything in me. Making the rounds of the sick, I made
friends. But the work had a bad effect on my health, particularly on my
nerves, because although I did a little reading in medicine, my attitude
was still "unscientific," and every new disaster in the hospital horrified
me. When the typhoid epidemic passed, and things were easier, I began
to feel how exhausted I was. My *haverim* began to persuade me to leave
the work. The doctor was opposed, but I did not listen to him, and "ran
away" to Kfar Giladi. There, too, I didn't want to work in the kitchen;
so I joined the builders—and I did well.

And you know, every time you do well at a particular kind of work, you
begin to think: Suppose I stayed on at this? Suppose I became a specialist?

But while I was in the building work, I didn't once forget my original
aim—agriculture; and I made up my mind to return to it at the first opportunity. Then [Avraham] Harzfeld[86] suggested that I come to Nahlat

85. The precise identity of Aharon is uncertain.
86. Avraham Harzfeld (1888–1973), a native of Ukraine, joined the Russian socialist
Zionist party in 1906, for which he was arrested by the tsarsit police and imprisoned. He

Yehudah and take charge of the *meshek hapoalot*. I would have agreed, but as a member of the Gdud Avodah I saw no future for me there. I therefore went to Ein Harod. I had hoped to realize my dream of working on afforestation but—they fooled me! Yehudah K.[87] asked me to go into the [secretariat] for a few days, to help him out. The Gdud Avodah conference was being held then, and there was much to do. [He] laid all the work on me, and instead of working there for a few days I worked a few months! As a matter of fact, I never regretted this work because there in the [secretariat] I got a full view of the Gdud, with its internal and external relations.

And now, at last, I am working in the *mashtelah* [plant nursery]. I work and am happy. The work interests me theoretically, too. During the day, I am outside and at night, I study. I have good books on botany. I have only one cloud hanging over me—the terror that they'll take me back into the [secretariat]. That would be simply a catastrophe.

Dov,[88] dear, I've had to write a whole history to explain why I changed jobs so often. Not every *haver* finds his place at once. How many *haverim* there are who long for agriculture and must go on working at building or at stone breaking!

II

You ask me, in your letter, why I have gone back to the *kibbutz*. To explain that, I should have to tell you why I left the *kibbutz* in the first place.

I know that since you left the *kibbutz* you consider the *kibbutz* society a false life-form. You think that human nature is opposed to it, and that the whole struggle of the individual to suit himself to the collective life is a futile one. But you also know how differently I feel about it. For me and for hundreds of other *haverim*, the collective life is a deep and earnest need.

For some time, we've been having a serious dispute here. Instead of a comradely discussion we've had a struggle, a war of two faiths.

---

was later sentenced to life imprisonment in Siberia, but eventually he escaped and immigrated to Palestine in 1914. He worked as an agricultural laborer in Petah Tikvah and became active in the labor movement. During World War I, he assisted Jews who had been arrested by the Turkish authorities. From 1919 he played a prominent role in Merkaz Hahaklai [Central Farmers' Association] and the Histadrut. He was instrumental in the establishment of numerous agricultural settlements.

87. The precise identity of Yehuda K. is uncertain.

88. This letter was written to Dov Zisle, the brother of Rahel Zisle-Levkovich.

Each faith is grimly determined to realize itself in the form of life around it, and this has led to a sharp quarrel.[89] And because of that quarrel I left.

I can recall meetings that were no longer meetings, but just wild shouting, a lava of emotion. There was no discussion, only enmity. I sat in a dark corner of the big dining room, far from the tumult, and my heart was shaken every time a hand was lifted in the midst of the argument. I wanted to run—but I was fastened to my place. I wanted to scream, to cry, but I sat dumb.

On one such evening, I said to myself: "No, this can't go on. Before long I shall have no more respect for my *haverim*. It's better to leave." And I left at the first opportunity. I did not go to look for another way of life. I neither wanted one nor could I have practiced it. I went away because of pain for all this effort which was being wasted and worn down. Wherever I went, the longing for the collective life on the soil went with me.

In the quarrel, I blamed less the leaders of the two parties than the mass of the *haverim*. The former had much power to create, and therefore much power to destroy. And just as the natural obstacles of our work had no terrors for them, so they were not afraid, either, of destruction. But it was the average *haver* whom I could not understand. I knew that our collectivist form of life was dearer than everything else to our *haverim*, dearer than all debatable points; and yet they took part in and assisted the work of destruction.

A storm broke out in our camp, and the clouds hid from most of our *haverim* the original beauty of the common life we had planned. Everyone felt that things could not go on in this fashion; we would succeed neither with our social nor with our economic work. Doubt began to eat into us. The meetings were given up and the storm was followed by a silence. Now *haverim* began to debate with themselves, everyone in his own corner. They began to understand whither the quarrel had

89. Starting in the early 1920s, a countrywide ideological debate arose among socialist Zionist pioneers concerning the variety of forms of Jewish colonization in Palestine and the agenda of the socialist Zionist movement. The debate revolved, in part, around contrasting Marxist interpretations of Zionist pioneering and led to a heated public dispute that caused rifts throughout the movement. Against this backdrop, three separate *kibbutz* movements emerged, each with its own distinct brand of socialist Zionist ideology, that remained largely intact until 1951: Kibbutz Arzi-Hashomer Hazair [Countrywide Kibbutz Federation of Hashomer Hazair]; Kibbutz Hameuhad [United Kibbutz Movement]; and Hever Hakvuzot Vehakibbutzim [Federation of *Kvuzot* and *Kibbutzim*]. For a full analysis in this regard, see Henry Near, *The Kibbutz Movement, A History: Origins and Growth, 1909–1939*, vol. 1 (Oxford: Oxford University Press, 1992), ch. 4.

brought them; they were standing on the brink of ruin. And out of their terror the *haverim* realized that their fate was still in their own hands. Gradually, a feeling of sanity and freshness came into them; they felt from the depths of their hearts the need of their life in common, and a new enthusiasm for the work returned.

It was hard for me to wait for the return of this spirit, but I knew all the time that it was bound to come.

III

I must confess that what filled me with enthusiasm at first was neither the work nor the life around me, but the books. As soon as the day's work was done, I ran to my books. And because I was exhausted by the day's work, I could get nothing out of my books. I began to feel an inner emptiness, and doubts began to arise in me. Often, I doubted whether I would be able to remain a Jewish worker.

When I first went to work on the land, I would look at every plant and every tree as through a lens—the lens of the book. And therefore I did not see them as they really were. But the deeper I went into the work, the less need I felt for the book. And at last the world of nature, which till then had been a dead and silent thing to me, opened suddenly and became alive and took me in—spoke to me, so that I felt and understood. It became marvelously intimate, so that I felt myself a part of it. Neither the house nor the tent was my home, but the wild field and the stony hill. I found company in the flowers and rocks, in the trees and birds. (Over here, the birds fly close up to people.)

Many old questions were answered for me, and many conflicts smoothed out. I felt that I had been born again, that new, clear concepts had come to me, and it was good to be in this beautiful world, this great, deep, boundless world. The further I went into it, the more it fascinated me. Toward the end of this period, I worked at the beehives. Those mobile, industrious, model bees, which filled all the air with the sound of their buzzing, were the last touch of harmony in the picture. I felt a wholeness around me, a unity into which all separate things were poured.

Darling brother Dov, it's a marvelous thing to feel oneself poured into nature, part of that firm harmony. It's good to live with the sun and moon, with the trees and flowers . . . The rains have just stopped; everything in nature awakens, grows, becomes beautiful and ready for a new life; and we ourselves begin to feel the influence of that beauty.

IV

Today, I was in the *mashtelah* [plant nursery] of the experimental station,[90] and spent a lot of time there. I hated to go away. Whenever I leave Ein Harod for a little while, I get a spasm of longing for agricultural work and the country landscape. The hours I spent in the *mashtelah* refreshed me. I walked between the beds and felt happy for the share that humanity has in nature, and I was happy, too, that I was helping. Isn't there something of an honor in this?

Do you know, [my] dear, that when I speak with experts about the *mashtelah* I find that I can very well hold my own? In fact, they don't tell me anything new—it's the other way round. I have convinced myself that I have a good eye for these things, and often note things in the *mashtelah* that the others miss.

V

Only now, because I've been away from you for a few days, do I begin to feel the effect of little children on a mother like myself. Whenever I think of them my heart fills suddenly with light, love, and joy. It seems to me that the whole world changes. Everything rejoices with me, and everyone I meet is intimate and friendly. It's as if the sunlight and the singing of the birds were meant for me only. I think it's only for the children's sake that love remains fresh in us. If I could only get a look at them now! I think that the bitterest curse in life is childlessness. And I thank God every day from the bottom of my heart for making me this gift.

---

90. In this period, several experimental stations tested possibilities for introducing new plants and crops into Palestine. Though trained botanists and agronomists supervised the stations, they were generally operated by Jewish laborers. Support for the stations was provided by the World Zionist Organization.

PART VI

In the Literature

Among Writers

Rahel Kaznelson [Shazar]

THE WOMEN OF Erez Israel have their share in the literature of the country not less than their sisters in other countries. But in the case of the Jews, the transition has been more abrupt than elsewhere. Until recently, the medieval character of Jewish spiritual creation excluded the woman almost completely.

The spiritual renaissance of the woman in Erez Israel is part of the springtime movement of the entire people; it has to do with Zionism, with pioneering, with work on the earth, with the rediscovery of the old-new land and the old-new language, with socialist ideals. For this reason, the majority of our women who take a share in literary creation are intimately associated with those spiritual values which labor in Erez Israel has inherited from the Jewish national and social movement, and which the woman has helped to strengthen in thirty difficult years in the country.

The foremost characteristic of the work of these women is its freshness. This springs in part from the newness of the situation itself. We are not accustomed to hearing a woman tell of herself in an art form and we are affected, too, by the newness of the woman's peculiar mastery of the Hebrew language.

The female Hebrew writer of Erez Israel devotes herself chiefly to poetry and stories. The poetry volumes of the last few years—by Rahel [Blaustein], [Yoheved] Bat-Miriam,[1] Esther Rav,[2] Elisheva [(Zhirkova)

---

1. Yoheved Bat-Miriam (1901–1980), a native of Belorussia, was a significant Hebrew poet. She attended the universities of Odessa and Moscow, and was strongly influenced by Russian symbolist poetry. Bat-Miriam began publishing poems in Russia in 1923. In 1928, she immigrated to Palestine, where she continued to write and eventually published six volumes of poetry. Her poetry, which employs a dreamlike landscape and is charged with images of nature, often explores her childhood in Russia, the backdrop of Jewish distress in Europe, and her life as a settler in Palestine.

2. Esther Rav (1899–1981), the daughter of Yehuda Rav (1858–1948), a First Aliyah pioneer and founder of Petah Tikvah, moved to Kibbutz Dagania at a young age. After five years in Egypt following her marriage, she returned to Petah Tikvah, her birthplace, and wrote poems, primarily about the Palestinian landscape.

Bikhovsky],[3] Anda Pinkerfeld [Amir][4]—have made a place for the Jewish woman in the world of Hebrew lyrics. Among the prose writers, Dvorah Baron is the only one who had established herself before she came to Erez Israel. But it is only in Erez Israel that the following women have come into their own—Nehamah Pukhachevsky,[5] Brakhah Habas,[6] Shulamit Kalugai,[7] D. Avrahamit.[8]

Not being able to reproduce here a complete anthology of women's Hebrew literature in Erez Israel, we have thought it proper, nevertheless, to reproduce in translation at least some representative material from the lyrics of Rahel and the stories of Dvorah Baron.

Among the poets of Erez Israel none has achieved the tenderness and simplicity which characterize the two little booklets *Safiah* [Aftergrowth] and *Mineged* [From Opposite] by Rahel [Blaustein].[9] This work of hers represents an extraordinary victory over the traditional burden of two thousand silent years and a triumph of the womanly spirit in

3. Elisheva is the pen-name of Elizaveta (Zhirkova) Bikhovsky (1888–1949), a non-Jewish Russian poet who was fascinated by Jewish culture and heritage and attracted to Zionism. She learned Hebrew and translated Hebrew literature into Russian. She also wrote original works in Hebrew. In 1925, she settled in Palestine with her husband Simon Bikhovsky, whom she had married in 1920. Known as "Ruth from the banks of the Volga," her stories and poems emphasize nature, love, and descriptions of the Russian and Palestinian landscapes.

4. Anda (Pinkerfeld) Amir (1902–1981), a native of Galicia, was born into an assimilated Jewish family. She attended a gymnasium in Lvov and published a book of Polish verse at age 18. After studying at the universities of Lvov and Leipzig, she immigrated to Palestine in 1923. Thereafter, strongly influenced by the Hebrew poet Uri Zvi Greenberg (1894–1981), she began to write in Hebrew. The themes of her verse are love of nature, romantic love, and the joys of motherhood.

5. Nehamah Pukhachevsky (1869–1934), a member of Russian Hovevei Zion [Lovers of Zion] and a First Aliyah colonist, was a Hebrew writer active in the public life of Palestine. She wrote under the pen name Nefesh [Soul]. Together with her husband Mikhael Zalman Pukhachevsky (1863–1947), an agricultural instructor specializing in viticulture in the Jezreel Valley, she established a farm in Rishon Lezion.

6. Brakhah Habas (1900–1968), a native of Lithuania, was brought to Palestine in 1907. She later worked as a teacher and then as a journalist, serving on the editorial board of *Davar* [The Word] and in the Am Oved [Working Nation] publishing house. She edited numerous books about the Zionist pioneers and the Palestine labor movement.

7. The Hebrew writer Shulamit Kalugai (1891–1972), a native of Poltava, Ukraine, immigrated to Palestine in 1911. Her brother was Yizhak Ben-Zvi, the Labor Zionist leader and second president of Israel.

8. The reference is to Dvorah Avrahamit, a Hebrew writer.

9. *Safiah* [Aftergrowth] (1927) and *Mineged* [From Opposite] (1930) are the two volumes of Hebrew verse that appeared during Rahel Blaustein's (1890–1931) lifetime. In 1932, a third volume entitled *Nevo* [Nebo] (1932) was published posthumously. (According to the Hebrew Bible, Mount Nebo, located east of the Jordan River and opposite of Jericho, is the site where the Israelites encamped on the last stage of their journey and the peak from which Moses beheld the Promised Land before dying; see Deuteronomy 34:6.) In 1935, the three volumes were collected and republished as *Shirat Rahel* [Poetry of Rahel].

Hebrew. She came to Erez Israel knowing not a word of either Hebrew or Yiddish; and perhaps this beauty was given to her because she sought it in the workers' *kvuzah*, from mother earth, and from the [Hebrew] Bible. But the lightness, naturalness, and richness of her modest lines make one think rather of the great Russian and European lyricists than of the typical Hebrew poetry. It had to be a woman and a "convert" who could bring this new, refreshing spirit of nature into Hebrew poetry. Still more strangely, the extraordinary gift of Rahel came to fruition only in the last part of her life, when she lay sick of an incurable disease.[10] Fastened almost constantly to her bed, she sent out her songs, which became always deeper and more richly human as her body became weaker and weaker. Her death took place in the spring of 1931.

Rahel came from a rich Jewish home in the heart of Russia, and was brought up in the Russian spirit in a great city of the Ukraine. Dvorah Baron is the daughter of a poor and distinguished father—a great rabbi in a small Lithuanian *shtetl*[11]—and she absorbed her Jewishness even in the cradle. She has a profound Jewish knowledge, of the type which few Jewish women were privileged to receive. All of Rahel's poetry concerns Erez Israel; but among Dvorah's stories, which appeared many years after she had settled in Erez Israel, there is not one that deals with the land itself. She was and remains one of the finest portrayers of the little Jewish *shtetl* and its culture. Her best pieces measure up completely with the finest to be found in [Isaac Leib] Perez,[12] [Avraham] Reisin,[13] and [Sholem] Asch.[14] Her true, deep-rooted village-folk spirit

10. Rahel Blaustein contracted tuberculosis during World War I, and soon became too ill for farm life. She spent the rest of her life in hospitals and sanitoria, and died in Tel Aviv in 1931.

11. The reference is to the town of Ozdah in Belarus.

12. On Isaac Leib Perez, see part V, note 54.

13. Avraham Reisin (1876–1953), a native of Kaidanovo, Minsk province, was an eminent Yiddish poet and short-story writer. He published his first poem at age 15 in Isaac Leib Perez's (see part V, note 54) anthology *Yidishe bibliotek* [The Jewish Library]. After serving in the Russian army, Reisin moved to Warsaw where, together with Sholem Asch (see note below) and Hersh David Nomberg (1876–1927), he became one of Perez's disciples. As his work gained recognition, he began to translate, edit literary journals, and travel widely. He played a leading role in the Chernovich Yiddish conference of 1908, which proclaimed Yiddish as the national language of the Jewish people. In 1914, he immigrated to New York City, where he made his permanent home and continued writing. In 1917, a twelve-volume edition of his poetry and stories was published. Reisen was a master of Yiddish prose and an innovator of the Yiddish short story. His writing centers on the individual but deals compassionately with the problems of groups, particularly the Jewish community and questions of Jewish peoplehood. His poetry is regarded as the first successful bridge between Yiddish folk poetry and the artistic Yiddish lyric.

14. Sholem Asch (1880–1957), a native of Kutno, Poland, received a traditional Jewish education. An autodidact, he later learned German and was thereafter influenced by the world of Hebrew, Russian, Yiddish, Polish, and German letters. Encouraged by Isaac

comes to strongest expression in her hatred of the smug, contented life of the rich Jew and in her motherly compassion for whatever is abandoned, innocent, and helpless. As an artist, she reaches her climax in the idealized pictures that she has drawn of her father and mother.

The symbolic picture of her father and of the Jewish mystery is contained in her story "The Genizah," one of the deepest studies of man and of religion to be found in our new *belles lettres*.

The Palestinian woman of the new generation has her place in publicistic writing as well as in *belles lettres*. Almost everything that has appeared in the Hebrew press on the question of the woman, and her relationship to work, has been written by women. *Tnuat hapoalot beerez yisrael* [*A History of the Women Workers' Movement in the Land of Israel*] (1929) has been written by Ada Fishman [Maimon].[15] From time to time, women also write in the labor press and for the local, hectographed journals which appear locally. For the most part, they are occupied with social and educational questions. We reproduce in this volume a woman's contribution to Palestinian publicistic writing in the article "From Language to Language," by Rahel Kaznelson which first appeared in the labor anthology *Baavodah*[16] [At Labor] in 1918.

Leib Perez (see part V, note 54), to whom he had shown his first Yiddish writings in 1900, he took up Yiddish literature as a profession. Asch's tone and focus evolved during his career. His early novels and plays focused on the lives of Jews in Eastern European villages. As time passed, his scope broadened and he concerned himself with the problems of worldwide Jewry. During World War I, he lived in the United States, returning to Poland after the war and later living in France. In 1938, he again made his home in the United States, where he published the bulk of his literary works. Although a noted Yiddish author by this time, Asch was something of a lightning rod for the American Yiddish-speaking milieu. In particular, he was publicly attacked for his trilogy *The Nazarene* (1939), *The Apostle* (1943), and *Mary* (1949) which, Jewish critics argued, promoted heresy and conversion to Christianity. Though he died in London, Asch spent the last years of his life in the Tel Aviv suburb of Bat Yam. He is credited with having linked the Yiddish world to the mainstream of European and American literature, and was the first Yiddish writer to enjoy an international reputation.

15. Ada (Fishman) Maimon (1893–1973), a native of Marculesti, Bessarabia, immigrated to Palestine in 1912. Two years later, she founded and taught at a girls' school in Safed. She was among the first to advocate the organization of a working women's movement in Palestine and helped found the Moezet Hapoalot [Working Women's Council], serving as its secretary general from 1921 to 1930. From 1931 to 1939, she represented the women of Palestine at the International Labor Organization at the League of Nations. Fishman was also was active in the broader labor movement. She was a member of the Central Committee of Hapoel Hazair [The Young Worker], the Actions Committee of the World Zionist Organization, and the Vaad Leumi [National Assembly] (see part V, note 57). Following the creation of the state in 1948, Fishman served as a Mapai representative in the first two Israeli goverments, devoting herself especially to women's issues; the Age of Marriage Law (1950) is known by her name. Her brother, Rabbi Yehudah Leib (Fishman) Maimon (1875–1962), an important religious Zionist leader and founder of the orthodox Zionist party Mizrahi, immigrated to Palestine in 1913.

16. On *Baavodah* [At Labor], see part V, note 17.

Poetry[17]

Rahel [Blaustein]

Idle Tales

Red gleams the western sky as day begins to fail,
    And evening settles downward desolate and slow;
In such an hour the heart recalls an idle tale:
    "A little girl there was, long, long ago . . .

A little girl there was, and young she was of will;
    Lightly she followed the plough from early until late;
And far across the fields she scattered grain until
    Her paths were closed by barricades of fate . . .

The barrier stands forever about those joyous days,
    From earth's four corners now the ancient storm wind
        wails."
Oh evening! I am sated with your desolate ways.
    I will recall no more these idle tales.

Perhaps

Perhaps these things have never been at all!
Perhaps that life was not!
Perhaps I never answered morning's earliest call
To sweat in labor on my garden plot!

Perhaps I never stood upon the loaded cart
To gather up the hay,

17. The poems reprinted here were originally translated from Hebrew into Yiddish by Zalman Rubashov-Shazar for the 1931 Yiddish volume. They were next translated from Yiddish into English by Maurice Samuel for the 1932 English volume. In order to preserve the integrity and artistry of Samuel's English translations, no emendations have been introduced to the poems that follow.

Nor heard the wild songs bursting from my heart
The livelong harvest day!

Perhaps I never made my body whole
In the blue and quiet gleam
Of my Kineret! Oh, Kineret of my soul,
Were you once true, or have I dreamed a dream?

In the Garden

Calm is the garden with blue and gray
In the peace of dawn,
I will rise from the dust of yesterday
To faith in the morn,
Accept with humble heart and free
The judgment that was given me.

A girl walks through the garden beds.
And scatters rain;
The withered leaves lift up their heads
And live again.
The bitter things that God must do.
I will forgive and start anew.

Comfort Me

In both your dear hands, loving as a brother's,
Take my own faltering hand.
You know and I know that the storm-tossed ship
Will never make the land.

Comfort my tears with words, my only one;
My heart is dark with pain.
You know and I know that the wandering son
Will never see his mother's door again.

In Sickness

To feel the darkness hammer on the eyeballs;
To thrust blind fingers into empty space;
To start in terror when the bushes rustle;
To pray for miracles and long for grace;

Seven times to hope what seven times was abandoned;
From "Never, never," to "But a little wait";
To alternate 'twixt waking and oblivion;
To curse my fate and to accept my fate;

To seek asylum in the lap of memory,
To cling to her dear, loving folds in vain;
To shake with pain, or lie in drunken stupor
Until the day breaks through the window pane.

To You

Morning and evening, toward you and you only,
Toward you and you only my singing must strain;
Wounded or healed, rejoicing or weeping,
In storm or in silence, in comfort or pain.

Instants may come when the magic seems broken,
My vision is blinded, my compass untrue.
Sudden awakens my jubilant singing,
Turns once again to its lode star, to you.

To you and you only, of you and you only—
My strings are a thousand, my song is but one:
In storm or in silence, in comfort or weeping,
When sunlight is shining, when sunlight is gone.

Barren

Oh, if I had a son, a little son,
With black, curled hair and clever eyes,

A little son to walk with in the garden
Under morning skies,
A son,
A little son!

I'd call him Uri,[18] little, laughing Uri,
A tender name, as light, as full of joy
As sunlight on the dew, as tripping on the tongue
As the laughter of a boy—
"Uri!"
I'd call him.

And still I wait, as mother Rahel waited,
Or Hannah in Shiloh, she, the barren one,
Until the day comes when my lips will whisper,
"Uri, my son!"

My Land

No deeds of high courage,
No poems of flame,
I bring you, my country,
To add to your fame;
By Jordan I planted
A tree in your soil,
And I wore out a path
In the field of my toil.

Well knows your daughter,
My own motherland,
How poor is her tribute,
How weak is her hand.
But my heart shouts with joy
When the sun shines upon you,
And in secret I weep
For the wrong that is done you.

18. The name "Uri" has important biblical connotations. It is a variant form of Ur, from the Hebrew meaning "my flame" or "my light." In Genesis 11:28, Ur is noted as the birthplace of the patriarch Abraham. It is also the name of the father of one of King David's warriors (I Chronicles 11:35).

The Genizah[19]

Dvorah Baron

O<small>N A SUNNY</small> Sabbath afternoon of summer, the *rav* [rabbi] of Zhu-zhikovka[20] stood on the pulpit of the *bet midrash* before the sacred ark, and preached a sermon on the weekly portion from the Book of Numbers, which had been read that morning at prayers.

He told of Balak, son of Zipor, King of Moab, who had been so terrified by the marvelous victories of the Children of Israel over Sihon, King of the Amorites, and Og, King of Bashan, that he did not go out to meet them in open war, as befitted a king, but sent to Pitor for Balam the magician to curse them.

And before the listeners rose the strange picture of the gentile prophet sitting on his ass in the narrow street with a wall on either side —a narrow street not unlike the street of the gentiles in Zhuzhikovka. And before the beast rose suddenly the angel of the Lord, so that in terror it pressed close to the fence, almost crushing Balam's leg.

Through the wide open windows of the *bet midrash* on that hot summer afternoon, there came glimpses of the neighboring meadow, which looked somehow greener and younger than usual, because the hay had been mown just a few days ago. And when the *rav* told of the seven altars which were raised in the field opposite the camp of Israel, the eyes of his listeners turned quickly and involuntarily to the huge stacks of hay which lifted up their rounded backs to God's heaven.

"*Kol kli yozer alekhah lo yizlah*"[21] [no weapon that is fashioned against you shall prosper], the *rav* cried, in his leonine voice, and the folds of his *talit* [prayer shawl] slipped downward from his shoulders, and flowed proudly over the length of his silken mantle, right and left.

---

19. A *genizah* is a depository for sacred books. According to Jewish law, articles cannot be destroyed which contain the name of God.

20. The *shtetl* Zhuzhikovka appears to have been located in Belarus.

21. The Hebrew quotation "*kol kli yozer alekhah lo yizlah*" is a variant of the biblical phrase "*kol kli yuzar alekhah lo yizlah*" (Isaiah 54:17). In its entirety, the passage reads as follows: "No weapon that is fashioned against you shall prosper, and you shall confute every tongue that rises against you in judgment." For a detailed explication of the text, see *The New Oxford Annotated Bible*, ed. by Michael Coogan, 3rd edition (Oxford and New York: Oxford University Press, 2001), p. 1055.

Then the *rav* spoke with fierce power of the strength of the people Israel and its Torah, which is *"ez hayim lemahazikim bah"* [a tree of life to those that hold fast to it].[22] And gradually he came nearer to the special content of the day's sermon, the two plans that he had for the Jews of Zhuzhikovka. The first was the ceremonious and reverential burial of torn books, fragments and defective scrolls of the law, in a *genizah*—after the ancient tradition of Israel which regards all printed and written paper on which the word of God has appeared, as eternally sacred, and entitled to decent interment when no longer in use; the second plan—more important—was the establishment of a little *yeshivah* in Zhuzhikovka.

But even before the *rav* had reached the details of his plans, the faces of his listeners were illumined so brightly, that the two creases on his forehead—one for each plan—were at once smoothed out.

The *rav* went on to mention "the days" which the poor students would have to eat in the houses of the various families of Zhuzhikovka. Then an excited murmuring and whispering came from the woman's section and the rustling of old satin was heard for some minutes through the length and breadth of the synagogue.

"What is there to think about? Are Mir[23] and Volozhin,[24] whose

22. The Hebrew phrase *"ez hayim lemahazikim bah"* [a tree of life to those that hold fast to it] comes from Proverbs 3:18. It is recited at the conclusion of the Torah service upon returning the Torah scroll to the ark.

23. Mir, a town in Belarus, was first settled by Jews in the early seventeenth century. During the rabbinate of Yosef David Eisenstadt (1776–1826), the famous *yeshivah* of Mir was founded. At the start of the nineteenth century, Hasidism acquired a strong influence over the community. In 1897, Mir's Jewish community of 3,319 souls made up 62 percent of the town's population. In 1903, Rabbi Elijah David Rabinowitz Teomim (1842/43–1905), then head of the *yeshivah*, immigrated to Palestine as part of the Second Aliyah. During the pogroms of 1904–05, Jewish self-defense of the community was organized and the Bund and Poalei Zion [Workers of Zion] gained strength.

24. The first Jews came to Volozhin, a town in Belorussia, in the sixteenth century. Volozhin acquired importance in Jewish life as a result of its *yeshivah*, which was created by Rabbi Hayim Volozhiner (1749–1821), a leading disciple of the *gaon* [genius] of Vilna (Rabbi Elijah ben Shlomo, 1720–1797), the spiritual leader of Lithuanian Jewry, in order to stop the spread of Hasidism. The *yeshivah* gained rapidly in prestige, serving as a model for other *mitnagdim* [opponents of Hasidism]. In subsequent decades, the head of the Volozhin *yeshivah* continued to be regarded as one of the most important figures in Russian Jewry; in 1813, during the Napoleonic Wars, the military governor of Lithuania specifically ordered the protection of the *yeshivah* and its leader. After 1824, the tsarist regime abruptly decided to close the *yeshivah*; however, it continued to operate illegally. The pervasive influence of the Haskalah [Jewish enlightenment] starting in the middle of the nineteenth century, followed by the rise of proto-Zionism in the region and, ultimately, the devastation of World War I brought about the *yeshivah*'s rapid decline. The famous Hebrew writers Hayim Nahman Bialik (see part V, note 28) and Mikha Yosef Berdichevsky (see note 77 below) both studied at the Volozhin *yeshivah*.

yeshivot are famous in all the corners of Israel, great cities? Are they not, too, like Zhuzhikovka, *shtetlakh* [little villages] in hungry Lithuania?"

"*Im yihiyeh reshithah mizar, aharitkhah yisgeh meod*"[25] [though thy beginnings be small, thy latter days shall be glorious]—the words of the *rav* flamed over his listeners, and he gathered together the corners of his *talit* in a last gesture of strength. Then he paused, being tired—for the sun had already sunk low and now stood over the river Zhuzhik—and passed on to the more beautiful part of his sermon, the parable; and the congregation, still trembling at the cry of his soul, breathed more easily.

With true affection the women looked at the young wife of the *rav*, where she stood in her dress of fine cotton with its long waist, fitting close to her figure, when the *rav* began to tell in glowing words of "that queen's daughter whom everyone loved with a great love."[26]

The golden wig on her head shone in the level rays of the sun; and when, at the ending of *minhah* [the afternoon prayer], she went down the steps from the women's gallery, and the long train descended after her, step by step, raising a faint cloud of dust, there was indeed a light as of royalty upon her.

From the *bet midrash* she turned down the narrow street to the cool storage cellar, and drawing her dress together with a graceful gesture, she descended, like the other women, to bring up the dairy dishes for the traditional Sabbath evening meal. Meanwhile the *rav*, his belt close about him, stood near the well, talking with his intimates, who had stopped there for a drink of water.

Now the last light of the sun died down and nothing was left but a faint redness above the *bet midrash*. The meadow nearby settled into a bluish darkness, and a faint mist came up from the river Zhuzhik. The full-uddered goats came back lazily from the pasture to drink their fill in the lake.

They stopped awhile, like self-conscious beings, at the end of the meadow, and then, without leader or guide, they went down the narrow street in single file. And each goat went straight up to its own house, and stood expectantly before the big pail where—as it well knew—was prepared its meal of rinds soaking in water, the peelings from the *shalesh sudes*[27] [third meal].

The summer was only at its beginning, and the vegetables had barely

---

25. The Hebrew phrase "*im yihiyeh reshithah mizar, aharitkhah yisgeh meod*" [though thy beginnings be small, thy latter days shall be glorious] derives from Job 8:7.

26. The provenance of this Yiddish phrase is unknown.

27. The Yiddish term *shalesh sudes* [third meal] (in Hebrew, *seudah shlishit*) is the closing meal of the Sabbath. It is customary, especially among traditional Jews and *hasidim* (see part V, note 51), to spend hours at the table, discussing rabbinic commentary, telling stories, and chanting hymns and wordless melodies.

begun to ripen in that district, few being yet obtainable in the market-place. Nevertheless, enough already grew in the street of the gentiles to make up the modest Sabbath evening meal of the Jews: little radishes, red or white, when cut into pieces, soaked in sour cream and sprinkled with salt, make a dish not to be despised in lean Lithuania. One could also get, by this time, spring onions, to be eaten raw, whole or cut up, and dipped in vinegar, and perhaps a cucumber, chopped up and added more for taste than substance. There might also be the red borscht, made from beet roots, in which was dropped the yolk of an egg. All in all, then, there was reason to thank God for *shalesh sudes* in Zhuzhikova, even on the Sabbath of the Torah portion of *Hukat*[28] [statute of the law] or Balak.[29]

And in fact, when the *rebezin* [rabbi's wife] stood an hour later at the oven, preparing the *"melaveh malkah"*[30] [escorting the queen] she was talking with her neighbor about these Lithuanian dishes. Her face lit up with its peculiar smile when she recalled how, when she first came into this district with her husband, she really could not look at these dishes, let alone eat them—and now she would not exchange them for the most elaborate crown in Poland.

She was still wearing the fine cotton dress with the long tight-fitting waist, but she had covered it with a house apron. In the neighbor's heart rose a motherly compassion, as she watched the little hands of the *rebezin*, shining white as they moved swiftly and lightly, peeling the big American potatoes.

28. The Torah reading known as *"Hukat"* [statute of the law] (Numbers 19:1–22:1) describes the ritual of the red heifer that purifies someone who is contaminated through contact with a corpse. In addition, the chapter portrays the death of the biblical characters Miriam and Aaron; Moses receives his own death sentence after striking a rock contrary to God's instructions. In chapter 21, many Israelites are killed by a plague of serpents when they complain about their fate. For a detailed explication of the text, see *The New Oxford Annotated Bible*, ed. by Michael Coogan, 3rd edition (Oxford and New York: Oxford University Press, 2001), pp. 214–218.

29. In the Torah reading known as "Balak" [from the Hebrew meaning "to destroy"] (Numbers 22:2–25:9), the Israelites are poised to enter the Land of Israel. King Balak, fearful of the Israelites' victory over the Amorites, summons the pagan prophet Balaam to curse this formidable enemy before they attack. At first, Balaam refuses to obey, but he changes his mind when God sanctions his mission. While en route, Balaam's donkey balks when it encounters an angel with a drawn sword. Balaam, who does not perceive the angel, beats the donkey until it speaks to him, after which the angel becomes visible to them both. Upon reaching Balak, Balaam—against his own will—blesses Israel instead of cursing it. For a detailed explication of the text, see *The New Oxford Annotated Bible*, ed. by Michael Coogan, 3rd edition (Oxford and New York: Oxford University Press, 2001), pp. 218–223.

30. The Hebrew term *melaveh malkah* [escorting the queen] refers to a customary meal occuring at the end of the Sabbath day. In traditional East European Jewish communities, especially among *hasidim*, the meal is prolonged and may last several hours in a deliberate effort to forestall the end of the Sabbath.

When the coals in the three-legged stove began to glow, the young wife placed on them two Holland herrings, to roast. But she first set aside the roe to pour on the potatoes as an appetizer—the year's store of pickled cucumber juice having already given out. Then she spread a weekday cloth on one half of the table and sat down to chat with her neighbor about the *genizah*, the burial of the fragments of sacred books, which was soon to take place, right in the midst of *"nein-tag"* [nine days of mourning].[31]

Early on Tuesday morning, when the *rav* went down between the gardens to the old *merhaz* [bath house], a heavy, dark mist still lay on the little street.

Dressed in his silk mantle, with the belt drawn tight, he passed, a tall, marvelous figure, through all the length of the big *bod-hoiz* [bath house], between the two rows of upended benches and the faucets which dropped water on the idle willow-switches. He came to the little room that contained the tubs and the *mikveh* [ritual bath].

Here he bent down to fix something in the stove, and lit himself a taper. Holding this in his hand he looked down doubtfully at the dark water in the plunge. Later, after he had dipped himself completely, he wrapped himself in a sheet by the light of the same taper and, though this was not the fitting place, he began to revolve in his mind the thoughts that he would weave into the sermon at the time of the *genizah*.

By now the windows of the *merhaz*, which had no shutters, were not as dark as before, and he could almost see the haystacks in the neighboring field.

On the narrow path, along which the goats went daily in single file, appeared suddenly the face of the bookbinder of Zhuzhikovka, who was carrying two bundles of newly plucked withes[32] with which to adorn his street on the day of festivity. And all the sad verses which the *rav* had thought of weaving into his burial sermon suddenly came to nothing.

The *rav* dressed himself, and lit his pipe—it was the one which he usually smoked on Sabbath evenings—and went out through the street where stood the *hekdesh* [shelter of Jewish wanderers]. He came to the vestibule of the *bet midrash*, and there the old *shamas* [sexton] stood in

31. *Nein-tag* [nine days] is the Yiddish designation for the nine days of mourning between the first and ninth days of the month of Av. See the explanation of Tisha Beav; part V, note 65.

32. A tough, supple twig, often from willows, used to bind handmade books.

the half-dark, surrounded by bundles and boxes of old fragments of books and parchments.

"Have they brought the clay pots?" the *rav* asked, and drew at his pipe, so that his face glowed back with light; and he went closer to the boxes and bundles.

Here, among the bundles of torn parchment, there was a package which he himself had brought last night from his old stores of books. He lit a candle and began to sort the torn leaves: fragments of the *Kabbalah*[33] [Jewish mystical tradition] in one heap, fragments of *hakirah*[34] [rabbinic investigations] in another. He even separated the fragments of the books of the Rambam[35] from fragments of the books of Rabad,[36] for in their lives, many centuries ago, they had been opponents and had carried on a war of words, and they might not lie in peace together. But, doing this, the *rav* thought it queer just the same.

This work done, the *rav* clambered up into the attic, where lay hidden a Torah scroll which was defective by reason of an error, and several fragments of sacred parchment which had been defiled some time ago during the *pogrom* in the neighboring *shtetl* of Semionovka.[37] When the *rav* came to the last step he paused, because the *shamas* who was lighting his way was weak, and the taper began to tremble in his hand; so waiting, the *rav* extinguished his pipe and put it in the pocket under his mantle.

33. The *Kabbalah* [Jewish mystical tradition] is a collection of Jewish esoteric teachings, mysticism, and theosophy based on meditation and enlightenment rather than intellectual seeking or logical reasoning. It treats God and creation as beyond the grasp of human comprehension. Although some parts of the *Kabbalah* can be traced to late antiquity, its core forms developed in the medieval period from the twelfth century forward.

34. The phrase "fragments of *hakirah*" [rabbinic investigations] refers to documentary material produced in the course of examinations of matters and affairs that fell within the juridical purview of the rabbis.

35. Moses Maimonides (1135–1204), known in rabbinic literature as Rambam (from the acronym Rabbi Moses ben Maimon), was the premier rabbinic authority and Jewish philosopher of the Iberian peninsula in the medieval period. His two most famous writings are *Mishneh Torah*, a codified collection of all rabbinic law, and *Guide of the Perplexed*, a synthesis of Aristotelian philosophy with Judaism. The latter sparked the two-hundred-year Maimonidean Controversy which pitted Jewish rational philosophers against traditionalists. Maimonides also conceived the thirteen fundamental principles of Jewish faith. Maimonides' enduring influence on Jewish thought is profound. Additionally, his works had considerable impact on philosophers of other faiths, including the Italian theologian and philosopher Thomas Aquinas (1225–1274).

36. Ibn Daud (c. 1110–1180), known in rabbinic literature as Rabad (from the acronym Rabbi Abraham ben David), was an eminent Spanish historian, philosopher, physician, and astronomer. *Sefer hakabbalah* (1160–61), Ibn Daud's major work, is essentially a history of Jewish tradition; it is oriented primarily against Karaism and seeks to demonstrate the primacy of rabbinic tradition. The latter is the best known of Ibn Daud's writings and has exerted significant influence over subsequent generations of Jewish thinkers.

37. There were several dozen villages and towns in the Ukraine bearing the name Semionovka. The *shtetl* noted here was probably a small town by that name located northeast of Chernigov in the Chernigov district, not far from Kiev.

"Reb Motte," he asked the *shamas*, "has a burial of sacred fragments taken place in your days?" And he was astonished to see suddenly the golden sunlight poured out on the forest of birches beyond the town.

"Not in my days," the *shamas* answered with a sigh, as he felt with his foot for the last step. "But one took place in my grandfather's days." And he followed the *rav* into the corner that was filled with the peculiar odor of dusty sanctities. He held up the candle, and they saw the old *aron kodesh* [sacred ark] with the wooden carvings, from the midst of which stared out—as if quite alive—the frightened face of the voiceless dove in the teeth of the lion: the parable of Israel among the peoples of the world.

"Wonderful, wonderful," the rav whispered, straightening out his back, though he really did not know what was so wonderful; and yet the shudder which passed through all his body was more than he could bear. But the legend of the Talmud came to his mind: "As the dove stretches out its neck to the knife, and does not tremble, so Jews give up their lives for their sanctities."[38] And as the words went through his mind, confused and dark, he opened the drawer above the ark, where lay the fragments of parchment saved from the *pogrom* of Semionovka.

But suddenly the *shamas* sprang back in terror and cried out:

"Rabbi! Rabbi! She is naked!"

"Who?" the *rav* asked, startled, and did not recognize his own voice, which sounded so dead and brought back no echo from the walls.

"The glory herself!" The *shamas* lowered the taper and they saw the little Torah scroll, naked indeed, without velvet mantle and without cover. The *rav* slowly lifted the scrolls by the *ez hayims*[39] [staves] and

38. This phrase derives from Song of Songs Rabbah (also known as *Midrash Hazita* or, more generally, *Midrash Rabbah*). The segment noted here is a Yiddish variant drawn from the following midrashic passage (I:15,2):

DOVES. As the dove is innocent (so Israel are innocent; as the dove is graceful in its step), so Israel are graceful in their step, when they go up to celebrate the festivals. Just as the dove is distinguished [by its coloring], so Israel are distinguished through [abstention from] shaving, through circumcision, through fringes. As the dove is chaste, so Israel are chaste. *As the dove puts forth her neck fort slaughter, so do Israel,* as it says, For they sake are we killed all the day (Psalm 44:[22]). As the dove atones for iniquities, so Israel atone for other nations . . . (*Midrash Rabbah,* trans. H. Freedman and Maurice Simon [London: Soncino Press, 1961], p. 86; emphasis added)

The foregoing text, like others in the midrashic tradition, provides a running rabbinic commentary on the Hebrew Bible. Compiled by the *amoraim,* Palestinian rabbinic scholars who lived between 200–500 C.E., the text as a whole was edited in the fifth and sixth centuries C.E. Written in Aramaic and Hebrew, with a sprinkling of Greek, it consists of homilies, sayings, and parables (many of which lean toward mystical interpretations). In general, *Midrash Rabbah* seeks to explicate each chapter and verse of the Hebrew Bible, including numerous specific terms.

39. The Yiddish designation *ez hayims* [literally, trees of life] refers to the staves (in Hebrew, *ezei hayim*) on which the Torah scroll is rolled.

placed the Torah tenderly under his cloak, like a father taking his child to his breast. He went downstairs perturbed, feeling with his feet for the steps. At the foot of the stairs already waited the first *davener* [worshipper].

Mina, the old childless widow Mina, who came from the family of *kohanim*[40] [priests], had risen specially early on this day, so as to lead her goat to pasture before the first *minyan* [prayer quorum] was through.

But it fell out otherwise, and by the time she had come back from the shed, had passed the milk through the sieve and had boiled it, the rays of the sun were already on the copper tray which stood on the shelf of her room. Nevertheless, she put on her dress of stiff satin, which rustled with a sound of proud generations long dead, put her *heibl* [bonnet] on her head, drawing out both points (she had to do this without a mirror, being without one) and took out from under the rafter—God help her, she was only a woman!—a bundle of pages belonging to an old *Zenah urenah*[41] [Come and See] printed, alas, in plain Yiddish! An inheritance it was, the remnants of the book from which her grandmothers and great-grandmothers had read, being unable to read Hebrew like the menfolk. And this was Mina the widow's contribution to the collection of sacred pages which the *shtetl* was to bury in pomp. Quickly, she took up the bundle, went out of the house, and locked the door behind her.

She perceived at once that she could not have chosen a more unfortunate moment. For just then there came, out of the house opposite, the *gabai* [chief trustee] of the *bet midrash*. He wore a coat of wool, drawn close about him; behind him came his two sons, and each one carried a bundle of genuine fragments, remnants of illustrious and scholarly books, and no pitiful make-believe stuff like her own.

Her heart sank within her. But she went on. In one hand, she held the rope that was tied to the horns of the goat which followed her along the narrow street, and in the other she carried the bundle of dubious documents. She came at last to the well, tied the goat to the post, and, bent deeper than before, turned toward the women's entrance of the *bet midrash*.

40. Jews who trace their ancestry to Aaron and the priests of ancient Israel.

41. *Zenah urenah* [Come and See] (Yiddish pronunciation *Zenerene*; title taken from Song of Solomon, 3:11) by Rabbi Jacob ben Isaac Ashkenazi was a very popular work of miscellany including folk tales, homilies, *midrashim* [textual interpretations], and exegetical commentaries woven around a Yiddish rendering and paraphrasing of the Pentateuch and other Jewish texts. The work is written in a lively and flowing style. Notwithstanding the author's original intention, it became a book for women.

A crowd of young rascals blocked her path, and threatened to untie the goat and ride it through the town.

"Look! look!" they yelled in chorus, "Mina's got a *tehineh* [supplication]!"[42]

In the *bet midrash*, the second *minyan* had ended its devotions, and the worshippers were out on the street. In her extremity, Mina the widow fled into the vestibule, and there she perceived the *rav*, who was standing by the boxes of manuscripts, splendid in his mantle. And it seemed to her that she had escaped out of a flaming desert into the shadow of a cool grove.

"Make way for Mina, of the family of the *kohanim!*" the *rav* cried, stretching out a hand to take the bundle of fragments from her.

Before his eyes, there had appeared, as if revealed by a lightning flash, the image of the widow who, many, many centuries ago, had brought a handful of meal to lay upon the altar, and he heard the voice that declared to the priest: "Despise not her offering, for it is as if she had brought her soul to lay upon the altar."[43] And the eyebrows of the *rav* trembled, and he looked down into the box of fragments.

In an hour's time, the work had so far progressed that they could send the draymen for the horses which were out to pasture.

When the thirty clay pots had been filled with fragments, covered, and set out in a row, the old *shamas* laid on them an old altar curtain. Suddenly Barukh Bren—the oldest and most respected community leader in the town, and the second scholar to the *rav* himself—remembered that in his house, behind the big cupboard, there was a package of

---

42. The term *tehineh* [supplication] refers to a specific form of prayer usually said quietly, its subject being the relationship between God and the people of Israel. It is sometimes constructed in rhymed verses. In addition to traditional Hebrew *tehinot* (pl.), Yiddish-German *tehines* (pl.), as noted here, were published in booklet form and produced especially for women, a custom that dates to the beginning of the eighteenth century.

43. This phrase is a Yiddish variant of the well known commentary by Rabbi Solomon Yizhak (1040–1105), the important French Jewish theologian and biblical scholar (known by the acronym Rashi), concerning Leviticus 2:1 which reads: "When anyone presents a grain offering to the Lord, the offering shall be of choice flour . . ." Like some earlier sources, Rashi's commentary discusses the significance of modest ritual offerings brought to the priests by poor persons. Rashi asserts:

Nowhere is the word *nefesh* [soul] employed in connection with free will offerings, except in connection with the meal offering. For who is it that usually brings a meal offering? The poor man! The Holy One, blessed be He, says, as it were, I will regard it for him as though he brought his very soul as an offering . . ." (*Pentateuch with Targum Onkelos, Haphtaroth and Rashi's Commentary: Leviticus*, trans. M. Rosenbaum and A. M. Silbermann [New York: Hebrew Publishing Company, 1934], p. 5b)

sheelot utshuvot[44] [queries and replies] which his grandfather—may his soul rest in peace!—had put there years ago. And eager to do the good deed himself, and bring these fragments, too, to a decent burial, he set out at a run for his home, his coat tails lifted behind him, flying so fast that even his grandsons could not keep pace with him.

Now the musicians were instructed to arrange themselves in two rows, and the draymen—a father and his son—mounted on the box of the cart. They had neither whip nor switch in their hands, and they turned their horses down the alley which lies between the *bet midrash* and the market place.

A shy smile hovered on the face of the *rav*'s wife when she came into the yard of the *bet midrash*, dressed in a woolen dress, and with a light, transparent shawl on her shoulders. Most of the women, true house-wives of the town, wore the accepted holiday uniform of Zhuzhikovka, a stiff satin dress covered by a pleated apron and a smooth black bonnet with two points which stuck out and trembled as they walked.

But when the assembly reached the market place, and the musicians began to play on their instruments—two drums, a trumpet, and a vio-lin which pierced to your insides—no one had a mind any more for the dresses and bonnets of the women.

Earnestly and solemnly, as conscious of their own importance as were the young oxen of Samuel the prophet which brought the holy ark from the field of the Philistines to Bet Shemesh,[45] the horses strode across the market place between rows of closed shutters through the clouds of dust and the excited crowd. Great was the astonishment of the Russian postmaster and the clerks of the town hall, who followed the procession with uncovered heads and staring faces as far as the cemetery itself; and there the voice of the *rav*—and the voice was enough!—changed the look of amazement on their faces to one of indefinable terror.

But the voice of the *rav* was enough to make anyone tremble. There he stood wrapped in his *talit* [prayer shawl]. A faint green luster was on his face. He spoke of the marvelous and eternal union of souls between Israel and the Torah. He also spoke of the time of the redemption,

44. The reference here is to rabbinic responsa or, in Hebrew, *sheelot utshuvot* [queries and replies], a term denoting an exchange of letters in which one party consults another on a matter of Jewish religious law.

45. The reference here is to the biblical account of the return of the ark of the Lord from captivity, found in I Samuel 6:1–21. In this passage, the Philistines consult with the priests and resolve that a "guilt offering" should accompany the ark's return, with the ultimate goal of avoiding future collective punishment. For a detailed explication of the biblical text, see *The New Oxford Annotated Bible*, ed. by Michael Coogan, 3rd edition (Oxford and New York: Oxford University Press, 2001), pp. 407–408.

when all the dead would rise to life; at that time, he recalled, the sacred fragments that they were burying now would also rise.

"And I will open your graves and I will lift you up and I will bring you unto the Land of Israel."[46] The *rav* stretched out his hand now over the graves and the monuments of the fathers, and now over the stones and wooden headpieces of the children; and it seemed that a sigh came from the trees that shook themselves and bowed their heads.

Oh, this was no longer the *shtetl* of Zhuzhikovka, which the young people had been abandoning during the last few decades, in favor of the great world outside. No! Here stood a congregation of Israel, four hundred years old, headed by a long line of fifteen illustrious rabbis, adorned with families of the *kohanim*, and sanctified by the presence of martyrs who had died for *kidush hashem* [sanctification of the name of the God of Israel]. And in this transformation, a cry of mourning, altogether unlike the mourning of bereaved ones, rose over the holy field and lingered above the heads of the assembled.

Barukh Bren, the greatest scholar among the *baalei batim* [household leaders] of the town, had laid his barred kerchief across the gravestone of his father, and pressed against it his face which was distorted with sobbing. And Mina, of the family of the *kohanim*, had pushed her way through to her "portion," the four ells of earth which she had bought herself next to the grave of her husband. There she threw herself on the grave of her husband and clung convulsively to the grass, just as if she did not have a little house of her own, with a little barn to the side, in the middle of the town, and a milk goat on the pasture behind the *bet midrash*.

But just at this point, the *rav* ended his sermon with the dry, closing formula *"uva lezion"*[47] [come to Zion] and, stepping forward, was the first to throw a spadeful of earth on the manuscripts in their grave.

46. This English phrase is a translation from the Yiddish by Maurice Samuel, which derives from the original biblical Hebrew found in Ezekiel 37:12. The phrase is part of Ezekiel's vision of the valley of dry bones, a critical moment in his prophetic career, which relates to the restoration of the Jews to the Land of Israel and the rebuilding of the Holy Temple in Jerusalem. For a detailed explication of the biblical text, see *The New Oxford Annotated Bible*, ed. by Michael Coogan, 3rd edition (Oxford and New York: Oxford University Press, 2001), pp. 1233–1235.

47. The Hebrew phrase *"uva lezion"* [come to Zion] is a conglomeration that appears in various biblical verses and passages throughout Jewish liturgical tradition. It is recited at the end of the weekday morning service, just prior to the *kadish shalem* [complete reader's *kadish*], a largely Aramaic doxology, and the prayer *"Aleinu Leshabeah"* [It is our duty to praise], which concludes the statutory services. Though there does not appear to be a traditional prescription for the ceremony of burying a Torah scroll or documents that might contain God's name, *"uva lezion"* could be recited in the context of such a ceremony. Moreover, the Talmudic sources *Babylonian Talmud Megillah* 26b and *Baba Kama* 17a mention the practice of placing holy books alongside the coffin of a

In groups, the congregation drifted down behind the musicians toward the ferry, and there, on the edge of the river, while the trumpet was pealing and the fiddle was singing, they saw the *rav* step up to the old drayman and, giving him his hand, exclaim heartily, "Happy journey!"

"He's going to Tukhanovka,[48] to bring the first Talmud students!" This was clear to everyone who beheld how the face of the *rav* lit up, while the wind lifted playfully the points of his mantle. And they stood, petrified and silent, watching the drayman erect on his cart disappearing slowly among the fields of wheat which lay on his right and left.

dead man prior to his burial. The phrase "*uva lezion*" also features prominently in Psalm 20, a prayer for the king's victory in battle. For a detailed explication of the latter, see *The New Oxford Annotated Bible*, ed. by Michael Coogan, 3rd edition (Oxford and New York: Oxford University Press, 2001), p. 791.

48. The *shtetl* Tukhanovka appears to have been located in Belarus.

From Language to Language

Rahel Kaznelson [Shazar] (Jerusalem, 1918)

I

IT WAS IN Kineret, during one of our comradely conferences, that I first clarified in my own mind the two concepts: revolutionary movement and revolutionary literature. It was then, too, that I became conscious of the revolutionary character of Hebrew literature and began to understand why we had passed from Yiddish to Hebrew and wherein, for us, lay the difference between these languages.

Fifteen years ago we began, of our own free will, to speak Yiddish just as later, of our own free will, we began to speak Hebrew. I believe that we have not as yet evaluated the significance of this period in our lives. We were then just a handful of people (in Erez Israel, too, we learned not to become enthusiastic about numbers) who felt that we had to begin speaking Yiddish. The language was like a homeland in exile. Every word we uttered in Yiddish seemed to be a reminder of a home—a street, a labor group. This mystery of being Jewish lived for us only in the poverty-stricken hovels; somehow, it seemed contrary to common sense to believe that in the houses of the rich there were Jews, too. The secret and the beauty of the race[49] lay for us in the little children's faces on the streets of the poor. On summer evenings, we walked in those streets to listen to the murmur of the thousands of voices of the workers, just as we might have walked in the forest to hear its thousand voices. We felt that here was life. The first time we listened to a reading in Yiddish, the whole of this world was unveiled to us. Then we found the writers of this world, too, Morris Rosenfeld,[50] [Isaac

---

49. The term "race" is used in the original Yiddish text.

50. Morris Rosenfeld (1862–1923), a pioneer of Yiddish poetry, hailed from Warsaw and began to publish his work at age fifteen. In 1882, he moved to London where he learned tailoring and wrote for Jewish socialist and anarchist journals. He immigrated to the United States in 1886 and found work in a sweatshop as a presser. His sweatshop poems and songs captured the hearts and minds of Yiddish-speaking workers. His writing focused on proletarian, national, and romantic themes. Regarded as the premier poet of the Jewish immigrant labor movement, Rosenfeld's literary accomplishments did not bring financial success. He worked for a meager living in sweatshops for much of his

Leib] Perez,[51] and the younger ones of our own generation. The simplicity of Avraham Reisin[52] appealed to us only later, and last of all we unlocked the door that opened on the riddle of Sholem Aleikhem.[53]

Every Yiddish word, spoken or written, that was touched with emotion, youth or art, we received in us as if it were a separate greeting from home. The language was new to us, and therefore poor in vocabulary, and yet we never felt "a lack of words." This was, perhaps, the one short period in our lives when our speech was dominated by truth. The language was indeed poor, and each one of us knew two or three richer languages, but all our inmost life found, without seeking, its full expression in Yiddish. For the first and, perhaps, only time, we felt the pride of language and of its music, knew that this tongue was an intimate secret between ourselves and our people, knew that for every experience of the soul an expression had been prepared, and that this expression lay stored up somewhere, ready to be called into instant use. And how we used to suffer when someone spoke a false, artificial Yiddish! We simply could not understand how anyone could be unaware of the un-authenticity of that speech—with all those good teachers around him.

Many of us, particularly among the young, knew Hebrew, too. Interest in Hebrew awakened almost simultaneously with interest in Yiddish. But for most of us, the knowledge of Hebrew was a dead or paralyzed thing. Even those who did not know Hebrew felt that in this language, too, there lay a great national treasure, and they wanted to learn about it. This was the time when [Hayim Nahman] Bialik's[54] poetry was

---

life. He published twenty volumes of poetry and prose, and he wrote biographies of the Hebrew poet and philosopher Judah Halevi (c. 1075–1141) and the German Jewish poet and essayist Heinrich Heine (1797–1856), both of whom exerted a strong influence over him.

51. On Isaac Leib Perez, see part V, note 54.

52. On Avraham Reisin, see note 13 in this section.

53. Shalom Aleikhem (a greeting that means "How do you do?") was the pen name of the famous Yiddish humorist writer Shalom Rabinovich (1859–1916), a native of Ukraine. Rabinovich showed much artistic promise as a youth. He began to write in Hebrew, but eventually turned to Yiddish as the central medium of his artistic efforts. His fame spread rapidly and, in a short time, his pen name became a household word. During his lifetime, the Jewish intelligentsia was scornful and even hostile to Rabinovich, treating him as a popular writer for the masses and even merely as an entertainer. Several of the best authors of the period, however, including Hayim Nahman Bialik (see part V, note 28), Yosef Hayim Brenner (see glossary), and Mikha Yosef Berdichevsky (see note 77 below) perceived his genius. In time, he came to be recognized as the most important Yiddish story writer of his generation. Sympathetic to Zionism, he eventually joined Hovevei Zion [Lovers of Zion], and wrote two Zionist pamphlets, a novel, a play, and a biography of Theodor Herzl.

54. On Hayim Nahman Bialik, see part V, note 28.

shaking the Hebrew world. His [*Al hashekhitah*] [On the Slaughter],[55] the song of pain and rage awakened in him by the massacre of Kishinev,[56] and "*Habrekhah*" [The Pool][57] had recently appeared. To the ears of those who could not read Hebrew, came nevertheless the news of the existence of such poets and writers as [Shaul] Chernikhovsky,[58] [Mordecai Zeev] Feierberg,[59] and [Gershon] Shofman.[60] They were translated and read. But it occurred to none of us to want to speak Hebrew; Yiddish seemed to us our natural medium of speech. And how could we turn from a natural to an artificial medium?

55. The Kishinev *pogroms* in 1903 deeply shocked the civilized world. Bialik went to Kishinev to interview survivors and prepare a report on the atrocities perpetrated there. Before leaving, he wrote *Al hashekhitah* [On the Slaughter] (1903). In the poem, he calls on heaven to exercise immediate justice and, if not, to destroy the world. Later he wrote *Beir haharegah* [In the City of Slaughter] (1904), a bitter denunciation of the Jews' meek, submissive, and cowardly behavior during the massacre as well as a cry against the indifference of nature and the cosmos: "The sun shone, the acacia blossomed, and the slaughterer slaughtered."

56. The Kishinev *pogroms*, which took place during Easter on April 6–7, 1903 and October 19–20, 1905, sent shock waves through the Jewish world. See part I, note 12.

57. "*Habrekhah*" [The Pool] (1905) was written during Bialik's stay in Warsaw, where he came under the influence of Isaac Leib Perez (see part V, note 54). The pool, guarded by the forest, illustrates the changing moods of nature and the observer. It also symbolizes the paradox of objective reality and reality as reflected in the pool.

58. Shaul Chernikhovsky (1875–1943), a native of Mikahelovka, Russia, received a traditional Jewish education but was also exposed to the Haskalah [Jewish enlightenment] and Hibbat Zion [Lovers of Zion]. He lived in Odessa, Heidelberg-Lausanne (where he completed his medical studies in 1905), St. Petersburg, Berlin, and finally Tel Aviv. In his work as a poet, essayist, and translator, Chernikhovsky pioneered new literary forms and expanded the arena of Hebrew letters. His ideology was essentially a rejection of life bound by ideology, and his poetry emphasized earthy love and nature. His poems evoked an especially enthusiastic response from contemporaries in the Palestine labor movement.

59. Mordecai Zeev (Feuerberg) Feierberg (1874–1899), a famous Hebrew writer whose works deal with the conflict between Jewish modernity and tradition, was born in Volhynia, Russia, to a Hasidic family. He received a traditional Jewish education but soon came under the influence of the Haskalah [Jewish enlightenment]. Thereafter, he became an active member in local circles of *maskilim* [Haskalah adherents] and Hovevei Zion [Lovers of Zion]. In 1896, he submitted poems and stories to *Hazfirah* [The Dawn], headquartered in Warsaw. The Zionist leader Nahum Sokolow (1859–1936) persuaded him to give up poetry and concentrate instead on prose. Around the same time, the eminent Zionist philosopher Ahad Haam (1856–1927) (see note 76 in this section) discovered Feierberg's work and realized its merit. He obtained a stipend for Feierberg in order that he might write full-time, but Feierberg's career was tragically cut short when he died from tuberculosis three years later.

60. Gershon Shofman (1880–1972), a native of Orsha, Belorussia, was a significant Hebrew writer distinguished for his short stories, didactic sketches, and epigrammatic essays on literature and life. He received a traditional Jewish education, but was also deeply influenced by Russian letters, European culture, and emerging trends in Hebrew literature. He served in the Russian army from 1902 to 1904, but fled to Galicia during the Russo-Japanese War where he lived for three years until moving to Vienna. In 1938, he immigrated to Palestine and settled in Haifa.

Yet it was this deep and natural bond which we severed on coming to Erez Israel. None of us here feels any longer that he is a child of Yiddish! And when we speak Yiddish sometimes, or hear it spoken and listen with joy to the sure, unfaltering words, it gives us such pleasure as one may feel in hearing someone speak a language well, having all its secrets at his command—yet not a language to which we are intimately bound! The passionate attachment to Yiddish no longer exists for us. We master the language, but it does not master us.

For this betrayal we paid dearly, as one pays for every betrayal. And yet we had to make the betrayal and pay the price. And we feel the need to explain and make clear to ourselves why this had to happen.

The fact that Hebrew was the old national language could not influence us; such theoretical considerations have never prompted people to leave a living tongue. Nor could we be influenced by the fact that there are Jews in the world who do not understand Yiddish and that Yiddish is declining. After all, there are many Jews who do not know Hebrew either. And if there are some who are forgetting their Yiddish, there are others who are just beginning to love it. Moreover, are we not the children of our generation, and is not our principal concern the consciousness of being true to ourselves and achieving inner peace? Certainly, the fact that we were few in number (we were fewer when we turned to Yiddish than when we turned to Hebrew) meant nothing to us. We had seen with our own eyes how minorities grow to majorities. Nor could we be bribed by the richness of Hebrew. For, in the first place, what had become of that richness? It was not apparent in the Hebrew we spoke. Was it not a dead language, without a soul, filled with strange expressions and a strange spirit? And was not every beautiful Hebrew expression a sort of miracle to us? And in the second place, "poverty is no shame," and the poor man loves even his bit of poverty—his true possession.

How was it, then, that we so swiftly threw overboard that which had been the very content of our lives?

II

When we consider the hopes that our generation reposed in the Yiddish language, and the respect which we felt for Hebrew, it seems that the division of the writers between Hebrew and Yiddish should have been other than it actually was. [Yosef Hayim] Brenner should have written his stories of Yiddish town life in Yiddish, while [Sholem] Asch should have written his idyll of the Jewish *shtetl* in classical Hebrew.

What happened was the opposite. And it was characteristic of the young generation of writers, Yiddish and Hebrew, who were brought up on the same street, often as boyhood friends, and knew both Yiddish and Hebrew, that they should part company in this fashion. [Yosef Hayim] Brenner, [Gershon] Shofman, and [Uri Nissan] Gnessin[61] wrote only in Hebrew; [Avraham] Reisin, [David] Einhorn,[62] and Der Nister[63] only in Yiddish. The difference between these groups began only when it came to the choice of language, and this was dictated by an organic, inner impulse. We must bear this in mind when we examine the question as a whole.

A language has its own atmosphere. It is impossible to learn a language thoroughly without being influenced by its spirit. For the language is the storehouse of a people's energy. The history of the people —not the written history alone, but the history which has been lived and felt, the totality of its aspirations and experiences—is enclosed forever in its language. He who knows the people, its history and its language, knows at once what words have their peculiar sound and sense, such as cannot be found in another language. And this peculiarity of sound or timber is related to a specific characteristic of the people, or to a specific incident in its history, or to a specific association born of its utterance by a national hero in a moment of crisis. The memory of the people is loaded with these expressions of exceptional circumstances, some national catastrophe, a moment of national religious ecstasy, of national danger, of national creativity. And even though only a handful were present when the expression was coined or the word uttered, the sound of it is carried like seed across the length and breadth of the people.

But it is not only the unusual that leaves its mark on the language; the usual, the ordinary also wear their grooves, and therefore a language continues to grow as long as people speak it and think it. And the

61. On Uri Nissan Gnessin, see part V, note 21.

62. David Einhorn (1886–1973), a native of Korelichi, Belorussia, made his debut as a Yiddish poet in the publications of the Bund. In 1912, after serving a six-month prison sentence for suspected revolutionary activity, he was forced to leave tsarist Russia. Next, he lived in Switzerland, Warsaw, Berlin, Paris, and New York City. Einhorn's poetry is characterized by national themes and lyric modes of expression.

63. Der Nister, Yiddish for "the concealed one," is the pen name of the Yiddish author Pinhas Kahanovich (1884–1950). A native of Berdichev, Ukraine, he was strongly influenced by Hasidism and socialist Zionism. In 1905, he fled Berdichev in order to evade forced conscription into the Russian military. Until World War I, he led a largely fugitive life, chiefly in Zhitomir, using false papers and giving private Hebrew lessons. Subsequently, he lived in Berlin, Kharkov, and Tashkent. Kahanovich's novels and poems are at once mystical and romantic. His wartime and postwar writings are distinguished by strong Jewish nationalist sentiments. He was killed in the Stalinist purges.

richer our inner life is, the richer is the heritage we bequeath to the language, the richer the atmosphere in which we move, and in which those coming after us will move. The words that we have used to convey deep thought and feeling will have had their effect on someone; he will never be able to use those words again without remembering what we have put into them. And the converse is also true: every flabby or stereotyped thought impoverishes the spirit and lowers the level of the people.

Every language has its magic circle, within which the listener—once he has entered the circle—becomes sensitive to the echoes of all words. Anyone who has mastered several languages thoroughly knows how one changes with each new language. For a language is not merely a collection of words and expressions; it is the whole of the past in living form.

"In times of doubt, in days of dark thoughts for the fate of my fatherland, you, my language, are my only support. Only you, our vast, powerful, true, free Russian speech! For it is imposible that so mighty a language should have been given to any but a mighty people." ([Ivan] Turgenev,[64] "The Russian Language."[65])

Every language has its own boundaries and limitations, according to the intellectual and emotional stores it contains. And these limitations determine the heights that the language can attain. Beyond this height, the artist himself cannot reach. And the converse is again true: no expression can sink lower than a given limit for a given language.

The heavier the heritage is, the more difficult the life. The children of a people with a great past do not fit easily into the ways of life, because a language exacts as well as endows. But Jews have never declined this difficulty; they have continued to increase their heritage.

The national energy that is deposited in the Hebrew language has not ceased to live through the thousands of years in which Jews have not spoken the language. Religion was its guardian. It is perhaps because of this religion that, after two thousand years, Chernikhovsky should have been able to write in Hebrew. The religious life filled and refilled the heart of the Jewish people with perpetually renewed confidence, flooding every corner of it with spirit. It was this religious life which returned to the Hebrew language that intimacy of which it had been deprived by the other language—the language of the home and street. And per contra, the religious idea (either in the form of philoso-

64. Ivan Sergeevich Turgenev (1818–1883), the great naturalist Russian writer and advocate of liberal western ideals, is credited with hastening certain social reforms in the tsarist empire, particularly the emancipation of the serfs. He is best known for his stories, plays, and novels, especially *Fathers and Sons* (1862).

65. See Ivan Turgenev, *Stories and Poems in Prose*, trans. Olga Shartse (Moscow: Progress Publishers, 1982), especially "The Russian Language," p. 415.

phy, or of science, or of poetry—everything was then religion) was strengthened from the inexhaustible sources of the Hebrew language. In this beneficent interaction the life of the people, touched always with new concepts, new intentions and new secrets, was carried from generation to generation.

And here our people has been speaking Yiddish for several hundred years, and in this language, too, we have accumulated great stores of national energy. We are fed from these stores in their various forms— the mother, childhood, our history in exile; things that are true and dear and belong to us. And these are the two worlds that lie before the young generation of Jewish writers.

In the time through which we are living, our national possessions have become dearer than ever to us, and our pride will not permit us to treat with contempt one of our high possessions simply because it is not perfect and harmonious. And only in a time of such jealous love could the war of languages have broken out in our midst in the manner that it actually assumed.[66] But we should know that if a writer has made his definite choice of one of the languages and not of the other, it was not through accident. He has merely obeyed an inner command, itself the inevitable result of his relationship to the tradition which the language contained. Each one of us carries on the tradition of the language in which he lives, not knowing it and sometimes even not willing it.

III

When we tried to characterize the original Yiddish literature we used to say: "The Yiddish literature is more national than the Hebrew." What we wanted to say was that the warmth which we felt in the Yiddish literature was absent from the Hebrew. It was in Yiddish that we were

66. The impact of modernity on East European Jewish life, which stimulated the development of modern Hebrew, gave rise to a modern literature in Yiddish. As the most widely spoken and highly developed Jewish vernacular in the late nineteenth and early twentieth centuries, Yiddish found its champions who proclaimed it as the national language of the Jewish people. As a rule, most Zionists championed Hebrew, while Yiddishists and anti-Zionists, if they did not advocate assimilation into Russian or Polish culture, favored Yiddish. There were, however, many Zionists, especially socialist Zionists, who favored Yiddish as well. For example, Ber Borochov (1881–1917), the premier theoretician of Marxist Zionism, was an ardent Yiddishist. Of the two main labor parties in Palestine, Hapoel Hazair was committed to Hebrew, while Poalei Zion was divided, with a slim majority favoring Hebrew. Even Yizhak Ben-Zvi, the Russian Poalei Zion leader, was originally a proponent of Yiddish; in 1908, he founded the country's first Yiddish workers' weekly, *Der anfang* [The Beginning]. In time, a fierce struggle ensued over the place of Hebrew in the Yishuv (see note 75 in this section).

loved as we were, in our Jewish street and in our *shtetl*. And this was one of the main virtues of Yiddish.

A Yiddish writer on a Warsaw newspaper once made the round from *shtetl* to *shtetl* within the Pale, and found in each *shtetl* treasuries of poetry—in the life of the places, in their inhabitants, in their past. This would have been impossible in the Hebrew literature; even Levinsky[67] would have been unable to find it.

The impression produced on us by Perez's *Folkstimlikhe geshikhtn*[68] [Yiddish Folk Tales] was in its way not less profound than that produced by Bialik's *Beir haharegah* [In the City of Slaughter].[69] In our hearts, we gave all these stories one name: *mesirat nefesh* [devotion unto death], for this was the poetry of our martyrdom, and our faithfulness in exile.

The relationship of Yiddish literature toward us was like that of a mother who, out of deep love for her child, is unable to understand its inner struggles, its faults and complexities, simply because it is her child and she is only the mother.

And in those years, soon after the Russian Revolution [of 1905], when everything within us was so tense, we felt in Yiddish literature something too soothing, something that holds down the wings, something that prevents one from drawing deep, free breath.

There was a time when the *shtetl* was to us what it was for Sholem Asch,[70] a world in itself, locked in, sustaining itself in its own beauty. But this was not what we now needed. If it had been possible for us to see Jewish life only as it was mirrored in the Yiddish literature, we could not have considered ourselves a great people.

There is a touch of bitterness in what I want to say about Yiddish— the bitterness of a disillusioned first love, which leaves behind it, together with its pain, the clear realization that the early freshness of relationship which is found but once in life is gone forever. And even the knowledge that Yiddish bound us to the life of the people and helped us to remain true to it can no longer console us.

Great and honest talents belonged to Yiddish. But why was it that only the Hebrew literature could restore to us the feeling of self-respect?

67. The identity of Levinsky is uncertain. The reference may be to the Hebrew publisher and writer Elhanan Loeb Levinsky (1857–1910).

68. Neither a follower of Hasidism nor a naive folk poet, Isaac Leib Perez (see part V, note 54) used Hasidic material and folk tales as a vehicle for his own beliefs and views. In his masterpiece *Folkstimlikhe geshikhtn* [Yiddish Folk Tales] (1909), translated and published in Hebrew in 1918 as *Mipi haam* [From the Voice of the People], Perez artfully shaped such material into new forms of secular aesthetic expression. His short stories opened up new vistas for Hebrew and Yiddish *belles lettres*.

69. See note 55 above.

70. On Sholem Asch, see note 14 in this section.

Why was Yiddish utterly devoid of that hypnotic power which characterized a Bialik, a Feierberg, a Gnessin? It is not a question of talent, but of personality. The magic of Hebrew was in the freshness of its people; and it was for living persons that we longed. For us Bialik's poem *"Zanah lo zalzal"* [71] [A Twig Fell], Chernikhovsky's introduction to the translation of "The Song of Hiawatha," [72] the problems in Feierberg, and women and nature as they appeared in Gnessin—were human, personal utterances. And where there are people, there is the folk. But the Yiddish literature was touched throughout with modesty, softness, and the fine eroticism and love which had flooded the Yiddish writing in Poland. This love, which is to be found in the Yiddish stories of Hasidism, and in [Sholem] Asch's "The Shtetl," [73] and which accounts perhaps for the magic of Perez's *Folkstimlikhe geshikhtn* [Yiddish Folk Tales]—this love may possess the power to uncover the secrets of life and to create a complete life philosophy. But there are times in the life of a people, and in the life of a man, when nothing is more dangerous than the idyllic and the intellectually narrow. Such a time had come for us, in fact, when each of us had to find his own answer to the question of a language.

A wide gulf lay between the actual difficulty that faced the individual Jew and the manner in which this difficulty was treated in the Yiddish literature and press of the time. (By "the Yiddish literature and press of the time" I mean the main current of Yiddish writing, and not that small part of it which was a reflex of the Hebrew literature and press.) On the one hand, the reforms that certain Yiddishist [74] writers wanted to introduce into our life wounded us by their tactlessness and lack of comprehension—like the interference of a stranger in one's most intimate affairs. Who of us has forgotten, for instance, the solemn debates on the subject of substituting Latin for Hebrew letters, or of dropping Hebrew from the curriculum of the Jewish schools? [75] And on the other

71. In *"Zanah lo zalzal"* [A Twig Fell] (1911), Hayim Nahman Bialik's (see part V, note 28) poetry becomes acutely personal. Having lost the purity of childhood and the ambition of early adulthood, he is preoccupied with death and considers himself a broken, useless twig, dangling from its branch.

72. Shaul Chernikhovsky's (see note 58 above) translation of "The Song of Hiawatha" (1855) by Henry Wadsworth Longfellow (1824–1884), the best known nineteenth century poet in the United States, first appeared in Odessa in 1912–13. In 1931, it was reprinted in Palestine with a new introduction by Chernikhovsky.

73. On Sholem Asch, see note 14 in this section. *The Shtetl*, published in 1904 in the Russian Yiddish socialist daily *Der fraynd* [The Friend], is regarded as a breakthrough in Yiddish literature. In place of a somber and gloomy depiction of East European Jewish life, it conveys a sense of warmth, vitality, and congeniality.

74. A Yiddishist is a protagonist of Yiddish language, literature and culture.

75. Starting in the late nineteenth century, the Zionist movement sought to make Hebrew the language of the Yishuv. To this end, Hebraization of the educational system became a primary objective. Initially, the various educational institutions in Palestine

hand there was a kind of terror when we spoke of national affairs in Yiddish, a fear of taking a free step lest the old dress we wore would rip apart. Yiddish was conservative, and could only see the things of the immediate hour.

Only in Hebrew literature and in the best Hebrew literature, did we feel ourselves freed from the yoke of the national censorship that crushed Yiddish literature everywhere. Here people could speak freely about themselves, about Jews, about the world at large—and it was thus that Ahad Haam,[76] [Mikha Yosef] Berdichevski,[77] and Bialik spoke.

Our nationalism interfered with our life. Thought and emotion were pointed only to one end, and we lacked the freedom of other human

---

reflected the language preferences of their sponsoring French, German, and English agencies. Likewise, Yiddish emerged as the vernacular of many Jewish colonies and Zionist political parties in Palestine. Over time, Hebrew made inroads into all strata of the Yishuv and the Zionist movement gradually created a network of Hebrew language schools. In 1913, the Histadrut Hamorim [Teachers Association] spearheaded a campaign to challenge the overseers of the Tehnion, a German-sponsored engineering school on Mount Carmel, Haifa. They sought to replace German with Hebrew as the language of instruction. Protests, student strikes and a boycott were organized. The so-called "language war" and the outbreak of World War I delayed the opening of the Tehnion. A decade later, it opened in December 1924 as an all-Hebrew institution. See also note 66 in this section.

76. Ahad Haam [One of the People] is the pen name of the Hebrew essayist and foremost cultural Zionist philosopher Asher Zvi Ginsberg (1856–1927), a native of Skvira, Kiev province. Following a traditional upbringing, Ginsberg was profoundly affected by the Haskalah [Jewish enlightenment] and abandoned religious orthodoxy for the secularism of Hibbat Zion [Love of Zion]. He soon found himself at odds with Hibbat Zion's ideology, particularly the notion of mass Jewish resettlement in Palestine, and withdrew from the organization. Thereafter, he wrote articles criticizing Hibbat Zion that brought him widespread attention. He argued that Zionism could not solve the "problem of the Jews"—their social, economic, and political plight—but rather the "problem of Judaism" (i.e., the trend of Jewish assimilation into European gentile society). In his view, cultural and spiritual renewal was a necessary precondition to creating a new Jewish society. He urged the use of Hebrew as a secular language and the Hebrew Bible as a basis for morality and culture rather than religiosity. Later, he clashed with Theodor Herzl (see part V, note 12), viewing the latter's program of diplomatic and political Zionism to be fundamentally flawed. Ahad Haam exerted a profound influence on younger generations, especially the Zionist intellectuals and political leaders of the post-Herzlian period. In 1922, he settled permanently in Tel Aviv.

77. Mikha Yosef Berdichevsky (later, Bin-Gorion) (1865–1921) was a Hebrew novelist and essayist who hailed from Podolia. Descended from a long line of Hasidic rabbis, Berdichevsky received a traditional education and studied at the Volozhin *yeshivah* (see note 24 in this section). As a youth, he was deeply influenced by the Haskalah [Jewish enlightenment] and secular European culture, particularly the writings of the German philosopher Fredrich Wilhelm Nietzsche (1844–1900) who argued the necessity of establishing a new basis for social values. In opposition to the ideas of Ahad Haam (see previous note) and Theodor Herzl (see part V, note 12), Berdichevsky asserted a Nietzschean demand for the "transvaluation" of Judaism and Jewish history. He lived in Volozhin, Breslau, Berlin, and Warsaw, and sustained contact with the major Jewish writers of his day.

efforts. Every enthusiasm for general, not specifically Jewish matters, pulled us or tried to pull us closer to the alien world. It was impossible to be a socialist, a Tolstoyan, an artist, a politician, or a scientist without the fear of falling a victim to assimilation. If you took one step toward human freedom, you felt yourself alienated from your people; one step toward social interests—alienation again. And that was why, in the fierce impulse toward Erez Israel, we also felt the fierce impulse to get rid of the *idée fixe* of nationalism. For in Erez Israel we would be Jews anyhow, and that was what we wanted. It was this assurance that we found in the Hebrew language. In this language, the writer feels himself more a citizen of the world than he does in Yiddish. His national certainty is stronger in it, his consciousness of his own peculiar character deeper-rooted; and therefore he feels a wider freedom in it, too. In this language he feels that, whatever he does, whatever interests he has, whatever activities he pursues, he still spins in a mysterious way, tacitly and without attention, the eternal thread of his people.

IV

The revolutionary character of the Hebrew literature is revealed both in its affirmations and in its negations.

Two years after the appearance of [Perez's] *Folkstimlikhe geshikhtn*, appeared [Yosef Hayim] Brenner's *Mikan umikan*[78] [From Here and There]. I wonder if Brenner ever suspected that his book would be a deeper and richer well of hope and security than the *Folkstimlikhe geshikhtn*. In any case, we felt one thing: if a man could write about us— as Brenner did—without the slightest touch of pity, it was a sign that we still lived. And the hope with which he presented us in *Mikan umikan* is our only one—but our true one. It was just at this moment, too, that the Yiddish, the Russian Jewish, and even a part of the Hebrew press were dominated by such a spirit of caution, of timidity, and of apology that they seemed to be concerned not with a living people, concerning which one may speak freely, but a dead people, concerning which one may say only the kindliest, most meaningless things.

But the power of Hebrew lay in something more than its negations. There are great negators whose lives have been one great affirmation. And there are some men who are so secure in themselves that they do

78. *Mikan umikan* [From Here and There] (1911), like many of Yosef Hayim Brenner's stories, is based on the author's personal life and experiences. In the latter, which depicts everyday reality and hardship in a struggling Jewish colony in Palestine, the protagonist is the editor of a Hebrew newspaper, as Brenner had been.

not need the tonic of negation. Such a one was [Aharon David] Gordon, who issued his challenge to Brenner's savage analysis of Jewish reality.

Another great affirmer of life was Feierberg, who was something more than a mere guide. Most of us have not yet learned to evaluate him properly. And it is indeed difficult to grasp him. If Bialik, for instance, had written only for three years, would we have known anything about him? But even in the stammering of the young Feierberg—for all his speech, concentrated flame and passion though it is, is only a stammering in comparison with what he had to tell us—there is hidden something that has no parallel in Hebrew literature. His stories have a natural power of attraction because there was, between him and Jewish history, a type of relationship that no one else had. If he had lived long enough to write the life of the Baal Shem Tov,[79] as he intended to, he would have given us a new vision of Hasidic and Jewish history, and not the cleverly thought out, artificial stories of Hasidism which (in comparison to Feierberg's relationship to Jewishness) are Perez's.

And thus the spirits came to the parting of the ways. Had Brenner at least written in Yiddish, the picture would have been different; not simply because another great talent would have been added to Yiddish literature, but because the incident itself would have been symptomatic. But the division of talents took place so clearly and unmistakably, all our dissatisfaction with our life of today, all our demand for a complete change swung over not to the "living" language, but to the "dead" one!

Yiddish was the language of the folk, of democracy; but in Yiddish literature there reigned narrowness, inertia and—as seen by our generation—the spirit of reaction. The stream of thought that meant revolution for us found its expression in Hebrew literature. And every person of living thought—and this is truest for the children of our generation, our people and our situation—feels himself drawn toward the sources of revolution.

79. Israel Baal Shem Tov (1669–1761), also known by his acronym the Besht, was the founder of Hasidism, the Jewish religious and mystical revival movement that first emerged in the Ukrainian regions of Volhynia and Podolia and swiftly spread to other parts of Eastern Europe. His brand of Jewish mysticism gave rise to a new type of spiritual leader called the *zadik* [righteous person] in Hebrew or *rebbe* [teacher] in Yiddish. After the death of Israel Baal Shem Tov, Rabbi Dov Baer of Mezhirech (d. 1773) assumed the leadership of the movement.

Glossary of Terms

Agudat Netaim. Hebrew for "Planters Association," an organization of Jewish shareholders in Palestine and the diaspora, established in 1905 for the purpose of promoting rural settlement and education in the Land of Israel.

Ahdut Haavodah. Hebrew for "Unity of Labor," a non-Marxist all-inclusive labor organization established in Palestine in 1919, that served as both a trade union and a framework for uniting rival socialist Zionist factions as well as various nonpolitical workers' groups; it was the leading Labor Zionist group in Palestine in the 1920s.

aliyah (pl. *aliyot*, Hebrew for "ascent"). A term used to indicate Jewish immigration to the Land of Israel. The First Aliyah is usually dated 1881–1903; the Second Aliyah, 1903/4–1914; the Third Aliyah, 1919–1923; the Fourth Aliyah, 1924–1928; and the Fifth Aliyah, 1929–1939.

Ashkenazi Jews. The term used to identify Yiddish-speaking Jews of East European ancestry.

bet midrash. Hebrew for "house of study," which, since the Middle Ages, served as a center of instruction for Jewish scholars and the public; although usually merged with the synagogue, study and discussion of Jewish law and problems concerning Judaism were paramount, whereas prayer was a secondary activity.

dunam. Term for one thousand square meters, approximately one-quarter of an acre.

Erez Israel (Hebrew), *Erez yisroel* (Yiddish). According to the social, religious, or political context, the term may denote the Land of Israel, Holy Land, or Palestine.

galut. Hebrew for "exile" (*golus* in Yiddish), it is a pejorative term used to describe both spiritual and geographic conditions.

Gdud Avodah. Hebrew for "Labor Legion," a countrywide commune established in 1920 by Third Aliyah pioneers who were disciples of the socialist Zionist leader Yosef Trumpeldor; although the members initially contracted to build roads, lay railway tracks, and work in construction and quarrying wherever Jewish labor was required, they subsequently resolved to establish permanent rural settlements throughout Palestine.

hagshamah azmit. Hebrew for "self-fulfillment."

Hahoresh. Hebrew for "The Plowman," the first Jewish laborers' association in the Galilee, which was established in 1907.

hakhsharah (pl. *hakhsharot*). Hebrew for "training," usually in reference to agricultural and/or manual skills required for life in the Jewish colonies of Palestine, including communal values, conversational Hebrew, and self-defense.

halukah. Hebrew for "distribution"; the traditional system for the distribution of financial contributions from abroad to the Jewish community of Palestine, particularly the "Old Yishuv" (see below) centers in Jerusalem, Hebron, Safed, and Tiberias.

haluz (pl. *haluzim*). Hebrew for "pioneer," used to describe the Labor Zionist pioneers in Palestine.

haluzah (pl. *haluzot*). Hebrew term for "women pioneers," used to describe the Labor Zionist female pioneers in Palestine.

haluziut. Hebrew for "pioneering."

Hamashbir. Hebrew for "The Provisioner," it was founded during World War I as a cooperative purchasing and consumer agency of the workers' movement, it became part of the Histadrut (see below).

Hapoel Hazair. Hebrew for "The Young Worker," a moderate non-Marxist Labor Zionist party established in Palestine in 1905 and the Palestinian sister organization of Zeirei Zion Hitahdut (see below).

Hashomer. Hebrew for "The Watchguard," an organization formed in the Galilee in 1909 to take over guard duty in the Jewish colonies of Palestine.

Hashomer Hazair. Hebrew for "The Young Guard," a worldwide Marxist Zionist youth movement established in Vienna in 1916, that stressed class struggle and pioneering settlement in Palestine; it later gave rise to a left-wing Zionist party in Palestine by the same name as well as a framework of communitarian rural settlements.

hasid (pl. *hasidim*). An adherent of Hasidism, a popular East European Jewish religious movement inclined to mysticism.

Haskalah. Hebrew for "enlightenment," the Jewish enlightenment movement in Europe, particularly that using the Hebrew language.

havurah (pl. *havurot*). Hebrew for "collective work groups," usually employed on the roads or in Jewish plantation villages, towns, and colonies.

havurat hapoalot. Hebrew for "women workers' collective," established by women leaders of the workers movement in Palestine in order to ensure female training and employment on the roads as well as in Jewish plantation villages, towns, and colonies.

heder (pl. *hadarim*). Term used to describe an East European elementary school conducted in Yiddish to teach the Hebrew Bible, homiletic literature, etc.

Hehaluz. Hebrew for "The Pioneer," an organization that emerged after World War I in Russia and became a nonpolitical body embracing all factions of the Zionist movement dedicated to *aliyah* (see above) and pioneering values.

Hibbat Zion. Hebrew for "Lovers of Zion," a philanthropic, proto-Zionist society that originated in Eastern Europe, used interchangeably with the name Hovevei Zion.

Histadrut. A shortened form of Histadrut Haklaklit Shel Haovdim Haivrim Berez Israel, Hebrew for "General Federation of Jewish Workers in the Land of Israel," the umbrella framework of the Labor Zionist movement in Palestine, established in 1920.

hora. Hebrew term for a vigorous circle dance (mostly of Rumanian origin), very popular among the Zionist pioneers.

Hovevei Zion (see *Hibbat Zion*).

Jewish Colonization Association (JCA/ICA). The Jewish Colonization Association founded in 1891 by the German Jewish philanthropist Baron Maurice de Hirsch (1831–1896) to promote and support the mass emigration of Jews from Russia and to encourage their rehabilitation in agricultural colonies, particularly in Brazil and Argentina.

Jewish Legion. The military formation of Jewish volunteers in World War I who fought in the British army for the liberation of Palestine from Turkish rule.

Jewish National Fund (JNF). Known in Hebrew as Keren Kayemet Leyisrael and founded at the Fifth Zionist Congress in 1901 to further the acquisition of land and development of Jewish colonies in Palestine.

kibbutz (pl. *kibbutzim*). Hebrew term for a cooperative rural settlement in Palestine.

kibush haavodah. Hebrew for "conquest of labor," the notion of Jewish spiritual renewal and revolution through physical toil developed by the Labor Zionist philosopher A. D. Gordon (1856–1922), in particular, by substituting Jewish labor for Arab wage workers in the Jewish colonies of Palestine.

Kupat Holim. Hebrew for the "Workers' Sick Fund," the first Jewish health insurance fund and medical network in Palestine, founded in 1911 by a small group of agricultural laborers and taken over in 1920 by the Histadrut (see above).

kvuzah (pl. *kvuzot*). Hebrew term for a communal rural colony in Palestine.

Labor Zionism. The colonizing movement of socialist Zionist pioneers that created an intricate countrywide network of social, economic, and political institutions that shaped the infrastructure of the Jewish state-in-the-making; comprising a variety of rival factions, each with a different emphasis on Marxism, Hebraism, Yiddish, etc.

Mapai. An acronym for the Hebrew Mifleget Poalei Erez Israel (Workers Party of the Land of Israel), established in Palestine in 1930; the party dominated Labor Zionism in the British Mandatory and early state periods.

maskil (pl. *maskilim*). Hebrew for "enlightened Jew," referring to an adherent of the Jewish enlightenment movement (see *Haskalah* above).

Merkaz Hahaklai. Hebrew for "Central Farmers' Association," an outgrowth of Hapoel Hahaklai [Land Workers' Association], was established in 1911 by Second Aliyah pioneers. Absorbed into the Histadrut (see above) after 1920, it was the central organizational body of agricultural workers in the pre-state era.

meshek hapoalot. Hebrew for "women pioneers' farm," usually a training farm or nursery attached to a Jewish settlement, at which women acquired manual skills needed for pioneering life in Jewish plantation villages, towns, and colonies.

Moezet Hapoalot. Hebrew for the "Women Workers' Council," established in 1922 as part of the Histadrut (see above) and the sister organization of Pioneer Women in the United States.

moshav ovdim. Hebrew for "workers' settlement," a rural Jewish colony in Palestine incorporating some cooperative principles.

moshavah (pl. *moshavot*). Hebrew for "plantation village," usually associated with the private landholding Zionist pioneers of the First Aliyah (see *aliyah* above).

Palestine Jewish Colonization Association (PICA). A society for Jewish settlement in Palestine active between 1924 and 1957, it was created by Baron Edmond de Rothschild (1845–1934) and was taken over from the Jewish Colonization Association (see above), which had managed the plantation villages assisted by Rothschild since 1900. PICA was recognized officially by the British Mandatory authorities in 1924.

Poalei Zion. Hebrew for "Workers of Zion," a Marxist Zionist party that originated in Russia in 1901–1903 and subsequently established branches in other countries, including Palestine.

pogroms. Russian term for anti-Jewish riots perpetrated by the Christian population against East European Jews; widespread in Russia between 1881 and 1921 and generally accompanied by destruction, looting of property, murder, and rape.

rebbe. a Yiddish term, usually refers to a Hasidic rabbi.

Sephardi Jews. Term used to identify Ladino-speaking Jews of Iberian ancestry.

shomer (pl. *shomrim*). Hebrew for "watchman" or "guard."

shtetl (pl. *shtetlkh*). Yiddish for a small town or village in Eastern Europe.

shul. Yiddish term for "synagogue."

Talmud Torah. Yiddish term for a traditional school, usually supported by the Jewish community, that taught boys the basics of biblical and rabbinic literature.

World Zionist Congress. The representative body and highest authority in the World Zionist Organization (see below), created by Theodor Herzl (1860–1904), the founder of modern political Zionism. The First Zionist Congress was held in 1897; between 1898 and 1939 the Congress convened every one to three years on twenty-one occasions. Only after World War II did the twenty-second Zionist Congress convene, thereafter meeting every four to six years in the early decades of the Jewish state.

World Zionist Organization. The political organization established by Theodor Herzl and the World Zionist Congress (see above) that was responsible for coordinating and implementing the political, financial, and development strategies of the Zionist movement in the diaspora and Palestine.

yeshivah (pl. *yeshivot*). Yiddish term for a school for advanced Talmudic study.

yeshivah bokher. Yiddish term for a male student in a *yeshivah* (see above).

Yishuv. Hebrew term for the Jewish community in Palestine before the creation of the State of Israel in 1948; the "Old Yishuv" refers to the traditional, religiously observant Jewish community established prior to 1881 whose four chief centers were Jerusalem, Hebron, Safed, and Tiberias.

Zeirei Zion Hitahdut. Hebrew for "United Youth of Zion," a European non-Marxist Labor Zionist party established in Russia in 1903 and affiliated with the moderate Palestinian party Hapoel Hazair (see above).

Glossary of Names

ABRAMSON, PESSIE (1893–1922). In 1905, Pessie Abramson immigrated from
Russia to Palestine with her parents. Her family settled in Rishon Lezion.
In 1908, she was accepted into Hannah Meisel-Shohat's (see below) newly
established *meshek hapoalot*. In 1914, she undertook work as an agricultural
laborer at Merhavyah and then Tel Adashim (Tel Adas). Two years later, she
joined the *kvuzah* of women workers in Petah Tikvah and subsequently
sought employment in Hederah. In 1918, after another brief stay in Tel
Adashim, she returned to Merhavyah and married Meyer Spektor (1893–
1955) (see part V, note 41), who had enlisted in the Jewish Legion. Their
eldest son Yizhak was born a year later. In 1920, Spektor moved the family
to Kfar Giladi, where their second child Uri was born. Meanwhile, he took
on assignments with Hashomer at distant colonies for weeks and even
months at a time. Lonely and depressed, Pessie Abramson committed suicide in May 1922. The child Uri died a few months later.

BARON, DVORAH (1887–1956). A native of Ozdah, Belorussia, Dvorah Baron,
was a significant Hebrew author. She began her writing career by publishing
articles in the Russian Hebrew periodicals *Hameliz* [The Interpreter] and
Hazfirah [The Dawn]. Baron immigrated to Palestine in 1911 and became
literary editor of the first Palestinian labor newspaper *Hapoel hazair* [The
Young Worker]. Her first anthology *Sipurim* [Stories] was published in 1927.
In 1934, she was the first to receive the newly created Bialik Prize. Her writing consists mainly of short prose, and her collections *Leet atah* [At the Present Time] (1943) and *Parshiyot* [Portions] (1951) won literary awards. Baron's
fiction frequently deals with personal experience, including memories from
her childhood. In addition to her own work, she translated Gustave Flau-
bert's *Madame Bovary* into Hebrew. She was married to Yosef Aharonovich
(1877–1937), the Labor Zionist leader and editor of *Hapoel hazair*.

BASEVICH, LILIYAH. A leading member of Ein Harod, Liliyah Basevich was
born in Russia and immigrated to Palestine in her youth. She was a proponent of radical measures related to communal child rearing in *kibbutz* life.
She was also a fierce critic of the opponents of women's liberation in modern Jewish society. She served on the editorial board of *Dvar hapoelet* [The
Woman Worker Speaks].

BECKER, ESTHER (SHTURMAN) (1891–1973). A native of Yekaterinoslav,
Ukraine, Esther (Shturman) Becker (later, Rainin), immigrated to Palestine

in 1905 and was a founder of Hashomer and the settlement Merhavyah. She also played a leading role in Ahdut Avodah. Her brother Hayim Shturman (1891–1938), who immigrated in 1906, was a founder of Ein Harod and a leader of the Palestine labor movement. See the information about her sisters Shifra (Shturman) Bezer and Sarah (Shturman) Krigser (Amidar).

BEN-ZVI, YIZHAK (1884–1963). A native of Poltava, Ukraine, Yizhak Ben-Zvi was a Yishuv leader and the second president of the State of Israel. As a youth, he became active in Russian Poalei Zion and Jewish self-defense activity. He immigrated to Palestine in 1907, where he joined Hashomer and helped found *Ahdut* [Unity], the first Hebrew language socialist journal. Expelled from Palestine in 1915 as a Russian foreign national, Ben-Zvi helped found the Hehaluz organization in New York. At the end of World War I, he returned to Palestine and shortly thereafter became chairman of the Vaad Leumi [Elected Assembly]. When the Zionist leader and first president of the State of Israel Chaim Weizmann (1874–1952) died, Ben-Zvi became the second president; he was re-elected twice. He was married to the Labor Zionist leader Rahel Yanait Ben-Zvi (see below).

BEZER, SHIFRA (SHTURMAN) (1885–1962). A native of Yekaterinoslav, Ukraine, Shifra (Shturman) Bezer settled in Palestine in 1906. Together with her husband Israel Bezer (1883–1963), she was a founder of Dagania. Her brother Hayim Shturman (1891–1938), who immigrated in 1906, was a founder of Ein Harod and a leader of the Palestine labor movement. See the information about her sisters Esther (Shturman) Becker and Sarah (Shturman) Krigser (Amidar).

BLAUSTEIN, RAHEL (1890–1931). A native of Saratov, on the Volga in northern Russia, and raised in Poltava, Rahel Blaustein was the central poet of the Second Aliyah. She immigrated to Palestine 1909, where she became known by the pen name Rahel. She was among the first trainees at Hannah Meisel Shohat's *meshek poalot* at Kineret, and there she also came under the influence of the Labor Zionist philosopher A. D. Gordon. In 1913, she traveled to France to study agriculture. Upon completing her studies, she returned to Russia, where she taught refugee children during World War I. In this period, she also contracted tuberculosis. She returned to Palestine after the war and settled at Dagania. Shortly thereafter, her illness forced her to leave, and she spent the remaining years of her life in sanitoria and hospitals; she died in Tel Aviv. Rahel was among the first Hebrew poets who wrote in a conversational style. Her wistful and nostalgic poetry captured the hearts of the Yishuv pioneers. A complete collection of poetry was published as *Shirat Rahel* [The Poetry of Rahel] (1935).

BOGEN, SHOSHANAH (1898–1918). A native of Russia, Shoshanah Bogen immigrated to Palestine in 1913. She was a leader of the women's *kvuzah* at Ben Shemen. Following the outbreak of World War I, she was among the organizers of a campaign by Jewish women who wished to volunteer for service in the British military. When the British refused to accept women into the army, she committed suicide.

BRENNER, BATYA. A native of Ukraine, Brenner was leader of the Second Aliyah. In her lifetime, she was regarded as a symbol of the woman worker in Palestine. Her brother was the famous writer, Yosef Hayim Brenner (see below).

BRENNER, YOSEF HAYIM (1881–1921). A native of Ukraine, Yosef Hayim Brenner was a central Hebrew writer of the Second Aliyah. He published his first short story collection in Russia, before departing for London in 1904 to escape forced conscription during the Russo-Japanese war. In London, he was active in the Poalei Zion party and published the Hebrew periodical *Hameorer* [The Awakener], which influenced many Second Aliyah pioneers. In 1909, he immigrated to Palestine, first working as a laborer in various settlements and continued writing fiction. He was also a journalist and became a leading intellectual influence in the Palestine labor movement. During World War I, he taught at the Herzliyah gymnasium. Thereafter, he devoted himself increasingly to translation work, literary criticism, social commentary, and writing fiction. Brenner's writings are frequently concerned with the problematic of modern Jewish identity, the tension between secular and traditional Jewish life, and the hardships of Jewish life in Palestine. Among his most famous works is the novel *Shekhol vekishalon* [Breakdown and Bereavement] (1920). In 1921, he was killed by Arab rioters in Jaffa. On his sister Batya Brenner, see above.

BROIZMAN, RIVKAH. Broizman was from Eastern Europe and served for many years as the principal of the agricultural training school operated by Moezet Hapoalot in Petah Tikvah.

BUSEL, HIYUTAH (1890–1965). A native of Lakhovich, Minsk province, Belorussia, Hiyutah Busel was an agricultural laborer, educator, and leader of the working women's movement in Palestine. As a child, she received a traditional Jewish education as well as private secular instruction. She joined the Zionist movement as a youth. In 1908, she immigrated to Palestine with her future husband, Yosef Busel (see below). She initially worked as a laborer in several Jewish colonies and subsequently worked as an agricultural teacher in Jaffa, Tel Aviv, Hederah, and Rishon Lezion. In 1912, she relocated to Dagania for several months; she soon left the *kvuzah* and expressed serious doubts about communitarian life. She next became active in the Zionist settlement efforts throughout the Galilee, especially those groups of women pioneers and others in the Kineret and Metulah areas. In 1917, she married Yosef Busel, who was to die suddenly just two years later. In 1925, she served as the Jewish National Fund's emissary in Poland. For much of her adult life, she was politically active in the Histadrut and the Mapai party and was a central figure in the leadership of Moezet Hapoalot. In 1925 and 1935, she served as a Labor Zionist delegate to the World Zionist Congress.

BUSEL, YOSEF (1891–1919). A native of Lakhovich, Minsk province, Yosef Busel was one of the originators of the idea of the *kvuzah*. He immigrated to Palestine in 1908 with his future wife Hiyutah Busel (see above), where he joined the group cultivating land at Kineret. In 1910, he helped to found

Dagania. Busel was a leading member of Hapoel Hazair and during World War I emerged as a leader of the Palestine labor movement. He drowned while crossing Lake Kineret from Tiberias to Dagania.

CHIZHIK, HANNAH (1889–1951). A native of Tomashpol, Ukraine, Hannah Chizhik immigrated to Palestine in 1905 with her brother Barukh Chizhik. Active in Poalei Zion and Ahdut Avodah, she worked as a laborer in the Jewish colonies and became a leader of the Histadrut. In 1922, she founded a *meshek hapoalot* in Nahlat Yehudah. She devised the idea of the *havurah* in 1926 to relieve female unemployment in Palestine. She was a central figure in Moezet Hapoalot and served in 1930–31 as an emissary to the Pioneer Women's Organization in the United States. On her younger sister Sarah Chizhik, see below.

CHIZHIK, SARAH (1899–1920). A native of Tomashpol, Ukraine, Sarah Chizhik immigrated to Palestine in 1906 with her parents, one year after her elder sister, Hannah Chizhik (see above). She worked initially on her parents' farm near Lake Kineret and subsequently at various Jewish settlements. She was killed with Yosef Trumpeldor at Tel Hai in 1920.

DANIT, RIVKAH (1896–1954). Danit was from Russia and immigrated to Palestine in 1913. She was among the first women laborers to be accepted into the Gdud Avodah and work on road construction near Tiberias. She later became a founder of Ein Harod.

DAYAN, DVORAH (1891–1956). A native of Ukraine, Dvorah (Zatolovsky) Dayan studied at the university in Kiev. She immigrated to Palestine in 1913 and soon joined Dagania. In 1914, she married Shmuel Dayan (1891–1968), a pioneer of cooperative Jewish settlement and founder of Dagania. In 1921, Dayan and her husband were among the founders of the first *moshav ovdim*, Nahalal. She became known as a writer of short stories and editor of *Dvar hapoelet* [The Woman Worker Speaks]. She also contributed to the Jewish labor press. Her articles were collected in the books *Asaper* [To Tell] (1952) and *Beosher uveyagon* [In Wealth and Sorrow] (1959). Her son was Moshe Dayan.

EDELMAN, YEHUDIT (1893–1959). A native of Ukraine, Yehudit Edelman immigrated to Palestine in 1913. She was a founder of the Gdud Avodah and helped to establish Ein Harod.

GILADI, ISRAEL (1886–1918). A native of Calarasi, Bessarabia, Israel (Butelbroit) Giladi was a member of Poalei Zion and an advocate of Jewish self-defense. In 1905, he immigrated to Palestine, where he helped to found the secret defense group Bar Giora. He later joined the workers' collective at Sejera and played a leading role in Hashomer, serving as its commander in 1913. During World War I, he proposed the establishment of an agricultural base for Hashomer and in 1917 he helped found Kfar Bag (named for the Bar Giora society) south of Metulah. Following Giladi's death during an influenza epidemic, the settlement was renamed Kfar Giladi in his memory.

GORDON, A. D. (1856–1922). A native of Troyanov, Russia, Aharon David Gordon (known as A. D. Gordon) immigrated to Palestine in 1904 at the relatively old age of 48. He soon emerged as the leading Zionist philosopher of the Second Aliyah. He worked as a laborer in Petah Tikvah, Rishon Lezion, Ein Ganim, and Dagania. While working during the day, Gordon wrote at night, principally about his mystical beliefs connecting God and worship with agricultural work. Although he avoided the term "socialism," he believed strongly in communal ownership and is credited with developing the concept of *kibush haavodah* [conquest of labor]. He was a strong advocate of Arab-Jewish reconciliation and exerted a powerful influence on the Zionist pioneering movement. His daughter was Yael Gordon (see below).

GORDON, YAEL (1879–1958). The daughter of A. D. Gordon (see above), Yael Gordon, a native of Ukraine, received a traditional Jewish education and was also instructed by private tutors. She completed her advanced training as a teacher in 1908 and subsequently immigrated to Palestine with her mother Faygl (Tartokov) Gordon. A year after their arrival in Palestine, Faygl Gordon died. During Yael Gordon's first years in Palestine, she worked as a teacher and laborer in Rehovot, Ein Ganim, Kineret, Migdal, Merhavyah, and Poriyah. In 1913, she was among thirty delegates to a countrywide conference of women pioneers. The conference elected her to a central committee—along with Hannah Meisel-Shohat (see below), Sarah Malkin (see below), and Leah Meron—which spearheaded the establishment of the organized women workers' movement in Palestine. After World War I, she lived in Petah Tikvah and Tel Aviv. When her father became ill with cancer in 1919, she settled temporarily in Dagania in order to care for him. After his death in 1922, she lived elsewhere for short periods. In 1929, she returned to Dagania permanently, where she worked as a teacher and continued her political activity in the Mapai party.

HANKIN, HAYA-SARAH (1882–1970). Hayah-Sarah Hankin immigrated to Palestine in 1903 and was an early member of Hashomer. Her husband, Yehezkel Hankin (1881–1916), was a founder of Hashomer and was killed in a skirmish with Arab attackers. Thereafter, she served as the head of an association of widows of former Hashomer members.

HANKIN, YEHOSHUA (1864–1945). A native of Kremenchug, Ukraine, Yehoshua Hankin was brought to Palestine in 1882 by his parents, who were First Aliyah settlers. Later, Hankin was instrumental in land acquisition and the settlement of large tracts of land, including the Jezreel Valley. He was known as the "Redeemer of the Valley."

IDELSON, BEBA (1895–1975). A native of Ukraine, Beba (Trachtenberg) Idelson, immigrated to Palestine in 1926. In 1930, she was elected secretary general of Moezet Hapoalot. She was also elected to all the central bodies of the Histadrut and Mapai from 1930 on. In 1949, she was elected a member of the Israeli Knesset and from 1955 to 1961 she served as deputy speaker of the Knesset. She traveled widely as an emissary of Moezet Hapoalot and published numerous articles on women and labor, mostly in the periodical *Dvar hapoelet* [The Woman Worker Speaks].

KAZNELSON, FRIEDA (1892–1979). A native of Bobruisk, Russia, Frieda Kaznelson was a Second Aliyah pioneer. She was the sister of Rahel Kaznelson-Shazar (see below) and was married to Zvi Chomsky. Shortly after World War I, Kaznelson and Chomsky moved to the United States, where he studied agriculture. They returned to Palestine and settled permanently in Kfar Azar, a *moshav* east of Tel Aviv, which was founded in 1932 by veterans of the Second and Third Aliyah.

KAZNELSON-SHAZAR, RAHEL (1888–1975). A native of Bobruisk, Russia, Rahel Kaznelson-Shazar immigrated to Palestine in 1912. Her sister was Frieda Kaznelson (see above). She initially taught Hebrew in the *meshek hapoalot* founded at Kineret by Hannah Meisel-Shohat (see below). She quickly emerged as a leader of the struggle for women's rights in the Yishuv. In 1914, she joined Tel Adashim (Tel Adas) located in the Jezreel Valley. In 1919, she moved to Tel Aviv to participate actively in the newly established Ahdut Haavodah party, and the following year she played a central role in the creation of the Histadrut. In 1920, she married Zalman Rubashov (later, Shazar), a former classmate at the Academy for Jewish Learning in St. Petersburg, who was later to become the third president of the State of Israel. She served as editor of the monthly *Dvar hapoelet* [The Woman Worker Speaks], a position she held for over twenty-five years. In 1928, she edited a collection of memoirs, letters, and prose by Zionist women pioneers entitled *Divrei poalot* [Women Workers Speak] (1928). (The anthology was to serve as the basis for *The Plough Woman*.) In the 1930s and 1940s she frequently undertook missions to diaspora communities in behalf of the Histadrut and Moezet Hapoalot. She was also a delegate of the Labor Zionist movement to several World Zionist Congresses. Following World War II, she spent time in the Displaced Persons camps of Germany and assisted Holocaust survivors in their immigration to Palestine. She testified before the United Nations Special Committee on Palestine (UNSCOP). In 1958 she was awarded the Israel Prize in the field of social sciences for a "half century's work in the educational and cultural absorption of the working women in Israel." She continued to be an outspoken feminist and Zionist leader after 1963, when her husband became president of Israel. Her books include *Tnuat hapoelet: mifalehah ushifotehah* [The Working Women's Movement: Projects and Aspirations] (1941); *Masot ureshimot* [Essays and Notes] (1945); *Im paamei hador* [The Footsteps of a Generation] (1964); *Al adamat ivrit* [On Hebrew Soil] (1966); and *Shelivuni veeinan* [My Companions Who Have Gone] (1969).

KRIGSER (AMIAD), SARAH (SHTURMAN) (1888–1966). A native of Yekaterinoslav, Ukraine, Sarah (Shturman) Krigser (Amiad) immigrated to Palestine in 1906. She worked as a laborer in several Jewish colonies, eventually settling permanently in Nahalal. See the information about her sisters Esther (Shturman) Becker and Shifra (Shturman) Bezer.

KROLL, ELIEZER (1897–1958). A native of Kremenchug, Ukraine, Kroll was active in socialist and Zionist activity as a youth. He immigrated to Palestine in 1908 and immediately joined the ranks of the labor movement. During his first two years in Palestine, he worked as an itinerant guard and a laborer in several Jewish colonies and settlements. In 1910, he was inducted into Hashomer and thereafter worked regularly as a guard. During World War I, he served in the Jewish Legion. Following the war, he was among the founders of Tel Adashim (Tel Adas). In 1921, he helped to revive the *kvuzah* of Kfar Giladi, where he settled permanently. In 1947, he was sent to Latin America as a Histadrut emissary. He played a key role in establishing the development town of Kiryat Shmonah, which is adjacent to Kfar Giladi. He was married to Haya (Drakhler) Kroll.

KUPERMINZ-DRORI, HASIA (1899–1976). Kuperminz-Drori was a member of the *moshav* Kfar Yehezkel and a leader of Moezet Hapoalot. She later served in the Israeli Knesset.

LAVI, SHLOMO (LEVKOVICH) (1882–1963). A native of Plonsk, Russian Poland, Shlomo Levkovich (later, Lavi) immigrated to Palestine in 1905. He worked as a laborer in several Jewish colonies. In 1909, he moved to the Galilee, where he worked as a *shomer* in Hederah and Rehovot. He conceived of the idea of the large collective, later called the *kibbutz*. In 1920, he organized a group of workers from the Gdud Avodah and helped to establish the first large collective in the Jezreel Valley, which subsequently split into Ein Harod and Tel Yosef. He was a leader of the Mapai party.

LIEBERSON, TEHIYAH (1886–1975). A native of Russia, Tehiyah Lieberson immigrated to Palestine in 1905. She was among the first Zionist women pioneers who performed agricultural labor in Petah Tikvah and Um Djuni (Dagania). She also worked in the *meshek hapoalot* at Kineret. Later, she was a founder of the first *moshav*, Nahalal. She eventually settled permanently in Tel Aviv, where she played a leading role in Moezet Hapoalot.

LISHANSKY, SARAH (1882–1924). A native of Malin, Ukraine, Sarah Lishansky received a traditional Jewish education. She later completed formal secular studies in Russian language and accounting. As a youth, she was active in Russian Poalei Zion circles. From 1904 to 1906, she undertook emergency medical training in Kiev. During the pogroms of 1905, she participated in Jewish self-defense efforts in Kiev. In 1906, she returned to Malin, where she engaged in local Zionist activity, but fled shortly thereafter due to the harassment of local tsarist authorities. In 1907, she relocated to Vilna, to be with her sister, Rahel Yanait Ben-Zvi (see below), and then to St. Petersburg. She eventually returned to Malin and continued her political work. Between 1908 and 1910, her family members immigrated to Palestine. In 1909, she immigrated to Palestine. Initially, she worked as a nurse at hospitals in Jerusalem. With the outbreak of World War I, she traveled to Karkur, Tel Adas (Tel Adashim) and other Hashomer outposts in the Jezreel Valley providing health care assistance. She later organized the first infirmary of Kupat Holim [Workers' Sick Fund] in Tel Aviv. She also worked with Kupat Holim in Jerusalem. She was an active member of Ahdut Haavaodah and was elected to the Jewish city committee of Jerusalem. After falling ill with cancer, she left the country for treatment in Berlin and Vienna. There, too, she remained active in Zionist activity. She subsequently returned to Jerusalem and continued her work with Kupat Holim. Within a short period, however, she experienced a relapse that caused her death.

MALKIN, SARAH (1885–1949). A native of Russia, Sarah Malkin immigrated to Palestine in 1905. She was a founder of Dagania and played a leading role in the development of the settlement's approach to communal child-rearing. Later, she worked as a nurse in the first hospital in Zikhron Yaakov. She was also a leader of Hapoel Hazair and Moezet Hapoalot.

MEISEL-SHOHAT, HANNAH (1890–1972). A native of Russia, Hannah Meisel-Shohat represented Poalei Zion in Odessa at the Seventh Zionist Congress. She immigrated to Palestine in 1909, and in 1911 she founded the first *meshek hapoalot* [training farm for women pioneers] in Palestine in Kineret. The following year she married Eliezer Shohat (1874–1971) and later became a delegate to the Eleventh Zionist Congress. In 1919, she founded a workers' kitchen in Tel Aviv and taught cooking to members of the Third Aliyah. She also helped found the womens' agricultural school of Nahalal and served as its principal until 1960. In 1920, Meisel-Shohat became a member of the world executive of the Women's International Zionist Organization (WIZO).

MEYERSON (MEIR), GOLDA (MABOVICH) (1898–1978). A native of Russia, Golda Mabovich was brought to Milwaukee, Wisconsin, in 1906 by her parents. She joined Poalei Zion in the United States in 1915 and immigrated to Palestine in 1921. She worked as a laborer and eventually joined Merhavyah. She soon left, however, because of the ill health of her husband, Morris Meyerson. She rose through the ranks of the Histadrut, becoming secretary general of Moezet Hapoalot in 1928 and a member of the World Zionist Organization executive committee in 1934. She also helped found the Palestine labor party Mapai in 1930, where she gained increased respect for her loyalty and ability. Her political role continued to grow in the years leading up to independence; she became head of the Political Department of the Jewish Agency in 1946 and, as such, negotiated with the British regime and King Abdullah of Jordan to try to convince the latter not to participate in the imminent war. During the War of Independence, Meir went to the United States, where she raised considerable funds for the war effort. After Israel was established, she was appointed minister to Moscow. She subsequently became a Knesset member and David Ben-Gurion's (1886–1973) minister of labor and housing. Thereafter, she served as foreign minister for ten years, finally becoming prime minister in 1969. She resigned in 1974 in the midst of the humiliation brought on by the nearly calamitous Yom Kippur War even though the investigating commission lauded her handling of the conflict. Her memoir is entitled *My Life* (1975).

REKHTANT-YAFEH, SHOSHANAH (1889–1956). A native of Poland, Shoshanah Rekhtant-Yafeh immigrated to Palestine in 1911. She worked as a laborer in Petah Tikvah and Mikveh Israel and later settled with her husband, Eliezer

Lipa Yaffe (1882–1942), in Nahalal. The latter, who emerged as the leading ideologist of the *moshav* movement, immigrated from Woodbine, New Jersey, to Palestine in 1909 with a group of American Zionist pioneers. He served in the Jewish Legion during World War I and helped to found the marketing cooperative Tnuvah [Yield].

DE ROTHSCHILD, BARON EDMOND (1845–1934). Rothschild was the key philanthropist for the emerging Jewish settlements in Palestine at the turn of the nineteenth and in the early twentieth centuries. Initially, Rothschild donated 30,000 francs to save the beleaguered settlement of Rishon Lezion. In 1883, he purchased the land for and set up Ekron as a model agricultural settlement. When the *moshavot* of the First Aliyah appeared on the verge of collapse, he sent money and administrative experts. Although, at first, there was some resentment of Rothschild and his experts, the settlers warmed to them as the newly implemented programs began to succeed. In 1899, Rothschild gave his enterprises over to the control of the Jewish Colonization Association (ICA) and established the Palestinian Jewish Colonization Association (PICA). In total, he founded more than thirty settlements, a glass factory, an olive oil plant, a salt refinery, and a dairy plant. He was also a cosponsor of the Palestine Electric Corporation, provided aid for swamp drainage, and donated the funds to establish the Hebrew University of Jerusalem. Although Rothschild strongly supported Jewish settlement in Palestine and advocated the eventual creation of a Jewish state there, he was always deliberate and cautious, warning against the establishment of a state that did not yet possess the means to survive.

SAMUEL, MAURICE (1895–1972). Born in Rumania, Maurice Samuel was brought to England as a child and then the United States where he lived most of his life. From 1917 to 1919, he served in the United States Army, spending time in Poland on the Pogrom Investigation Commission. Later, he worked for the Zionist Organization of America, and from 1927 to 1929, he was on the Zionist Actions Committee. A widely known writer, translator, and lecturer, Samuel was a strong supporter of socialism, Zionism, and Labor Zionism.

SHAZAR, ZALMAN (RUBASHOV) (1889–1974). A native of Belorussia, Zalman (Shneur Rubashov) Shazar, was a scholar, writer, Labor Zionist leader, and the third president of the State of Israel. He became involved as an adolescent in Jewish self-defense and the Poalei Zion movement. In 1907, he was arrested and imprisoned for his role on the Poalei Zion newspaper *Der proletarisher gedank* [Proletarian Thought]. After his release, he studied in St. Petersburg at the Academy for Jewish Studies and served on the editorial staff of *Der yidisher imigrant* [The Jewish Immigrant], a publication of the Jewish Colonization Association. While a student of history and philosophy at Freiburg and Strasbourg, and later at Berlin, he helped organize Hehaluz in Germany. He attended the Twelfth Zionist Congress; at the Thirteenth, he was elected to the Actions Committee. In 1924, he immigrated to Palestine and soon thereafter became editor of the labor newspaper *Davar*

[The Word], a position he held until 1949. He also played a leading role in the Palestine labor movement, participating in the founding of Mapai and becoming a member of the executive of the Vaad Leumi. Prior to Israel's independence, Shazar participated in the Jewish delegation that negotiated with the United Nations Special Committee on Palestine, and he drafted the resolution adopted by the Zionist General Council that declared the Jewish state's independence when the British Mandate ended. After the creation of Israel, Shazar was elected to the Knesset and served for ten years, part of the time as minister of education and culture, and in 1963 he succeeded Yizhak Ben-Zvi (see above) as the third president. He was re-elected in 1968. He was married to Rahel Kaznelson-Shazar (see above).

SHOHAT, MANYA (WILBUSHEVIZ) (1880–1961). A native of Grodno, Lithuania, Manya Wilbusheviz (later Shohat) immigrated to Palestine in 1904 to join her brother Nahum Wilbusheviz (1879–1971). In Russia, she was deeply involved in clandestine revolutionary activity and the defense of Jewry. Upon her arrival in Palestine, Shohat became a leading figure in the labor movement and raised considerable sums for nascent Jewish self-defense activity. With her husband Israel Shohat (1886–1961), she was a founder of Hashomer. As a Russian foreign national, she was expelled from Palestine by the Turks during World War I. From abroad, she aided the flow of "illegal" Jewish immigrants to Palestine. In addition, she worked in the United States for the Histadrut and the Haganah, and she helped establish the League of Arab-Jewish Rapprochement.

SYRKIN, MARIE (1899–1989). Born in Berne, Switzerland, Marie Syrkin was brought to New York City at the age of eight. Her father, Nahman Syrkin (1868–1924), was a preeminent socialist Zionist theoretician and leader. As a youth, Syrkin became active in socialist Zionist affairs in the United States. She worked closely with the Zionist thinker Hayim Greenberg (1889–1953), founding editor of the Labor Zionist journal *Jewish Frontier*, and she herself played an active role in the publication for many years. She was also a close associate of Golda Meir (see above), about whom she wrote a biography. From 1955 to 1966, she was a professor of English at Brandeis University.

TABENKIN, EVA (STASHEVSKY) (1889–1947). A native of Warsaw, Eva (Stashevsky) Tabenkin received a traditional Jewish education as well as formal instruction in general Russian-Polish studies. She joined the Poalei Zion party as a youth and participated in clandestine political activities for which she was twice imprisoned. In this period, she also underwent training for Zionist pioneer life in Palestine and played an active role in Jewish self-defense efforts in Warsaw. In 1907, she completed an advanced teaching degree. She studied philosophy and medicine at the University of Kharkov. In 1912, she immigrated to Palestine with her husband Yizhak Tabenkin (1887–1971), who emerged as the leading ideologist of the Kibbutz Hameuhad [United Kibbutz] movement. Eva Tabenkin worked as a laborer in Kfar Uriah, Kineret and other Jewish settlements. She was one of the first to champion the cause of working women in the Yishuv. She was a founder of Ein Harod and was especially active in the educational divisions of Kibbutz Hameuhad and the Zionist movement.

TIOMKIN, VLADIMIR (1861–1927). An assimilationist until he witnessed the devastation of the pogroms in 1881–82, Vladimir Tiomkin was a member of Hovevei Zion and helped to found the St. Petersburg Ahavat Zion Society. In 1891, he was elected to the Greater Actions Committee of the World Zionist Organization by the Second Zionist Congress. He subsequently became the first director of the Jaffa Office of the Hovevei Zion. In 1903, he was an outspoken opponent of Theodor Herzl's Uganda plan. During World War I, he headed relief projects in southern Russia. After the Russian Revolution, he resumed his Zionist activity in Eastern Europe for a brief period. In 1920, he left Russia and settled in Paris, where he became a close associate of the right-wing Revisionist Zionist leader Vladimir Zeev Jabotinsky. Tiomkin himself emerged as a leader of Revisionist Zionist movement.

YANAIT BEN-ZVI, RAHEL (1886–1979). A native of Russia, Rahel Yanait Ben-Zvi became engaged in Zionist activity as a student in Kiev. In 1908, she immigrated to Palestine, where she worked as a laborer in the Jewish colonies. She helped found Hashomer and the Hebrew gymnasium in Jerusalem. She played a leading role in the Histadrut and Moezet Hapoalot. She also served as an emissary to the Pioneer Women's Organization in the 1930s. Her husband Yizhak Ben-Zvi (see above) was the second president of Israel.

ZEID, ALEXANDER (1886–1938). A native of Balagansk, Siberia, Alexander Zeid moved to Vilna as a youth, where he joined the socialist Zionist movement. He immigrated to Palestine in 1904 and initially worked as a laborer and wagoner in Rishon Lezion and Petah Tikvah. He subsequently worked for over a year as a stonemason in Jerusalem. In 1907, he was one of the founders of the secret defense society Bar-Giora, from which stemmed the Hashomer organization in 1909. In ensuing years, Zeid worked as a guard at numerous Jewish settlements. In 1916, he joined a group of Hashomer veterans who settled at the location that would later become Kfar Giladi. In 1926, he relocated to Tel Hai and then to Sheikh Abrik in the Jezreel Valley. He was wounded on several occasions in the line of duty. He was among the organizers of the Beit Shearim archeological excavations near Sheikh Abrik. In 1938, he was killed by Arab attackers while on guard in the Jezreel Valley. The settlement Givat Zeid, established in the Jezreel Valley in 1943, is named in his memory. He was married to Ziporah Zeid (see below).

ZEID, ZIPORAH (1892–1968). A native of Vilna, Ziporah Zeid immigrated to Palestine in 1907. She worked as a laborer in the Jewish colonies and was active in the establishment of Moezet Hapoalot. Her husband Alexander Zeid (see above) was a founder of Hashomer. She was a staunch advocate of Arab-Jewish reconciliation.

ZIZER (ZAR-ZION), NEHAMAH (1891–1981). A native of Groslovo, Russia, Nehamah Zizer received a traditional Jewish education and instruction at a local gymnasium. Her parents, who were active Zionists, immigrated to

Palestine and established a farm in Nahlat Yehudah; they were among the first observant Jewish pioneers to raise tobacco and plant trees for afforestation. In 1913, Nehamah abandoned her studies and immigrated to Palestine. She initially worked as an agricultural labor in Merhavyah. In 1915–1916, she went to work with A. D. Gordon (see above) as a laborer in Sharonah, a *moshav* in the Lower Galilee. She next moved to Poriyah, Tel Hai, and then to Kineret, where she contracted malaria. During World War I, she joined a group of women vegetable farmers in Galilee and helped to coordinate cooperative relief efforts in the area. During this period, she married a pioneer named Carmin. From 1921–1925, they lived in the United States, where she studied agriculture. While in America, she gave birth to a daughter. She returned to Palestine with the child and joined the Gdud Avodah. From 1926–1928, she lived and worked on her parents' farm at Nahlat Yehudah. After 1929, she resided in Tel Aviv, where she raised two children and worked as a seamstress and housekeeper. She was politically active in the Histadrut and the Mapai party.

Glossary of Places

Afulah. A Jewish town in the Jezreel Valley founded in 1925 with aid from the American Zion Commonwealth and intended to be an urban center for the outlying Jewish colonies. Nearby settlers, however, showed little interest in the town except for its hospital.

Akko (Acre). An ancient port city situated on a promontory at the northern end of Haifa Bay. The Jewish community of Akko reached its lowest ebb before World War I but grew slowly during the British Mandate period. The Jewish residents abandoned the town when Arab riots broke out in 1936. The British used the local fortress as a prison. Several prominent Zionist leaders were held as political prisoners there, including a few right-wing Zionist underground fighters who were executed by the British authorities.

Ayelet Hashahar. A *kibbutz* to the south of the Huleh Valley, founded by Second Aliyah pioneers in 1918 and joined by members of the Gdud Avodah who believed its location useful for protecting remote Jewish Colonization Association lands.

Beersheva. Known as the "capital" of the Negev. During World War I, the town became a principal base for the Turkish-German military forces fighting on the Suez and Sinai fronts. In this period, many Jews came to Beersheva and provided services to the military. In 1917, the town was captured by the British troops. As a result, Beersheva's strategic role ended and its economy dwindled. Soon, however, a small group of Jewish pioneers settled in Beersheva, planted a tree nursery, and experimented with cultivating vegetables and other crops. During the Arab riots of 1936–39, the Jewish residents abandoned the town. Thereafter, the Zionist Organization intensified efforts to purchase land for Jewish settlement in the region.

Dagania. The first *kibbutz*, founded in 1910 (at a site known in Arabic as Um–Djuni) after a small group of pioneers separated from the Kineret farm to establish a communal settlement of their own. Later, Dagania Alef, the older segment of Kibbutz Dagania, separated from the newer Dagania Bet to maintain the ambiance of a *kvuzah* while accommodating to the realities of population growth.

Ein Harod. A *kibbutz* in the northern Harod Valley. The Jewish National Fund acquired the land to establish Ein Harod in 1921, and pioneers associated with the Gdud Avodah drained the malarial swamps in the region. The settlement later split into two *kibbutzim*, giving rise to its sister settlement Tel Yosef.

Galilee. The northernmost part of the Land of Israel, a hilly region between the Judah Valley and the coast. Many early Zionist settlement were established in the Galilee, especially around the south and west shores of Lake Kineret.

Haifa. A primary Mediterranean port and the third largest city in Israel. Prior to World War I, Jews acquired land on the slope of Mt. Carmel on which most of the city was later constructed. In 1912, work on the Tehnion, the region's foremost science and technology institution, was begun. The town gained importance with the construction of the railway.

Hauran. A region of Syria, northeast of Transjordania, with very rich farmland. It was described by the prophet Ezekiel as one of ancient Israel's boundaries to the north. Baron Edmond de Rothschild unsuccessfully attempted to launch a Jewish colonization effort there.

Hederah. Founded in 1890 by First Aliyah immigrants in the Sharon plain. Baron Edmond de Rothschild aided the colony to construct drainage channels and plant eucalyptus groves. Situated near a road junction and a rail station, it became one of the largest Jewish settlements in Palestine. During World War I, Hederah took in Jews who had been expelled from other areas of Palestine by the Turks.

Hefzibah. A kibbutz at the base of Mt. Gilboa, founded in 1922 by Zionist pioneers from Germany and Czechoslovakia.

Huleh Valley. Region in the upper eastern Galilee, located in a section of the Syrian–East African rift. Bound by a geologic barrier of basalt, alternating layers of peat and chalk gave rise to a shallow lake and stagnant waters that formed swamp marshes. Until the 1940s, Lake Huleh covered five square miles (fourteen square kilometers) and the swamps about a sixth of the valley's sixty-five square miles (177 square kilometers). Malarial conditions in the region affected Arab villages in the valley, which had, as a result, the highest mortality rate and the lowest living standard in Palestine at the end of the nineteenth century. In 1934, the Palestine Land Development Corporation acquired the Huleh Concession from the British Mandatory. The Jewish National Fund made efforts to acquire additional land in the Huleh Valley, and from 1939 on new Jewish settlements were established there. Drainage of the region was completed in 1958 by the Jewish National Fund.

Jaffa. A city on the Mediterranean Sea, which, since ancient times, had served as a major port. The first Jewish settlers in Jaffa established the Jewish quarters Neveh Zedek and Neveh Shalom. By 1914, Jews made up more than a third of Jaffa's 40,000 inhabitants. World War I brought numerous difficulties to Jaffa. Economic life was paralyzed and residents were conscripted into the Turkish army. These events were followed by hunger and deprivation, and consequently considerable numbers of inhabitants abandoned the city. Under the British Mandate, Jaffa recovered, expanded, and developed. However, the inner parts of Jaffa were gradually deserted by Jews after the

Arab riots of 1921, 1929, and 1936–39 and were entirely abandoned at the end of 1947. Only after the State of Israel was established in 1948 did Jewish immigrants again settle in Jaffa in appreciable numbers.

Jezreel Valley. One of the largest inland valleys in the Land of Israel, located between the Mediterranean Coast and the Jordan Valley. To the south, it is bounded by the lower Galilee, and to the north it reaches Mt. Hermon. Soon after the establishment of the British Mandate, large tracts of the valley were acquired by the Jewish National Fund. In the 1920s, the valley, known in Zionist parlance as the *"emek"* [valley], was drained and settled, making it a showpiece of Zionist pioneering and progressive regional development.

Judea. Latin form of Judah; site of the Kingdom of Israel, the southern province of Palestine during the period of Roman hegemony. The region of Judea lies between the Jordan Valley and the Mediterranean Sea and includes the southern part of Israel's central mountain range. Judea, which provided a foothold for early groups of Zionist pioneers, is also known today as the West Bank.

Karkur. Located in the Sharon Valley northeast of Hederah, Karkur was founded in 1913 by a group of English Jews called Ahuzat London. In 1912, the site for Karkur was acquired by the Palestine Land Development Company. The settlement was guarded by members of Hashomer who remained and worked at the colony, together with other Jewish laborers, until the 1920s. A group of Anglo-Jewish settlers joined Karkur in 1925–1926. In 1927, Karkur numbered some 300 inhabitants, and the intially hard conditions improved after abundant groundwater was discovered. Thereafter, citrus became a key agricultural product in the area. In 1969, the settlement combined with Pardes Hannah, which was established in 1929, to become Pardes Hannah-Karkur.

Kfar Giladi. Situated in the northwest of the Huleh Valley, it was established in 1916 by Hashomer as an outpost on the land of the Jewish Colonization Association. This settlement, along with Tel Hai, was attacked in 1920 by Arabs who were under the mistaken assumption that French soldiers were being hidden there. It was subsequently abandoned but resettled only ten months later, and it merged with Tel Hai in 1926.

Kfar Tavor (known in Arabic as Meshah). A *moshavah* in the lower Galilee, southwest of Tiberias, it was founded in 1901. The settlement was created by the Jewish Colonization Association as a grain-growing enterprise, but the scarcity of water hindered its progress. It was an important center for Hashomer.

Kineret. Location of early Zionist pioneer settlements to the southeast and southwest of Lake Kineret (at a site known in Arabic as Daleika). In 1908, a training farm was established there by the Zionist Organization's Palestine Office. Following a strike by Jewish workers, the Palestine Office allocated land east of the Jordan River to a restless cohort of socialist Zionist pioneers, who subsequently established Dagania (see above). Following a second strike in 1912, a womens' agricultural training farm was added to Kineret under the direction of Hannah Meisel-Shohat. Soon thereafter, a group of Jewish pioneers from America established a *moshav*, and a large *kvuzah* (later called a *kibbutz*) also emerged. Outstanding leaders of the Yishuv all worked and lived at Kineret prior to and during World War I. The settlement was a spiritual center of the Labor Zionist movement in the prestate period and served as a focal point of Hapoel Hazair and Mapai activity.

Lake Kineret. Freshwater lake in northeastern Israel. The Jordan River enters its north shore and flows out via its south shore. The lake occupies a section of the central Jordan Rift Valley. It covers an area of sixty-four square miles (165 square kilometers). Beginning in the first decade of the twentieth century, Jewish settlements were founded on and near the lake's west and south shores. The frontier drawn between the British Mandate over Palestine and the French Mandate over Syria included the entire lake in the former territory, giving rise to a settlement chain of Jewish colonies in the region.

Mahanayim. A *kibbutz* located in the Upper Galilee, it was first established as a plantation village by Orthodox Jews in 1898. In 1902, the Jewish Colonization Association also helped to settle a small group there. These attempts failed as did a further effort in 1918 when a workers' group set out to establish a *moshav*. On the eve of World War II, a *kibbutz* was permanently established on the site as part of the Zionist movement's strategic and symbolic response to the British White Paper of 1939, which severely curtailed Jewish immigration and land acquisition in Palestine.

Merhavyah. Kibbutz in the Jezreel Valley, east of Afulah. In 1909, the first landholding in the valley was acquired at Mahanayim by the Palestine Land Development Corporation. In 1911, a group of Hashomer pioneers established a farm there. They persevered in spite of malaria and attempts by the Turkish authorities to force them to leave. The colony evolved into a cooperative during World War I but dispersed shortly thereafter. Later, an unsuccessful attempt to establish a permanent settlement at the site was undertaken by former members of the Jewish Legion. In 1929, a group of Hashomer Hazair pioneers from Poland established a permanent *kibbutz* at Mahanayim. It soon became the organizational center of the left-wing Hashomer Hazair *kibbutz* movement.

Meshah (see Kfar Tavor).

Metulah. Northernmost Jewish colony in the country, located on the Israel-Lebanon border. Founded in 1896 by Baron Edmond de Rothschild as a defensive outpost, it was settled by pioneers specially chosen for their ability to guard the isolated site and help demarcate the Yishuv's northern frontier borders. Metulah grew very slowly until the 1950s.

Migdal. A *moshavah* in the Ginosar Valley, northwest of Lake Kineret, founded in 1910 by Russian Jewish pioneers. In 1921, it became the site of a camp of Third Aliyah pioneers who worked on the Tiberas–Rosh Pinah road. These laborers founded the Gdud Avodah at Migdal. Beginning in 1924, Jews from England and America acquired parcels of land at Migdal, and some of them went to settle there. After 1948, the *moshavah* was significantly enlarged by an influx of new immigrants.

Mikveh Israel. A rural Jewish community located east of Tel Aviv–Jaffa, it was founded in 1870 by the Alliance Israélite Universelle. It served as a precursor to the establishment of Jewish colonies during the First Aliyah. Maintained by Baron Edmond de Rothschild, the training school at Mikveh Israel attempted to attract and prepare Jews for agricultural life in Palestine.

Nablus (Hebrew: Shekhem). The largest city in Samaria, Nablus is holy to religious Jews as the burial site of the patriarch Joseph. The city was established in 72 c.e. by the future Roman emperor Vespasian (c. 9–79 c.e.) during his conquest of ancient Palestine in 67–68 c.e. It prospered due to the area's favorable geographic conditions and groundwater sources. After the seventh century c.e., Nablus came under Islamic rule and emerged as home to a mixed population of Muslims, Persians, Samaritans, and Jews. The first mention of a significant Jewish presence in the city dates back to 1522. The fortunes of the Jewish community varied considerably and the Jews abandoned Nablus completely after 1900. An attempt after World War I to reestablish a Jewish community there failed, owing especially to the Arab riots of 1929. In 1927, a severe earthquake destroyed much of the city. The British Mandatory aided in the rebuilding of Nablus, but sought to preserve its Arab character. From 1948 to 1967, Nablus became an administrative center of the Jordanian regime. The area was captured by Israel during the Six-Day War (June 1967).

Nahalal. The first *moshav*, it was established in 1921 in the western Jezreel Valley by veteran pioneers of the Second Aliyah. It was the beginning of the development of the Jezreel Valley, and some of its attributes served as models for future *moshavim*, including its physical layout in concentric circles. In 1929, a womens' agricultural training farm was founded in Nahalal by Hannah Meisel-Shohat. Nahalal quickly became a principal center of the emergent countrywide *moshav* movement.

Nahlat Yehudah. A *moshavah* contemporary with the Second Aliyah, it was founded by members of Hibbat Zion from Russia in 1914 on the coastal plain, contiguous with but independent from Rishon Lezion. The settlement was characterized by auxiliary farmsteads whose owners were employed in Rishon Lezion or in Jaffa and Tel Aviv.

Petah Tikvah. A *moshavah* located east of Tel Aviv, it was first settled in the 1870s by religious Jews from Jerusalem. These settlers hoped to use the 850 acres for a farming village. However, Petah Tikvah was abandoned in 1881 because of a poor harvest, the threat of malaria, and problems with the local Arabs. The abandonment did not last long. The First Aliyah settlers, with the aid of Hovevei Zion, colonized the area. Although at first it faltered, the *moshavah* received assistance from Baron Edmond de Rothschild and gradually became a productive vineyard. It was also a focal point of the Palestine labor movement, and in 1905 the party Hapoel Hazair was created there.

Poriyah. A Jewish colony located on a mountain ridge just south of Tiberias. Poriyah was established in 1912 as a fruit farm, mainly based on almond plantations, by a group of American Zionists. Abandoned during World War I, it was temporarily resettled as a *kibbutz* in 1940. In 1949, Yemenite immigrants established a work village there. It subsequently served as a training farm and youth hostel.

Rehovot. Originally a *moshavah* to the south of Tel Aviv, it was founded in 1870 by First Aliyah immigrants from Poland on land purchased by Yehoshuah Hankin. For a time, it was the only Jewish village that survived without assistance from Baron Edmond de Rothschild. Those who lived in Rehovot exhibited a high level of cooperation despite the settlement's individualist orientation. After World War I, the colony swiftly expanded and gained municipal status. In the 1930s and 1940s, Rehovot became one of the country's principal citrus growing regions and an important center of industry and technology.

Rosh Pinah. A *moshavah* located in the Upper Galilee, it was founded originally in 1878 under the name Gei Oni [Valley of My Strength] (adapted from the name of the nearby Arab village Jauna), not by pioneers but by religious Jews from Safed seeking to make a living for themselves rather than relying on the *Halukah* system. It was briefly abandoned because of a lack of money and experience as well as the colonists' inability to defend the settlement against Arab attacks. Resettled by First Aliyah pioneers in 1882, it was supported by Baron Edmond de Rothschild but proved unsuccessful. The British Mandatory maintained a police station and customs office near Rosh Pinah. In the 1936–39 Arab riots, the *moshavah* suffered from repeated attacks. After 1948, the *moshavah* grew slowly and steadily as a result of the absorption of new immigrants.

Safed. An ancient city in the Upper Galilee, with a long history of Jewish scholarship and mysticism. Many Jews fled during the Arab riots of 1929, but the Jewish quarter was rebuilt in the early 1930s. When Safed was taken by Jews during the War of Independence in 1948, the Arab majority in the city fled.

Samaria. The northern capital of the ancient Kingdom of Israel, it also refers to the region between the Jezreel Valley and Judean mountains. Although Samaria provided a foothold for a few groups of early Zionist pioneers, there was little modern Jewish settlement there until the area's capture by Israel during the Six-Day War of 1967. Samaria is also known today as the West Bank.

Sejera (Ilaniyah). A *moshavah* in the eastern Lower Galilee established in 1902 by the Jewish Colonization Association. It served as a training ground for many of the outstanding leaders of the Second Aliyah. The Jewish laborers' association Hahoresh was founded there in 1907, with the aim of contracting for farm work as a collective. Sejera later became a *moshav* known by the Hebrew name Ilaniyah.

Shekhem (see Nablus).

Shekhunat Borohov. A suburb of Tel Aviv named for the socialist Zionist thinker Ber Borohov (1881–1917), it was originally built as a workers' garden city. It served as a hub of the urban workers' movement in the Yishuv. A women's agricultural training farm was established there in the 1920s. There were three other large workers' garden cities in the pre-state era: Kiryat Haim and Kiryat Amal, both of which were near Haifa, and Kiryat Avodah, which was also located in Tel Aviv.

Tel Adas (also, Tel Adashim). *Moshav* in the Jezreel Valley north of Afulah. In 1913, the site became Jewish property and members of Hashomer set up a camp there. In 1923, pioneers from Eastern Europe and Hashomer veterans founded the *moshav*. Soon thereafter, it was joined by former members of the Jewish Legion. The *moshav* grew slowly and expanded after Israel's War of Independence in 1948, with the absorption of new immigrants.

Tel Aviv. Located in the central part of the coastal plain, was established in 1909 as a garden suburb of Jaffa. Known as the "first all-Jewish city," Tel Aviv evolved rapidly over the course of a few decades, particularly from the 1930s on, to become the largest urban settlement of the Yishuv. It served as an important center of the Palestine labor movement.

Tel Hai. Settlement located on the northwest rim of the Huleh Valley, founded in 1918 as one of three outposts to guard the northern frontier borders of the Yishuv. Originally settled by shepherds, the site eventually served as an outpost for Hashomer. After World War I, the territory came under French rule, and local Arabs, believing that French soldiers were being hidden by the colonists, attacked the settlement in 1920, killing several Jews, including Yosef Trumpeldor and Sarah Chizhik. The defense of Tel Hai and its sister settlement Kfar Giladi became synonymous with Zionist heroism and Jewish self-defense in Palestine.

Tel Yosef. Kibbutz in the Harod Valley southeast of Afulah, founded in 1921 as a work camp for the Gdud Avodah. Its members participated in draining local malaria-infested swamps. In 1929, following the decline of the Gdud Avodah, Tel Yosef moved (along with Ein Harod) from its original site at the foot of Mt. Gilboa to the Harod Valley.

Tiberias. Ancient town on the western shore of Lake Kineret, near Poriyah. The city has a long history of serving as a center of Jewish learning and traditional Jewish life in the Land of Israel. The first Jewish settlement outside of Tiberias was constructed at Migdal in 1910 and became a base of the Gdud Avodah.

Yavniel. *Moshavah* located in the Yavniel Valley of the eastern Lower Galilee, founded in 1901 by the Jewish Colonization Association on land purchased by Baron Edmond de Rothschild. The settlement's economy was based on grain farming, and it struggled for many years with a drastic shortage of water. After Israel's War of Independence in 1948, the settlement grew with the absorption of new immigrants. Three neighboring villages were united with Yavniel in the 1950s.

Zikhron Yaakov. A plantation village located on the southern spur of Mount

Carmel, it was one of the earliest settlements of Hovevei Zion. Founded as a *moshavah* in 1882 by Rumanian Jewish pioneers and aided by Baron Edmond de Rothschild, Zikhron Yaakov emerged as a principal site of large-scale experimental viticulture and later a center of Palestine's wine industry. Several outstanding nonsocialist leaders of the Yishuv lived in Zikhron Yaakov, and the *moshavah* served as a hub of clandestine anti-British political activity following World War I.

Selected Bibliography

There is a rapidly growing corpus of scholarly literature on Jewish women, Zionism, and the State of Israel. To date, however, no effort has been undertaken to compile a comprehensive guide to this emerging field of study. The following selected bibliography attempts to trace the broad outlines of scholarship past and present (in English) that best illustrates the nexus between Jewish women and the campaign to create an independent Jewish national home in Palestine. It begins with suggestions for reference sources, leading periodicals that include articles on women and Zionism, and historical works that serve as a backdrop to the role of women in Zionist affairs in the prestate period. Finally, the bibliography lists significant monographs related to women, Judaism, and Zionism, including some primary sources.

I. REFERENCE SOURCES

American Jewish Year Book
Encyclopaedia Judaica
Encyclopedia of Judaism
Encyclopedia of Zionism and Israel
Herzl Year Book
Jerusalem Cathedra
Jewish Women in America: An Historical Encyclopedia
The Jew in the Modern World: A Documentary History, 2d edition (1995)
Universal Jewish Encyclopedia

II. LEADING PERIODICALS

American Jewish Archives
American Jewish History
Jewish History
Jewish Journal of Sociology
Jewish Social Studies
Judaism
Journal of Israeli History (formerly *Studies in Zionism*)
Modern Judaism
Proceedings of the World Congress of Jewish Studies
Studies in Contemporary Jewry

III. ZIONISM, PALESTINE, AND ISRAEL

Almog, Shmuel, Jehuda Reinharz, and Anita Shapira, eds. *Zionism and Religion*. Hanover: University Press of New England, 1998.

Avineri, Shlomo. *The Making of Modern Zionism: The Intellectual Origins of the Jewish State*. New York: Basic Books, 1981.

Brown, Michael. *The Israeli-American Connection: Its Roots in the Yishuv, 1914–1945*. Detroit, Mich.: Wayne State University Press, 1996.

Cohen, Mitchell. *Zion and State: Nation, Class and the Shaping of Modern Israel*. New York and Oxford: Basil Blackwell, 1987.

Diament, Carol, ed. *Zionism: The Sequel*. New York: Hadassah, The Women's Zionist Organization of America, 1998.

Frankel, Jonathan. *Prophecy and Politics: Socialism, Nationalism and the Russian Jews, 1862–1917*. Cambridge: Cambridge University Press, 1981.

Halperin, Samuel. *The Political World of American Zionism*, reprint. Silver Spring, Md.: Information Dynamics, 1985.

Halpern, Ben. *The Idea of the Jewish State*. 2d ed. Cambridge, Mass.: Harvard University Press, 1969.

Halpern, Ben and Jehuda Reinharz. *Zionism and the Creation of a New Society*. Hanover and London: University Press of New England, 2000.

Hertzberg, Arthur, ed. *The Zionist Idea: A Historical Reader and Analysis*. Reprint. New York: Atheneum, 1984.

Laqueur, Walter. *A History of Zionism*. 2d rev. ed. New York: Schocken Books, 1989.

Mendelsohn, Ezra. *Zionism in Poland: The Formative Years, 1915–1926*. New Haven and London: Yale University Press, 1981.

Near, Henry. *The Kibbutz Movement: A History*. Vol. 1, *Origins and Growth, 1909–1939*. Oxford: Oxford University Press, 1992.

———. *The Kibbutz Movement: A History*. Vol. 2, *Crisis and Achievement, 1939–1995*. Oxford: Oxford University Press, 1997.

Penslar, Derek J. *Zionism and Technocracy: The Engineering of Jewish Settlement in Palestine, 1870–1918*. Bloomington and Indianapolis: Indiana University Press, 1991.

Raider, Mark A. *The Emergence of American Zionism*. New York and London: New York University Press, 1998.

Reinharz, Jehuda and Anita Shapira, eds. *Essential Papers on Zionism*. New York and London: New York University Press, 1996.

Schweid, Eliezer. *The Land of Israel: National Home or Land of Destiny*. London and Toronto: Associated University Presses, 1985.

Shapira, Anita. *Berl: The Biography of a Socialist Zionist*. Cambridge: Cambridge University Press, 1984.

———. *Land and Power: The Zionist Resort to Force, 1881–1948*. New York and Oxford: Oxford University Press, 1992.

Shapiro, Yonathan. *The Formative Years of the Israeli Labor Party*. London: Sage, 1976.

Shimoni, Gideon. *The Zionist Ideology*. Hanover and London: University Press of New England, 1995.

Stein, Kenneth W. *The Land Question in Palestine, 1917–1939*. Chapel Hill and London: University of North Carolina Press, 1984.

Tessler, Mark. *A History of the Israeli-Palestinian Conflict*. Bloomington and Indianapolis: Indiana University Press, 1994.

Urofsky, Melvin I. *American Zionism from Herzl to the Holocaust*. Reprint. Lincoln: University of Nebraska Press, 1996.

IV. WOMEN, JUDAISM, AND ZIONISM

Baron, Dvorah. *"The First Day" and Other Stories*. Chana Kronfeld and Naomi Seiden, eds. Berkeley and Los Angeles: University of California Press, 2001.

Baskin, Judith R., ed. *Jewish Women in Historical Perspective*. 2d ed. Detroit, Mich.: Wayne State University Press, 1998.

Baum, Charlotte, Paula Hyman, and Sonya Michel, eds. *The Jewish Woman in America*. New York: Schocken, 1976.

Bernstein, Deborah S. *The Struggle for Equality: Urban Women Workers in Pre-state Israeli Society*. New York: Praeger, 1987.

Bernstein, Deborah S., ed. *Pioneers and Homemakers: Jewish Women in Pre-State Israel*. Albany: State University Press of New York, 1992.

Caspi, Mishael M. *Daughters of Yemen*. Berkeley: University of California Press, 1985.

Dash, Joan. *Summoned to Jerusalem: The Life of Henrietta Szold*. New York: Harper & Row, 1979.

Ferguson, Kathy E. *Kibbutz Journal: Reflections on Gender, Race, and Militarism in Israel*. Pasadena, Calif.: Trilogy Books, 1995.

Freedman, Marcia. *Exile in the Promised Land: A Memoir*. Ithaca, N.Y.: Firebrand Books, 1990.

Gilad, Lisa. *Ginger and Salt: Yemeni Jewish Women in an Israeli Town*. Boulder, Col.: Westview Press, 1989.

Govrin, Nurit. *Alienation and Regeneration*. John Glucker, trans. Tel Aviv: MOD Books, 1989. (See chap. 12: "Dvorah Baron—Ignoring the Reality of *Erez Israel*: Back to the *Shtetl*.")

Hazleton, Leslie. *Israeli Women: The Reality Behind the Myths*. New York: Simon and Schuster, 1977.

Hyman, Paula. *Gender and Assimilation in Modern Jewish History: The Roles and Representation of Jewish Women*. Seattle: University of Washington Press, 1995.

Keren, Thea. *Sophie Udin: Portrait of a Pioneer*. Rehovot: published privately, 1984.

Las, Nelly. *Jewish Women in a Changing World: A History of the International Council of Jewish Women, 1899–1995*. Jerusalem: Avraham Harman Institute of Contemporary Jewry, 1996.

Levin, Marlin. *Balm in Gilead: The Story of Hadassah*. New York: Schocken Books, 1973.

Lieblich, Amia. *Conversations with Dvorah: An Experimental Biography of the First Modern Hebrew Woman Writer*. Naomi Seidman, trans. Berkeley and Los Angeles: University of California Press, 1991.

Lipman, Beata. *Israel: The Embattled Land. Jewish and Palestinian Women Talk about Their Lives*. Cambridge, Mass.: Harvard University Press, 1988.

Lowenthal, Marvin. *Henrietta Szold: Life and Letters*. New York: Viking Press, 1942.

Maimon, Ada. *Women Build a Land*. New York: Herzl Press, 1960.

Marcus, Jacob Rader. *The American Jewish Woman, 1654–1980*. New York: Ktav, 1981.

Masnik, Ann S., ed. *The Jewish Woman: An Annotated Selected Bibliography, 1986–1993*. New York: Biblio Press, 1996.

Meir, Golda. *My Life*. New York: Dell, 1975.

Reinharz, Shulamit, and Mark A. Raider, eds. *Partners to Palestine and Israel: American Jewish Women and the Zionist Enterprise*. Hanover and London: University Press of New England, forthcoming.

Reinharz, Jehuda, and Shulamit Reinharz, eds. *The Letters and Papers of Manya Shohat*, forthcoming.

Rogow, Faith. *Gone to Another Meeting: The National Council of Jewish Women, 1893–1993*. Tuscaloosa: University of Alabama Press, 1993.

Shepherd, Naomi. *A Price Below Rubies: Jewish Women as Rebels and Radicals*. Cambridge, Mass.: Harvard University Press, 1993.

Spiro, Melford E. *Gender and Culture: Kibbutz Women Revisited*. New York: Schocken Books, 1980.

Swirski, Barbara, and Marilyn P. Safir. *Calling the Equality Bluff: Women in Israel*. New York: Teachers College Press, 1993.

Tiger, Lionel, and Joseph Shepher. *Women in the Kibbutz*. New York and London: Harcourt Brace Jovanovich, 1975.

Weinberg, Sydney Stahl. *The World of Our Mothers: The Lives of Jewish Immigrant Women*. Chapel Hill: University of North Carolina Press, 1988.

Talmon, Yonina. *Family and Community in the Kibbutz*. Cambridge, Mass.: Harvard University Press, 1972.

Yanait Ben-Zvi, Rachel. *Before Golda: Manya Shohat. A Biography*. New York: Biblio Press, 1989.

Yishai, Yael. *Between the Flag and the Banner: Women in Israeli Politics*. Albany: State University of New York Press, 1996.

Zacks Bar-Yishay, Hanna. "Female Labor Force Participation in a Developing Economy, Pre-State Israel as a Case Study." 2 vols. Ph.D. diss., University of Minnesota, 1991.

Index